Successful Marketing
Secrets & Strategies

First Edition

Rhonda Abrams
with Julie Vallone

thePlanningshop

The Planning Shop
Palo Alto, California

Praise for Books from The Planning Shop

"User-friendly and exhaustive … highly recommended. Abrams' book works because she tirelessly researched the subject. Most how-to books on entrepreneurship aren't worth a dime; among the thousands of small business titles, Abrams' [is an] exception."
—*Forbes Magazine*

"Rhonda Abrams knows her target market. She did not try to be all things to all readers. This book is for people who want to be serious entrepreneurs … It comes down to the numbers … Rhonda Abrams makes sure you'll take care of the Bottom Line numbers."
—*Sean Murphy, Ernst & Young, LLP, New York*

"If you'd like something that goes beyond the mere construction of your plan and is more fun to use … this book can take the pain out of the process."
— *"Small Business School" (PBS television show)*

"This book stands head and shoulders above all others … and the perfect choice for the beginner and the experienced business professional."
—*BizCountry*

"It is my No. 1 recommendation to SBDC clients … I have always liked the layout, order of presentation, sidebar notes, and real-world perspective on the planning process, components of the plan, etc."
—*David Gay, Small Business Development Center, College of DuPage*

"I have to say—I reviewed several options on the Internet, and after much searching, ordered four different books that I thought would be the best to consider using in the course. The other three didn't even come close. This is a great book, especially for non-native speakers of English. Good work over there!"
—*Julie Carbajal, Fonty University of Applied Sciences, The Netherlands*

"You have done a great service in establishing your publishing company and in helping so many people to learn all the ins and outs of what can be a daunting experience. You've also saved people like me lots of money in the interim, as we learn and do what we can to realize our dreams."
—*S.M. Lourenco, VP, Imaginas, LLC, New York*

"There are plenty of decent business-plan guides out there, but Abrams' was a cut above the others I saw. *The Successful Business Plan* won points with me because it was thorough and well organized, with handy worksheets and good quotes. Also, Abrams does a better job than most at explaining the business plan as a planning tool rather than a formulaic exercise. Well done."
—*Inc. Magazine*

"At last, a straightforward book that demystifies the process behind conducting effective business research … gives business practitioners and students an incredibly useful tool to enable them to find accurate and timely information for business plans, academic papers, and other business uses."
—*Molly Lavik, Practitioner Faculty of Marketing, Graziadio School of Business and Management, Pepperdine University*

"I'm growing my business by purchasing a commercial building, and I needed a real estate loan to make the purchase. *Business Plan In A Day* was THE source I used for writing my plan, and the bankers and brokers I spoke with all commended my plan as being very strong and well written. Thanks to you, I've secured my loan and the transaction is going through. I feel so fortunate to have found this book."
—*Lisa Stillman, GardenWalk Massage Therapy, St. Louis*

"As a small business advisor, I use the Electronic Financial Worksheet (EFW) tool extensively in analyzing my clients' financials. I recommend the Planning Shop's EFW for any small business. It's the best cash flow financial planning tool on the market today."
—*Joe Lam, Certified Business Advisor, Texas State University Small Business Development Center*

"Your book has been both an inspirational read as well as a comprehensive guide. … Being relatively inexperienced with entrepreneurship, your book has not only given me the ability to create a solid roadmap for planning, but has also provided an encouraging and easy way to cope with the enormous amount of information and organization needed."
—*Simon Lee, Entrepreneur*

"I just finished reading Rhonda's *Trade Show In A Day* and thought it was an excellent book and one that will stay close by my side during my next dozen shows. I highly recommend the book to anyone who wants to increase their productivity and profitability at their next trade event."
—*Gene Muchanski, President, Dive Industry Association*

Successful Marketing: Secrets & Strategies
©2008 by Rhonda Abrams. Published by The Planning Shop™

All rights reserved. No part of this publication may be reproduced, transmitted, stored in an information retrieval system, or used in any form or by any means, graphic, electronic, mechanical, photocopying, recording or otherwise, without the prior written permission of the publisher.

ISBN: 978-1-933895-05-5 (Trade)

ISBN: 978-1-933895-06-2 (Binder Edition)

Managing Editor: Maggie Canon
Project Editors: Mireille Majoor, Jill Simonsen
Cover and Interior Design: Diana Van Winkle, Arthur Wait

Excel Marketing Budget Templates Project Manager: Sue Raisty-Egami

Services for our readers

Colleges, business schools, corporate purchasing:
The Planning Shop offers special discounts and supplemental teaching materials for universities, business schools, and corporate training. Contact:

> info@PlanningShop.com
> or call 650-289-9120

Free business tips and information:
To receive The Planning Shop's free email newsletter on starting and growing a successful business, sign up at: *www.PlanningShop.com.*

> The Planning Shop™
> 555 Bryant Street, #180
> Palo Alto, CA 94301 USA
> 650-289-9120
>
> Fax: 650-289-9125
> Email: info@PlanningShop.com
> www.PlanningShop.com

The Planning Shop™ is a division of Rhonda, Inc., a California corporation.

"This publication is designed to provide accurate and authoritative information in regard to the subject matter covered. It is sold with the understanding that the publisher and author are not engaged in rendering legal, accounting, or other professional services. If legal advice or other expert assistance is required, seek the services of a competent professional."

— *from a Declaration of Principles, jointly adopted by a committee*
of the American Bar Association and a committee of publishers

Printed in Canada

10 9 8 7 6 5 4 3 2 1

Who This Book Is for

Successful Marketing: Secrets & Strategies addresses the entrepreneurial marketing techniques that work in the real world. The emphasis is on providing the practical, affordable marketing tactics that will give you the best return on your marketing investment and delivering the essential knowledge that will make your marketing plan a success.

Successful Marketing: Secrets & Strategies is for you if you want to:

- Sell more products or services
- Launch new products or services
- Establish or build a brand
- Attract the attention of investors or increase your visibility in the stock market
- Understand how to use online marketing techniques
- Find affordable ways to get the word out about your company, product, or services
- Develop a marketing plan, including a complete annual marketing budget

In particular, this book was designed for:

- Entrepreneurs starting new businesses
- Entrepreneurs looking to increase their sales at established companies
- Entrepreneurs seeking improved results from their marketing expenditures
- Entrepreneurs launching new products or services for existing companies
- Students of entrepreneurship who want to familiarize themselves with real-world marketing tactics for growing, new, or small companies
- Students of marketing who need a thorough grounding in marketing essentials and a complete overview of marketing techniques
- Corporate marketing personnel who need to create marketing plans and/ or develop marketing budgets
- Anyone trying to pinpoint the best marketing tactics and strategy for their business and budget

About The Planning Shop

The Planning Shop specializes in creating business resources for entrepreneurs. The Planning Shop's books and other products are based on years of real-world experience, and they share secrets and strategies from entrepreneurs, CEOs, investors, lenders, and seasoned business experts. Millions of entrepreneurs have used The Planning Shop's products to launch, run, and expand businesses in every industry.

Since chief entrepreneur and CEO Rhonda Abrams founded The Planning Shop in 1999, more than six hundred business schools, colleges, and universities have adopted The Planning Shop's books. In addition, The Planning Shop's first book—*The Successful Business Plan: Secrets & Strategies*—has sold more than 600,000 copies.

The Planning Shop's expanding line of business books includes:

- The **Successful Business series,** assisting entrepreneurs and business students in planning and growing businesses. Titles include *Six-Week Start-Up, The Owner's Manual for Small Business,* and *What Business Should I Start?*

- The **In A Day series,** enabling entrepreneurs to tackle a critical business task and "Get it done right, get it done fast.™" Titles include *Business Plan In A Day, Winning Presentation In A Day,* and *Trade Show In A Day.*

- The **Better Business Bureau series,** helping entrepreneurs and consumers successfully make serious financial decisions. Titles include *Buying a Franchise, Buying a Home,* and *Starting an eBay Business.*

At The Planning Shop, now and in the future, you'll find a range of business resources. Learn more at *www.PlanningShop.com.*

About The Authors

RHONDA ABRAMS

Entrepreneur, author, and nationally syndicated columnist Rhonda Abrams is widely recognized as one of the leading experts on entrepreneurship and small business. Rhonda's column for *USAToday,* "Strategies," is the most widely distributed column on small business and entrepreneurship in the U.S., reaching tens of millions of readers each week online and in print.

Rhonda's books have been used by millions of entrepreneurs. Her first book, *The Successful Business Plan: Secrets & Strategies,* has sold more than 600,000 copies. It was named one of the Top Ten business books for entrepreneurs by both *Forbes* and *Inc.* magazines. Rhonda's other books are perennial best-sellers, with three them having reached Bookscan's "Top 50 Business Bestseller" list.

Rhonda not only writes about business—she lives it! As the founder of three successful companies, Rhonda has accumulated an extraordinary depth of experience and a real-life understanding of the challenges facing entrepreneurs. In 1986, Rhonda founded a management consulting practice working with clients ranging from one-person startups to Fortune 500 companies. In 1995, she founded a Web content company for small businesses, which she later sold. And in 1999, Rhonda started a publishing company—now called The Planning Shop—focusing exclusively on topics of business planning, entrepreneurship, and new business development.

A popular public speaker and lecturer, Rhonda is regularly invited to address leading industry and trade associations, business schools, and corporate conventions and events. She conducts training workshops on business planning and delivers keynote speeches. Educated at Harvard University and UCLA, where she was named Outstanding Senior, Rhonda now lives in Palo Alto, California.

Register to receive Rhonda's free business newsletter at The Planning Shop's website, www.PlanningShop.com.

Other books by Rhonda Abrams include:

The Successful Business Plan: Secrets & Strategies

Six-Week Start-Up

Business Plan In A Day

The Owner's Manual for Small Business

Successful Business Research

What Business Should I Start?

Winning Presentation In A Day

Trade Show In A Day

Wear Clean Underwear: Business Wisdom

Julie Vallone

Julie Vallone has been answering the marketing needs of businesses ranging from startups to Fortune 500 companies for more than a decade. As president of Vallone Communications, she has created winning marketing campaigns and penned marketing copy for clients focused on everything from art to chocolate, computer components and peripherals, GPS technology, hotel services, luxury travel, nonprofit programs, restaurants, spas, sunglasses, and Web services.

Before starting Vallone Communications, Julie managed two Web content development teams for high-tech startups. She also served as editor-in-chief for Santa Cruz County's award-winning newsweekly *Good Times* and editor and marketing writer for the California Association of Nonprofits.

Julie is currently a freelance journalist and a regular, ten-year contributor to *Investor's Business Daily*. She has also written for *Entrepreneur* magazine, *Business Start-Ups*, *Santa Cruz Magazine*, *South Bay Accent,* and *Salon.com*.

Other Planning Shop Books that Julie has contributed to (either as a principal writer or contributor) include *Business Plan In A Day*, *Winning Presentation In A Day*, and *Successful Business Research.*

Julie currently lives in Soquel, California, with her husband, Rick; daughter Siena; and cat Charlotte.

How to Use This Book

Sccessful Marketing: Secrets & Strategies serves as an interactive tool for entrepreneurs seeking the most effective, efficient, and affordable means to get the word out about their company, products, and services.

As you will quickly come to realize as you work your way through this guide, there are almost as many marketing options today as there are products and services to sell. This book helps you make sense of them and assists you in finding the ones that are the best matches for your products or services and promise to provide the biggest bang for your bucks.

To that end, *Successful Marketing: Secrets & Strategies* covers all of the major marketing tactics in use today (as well as some more radical ones that have yet to be widely adopted), offering a wealth of worksheets and examples to help you turn your ideas into actions. By the time you reach the end of this volume, you will have developed a complete marketing plan as well as the overall marketing budget to support it.

Organization

Divided into six main sections and a concluding section, *Successful Marketing: Secrets & Strategies* leads you step-by-step through the process of developing, preparing, and implementing a marketing plan:

■ **Section I, Marketing Essentials,** provides the grounding you need to begin formulating your own marketing plan.

■ **Sections II through VI** provide in-depth guidance in the range of marketing tactics and techniques available to you.

■ **Section VII, Pulling It All Together,** demonstrates how to pull together everything you've learned into an overall 12-month marketing plan and marketing budget.

*Note: For a thorough overview of **online marketing activities**—including many that are just emerging—refer to Section V, Online Marketing.*

Marketing Essentials

Section I, Marketing Essentials, aims to help you achieve a thorough understanding of why people buy (and how you can increase the odds of them doing so), who your customers are (and how you can acquire and retain them), how you can best your competition, what you need to do to define your brand and core message, and your ultimate marketing goals. In the process, it provides a thorough grounding in the marketing basics you'll need to choose your marketing tactics and develop your marketing plan.

Traditional Advertising

Section II, Traditional Advertising, gets to the heart of the first thing people think of when they hear the word *marketing*—advertising. As you work your way through this section, you'll learn about the vast range of marketing options—for budgets large *and* small—available through print, radio, and TV advertising. In addition to the Brainstorming, Return on Investment (ROI), and 12-Month Budget worksheets you'll find throughout this volume, the chapters in this section include comprehensive tables comparing the myriad options available for each medium—including types of publications or stations, price scales for advertising in or on them, the benefits and challenges associated with each, the types of audiences they're best for targeting, and tips for making the most effective use of them.

Person-to-Person Marketing

Section III, Person-to-Person Marketing, is all about *connections*—the human interactions that drive people to buy your product or service. With chapters on networking, word-of-mouth marketing, trade shows, and public relations, this section shows you how to turn personal contacts and professional affiliations into key marketing opportunities for your business.

Print Marketing

Section IV, Print Marketing, explores the world of marketing opportunities available through printed materials. From business cards to brochures, printed marketing materials—often referred to as *collateral*—serve as the face of your business, both supplementing and supporting your online marketing presence. In chapters on print collateral and direct mail, you'll learn about the range of options—from penny pinching to budget busting—that ink-on-paper materials present for promoting your products and services and improving the credibility and visibility of your brand.

Online Marketing

Section V, Online Marketing, ushers you into the brave, new, and constantly evolving world of marketing on the Internet and the World Wide Web. Millions of people are going online every day to research potential purchases, socialize, seek entertainment, and find out the news of the day. And this means millions of marketing opportunities for your business—if only you could figure out how to reach these millions of online users. This section shows you how via chapters on website marketing, search engine optimization and marketing, email marketing, other forms of online advertising, and blogs, social networking, and other online tactics.

Other Types of Marketing

Section VI, Other Types of Marketing, reveals the wealth of additional marketing tactics—some tried and true and others a bit more radical—that don't fit neatly into any of the previously discussed categories. In chapters on in-store marketing and sampling as well as signs, other types of ads, and out-of-the-box marketing, you'll learn that the only true limit to your marketing options is you own imagination. In these pages you'll discover a variety of tactics (including sampling, sponsorships, transit ads, product placement, Yellow pages listings, guerilla marketing, and more) that you can use to get your product, service, or brand in front of customers—and indeed much closer to them than through most other forms of marketing.

Pulling It All Together

Section VII, Pulling It All Together, represents the culmination of your labors in working through this guide. In its single concluding chapter, "Completing Your Marketing Plan," you'll learn how to draw on the information you've gleaned from filling out the worksheets and budgets in earlier sections (as well as the In-House Marketing Staff budget in Section VII) to create an overarching annual marketing plan and budget. Even more importantly, you'll learn how to *execute* on that plan. Happy marketing!

Worksheets

To help you think through and plan your marketing activities, *Successful Marketing: Secrets & Strategies* includes a slew of worksheets for you to complete as you go through the text. These help to get your creative juices flowing and enable you to map out the goals, costs, and needs associated with your marketing plan. By the time you're finished filling out all the worksheets, you'll have a complete Marketing Plan!

Successful Marketing: Secrets and Strategies worksheets come in the following flavors:

- **Brainstorming.** Use these worksheets to do your internal planning and to gather and coordinate the information you will use to complete your overall marketing plan.

- **Return on investment (ROI).** Every marketing activity has associated costs; thus, it's important that you determine not only the financial and non-financial investments your marketing activities will require but also the *return* you can expect to get on that investment—whether it takes the form of increased sales, heightened visibility, increased brand awareness, or any number of other benefits. Only in this way will you be able to determine whether the marketing activity in question represents a good use of your time and money. To help you make that determination, this book includes an ROI worksheet for each type of major marketing activity covered.

- **12-month budget.** Since most marketing activities represent sustained efforts rather than one-time projects (and since many businesses develop annual budgets), this book includes worksheets that allow you to break down all of the costs associated with each major marketing activity for a 12-month period. At the end of the book, you'll find an overall budget that collates all of those marketing techniques (and their costs) into a single 12-month marketing budget.

- **Building your marketing plan.** At the end of each section (except Section I, Marketing Essentials), you'll find a worksheet that allows you to draw on everything you've learned in the section—including all of the information you've distilled from the Brainstorming worksheets—to put together a marketing plan for the techniques covered in that section.

Special Features

In addition to a plethora of worksheets—which you can use to turn ideas into actions—*Successful Marketing: Secrets & Strategies* offers the following tools to highlight important information and to help you refine your marketing goals and tactics:

- **Lingo.** Every industry, trade, profession, and social group has its own language, made up of terms and expressions that while meaningful to members of that group, may be all but incomprehensible to outsiders. *Successful Marketing: Secrets & Strategies* makes you an insider in the world of marketing by opening each section and chapter with a list of such terms and their definitions. After all, it's much easier to get by—and thrive—if you speak the language.

- **Myth Busters.** You've heard them a million times—sayings like, "If you build it, they will come." But what if *they* don't know about your brilliant invention, or even if they do, don't understand why it's relevant to them. These sidebar elements—scattered throughout the book—lay down the facts about some commonly held marketing misperceptions, making you think twice about your own marketing plan in the process.

- **Affordability Scales.** With an almost mind-boggling variety of marketing tactics and techniques available to you, sometimes the best and fastest way to start narrowing your options is by figuring out which you can actually afford. That's why *Successful Marketing: Secrets & Strategies* includes Affordability Scales. Found in all of the major sections as well as in some individual chapters in this book, these graphical tools provide an at-a-glance summary of the overall costs of each major marketing activity described. In this way, you can see how the various tactics stack up against each other price-wise.

- **Electronic Marketing Budget Tempates.** Let's face it: not many people enjoy preparing budgets—after all, collating the costs from myriad activities (which themselves require separate budgets) to come up with an accurate overall marketing budget is no small task. *Successful Marketing: Secrets & Strategies* makes the process a lot less painful by providing Electronic Marketing Budget Templates—pre-formatted Excel spreadsheets that automatically total the individual budgets from throughout the book to create an Annual Marketing Budget. These come free with the Deluxe Binder Edition or can be downloaded for a small fee by purchasers of the paperback version at www.PlanningShop.com.

Electronic Marketing Budget Templates

If you purchased the Deluxe Binder Edition of *Successful Marketing: Secrets & Strategies*, you have one additional flavor of worksheet—electronic marketing budget templates (Excel-based). These comprise all of the marketing budget worksheets from this book in electronic format—as pre-formatted Excel spreadsheets. These worksheets automatically total the individual budget worksheets to create an overall Annual Marketing Budget. Purchasers of the paperback version of this book can download the Electronic Marketing Budget Templates (for a modest fee) at www.PlanningShop.com.

CONTENTS

SECTION I

Marketing Essentials

Lingo

CAMPAIGN: A planned program of marketing activities and tactics executed over a specific period of time and established in line with an overall strategy; often planned to launch something new (product, service, or pricing).

CHANNEL: An avenue through which you will sell your products/services (such as through distributors, retailers, or online).

COLLATERAL: Printed marketing materials that describe your company, product, or service; these include brochures, catalogs, and product information sheets.

COMPETITION: Other companies that offer products or services similar to yours and/or other solutions that compete with yours for your target market's dollars.

COMPETITIVE ADVANTAGE: What differentiates you from your competition. The reason your customer would buy what you sell over what someone else sells.

MARKET SHARE: The proportion of the total market for a product or service that a business controls.

MARKETING MESSAGE: What you hope those who are the target of your marketing campaign will learn and remember about your company, products, or services; the specific content of what you say in your marketing materials and advertisements.

MARKETING PLAN: A thought-out program, in written form, delineating your overall marketing goals, strategy, and budget—and the marketing tactics you will use to achieve your goals; a blueprint for your marketing activities.

MARKETING TACTICS: The specific means and vehicles you use to reach customers, such as advertising, direct mail, or networking.

CHAPTER 1

Success Takes Marketing

Success in business requires marketing.

Marketing shapes the future of your business. Whatever industry you're in, whatever the quality or price of your product or services, you still need to market your business to succeed. A well-conceived marketing plan and well-executed marketing program make the difference between a thriving, growing business and one that never gets past the starting gate.

What Is Marketing?

You've developed a great new product. You've started a business, secured financing, created a product, or started a service. But where are the customers? How do you let people know about your offering? And what do you want them to know about you?

You need marketing—and a marketing plan.

There's a common misconception that marketing equals advertising. But marketing is much more than that. Simply stated, marketing is made up of the full range of a company's activities aimed at reaching and motivating customers. In addition to letting customers and potential customers know that you exist and describing what you offer and the benefits of your product or service, marketing enables you to:

Announce new products, services, or partnerships

Alert customers to new locations or places to buy your products

■ Attract new customers and more sales through special offers

Develop new sales and distribution channels

Determine the right prices for your products or services

Create a need or desire for a product or service that didn't exist before

Make potential partners aware of your business

Attract investors or other sources of funding

> **❝***Marketing is an organizational function and a set of processes for creating, communicating, and delivering value to customers and for managing customer relationships in ways that benefit the organization and its stakeholders.*❞
> **The American Marketing Association**

If You Build It, They will Come

MYTH: Customers will naturally be attracted to a great business, product, or service.

BUSTED: No matter how terrific your business, product, or service is, you need marketing.

Many entrepreneurs, especially those new to business, believe that if they build a truly great product, customers will find them. It's just not so. The fact is that you must make customers or clients aware of your products or services before they will buy. Indeed, you must not only let them know about you; you also have to help them understand why they would want to buy what you're offering: what makes your product, service, or company unique, special, better than the competition.

That's why marketing is a key component of business success. And that's why you have to plan—and budget— for marketing as part of the development of any company, product, or service.

Advertising—and other activities such as promotions, networking, search engine optimization, and the like—are *marketing tactics.* They make up the bulk of your marketing program. But before you can choose and engage in those marketing tactics, you'll need a framework for making choices about them.

A *marketing plan* is that framework. With a marketing plan, you establish your goals, evaluate and determine the best customers for your product or service, understand your competitors, and develop a clear strategy for distinguishing yourself in the marketplace. Then you need to set the right price, choose the best ways to reach your customers, and craft a compelling message to motivate them to buy your product or service.

A marketing plan helps you make sure you're spending your marketing dollars wisely and in the most effective way. A complete marketing plan guides you as you grow your business.

What Marketing Accomplishes

Marketing has two main objectives:

- **Building awareness.** All marketing activities are aimed at getting an audience's—usually prospective customers'—attention. If customers don't know you exist, they can't buy from you. You need to be sure, at a minimum, that they know about your company, product, or service—or at least remember your name. That's why some companies go to extraordinary lengths to attract customers' attention, especially since consumers are constantly bombarded by advertisements.

- **Driving sales.** The ultimate goal of marketing is to increase your revenues. There are significant differences between sales and marketing (see page 7). Marketing exists to generate customer demand, bring in prospects, and support the sales force and sales process. Within a company, marketing goals are often tied to, and evaluated by, the sales results achieved. It's all about making the cash registers ring.

But marketing also achieves a broader range of critical goals:

- **Shaping perceptions.** Why do consumers think of Apple products as particularly cool? Why are Volvos believed to be exceptionally safe? What we think of, and associate with, a company or product or service is substantially influenced by their marketing. Apple and Volvo, and most other successful companies, understand what makes them special—what distinguishes them—to their customers. To some degree, their actual products first established their image, but they make certain their marketing messages continually expand and reinforce their image or distinguishing characteristics. Good marketing helps customers perceive and remember what makes your business special, unique, and better than the competition.

- **Developing loyalty.** Because many marketing activities are aimed not merely at attracting new customers but also at retaining current customers, a complete marketing program actually enhances a customer's sense of loyalty to your business. In fact, some marketing activities are called "customer loyalty programs." These can be as simple as a sandwich shop giving customers one free sandwich after they've purchased ten or as complex as a major airline's mileage rewards program. The goal is to keep customers coming back.

- **Creating connections.** Great marketing does more than just convey a message to prospective customers or even compel them to buy. The best marketing actually creates a strong bond with them. Outstanding marketing helps a company, product, or service create a personality. Customers actually develop or enhance their sense of self by association with that company, product, or service. Many businesses achieve this bond by being known for their socially responsible character—they take steps to protect the environment or use environmentally sensitive manufacturing processes or treat employees exceptionally well or do no research on animals. Customers feel good about supporting such businesses.

- **Building brands.** What products have you purchased because you trusted their brand? What products have you paid more for because you respected their brand name? Brands have value, in some cases billions of dollars in value, because they motivate customers to buy. Building a brand takes time, money, and consistent, repetitive, careful marketing. But even a small, entrepreneurial business can build a successful brand—just think of MySpace, which started small and built a world-class brand.

- **Building businesses.** Effective marketing often results in a company increasing its market share (the proportion of the total market for a product or service that a company controls). Companies that can capture and retain a significant portion of a market are clearly important companies. They tend to have greater staying power and greater market value than their competitors.

Marketing Versus Sales

Many people use the terms *marketing* and *sales* interchangeably, but these two critical business functions are very different. All the same, they are very closely interrelated.

Briefly, here's the distinction between marketing and sales:

- Marketing encompasses all those activities designed to make customers aware of you and to explain your competitive advantage. It is not specifically transactional (as sales are). Marketing includes advertising, developing and maintaining a website, exhibiting at trade shows, and creating brochures and other marketing materials. Marketing also includes networking—meeting potential customers and referral sources through informal activities such as joining organizations, attending industry events, or taking people to lunch.

- Sales activities are direct actions taken to secure customer orders. They are aimed at a transaction. Sales activities include helping customers at your place of business make selections, submitting proposals and bids, making phone calls or in-person visits to solicit orders, and selling merchandise on your website.

It's clearly difficult to be successful in one area—either marketing or sales—if you neglect the other. How do you go out and make a sales call if

---

Not Just for Customers

While it's typical to think of marketing as communicating with customers, some of your marketing activities may be directed to different audiences. You may be looking for financing for a new venture, so you'll want to choose marketing activities that reach the attention of potential investors. Or you may want to increase your company's stock price, so you'll make sure Wall Street financial analysts know about the big deal you've landed.

What Marketing *Cannot* Do

Marketing is a critical component of your success, but it's not the only one. Great marketing can help launch a business or a product, but no matter how terrific your marketing is, it can't sustain a company, product, or service indefinitely.

If a company—or its products or services—are fundamentally flawed, marketing won't keep it alive, at least not for long. If your company makes poor products or provides bad service, sooner or later, customers will stop coming.

The Golden Rule: Repetition, Repetition, Repetition

Regardless of which marketing tactics you choose, a key rule of marketing is that you must repeat your message to the same audience in the same place, over and over and over again. It may be annoying to see the same TV commercial for the umpteenth time, but there's a reason for the repetition: it takes many exposures to a message before someone even notices it. By the time you become aware of any ad—whether on TV, on the Internet, in print, or elsewhere—you may already have been exposed to it at least a half-dozen times. It takes many more exposures before that message starts to sink in. It takes even more exposures before you actually remember it. Even if you use networking as your main marketing technique, you'll need to attend the same organization's meetings many times before others remember you.

you don't have a brochure to give a prospect or a website to add credibility to your company or explain your products? On the other hand, what good are all those great marketing activities if you don't have someone to actually close the deal?

Since both marketing and sales are designed to attract and secure customers, can they both be handled by the same department, or same person, in a company?

Generally, no. That's because these key activities require very different skills and appeal to very different personality types. The marketing ability required to evaluate market research, develop a brochure, or plan a website is much different than the sales talent it takes to cold call a prospect, generate leads, or ask a customer in person to make a purchase. The chart below compares the types of activities involved in marketing with those done in sales.

Marketing Tactics

The bulk of this book is devoted to *marketing tactics*—the specific activities you'll undertake to reach your marketing goals and get your message to its intended target audience. That's because most businesses spend the vast majority of their marketing time and money on tactics.

There's an almost unlimited range of techniques that can be used to market to customers and an equally wide range of costs associated with those efforts. Some of these techniques are familiar: advertising in print, radio, or TV advertisements are the most traditional. But other, less traditional marketing tactics are also considered fairly standard: Internet campaigns, exhibiting at trade shows, offering samples of products, and developing brochures and other marketing materials.

Some activities are frequently not considered marketing, yet they are actually marketing tactics: networking with prospective clients at industry association meetings, donating to public radio stations, getting involved with community not-for-profit organizations.

The chart on page 9 lists a range of marketing tactics. Keep in mind that this list doesn't include "outside the box" marketing ideas, such as having students shave your company logo into their hair, getting dog leashes printed with your company name, or having labels with your logo placed on bananas at your local supermarket. Marketing techniques and tactics are limited only by your imagination and budget.

Why You Need a Complete Marketing Plan

A complete marketing plan is a blueprint outlining the full range of activities you'll undertake to reach your marketing objectives. It explains how those objectives fit in with your overall business goals, what message you'll be communicating and to which audience, what marketing activities you'll be doing—and when, how frequently, and how much they'll cost—and how you'll measure your success.

You can spend a great deal of money on advertising, promotions, public relations, and other marketing activities and still not be effective. Bad marketing can leave your audience confused about your message and unsure of what you do or sell. Or it may convey the wrong image—you may want to let customers know that you're very competitive on price, but this may actually leave customers thinking your products are cheap and shoddy. You can reach the wrong audience: people who are not prospective customers. Poorly planned marketing wastes money.

That's why you need a complete marketing plan: a thorough program that establishes your goals, message, and target audience, along with the right marketing tactics and vehicles to reach them.

By developing a complete marketing plan, you'll have an action roadmap for success and a way to avoid potentially costly mistakes.

What Your Marketing Plan Should Accomplish

A complete marketing plan is a roadmap to success for your marketing efforts. It helps you to:

- Determine what you hope to achieve through this communication—in other words, establish your goals

- Identify the best potential customers for your products or services—your target market

- Understand that market—what they're like; where they are; what they do, watch, read; what and how they buy; what motivates them

- Match the right products or services to that market

- Understand who your competitors are and how you are distinguished from them

- Craft a message that clearly distinguishes you from your competitors, conveys your benefits, and will compel customers to buy

- Choose the right ways and places to reach your target market with your message—your marketing tactics and vehicles

- Budget the expenditure of your marketing funds to insure you make the best use of the resources you have available

- Evaluate whether you have, indeed, reached your goals

On top of all that, you have to build in a structure that enables you to continue to be able to communicate with those same prospects or customers repeatedly and build an ongoing customer relationship.

Throughout this book, you will find worksheets, highlighted in green, which will help you develop a complete marketing plan. Fill in these worksheets as you go through this book. By the end, you'll have a complete marketing plan for your business.

Most-used Marketing Tactics

- Traditional advertising
- Public relations
- Marketing collateral
- Websites
- Online marketing
- Networking
- Trade shows
- Public speaking
- Newsletters
- Direct mail
- Sampling
- Sponsorships
- Viral marketing
- Product placement

Lingo

ACTUAL NEEDS: What customers absolutely need to survive or function well in their current situations, such as air, water, food, a source of income, transportation, and a healthy living and working atmosphere.

AFFILIATE MARKETING: Partnering with another company as a way of gaining credibility through a positive association, in hopes of selling more products or services.

AWARENESS: The level of knowledge among customers and others regarding your company, product, or service.

BENEFITS: How a feature of a product or service answers customers' needs and wants. What a customer gains from using or owning a product or service; for example, increased productivity or improved appearance. These are not the product's features (see "Features" definition below).

BRAND: A trade name for a company, product, or service that distinguishes it from competitors. In a wider sense, a level of recognition and relationship that a company, product, or service builds with the public, and what a company, product, or service stands for.

FEATURES: The specific, objective attributes of a product or service. These are not the benefits (which are defined above).

GENERIC: A product or service without a brand name.

PERCEIVED NEEDS: What customers think or believe they need to function well in a situation, such as needing a younger, more muscular, or more beautiful appearance.

PRICE/COST: The amount you are charging (or were charged) for a product or service.

VALUE: The total worth of a product or service; often expressed as a combination of price and features and benefits. A product that offers more features than a similarly priced competing product is perceived to be a better value, even though the cost or price is the same.

CHAPTER 2

Why People Buy

People, businesses, the government, your dog—they all have needs and desires. Without needs and wants, real or imagined, no one would ever buy (or sell) anything. But having needs and knowing what they are, are two entirely different things. Customers may think they need or want one thing, but sometimes they actually need or want something very different.

Music fans may believe they want a T-shirt with the logo of a particular band on it, but what they *really* want is the acceptance and camaraderie of the peers who turned them on to the band in the first place. A sales executive might spend hundreds of dollars to fly first class because they believe they need the extra room to work on the plane. What they're *really* looking for is the sense of status they get from sitting in the front of the plane.

Why people buy from a certain seller is even more challenging to determine. Once again, buyers aren't always aware of all the reasons why they choose to do business with one company rather than another. They may think they patronize a business because the products or services are better when, in reality, it's because they trust and like the actor who's the company's spokesperson.

The more you understand why people buy—and from whom—the better you will be able to develop an effective marketing strategy and plan.

Customer Motivations

Successful marketing starts with figuring out the motivations of your customers, both the obvious ones and the deeper needs and desires that compel your customers to buy. Being aware of all customers' motivations enables you to better tailor your marketing efforts to appeal to all their needs and wants. In general, there are four kinds of needs and desires that drive customers to buy any kind of product or service:

- **Actual immediate.** These are short-term needs that customers must respond to right away. A hungry person with a 30-minute lunch break who needs to grab a sandwich or salad close by or an itchy person who needs to find something to relieve the symptoms of a run-in with poison oak will take action within a couple of hours. A business losing valuable orders because its phone system can't keep up with the call volume needs to upgrade its phone system pronto to avoid losing revenues.

An Italian restaurant whose pasta supplier just retired and moved back to the old country needs to find a new carb connection right away. These companies will need to find a solution within a couple of days. Customers with an actual, immediate need are less price-sensitive and will do little comparison shopping.

■ **Actual long-term.** These are reality-based needs and wants that must be responded to, but not necessarily right away. Customers do plan to fulfill these needs or desires at some point, but not in the next few hours. Consider a consumer whose car is starting to need constant repair and who realizes they'll have to replace it or a business that has an outdated e-commerce website and recognizes they'll have to improve its functionality. These customers know they'll benefit from a product or service and foresee making a purchase, but they do not need those benefits immediately and are not necessarily in a hurry to act. They will likely take several months to consider all the options and compare pricing before making a final decision on a product or service.

■ **Perceived.** These are needs a person believes or thinks they have, but are not, in reality, absolute needs. An individual may desire to have bright white teeth or a corporation may wish to have a big-name rock star perform at their new-product launch party, but it's unlikely either would suffer dire consequences if those needs were not met. Many people feel they absolutely must drive a snazzy sports car, but other than a race-car driver, no one really *has* to drive a Ferrari. The purchase of virtually all luxury goods is almost always motivated by perceived needs and desires. Yet customers make many purchasing decisions based on a desire to define their personal image or business reputation or a perceived need to improve their social standing, sense of well-being, or success. Perceived needs are just as real to customers as actual needs and can be powerful motivators to buy.

■ **Unrecognized.** These are desires and needs that customers don't yet—or can't yet—recognize, often developed in response to the creation of a new type of product or service. Nobody walked around thinking they needed to carry around ten thousand songs before the Apple iPod was invented. But innovation and invention create needs and desires that never existed before. Innovative companies that are developing new products or services have to shape their marketing campaign to help customers realize why they even need to, or would want to, buy what you're selling.

As you plan your marketing efforts, assess the motivations of your potential customers. Will the majority of them have an actual immediate need? Your marketing will need to clearly indicate you can solve their problem. Or will more of your prospective customers be meeting perceived, rather than actual, needs? If so, your marketing has to emphasize how you enhance customers' sense of well-being and fulfill their desires.

In most cases, of course, customers have a combination of actual and perceived needs and wants. If you build e-commerce websites, some customers will have an absolute, critical need for the fastest, best technology. Others will just want those features to feel like they have the latest and greatest on their site. It's a mistake to assume that all customers have the same motivations as you (or your immediate friends, family, and colleagues). Often, customers have very different reasons for making a purchase, and there's probably a wide range of motives. Conducting market research, such as surveys, interviews, and focus groups, can help you figure out some of the reasons why customers will want or need to buy your product or service.

Savvy marketers take advantage of both actual and perceived needs and desires. And when they are introducing something new, they can create a need or desire where none existed before. Tailor your tactics and message to meet the range of all their actual, perceived, and unrecognized needs.

SO YOU THINK YOU NEED A NEW CAR ...	
ACTUAL IMMEDIATE:	Your only car breaks down beyond repair. You must have a car to get to work, and there's no public transportation available. Renting cars is expensive.
ACTUAL LONG-TERM:	Your car is getting increasingly expensive to repair and maintain. It's becoming unreliable, and you need a car to get to work, run your errands, or get to school.
PERCEIVED:	You've been driving your 12-year-old economy car for years. You just got a new, high-paying job, and you can now afford a more expensive vehicle. You want to impress clients, neighbors, friends; more importantly, you feel you deserve it.
UNRECOGNIZED:	Hybrid cars and electric vehicles are introduced. You care about the environment, and you now realize you can operate a car that will reduce fuel emissions.

Why Customers Buy from YOU

When a customer is ready to make a decision, you naturally want to be the one they turn to. But other companies will also be ready to answer customers' needs and wants. So what makes a customer choose a particular company? More specifically, how do you convince a customer to overlook the competition and buy from *you*?

There are many factors affecting whether a customer chooses to buy goods or services from you rather than from your competition, including:

- Awareness
- Features and benefits
- Price
- Brand
- Convenience
- Word of mouth
- Online opinions/reviews
- Affiliation

BRAINSTORMING

YOUR CUSTOMERS' NEEDS

Why would people buy your product or service? Use this worksheet to brainstorm about the possible actual immediate, actual long-term, perceived, and unrecognized needs customers may have for what you have to offer.

Your product or service:

_____

_____

_____

_____

1. Actual immediate needs:

_____

_____

_____

_____

2. Actual long-term needs:

_____

_____

_____

_____

3. Perceived needs:

_____

_____

_____

_____

4. Unrecognized needs (if any):

_____

_____

_____

_____

Awareness

First and foremost, a customer has to know you exist before they can choose to patronize your business. Awareness is the most necessary, and often overlooked, component of motivating a customer to buy from you. Creating awareness is the *fundamental goal of any marketing campaign.* That means you need to somehow place yourself in front of, or at least in the mind of, your customer. How you do that depends on the type of business you're in.

If you're in a business where customers come to you (for example, a restaurant or retail business), the old maxim applies: *location, location, location.* For instance, you may be a loyal customer of a sandwich shop a block from your home. You might not even know the name of the shop, but they have good turkey sandwiches, and they're reasonably priced. There's another sandwich shop three streets over with better food and a nicer atmosphere, but that doesn't affect your choice, because you don't know about it.

But every place that wants your business can't be located near you. Some businesses (for example, service businesses and Internet sites) may not have a physical location at all. That's where advertising and other forms of marketing come in. Marketing puts your company, product, or service in front of your customer and makes them aware of you.

So if that sandwich shop three streets over runs an ad, complete with a discount coupon, in your local paper, you may suddenly become aware of it. You decide to try the place and find that their sandwiches are fresher and have better value than the BLTs at your old lunch place. Suddenly, you're now *their* loyal customer. You would never have made the change if the new sandwich shop hadn't advertised—and made you aware of their existence.

Features and Benefits

The terms *features* and *benefits* are often used interchangeably, but their meanings are actually quite distinct.

Features are the specific attributes of a product or service that distinguish it from competitive products or services. For example:

A head of lettuce is organic.

A car has a built-in navigation system.

A desk chair has five height settings.

The organic cultivation, the navigation system, and the height settings are all features of their respective products.

Benefits are the ways in which a product or service improves a customer's life or business. For example:

The organic origin of the lettuce helps the customer stay healthy (by avoiding pesticides).

The car's navigation system provides the customer with convenience and time savings (by helping drivers get to where they need to go).

Focus on Benefits

A cardinal rule of marketing is that customers buy *benefits*, not *features*. Of course, customers compare features while shopping, so you'll need to include features in your advertising and marketing materials. But you'll always want to emphasize the benefits those features bring. If you're selling laptop computers aimed at business travelers, for example, you may want to describe features such as how light-weight they are and how long their batteries last. But your marketing will be more effective if you also communicate how the customer will benefit, such as being able to stay powered up for a cross-oceanic flight.

■ The desk chair's variable height settings enable a business customer to make its employees more comfortable, improve productivity, and enhance their ergonomic well-being.

Improved health, convenience, time savings, productivity, and comfort are some of the benefits offered by these products due to their specific features.

Price

Depending on the type of product or service you're offering and who you're targeting as a customer, pricing plays a key role in swaying customers to choose *your* company's product or service. Setting the right price to motivate people to buy comes with knowing your customers' needs, desires, and purchasing patterns as well as your competitors' prices. Generally, there are three types of price levels that motivate customers:

■ **Low prices.** Price is the major motivator for highly cost-sensitive customers. Such customers are less concerned about service, prestige, product/service features, and sometimes even the quality associated with higher-priced options. They're more apt to buy a generic product (one without a brand name) over a higher-priced one produced by a better-known and respected competitor. Customers driven primarily by low prices shop at retailers such as Wal-Mart or Internet sites offering rock-bottom prices. If you're targeting these types of customers, emphasizing the fact that you are the "low-cost leader" is paramount.

■ **High—or premium—prices.** By contrast, some customers are actually motivated when goods are priced high, and a low price can dissuade this type of customer from making a purchase. That's because these customers tend to question the quality of a lower-priced product or service. Most luxury goods must carry a high price tag for customers to perceive their value or to meet their need for status. For instance, someone who pays thousands of dollars for a watch would not feel they reaped the same benefits (including prestige and quality workmanship) if they bought a watch costing less than $100—even though both watches keep time. In the corporate arena, some executives will pay higher fees for premium credit cards, because they believe that these cards indicate they're successful and in the same league as other elite executives.

Customers who are motivated by high/premium prices shop at upscale retailers such as Neiman Marcus or Bloomingdales, small boutiques, and upscale electronics retailers such as Bang & Olufsen. If you're targeting these types of customers, emphasizing the quality and luxurious nature of your products and the elite stature of your current customers is critical.

■ **Value prices.** The majority of customers are searching for the best return for their money. They will pay more than a highly cost-conscious customer but expect to receive many benefits in return. They will not pay premium prices just to be perceived as elite. For instance, a value-conscious business traveler will choose to stay at a motel that offers not just a room but also a suite with complimentary Internet access, breakfast, and cocktail hour even if the motel is not considered a prestigious brand. Customers who are value conscious shop at stores such as Costco, Best Buy, and Target. If you're targeting these customers, your marketing should emphasize the many benefits they receive for a relatively affordable price.

Brand and Reputation

Brands are powerful motivators for customers, because they enhance customers' familiarity and comfort level with your products or services. A brand is a promise—a promise of consistency of quality, service, image. When you get a hamburger from McDonald's, it may not be the best hamburger in the world, but it's the same as the last McDonald's hamburger you had and the same as the next McDonald's hamburger you'll eat.

Because branded products or services promise to be consistent, they inspire the trust of your customer. Since customers can be confident of what they'll get with a branded product, branding adds value to a product or service. That means people are willing to pay more for a well-known brand name product than they would for a generic or lesser-known brand. It's why a Sony laptop can command a higher price than a laptop with similar specifications: customers trust the quality.

An effective brand also embodies a certain personality or image that makes your customer relate to your company and feel good about themselves when they spend money with you rather than with another company. Think of a brand as a relationship a business builds over time with its current and potential customers. Brands build, and engender, loyalty.

Brands also have power with many others who may or may not patronize the business (such as investors, the media, potential strategic corporate partners, and the general public). In the same way that building a strong, recognizable brand makes it much easier to motivate a customer to buy from you, brands increase the media's willingness to cover your press releases, potential investors' receptiveness to financing your expansion, and a partner or other interested party's willingness to work with you.

In smaller companies, especially service businesses and one-person businesses, the company's *reputation* may be thought of as their brand. Over time, an individual or a business earns the confidence of customers and referral sources as a reliable provider of goods or services.

Convenience

Why would anyone walk down to the corner store to buy a gallon of milk when they could get it for a much lower price at a supermarket? Why would a business traveler add $5 to their bill for a bottle of water in the room or pay $15 an hour to access the hotel's wireless connection when they could get the water for $1 and the wireless connection for free at the café right next door to the hotel? Why will a business pay a heftier fee for consultants to come to their offices and train employees onsite rather than send employees to a lower-priced offsite training center?

It's all about convenience, which allows individuals and businesses to save time and lets them focus their energy on other things. Walking down to the corner store eliminates driving time, along with the need to navigate the supermarket aisles and wait in long lines. Buying the overpriced hotel amenities and working from their room gives business travelers more time to be

Myth ⦸ Buster

Price Is King

MYTH: Customers will always choose the lowest price for the same product.

BUSTED: Customers will often pay more for the exact same product, depending on other factors. Some factors that motivate customers to pay more include: the reliability and reputation of the seller, guarantees, level of customer service, association of the seller with causes the buyer supports, a desire to support local retailers, and even being golf buddies with the salesperson.

productive (and make the extra money for the company to afford the additional charges). For the corporation in need of trainers, keeping its employees onsite saves hours of travel time.

Convenience isn't only about location. Integrating more than one product or service together makes it more convenient for the customer. The ultimate in convenient packaging is the Swiss Army Knife—it's incredibly convenient to have all those tools in one handy package. Packing a product or service with features—whether it's a pocket knife, a cell phone, or accounting software that automatically integrates with your shipping, payroll, taxes, and other business functions—brings the benefit of convenience to customers and is highly motivating to many customers.

Customers will often pay more for convenience, and for a significant portion of many target audiences (for instance, harried working moms or overworked corporate executives), convenience is the most important factor.

That's why it's important, if your product or service is more convenient to buy or use than your competitor's, that you highlight these aspects in your marketing campaign and indicate the ways in which you save your customers time.

Word of Mouth

Looking to find a hairdresser or a plumber or an attorney? One of the first things you're likely to do is to ask others who they use and recommend. If you're looking to buy a new air conditioner for your home or a new accounting program for your business, you're probably going to ask others which products they use.

Personal referrals from someone you trust are one of the strongest motivators to customers. This is especially true when you are selling products or services where the prospective customer can't easily discern the difference between offerings. How do I know if an attorney will prove to be knowledgeable and responsive? How do I know whether an air conditioner will be reliable and quiet? If I talk to others who've already had a positive experience, I feel a lot more confident in my choice.

The Internet has multiplied the power of word-of-mouth marketing. Customer rating sites, such as TripAdvisor.com for travelers or Angie's List for building contractors, make it easy to find personal referrals and references for many types of businesses. A large percentage of buyers check these types of sites before making a purchase.

That's why personal referrals greatly enhance the chances of a customer buying your product of service. And that's why developing positive *word-of-mouth marketing* is critical for most businesses, especially service companies.

In fact, most smaller companies would say they get most of their new customers through word-of-mouth, even if they have not intentionally done anything to develop or create positive referrals. It's just that they've been in business long enough, and have provided quality products or services of high enough quality, that they've been able to build up a large number of past customers who spread the word.

For newer companies, however, word-of-mouth marketing can be intentionally developed and nurtured. Your marketing efforts can include word-of-mouth strategies such as:

- Rewarding current customers for referrals (through discounts or gifts)

- Using social networking websites to spread the word

- Encouraging satisfied customers to share their opinions on Internet customer rating sites (but don't pretend to be a customer; this can get you banned from these sites)

- Helping past customers remember you (and increasing the chance of their making referrals) through frequent emails, newsletters, or direct mail

- Using public relations programs to keep your business in the public eye

- Making it easy for customers to forward information about you to their friends

Affiliation

Like personal referrals and word-of-mouth recommendations, positive affiliations increase customers' confidence that their money will be well spent. Affiliations lend credibility to a company (and its product or service), as it benefits from its association with another respected company or organization. For example:

- A traveler with an AAA card picks an AAA-endorsed hotel, because they know they'll get a discount.

- A person selects a breakfast spot because it serves Starbucks coffee.

- A businessperson chooses a particular cell phone provider, because it comes with extra data services provided by well-known Internet companies.

- A parent takes a child to a fast food restaurant because the kids' meal includes a character from their child's favorite movie.

There's "merit by association" in these kinds of arrangements—affiliation programs or strategic partnerships. Your company, product, or brand gets added stature by being identified with a brand name prospective customers know and, ideally, trust.

What's important in these affiliations is that customers recognize the name or brand. Of secondary importance is how much customers value that brand. An affiliation with a brand name organization, company, product, or service can be worthwhile even if some customers are not crazy about the company with whom you're affiliated. That's because customers are more comfortable with the familiarity offered by your partnership with a company they already know, as opposed to taking a chance on a company with no recognizable ties at all. Of course, you'll want to avoid affiliations with names and brands that have bad reputations or that a large segment of your target market actively dislikes.

The Art of Building Credibility

Once your target market views you as a credible provider of products or services, you've won half the marketing battle. You can continue to build on that credibility through third party endorsements (or recommendations), which take many forms. Ways to capitalize on those endorsements include:

■ Asking customers to refer you to others they know who could use your products and services

■ Creating discount and other kinds of programs to reward customers for referrals

■ Including customer testimonials in marketing materials

■ Putting authentic Seals of Approval (Better Business Bureau or Good Housekeeping) on your website or other materials

■ Becoming an "Official Supplier" to a well-known sports team or other group affiliated with your clients

For a young company, seeking out positive affiliations can be a major help in gaining credibility. See which organizations you can join (such as the Better Business Bureau or trade associations) or marketing affiliations you can sign up for (such as the American Association for Retired Persons AARP). Look for strategic partnerships with well-known companies that have products or services that are complementary to yours. Highlight your affiliations in all your marketing materials: advertisements, websites, brochures, and the like. Leverage the cachet of another organization or company to enhance your stature with your prospective customers.

Get Inside Their Heads

Understanding what motivates your customers—why they buy your product or service and especially why they're likely to buy from you—is an important first step in developing your marketing message and plan. This will help you choose where, when, and if you want to advertise, what aspects of your competitive position you'll want to highlight in your marketing materials, and even how to price your service.

For instance, if you know that most of your customers are going to use your plumbing service because they have an actual immediate need for a plumber and the most important factor for them in choosing one company over another will be convenience, you're likely to advertise in the Yellow Pages and perhaps spend money to come up high in search engine results. You'll feature the fact that you're open 24 hours a day, 7 days a week.

On the other hand, if most of your customers are going to be remodeling high-end homes and the most important factor for them in choosing a plumbing contractor is the quality of their work, you're more likely to exhibit at home improvement trade shows and feature your ability to install unique plumbing fixtures or adapt newer plumbing to older homes.

As you plan your marketing, get inside your customers' heads. Naturally, that means you have to know what type of customers you're likely to have. To do that, you have to define your target market.

BUILDING YOUR MARKETING PLAN

WHY CUSTOMERS BUY FROM YOU

Why would a customer buy a product or service *from you?* Pick a product or service that you currently offer, or would like to offer, and use this worksheet to brainstorm about aspects of your company, product, or service that would motivate a customer to choose you rather than a competitor. Then use the right-hand column to make notes about what marketing activities relating to each aspect would enhance your ability to attract customers.

CUSTOMER MOTIVATION ASPECT	WHAT YOU HAVE NOW	WHAT YOU COULD DO TO ENHANCE THIS ASPECT
Awareness		
Features and benefits		
Price		
Brand		
Convenience		
Word-of-mouth		
Affiliation		
Other		

Lingo

B2B: A business that sells a product or service to another business, either for the company's own use or for that company to re-sell to consumers.

B2C: A business that sells a product or service directly to the consumer or end user.

CLIENT: A customer for a professional service. When used in a health care setting, the term *patient* is substituted.

CONSUMER: The individual who will actually use your product or service; this term is applied especially to goods and services aimed at non-business customers.

CUSTOMER: The individual or company that actually purchases your product or service. This can be the person who actually uses the product or service (the end user or consumer) or it can be an intermediary, such as a retailer or wholesaler, or it can be the person who buys on behalf of others, such as a parent purchasing for a child. However, the term *customer* is also broadly employed for anyone using or consuming your product or service, whether or not they actually make the buying decision.

DECISION MAKER: The person who actually chooses what product or service to buy, whether or not they actually make the purchase themselves. A college professor is the decision maker concerning which books their students will purchase, but the students make the actual purchase.

DEMOGRAPHICS: Basic objective characteristics of your customers, such as age, income, and occupation (for individuals) or company size, revenue, and industry affiliation (for businesses).

END USER: The customer who will actually use your product or service; this term is applied especially to technology-related goods and services and those aimed at business customers.

MARKET RESEARCH: Investigative techniques to discover information about your customer base or potential customer base, including such things such as customer preferences, buying patterns, and size and growth of total market.

NICHE: A specialized, clearly identifiable group within a larger target market that you choose to focus on and serve.

PRIMARY RESEARCH: Market research involving direct contact with your potential customers rather than a study of data collected by others.

PSYCHOGRAPHICS: Characteristics of your target market based on attitudes, values, lifestyle, desires, business style, and behavioral characteristics that may impact the buying decisions of your customers.

PURCHASING PATTERNS: How your customers make their purchasing decisions and how they prefer to make their purchases (with cash, credit card, or by other means).

SECONDARY RESEARCH: Research that relies on market data gathered by secondary sources rather than on direct contact with potential customers.

TARGET MARKET: The people, businesses, and organizations most likely to buy your product or service; the people, businesses, and organizations you are trying to reach so they will purchase your goods or services.

CHAPTER 3

Your Target Market

Before you can begin marketing to your prospective customers, you first have to know who they are. Are they old or are they young? Do they live in the city or in the suburbs? Are they more concerned about price or about quality? If you're selling to businesses, are they big companies or small? What industries are they in? How quickly do they make their buying decisions?

This information may not immediately seem important, especially when you're first getting started. After all, you want to sell to every customer you can. But narrowing in on exactly the type of customers you'd most like to reach—and the kind that are most likely to be willing, eager, and able to buy from you—is a key building block to success in marketing. Defining your target market gives focus to all your marketing and sales activities, helps you craft your advertising messages (and images), helps you choose where and when to advertise, influences which distribution channels you use, and perhaps even helps you decide on the color of your employees' uniforms or the type of music playing in your store.

A Target Is Something You Aim At

You're selling a new kind of energy bar. You know it would be good for a whole range of people: health buffs, office workers who can't get away for lunch, serious athletes, people who are sick and need more calories, harried moms who don't have time to stop for a meal, and just about anyone else who could use a quick, healthy pick-me-up.

If you tried to sell to everyone who might buy your product, you'd need a huge marketing budget to make them all aware of you. You'd probably have to spend a fortune on advertising. And even then, you'd have to decide what you would say in your ads and what kinds of people and images you would feature.

Instead, you need to select one or two market segments to pursue, especially since yours is a new company, with limited resources. But who should you sell to? How do you target your market? You have to narrow in on the

> *Most businesses don't have the foggiest idea who their target market is. Many business owners will say, 'Everyone's my target market.' In reality, every product or service has a target market, and if you're trying to talk to everyone, you're not talking to anyone. By excluding some people, and targeting others more likely to take an interest in your product, you greatly improve your likelihood of making the sale.*
>
> **Susan Schwartz**
> **Owner of You Who Branding**

Who's in the Bullseye?

When defining your target market, keep the image of an actual target in mind. The outermost ring of the target is the whole universe of potential customers—everyone who might ever possibly be interested in your product or service. As you get closer to the center of the target, narrow in on the customers who are more likely to actually make a purchase. The group at the center should be those who you would most like to have as customers, who you can reach and sell to affordably, and who are most likely to buy.

factors that best make you able to compete and to reach and sell to a specific type of customer. These are some of the factors you need to consider in closing in on the "bullseye" in your target market:

- **The actual features and benefits of your product or service.** Which group is your energy bar *best* suited to?

- **The competition.** Is there a segment of the market that other energy bar makers are not reaching or are underserving?

- **Market trends.** Is there a part of the overall market for energy bars that is growing?

- **Most motivated buyers.** Which part of the market has the most immediate need or desire to purchase energy bars?

- **Greatest ability to purchase.** What type of customer is most likely to have the disposable income to spend on energy bars?

- **Ease of reaching your prospects.** Is there a part of the market that is easiest to tell about your energy bars, because of trade shows, media (such as magazines), or other communications directed specifically at them?

- **Ease of selling to your prospects.** Are there any existing distribution channels (such as specific stores, websites, wholesalers) that make it easier or less expensive to reach one part of your market?

You've developed your energy bar to have particular benefits for people engaged in sports. It happens that you're located in a college town, filled with athletes on college teams: football, baseball, soccer, swim, field hockey, and more. Of course, there are even more recreational athletes: runners, swimmers, snowboarders, cyclists, skateboarders, hikers.

But after doing research, you realize athletes on the college's athletic team are the easiest and fastest to reach. After all, if you can just convince the coaches of each team that your energy bar can improve their players' performances, you can get the team to make large, repeated purchases. If they like your energy bars and the team wins, the star players may be your endorsers when you start to market to recreational athletes. And you may be able to get other college (and high school and professional) teams all over the country to buy your energy bars too. (That's basically the way that Gatorade got launched in 1965. It was promoted as an energy drink for athletes, and it now serves a much broader market.)

Decision Makers and Distribution Channels

Even once you've narrowed in on a specific target market, you'll likely realize that you have more than one "customer" to reach. When defining your market, explore the various channels of distribution that your product can go through before the final customer ever sees your product. Familiarize yourself with the details of the different ways your product gets into your customer's hands. From that, you will learn who you need to talk to and what message—besides saying what a great product you have—you need to get out there in front of your end users.

BRAINSTORMING

TARGETING YOUR CUSTOMERS

Pick a product or service you offer, or would like to offer, and fill in the target of potential customers for it, starting from the outer ring of the entire potential market for your type of product or service and narrowing in on the very best target market. Thus, to continue the energy bar example from the previous pages, you would begin with something like "Everyone who eats snack foods" in the outer ring, then put "Athletes who eat energy bars" in the next ring, and continue until you've worked your way in to your narrowest (that is, best) target: "Members of college teams."

Product: _____

Consider how the college athletes will actually get your energy bars:

As you consider your target market, include:

- ■ **End users/Consumers** (college athletes)

- ■ **Purchasers/Decision makers if different from end users** (coaches, cafeteria buyers)

- ■ **Influencers** (personal trainers, nutritionists)

- ■ **Retailer decision makers** (college store buyers, health food store buyers, Internet store buyers)

- ■ **Wholesalers/Distributors** (health food store distributors, mainstream supermarket distributors)

Any of these individuals or companies could make the primary decision to include the energy bars in their offerings to college athletes, so any or all of these must be considered part of your target market. Understanding where and how the bars will be sold—how they're *distributed* to the people who want them—provides the wider spectrum of your target market.

> **❝**For marketing to be effective, you need to understand your customer: who are you trying to serve and how and when are you trying to serve them? The further away you get from your customer, the less you understand what they want, the less success you'll have in your in-store and other marketing efforts. **❞**
>
> **James Parker**
> **Associate Global Coordinator for Produce—Whole Foods Markets**

Getting to Know You

MYTH: I've been doing this so long, I don't need to do any market research.

BUSTED: Customers change and evolve. What was true about your customer base when you first built your business may no longer be accurate. What's going on with them now may not be what motivated them to buy from you originally. Learning more about your present customers can help you keep them by letting you know if you should modify your marketing activities and perhaps even your products or services. You'll also learn how to bring in more new customers.

Understand Your Market

If you have a product or service, or an idea for one, you probably came up with it after recognizing that people or businesses would need or want it. Who are those people or those companies? What are they like? How many of them are there? Where do they live? How old are they? How do they like to shop? What are they buying now to meet their needs and wants?

To help you determine whether there is a market for your product or service, or find ways to improve either your product itself or the way you market it, you need to do some market research. Market research is the process of gathering data about your target market. Market research is critical to helping you understand your market, verify that your market exists in sufficient numbers to sustain your business, and grasp trends in your market that may affect you directly.

There are two kinds of market research: *primary research* and *secondary research*. They offer two different approaches to learning about your market, and each has advantages and disadvantages.

Primary Research

Primary market research is information that is collected for the first time, usually by you or by companies you hire on your behalf. Conducting primary research enables you to get insights and answers that are directly and specifically related to the concerns and questions you have for your business.

Typically, primary research gathers information through direct contact with customers or prospective customers. In most primary research, you are attempting to determine whether or not customers are interested in your product/service, what features they most want and will pay for, what price they'll pay, what competitive products or services they're using, and so on. Methods of primary research include:

- **Surveys/Questionnaires.** Opinions gathered from a large number of people either in person, on the phone, on the Internet, or by mail.

- **Interviews.** One-on-one, in-depth discussions that can get at deeper understanding of prospects' answers.

- **User testing**. Having individuals try or interact with the product to learn more about how customers will actually use it. (This approach is taken particularly in technology businesses.)

- **Focus groups.** Gathering a group of prospects together to conduct an in-depth discussion relating to the product/service in question.

In addition to primary research that is done by interacting with customers and prospective customers, you can gather information from other sources, including:

- **Industry research.** Contacting, interviewing, or surveying others in your industry to gain insights. This could include calling distributors and suppliers to find out what products sell well, what kinds of packaging are preferred, and other information about the market. It may also include going to industry trade shows to evaluate competitors and learn about trends.

■ **Competitive research.** Reviewing competitors' marketing materials to determine what market segments they're targeting. Examining their brochures, advertisements, direct mail pieces, email blasts, websites, and packaging to see how they are pitching their products to that market, including which features and benefits they deem important to the market.

Secondary Research

Secondary research involves analyzing information that has been gathered and compiled by other sources to determine how it applies to your company or business concept. You can find this information at a university or public library (or through their online resources), through the Internet, from industry trade associations, from government sources, and from private research firms. Examples of secondary research include:

■ Studying Census Bureau data, which enables you to drill down all the way to the zip code level to find demographic information such as the age, gender, income, and education level of your target market.

■ Delving into data compiled by market research companies (often available through university libraries) to find behavioral and lifestyle characteristics of your customers, where they shop, what magazines they read, and much more.

■ Obtaining media kits from consumer, business, or trade magazines geared to your market. Media kits are a marketing tool used by media outlets to attract advertisers. They include the outlet's advertising rates, but more importantly they contain detailed demographic and behavioral information (including typical job titles and income and education levels) about the people who read, watch, or listen to them.

Whether you decide to do primary or secondary research depends on the nature of your business and the time, energy, money, and other resources available to you. What's important is to find some way to support your assumptions regarding your target market or information that compels you to change those assumptions if the research doesn't support them.

What You Need to Know

Once you have defined your target market, you'll want to know as much about your potential customers as possible. This information is critical to designing your products or services. But it is also essential in helping you shape your marketing activities. Knowing exactly where your customers are located, for instance, helps you choose the right media (such as a local newspaper) for your ads. Knowing what motivates your customers helps you craft what you will say in your marketing materials, brochures, and ads. Knowing their income helps you determine whether you should emphasize price in your ads.

Demographics

For consumer-based markets, demographics refers to the objective, descriptive characteristics of customers: information such as age, income, gender, occupation, education level, race, and nationality. If your customers are businesses (rather than consumers), the term *demographics* can be broadly

---

B2C or B2B?

One key component of a company's business model—the basic structure of how they will make money—is whether they will be selling "B2B" or "B2C."

■ **B2C** (Business to Consumer). You sell a product or service directly to the consumer or end user.

■ **B2B** (Business to Business). You sell a product or service to another business, either for the company's own use or for that company to re-sell to consumers.

In your marketing, you will want to emphasize different features, depending on whether yours is a B2C or a B2B business. With a B2C business, you'll focus entirely on the benefits the end user will get from purchasing the product or service. The focus will be on the *personal* benefits. With a B2B business, you'll also have to emphasize the broader benefits the company will reap, especially when they re-sell your products or services to others. The focus will include how you meet a *business need*, such as by increasing efficiency or improving profits.

applied to objective company characteristics, such as number of years in business, number of employees, revenue, number of locations, and especially industry. Knowing these objective facts about your target market is key to virtually every aspect of your marketing plan. For instance, if you know your potential customers are more likely to be female than male, this will help you choose which magazines to advertise in. If you know that your customers are in a particular industry, you can choose to exhibit at a trade show serving that industry.

Geographics

Where are your customers located? What cities are they in? Even in a metropolitan area, are they in the city or a suburb? Which suburb? What's the density of the areas? Knowing where your customers are located is a basic requirement for choosing which marketing vehicles you'll use. For instance, if your customers are mostly in suburbs of a big city, instead of advertising in the metropolitan newspaper, you may want to advertise in local papers. Even if your business is online-based, it is helpful to know where your customers are located. This can assist you in choosing geographically appropriate messages or images for your website or other marketing materials.

Market Size

This is a critical piece of information, which can show whether a particular market is worth pursuing. If the market is too small, perhaps you need to widen the geographic area to reach enough potential customers. On the other hand, if it's too large, it's going to be costly to market to affordably, as the advertising vehicles will probably be prohibitively expensive (for instance, TV ads or buying highly desired keywords on Internet search engines). If your market is too large, you may want to focus instead on a segment of your target market; for instance, instead of to athletes, you'd direct your marketing to *college* athletes or *female* college athletes.

Psychographics and Motivations

What underlying emotional and lifestyle factors motivate your customers to buy? "Psychographics" is the term applied to the psychological, emotional, lifestyle, and values-based characteristics of your target audience rather than objective descriptive characteristics. In other words, an objective motivator is "I'm hungry; I need to eat." A psychographic motivator is "I want to look thinner; I need to eat low-fat food." Even business customers have "psychographics." One small business may want to look bigger; another may be very concerned about protecting the environment. Understanding your customers' psychographics is basic to shaping your marketing messages and choosing marketing images—and even to what type of package design and materials you use.

PSYCHOGRAPHICS MATCH

See how marketing messages for a new digital camera might change, depending on the emotional/psychographic motivations of target customers.

Baby boomers who want to feel young	*Capture your new adventures.*
Male college students who want to feel macho	*Our shutter moves as fast as you.*
Working parents who feel guilty about having to be away from their kids	*Connect while you're on the road.*
Single women who are looking to find a date or a mate	*See yourself in the best light.*
Seniors who love their grandchildren	*Capture those precious memories.*

Purchasing Patterns

How do your customers behave when it comes to actually making a purchase? How frequently do they buy? Where do they make their purchases? Who makes the actual purchase? Who influences the purchasing decision? How long does it take for them to make a decision? All these issues affect how you'll market to your customers and indicate issues, problems, or opportunities you may have. For instance, if you are selling washing machines, it's useful to know that customers buy a new machine only every eight to ten years, and then they buy when their current machine breaks down. That makes your marketing challenging, and you'll need to look for marketing vehicles that can reach prospects like that when they're at a decision-making moment.

Find Your Niche

A niche market is a group, or subset, of customers within a larger target market who have specialized needs or who can be identified easily by objective factors such as industry, age, life stage, activities engaged in, and so on. Finding a niche—and marketing to them—provides a simple and fast way of distinguishing yourself from competitors and generating greater awareness of your business.

Specializing may also enable you to charge more for your products and services. That's because many customers are willing to pay more for goods specially tailored for them, especially if those products or services are hard to find. Niche products and services also often generate powerful word-of-mouth activity. Just because the word *niche* is used doesn't mean the market has to be small, just that it is specialized and identifiable.

Examples of niche marketing:

- Focusing on hair care products for curly hair
- Providing accounting services for optometrists
- Creating bedding for people with allergies

When choosing your niche, keep these factors in mind:

- Define your niche objectively. Rather than saying you provide "extra gentle haircuts in a fun atmosphere," spell out your niche demographic target with "Kid-Friendly Haircuts."

- Make sure your targeted niche is large enough to sustain you. For example, cat-friendly hotels probably won't provide a big enough market, but pet-friendly hotels, which allow both dogs and cats, could.

- Serving a niche doesn't mean you can't serve a larger market as well. If the user-friendly approach of your senior computer classes starts generating a positive buzz among the under 65 set, you could develop complimentary offerings for younger clients.

Market Trends and Growth

What's going on with your market? What trends, fads, issues, and values are changing or shaping customers' purchasing decisions? What part of your market is increasing? What segments are declining? What's changing about the way your market gets information that affects their buying decisions? For instance, if you reach prospective customers primarily through coupons in your local newspaper, how will you respond as newspaper readership declines? Your marketing activities have to take into account what's going on with your customers *now*. Let's say you run a popular hamburger stand across from a college, but now a large number of college students are becoming more health conscious. You may want to add a veggie burger to your menu with a whole wheat bun and feature that on a big sign in your window or in ads in the college paper.

Market Research Resources

Need to do some secondary research on your target market? Here are some excellent resources likely to lead you to plenty of relevant data.

■ U.S. Census Bureau: American FactFinder

http://factfinder.census.gov

An easy-to-use portal for finding census data (mostly demographics and geographic information) on both people and businesses in the United States.

■ U.S. Census Bureau: County Business Patterns

http://www.census.gov/epcd/cbp/view/cbpview.html

Especially useful for gauging business activity within a particular area at the local, county, metro area, or state level. For example, you could use it to find the number of dry cleaners within a specific zip code.

■ U.S. Census Bureau: State and County Quickfacts

http://quickfacts.census.gov or through U.S. Census Bureau homepage at *www.census.gov*

A particularly helpful, easy-to-use site summarizing the most requested data for states and counties.

■ Statistics Canada

www.statcan.ca

The entry point to Canada's national statistics agency, a government agency providing a wealth of statistical information about Canada.

■ Industry Associations

www.planningshop.com/tradeassociations.asp

Or check search engines for an industry of interest. Industry associations typically conduct surveys of their members or of consumers, often providing substantial data on market behavior.

■ InfoTrac

Access through your public or university library. This popular database features millions of articles, mainly from magazines and reference books, from mainstream to specialized sources.

■ Mintel

www.mintel.com

Provides detailed information on consumer behavior, as it relates to a wide range of industries, products, and life stages. Reports are very expensive, but many colleges or universities offer use of this source for free (although you may have to pay a small fee to access the library if you're not a student).

■ Community Sourcebook America

Access at college/university libraries (on CD-ROM)

Shows you consumer spending patterns by geographic area for products ranging from home improvement equipment to take-out food.

■ LexisNexis

http://alacarte.lexisnexis.com

This for-fee site offers searches on more than 20,000 sources containing over 3.8 billion documents. It's especially good for finding updated company market share data and hard-to-find transcripts from TV and radio broadcasts.

■ Media Websites

In addition to news stories, media websites often provide a number of research resources, such as overviews on industries, companies, and products. Some sites to explore:

NewsLibrary.com: www.newslibrary.com

Library of Congress list of news resources on the Web: *www.loc.gov/rr/news/lists.html*

Internet Public Library list of newspapers worldwide: *www.ipl.org/div/news*

More information on these and additional research sources—and how to use them—is available through the Planning Shop guide *Successful Business Research*, available in bookstores and at www.planningshop.com.

BUILDING YOUR MARKETING PLAN

TARGET MARKET CHARACTERISTICS

Use this worksheet to identify the major characteristics of your target market.

1. What are the demographic characteristics of your target market? (For individuals, list age, gender, marital status, income, education level, and so on. For businesses, list years in business, annual revenue, and industry.)

_____

_____

2. Describe the geographic area you are targeting. (Country, region, state, province, city, suburb, zip codes, and so on.)

_____

_____

3. What are some of the psychographic aspects of your customers? (Their motivations based on emotions, desires, lifestyle, and values.)

_____

_____

4. How and where do your customers make their purchases? How long do they wait between purchases?

_____

_____

5. How many people/businesses fit the characteristics of your target market in the specific geographic location you're targeting? What is the size of your potential market in actual numbers?

_____

_____

6. How is your market changing? What are the trends and fads that are affecting your customers' buying decisions? Is your market growing or shrinking?

_____

_____

7. How can you use the specific characteristics of your target market to shape your marketing activities?

Think about your:

Marketing vehicles _____

Marketing messages _____

Marketing images _____

Lingo

BARRIERS TO ENTRY: The obstacles a new company faces when trying to enter a market.

BRAND LOYALTY: A customer's commitment to the same brand that they have come to know and trust, making them reluctant to change.

COMPETITIVE ADVANTAGE: The strengths that differentiate a company from its competitors.

DIRECT COMPETITION: Companies offering products and services like yours that can be viewed as viable alternatives to what you have for sale.

INDIRECT COMPETITION: Companies offering products or services that differ from yours but meet the same need.

MARKET SHARE: The portion or percentage of total market revenue controlled by a company.

TRADE ASSOCIATIONS: Organizations that serve members of a particular industry; they often have information and statistics on leading companies and competitors in a field.

CHAPTER 4

Taking On the Competition

Believe it or not, competition is a good thing. If your product or service is worth buying, rest assured that others will want to sell it, or something similar to it, too. As a marketer, it's critical to understand your competitors if you want to differentiate yourself from them. You want to see which markets they're targeting, what features and benefits they're promoting, where they advertise, and what advertising messages they're sending. Only then will you be able to differentiate yourself from the competition in your prospects' eyes and highlight your advantages.

So don't bemoan the fact that you have competition—even if you just want to beat the pants off them. When competition exists, it means you've tapped into a viable market. It shows you're on the right track with your business idea; it demonstrates that others have also identified the same market opportunity.

Competition also keeps you on your toes; it helps you consistently improve what you have to offer and find out exactly what it is that makes your business unique. It also provides an opportunity to learn from the mistakes of others. Your competition provides the information and motivation you need to make your business the best it can be and your marketing as effective as possible.

Even if you're selling a totally new type of product, such as a groundbreaking new technology, it's important to understand which other products are competing for your customers' dollars. There may be no products comparable to yours on the market, but there are probably other products that fit the same market need. If you're marketing a new financial Internet site to enable consumers to keep track of their finances, your competition wouldn't just be other Internet sites, but financial management software and even checkbooks and good ole pen and paper. To be able to craft an effective marketing campaign for your product, you must recognize that customers have these ways of meeting their needs too.

> ## Direct and Indirect Competition
>
> When thinking about competition, you're most likely to consider only *direct competitors*. Direct competitors are businesses that offer products like yours that customers perceive as acceptable alternatives—for example, Honda vs. Toyota, Burger King vs. McDonald's.
>
> But you've also got competition from *indirect competitors*. Indirect competitors are companies that offer products or services which differ from yours but fill the same need. For example, customers needing to travel a few hundred miles could take a plane, drive, or take a bus. If you have to entertain kids for an afternoon, you could go to the movies, a children's museum, a public playground, or Chuck E. Cheese.

> *Many businesses can't even point to exactly who their competition is. If you can't identify a competitor, you need to at least identify a competitive force that drives you. Sometimes it's just like setting goals; like saying 'We want to be the best in our industry at this!' The people inside your organization can much better respond to that kind of rallying cry than to 'Hey, we're just going to sell some more stuff today.'*
>
> **John Jantz**
> **Author**
> ***Duct Tape Marketing***

Just as important as knowing your competition is learning from it. Watch what your competitors are doing, especially how they are marketing their products. What marketing vehicles are they using? Where do they advertise? How frequently do they advertise? How do they find new customers? The more you know about your competition, including their marketing, the more effective your marketing can be. Understanding your competition enables you to:

- Identify which features and benefits of your offerings you can highlight in your marketing to differentiate yourself from others

- Determine which markets are not being served or are underserved by competitors and go after those markets

- Price your products or services appropriately

- Choose the marketing vehicles you need to keep your prospects—and your competition—aware of you

- Respond to needs that aren't currently being addressed by competitors

- Figure out what you're up against and prepare to take action!

What You Need to Know

To be an effective competitor, you have to scout out the competition. Just like an athlete, you've got to honestly evaluate your rivals' strengths as well as their weaknesses if you want to win. Successful marketers learn all they can about their competitors, including:

- Who they are

- Which benefits and features they claim to have

- The real benefits and features of their offerings

- Which benefits and features they highlight in their marketing

- What benefits and features their products or services are missing

- How much they charge and their pricing structure

- Why customers buy from them

- Why customers don't buy from them

- Which market they're trying to sell to (their target market)

- How and where they sell their products and services

- What types of marketing they do; how and where they market and advertise

- How much of the market they control (their market share)

- What message they're sending to their customers through their marketing efforts

Once you gather this information, you'll be better able to figure out what makes your competitors successful, what you can learn from this, and even more important, how to distinguish yourself from them in your marketing efforts.

Assess Your Competitors' Strengths

Once you gather the basic info on your competitors (such as what they offer, their prices and locations) you can begin assessing their strengths—their *competitive advantages*. What works for them? Let's face it: they're still in business for a reason. Whether it's their products' features, their prices, convenience, or just because they've been around a long time, there are actually compelling reasons why customers buy from them. Take a careful look at your competitors' products or services to try to figure out what they're doing right. Analyze their:

- Features and benefits
- Prices
- Convenience
- Customer service
- Distribution—where their product is sold/available
- Design, packaging, ease of use
- Established customer base
- Marketing program and budget

Keep in mind that their marketing program itself may be a key advantage. They may have a large budget to make customers aware of their offerings, and you may have far fewer funds. Do they have a great campaign that's winning the hearts of their customers?

Even if a competitor's strengths aren't immediately obvious, examine what makes customers stick with them. For example, let's say you're opening up a new, hip, healthy breakfast spot. Your main competitor is a diner that's been a hangout for local residents for more than 50 years. Their marketing is minimal, their equipment outdated, their food loaded with cholesterol, and the atmosphere dingy. But the place, for all its faults, continues to attract loyal customers.

Their competitive advantages are intangible. They've been there for a long time; they treat people, especially the old timers, right; they serve tasty food. They have the most powerful word-of-mouth marketing imaginable—a large number of satisfied customers. Moreover, people are comfortable with the familiar. The breakfast spot is like an old friend. You need to understand those competitive advantages as you begin to design your marketing campaign.

The 800-Pound Gorilla

Some competitors are more important than others. In particular, companies commanding the largest share of customer dollars—or *market share*—present the fiercest competition. Even though these companies may not necessarily provide the best products or most attentive customer service, they're going to be on your customers' minds and you're going to have to take them into account in your marketing efforts. If you're opening a neighborhood hardware store, you're going to have to watch what's going on at Lowe's and Home Depot. If you're launching a new, low-cost airline, you'll have to keep a close eye on the major carriers in your market, such as American or United. Always keep in mind that your customers and prospects will be checking out the big guys as well as you.

Determine which companies command the largest portion of your market. These competitors are significant because they:

- Tend to define the standard features of a product or service
- Influence customers' perceptions of products and services
- Have and spend significant resources to maintain market share
- Can offer consistently lower prices or undercut prices to maintain market share

It's tough—if not impossible—to compete against a huge market share leader—the eight-hundred-pound gorilla. It's going to take a huge budget to compete against Microsoft Office for office productivity software or Google for a new search engine. It's often wiser to go after niche markets (see page 29) that may be poorly served by major market leaders.

BRAINSTORMING

YOUR COMPETITORS' STRENGTHS

List your top three competitors and their primary strengths.

COMPETITOR	STRENGTHS
#1:	
#2:	
#3:	

BRAINSTORMING

YOUR COMPETITORS' WEAKNESSES

List your top three competitors and their primary weaknesses.

COMPETITOR	WEAKNESSES
#1:	
#2:	
#3:	

> ### Better, Faster, Cheaper
>
> When looking for your competitive advantage, the old mantra is that customers are looking for *"better, faster, cheaper."* What makes your product or service better than others? How does it meet their needs faster? And in what ways is it cheaper?

Assess Your Competitors' Weaknesses

Of course, you also want to be fully aware of your competitors' weaknesses. You probably already have some sense of their shortcomings; those weaknesses may have been what motivated you to start your business in the first place.

But as part of your marketing strategy, you'll want to take a complete inventory of your competitors' weaknesses. In particular, you'll want to determine their most important flaws—what their customers are most dissatisfied with or what keeps other customers away. Knowing where your competitors are vulnerable supplies you with a critical piece of information as you shape your marketing plan: why people would want to buy from you rather than others.

In the example of the old diner above, the diner's weaknesses included the facts that their food is not very healthy, the décor is shabby, and they do hardly any marketing

Define and Highlight *Your* Competitive Advantage

Once you've assessed your competitors' strengths and weaknesses, you're in a good position to figure out what you can say about your products or services to highlight the reasons why customers should buy from you instead. You'll want those differences that give you a competitive advantage to be a key part of your advertising message and drive your marketing campaigns.

Some of the types of competitive advantages you can feature include:

- **Better price.** Sample advertising message: "Find it here for less." When price is a factor, it helps to explain *why* your price is better, so your goods/services aren't perceived as cheap or inferior. For example, if you sell fine jewelry at a discount because you import directly and eliminate the middlemen, say so in your ads.

- **More features.** Sample message on your packaging: "Includes three free bonus CDs." Sample advertising message: "Shampoo & conditioner in one bottle!" These features can be attributes of the product itself (it performs more functions), or you can bundle more products together. One of the most important ways to distinguish yourself from others is by offering more to your customers for the same price.

- **Convenience.** Sample advertising messages: "Photo enlargements in 50 minutes" or "Drop it off on your way to work; pick it up on your way home" or "We come to you." Time is of critical importance to many customers when making their purchasing decisions. If you are faster, closer, or easier than competitors, emphasize those things in your marketing messages.

- **Hard-to-find niche or specialty.** Sample advertising message: "Exclusively available here." Sample tagline: "Secure, Bonded Janitorial Service for Banks & Other Financial Institutions." You cater to a smaller, better defined target market, who buys from you because you are the only company or one of the few companies that offers what they want. For more on niche marketing, see page 29.

■ **Higher performance/Quality/Durability.** Sample advertising message: "Zero to 60 in 7 seconds" or "Guaranteed to last 10 years" or "Handcrafted of genuine leather." Showing that your product or service outperforms the competition is particularly important if you are charging more than they are.

■ **Credibility/Proven model/Longevity.** Sample advertising message: "Tom Smith, DDS: Brightening Saratoga Smiles for over 50 years" or "The choice of over 100 of the Fortune 500 Companies." Customers who are hesitant to make a buying decision are reassured by the fact that your business has been chosen by others—especially others they respect—before. It increases their sense of trust that you can do the job and will be around to handle any future needs.

■ **Newer/More innovative.** Sample advertising message: "Our state-of-the-art technology blows away the competition" or "The first fully electric sports car on the market." A younger or more innovative business appeals to a large segment of customers who want to be at the forefront of technology or trends or who just don't want to purchase outdated products or use old-fashioned service providers.

BRAINSTORMING

YOUR ADVANTAGES OVER THE COMPETITION

List your advantages over your competitors in the following areas:

Better price _____

More features _____

Convenience _____

Hard-to-find niche or specialty _____

Higher performance/Quality/Durability_____

Credibility/Proven model/Longevity_____

Newer/More innovative _____

Association with positive role models _____

Design _____

Social responsibility _____

Other _____

_____

_____

SWOT Marketing Analysis

"SWOT" analyses are carried out to develop both marketing and business strategies. These are ways of developing your business's:

Strengths

Weaknesses

Opportunities

Threats

By identifying your strengths and weaknesses, you're in a better position to look at the opportunities you can exploit—and the threats you need to hold off—in your marketing campaign. Use the SWOT analysis worksheet on page 41 to create a marketing SWOT analysis for the business you are in or would like to start.

- **Association with positive role models.** Sample advertising message: "Be a Tiger" (for business consulting firm Accenture's advertising campaign with Tiger Woods) or "The choice of celebrities." Customers are often influenced to purchase products or services because they believe those products or services will help them achieve a desired self-image or goal—or just because they like being associated with winners.

- **Design.** Sample advertising message: "21st century design for 21st century tastes" or "A vacuum so beautiful, you won't want to put it in the closet." Design has become an increasingly important factor in determining customer preferences. If you have particularly attractive or functional design for your product or retail/restaurant location, you'll want to emphasize that in your marketing.

- **Social responsibility.** Sample advertising message: "Our dry cleaning is great for your clothes and good for our planet" or "Giving 5% of income to the community" or "No animal testing—ever!" A large segment of customers want to choose products, services, and companies they can feel good about supporting. If you are honestly committed to social responsibility as part of your company's practices, let customers know.

Use Your Competitive Advantage in Your Marketing

Once you've examined how you are different from—and better than—the competition, use this information as a foundation for your marketing activities. You'll certainly want to highlight your competitive advantages in your advertising messages. You'll also want to make sure you choose the appropriate marketing vehicles to take advantage of your strengths and exploit their weaknesses. And you'll want to find ways to imitate some of the things they do best.

For instance, in the example above, where you were launching a new breakfast restaurant, trying to compete against an established, familiar diner, you'd want to point out the advantages customers would get from eating at your restaurant while reassuring them that they'd still find the positive things they'd expect from the diner, such as a friendly neighborhood place where they would be treated like a regular. Here's how it might affect your marketing efforts:

- Advertising message: The Healthy Breakfast Spot with a Heart

- Where you advertise: neighborhood newspapers as well as local publications aimed at health-minded customers, such as recreational athletes (e.g., South Bay Runner) and seniors

- Signage: signs in your restaurant saying, "Eat healthy; Eat here."

- Brochures: pamphlets in the restaurant giving nutritional information about your offerings

- Loyalty program: "healthy neighbors" punch card giving the tenth breakfast free, to encourage locals to become regular patrons

- Other marketing activity: sponsor a local foot or bike race to reach health-minded consumers

BRAINSTORMING

YOUR MARKETING SWOT ANALYSIS

Fill out the worksheet below to identify your marketing opportunities and threats in comparison to those of your competitors.

STRENGTHS

What do you do better than your competitors? What features or benefits do you offer that they don't? Why would customers buy from you instead of others?

WEAKNESSES

What do other companies do better than you? What features or benefits do they offer that you don't? Why would customers buy from them instead of you?

OPPORTUNITIES

Based on your strengths compared to those of your competitors, how could you shape your marketing campaign? What messages would you choose? What markets would you target?

THREATS

Based on your weaknesses, how can you shape or change your marketing campaign to best hold off competitors?

- Other: train your staff concerning the importance of customer service and get to know the names of your customers as quickly as possible

- This type of marketing highlights your competitive advantage: the fact that you offer much healthier food. But it also shows that you're going to exploit one of your competitor's strengths: offering a welcoming atmosphere. You may never get the old timers to switch over, but you'll attract the more health-conscious members of your community who'll be delighted to have found the best of both worlds.

BRAINSTORMING

USING YOUR COMPETITIVE ADVANTAGE

Use this worksheet to list ways you can highlight and exploit your competitive advantage in your marketing activities.

My competitive advantage is: _____

I can feature that in my marketing efforts in:

Advertising messages: _____

Choice of where I advertise: _____

Marketing materials: _____

Packaging: _____

Signage: _____

Special promotions: _____

Public relations, including community sponsorships: _____

Other marketing activities: _____

Your Competitors' Marketing

In addition to understanding why you are different from—and better than—your competitors, you have to be aware of what kind of marketing they are doing. How are they trying to reach customers? Where and when do they advertise? What kinds of non-advertising marketing do they do? The goal is not to copy your competitors' marketing strategy but to either:

Choose entirely different marketing strategies and marketing vehicles so you can reach a market distinct from your competitors'

or

Take them on directly, so customers know about you as well as your competitors

If you can compete for somewhat different target markets, it may be best to avoid the same marketing approach as your competitors'. Let's say you're launching a new furniture line. Your competitors target their marketing efforts to interior designers and consumers, advertising heavily in home design magazines and exhibiting at national furniture trade shows. That's expensive. You could choose instead to target your marketing to younger furniture buyers and spend your marketing dollars on a terrific website and extensive online marketing campaign.

On the other hand, if you're competing for a limited audience, you have to make sure you're doing much of the same marketing as your competition. For instance, if you're selling an expensive, high-performance ski boot and must reach avid skiers, you need to know which ski magazines your competitors are advertising in, which winter sporting goods trade shows they're attending, and which ski races they're sponsoring. You can't afford to let your competitors be the only ones visible in those arenas.

Just as important, you need to know what messages your competitors are sending to their customers. Which of their features, benefits, and advantages do they highlight? You'll need to know this information as you craft your advertising message and your marketing strategy so you can differentiate yourself from the competition in your customers' eyes.

Finally, analyze your competitors' marketing efforts honestly. What works and what doesn't? By looking at their successes and failures, you can learn how to improve your own marketing tactics and avoid costly mistakes.

The only way to beat the competition is to understand them. So as part of your marketing plan, you need to include an analysis of your competition. This will help you know and understand what and who you're up against.

Myth Buster

If You Can't Say Something Nice ...

MYTH: To beat the competition, let customers know about their failings.

BUSTED: In your marketing, focus on your strengths rather than dumping on your competitors. It can be tempting to take them on, by name, especially when you know they're not telling the whole story. For instance, let's say your competitor trumpets the fact that they have lower prices. But you know they tack on a slew of fees that actually make their product more expensive than yours. So in your advertising, use language like "No Fees!" or "Total Price—no hidden charges" rather than "Our widgets are less expensive than Smith widgets because of their added fees." Avoid mentioning your competitors' names; if you do, you'll be giving them free publicity.

Barriers to Entry

In addition to evaluating the competitors you've already identified, it's useful to consider whether any new companies can come in and compete against you. What obstacles, if any, prevent new competitors from entering your market? In other words, what *barriers to entry* keep new competition from coming after you?

Barriers to entry can include:

- Obtaining patents and trademarks
- High startup costs
- Procuring substantial, hard-to-find technical or industry expertise

- Restrictive licensing or certification requirements or regulations
- Acquiring limited or high-priced office or retail space in an area

Barriers to entry won't prevent new competition, but it could delay it. In any case, prepare yourself for it. Check for articles in local or industry media. Look at companies in related fields and examine their websites for press releases about new product offerings. These can provide clues on what, or who, is coming down the pike.

BRAINSTORMING

YOUR COMPETITORS' MARKETING

Use this worksheet to analyze the kinds of marketing your competitors do.

What kind of marketing do your competitors do?

_____

_____

_____

What message are they sending to their customers through their marketing efforts?

_____

_____

_____

Where and when do they advertise?

_____

_____

_____

What other marketing activities do they engage in?

_____

_____

_____

What's working for them?

_____

_____

_____

What's not?

_____

_____

_____

BUILDING YOUR MARKETING PLAN

COMPETITIVE ANALYSIS

Drawing on the information you gathered in the Brainstorming Worksheets in this chapter, use this worksheet to prepare the competitive analysis portion of your marketing plan.

1. Who are your major competitors?

_____

_____

2. What are their major strengths? What aspects do they highlight in their marketing?

_____

_____

3. What are their weaknesses? How are they vulnerable?

_____

_____

4. What is your competitive advantage compared to that of others? Why would customers buy from you rather than from the competition?

_____

_____

5. How do you plan to highlight/exploit your competitive advantage in your marketing campaign?

_____

_____

6. How and where do your competitors market their products or services?

_____

_____

7. How will you respond to their marketing efforts?

_____

_____

Lingo

CRM (CUSTOMER RELATIONSHIP MANAGEMENT): A systemized plan, using a computer database, for acquiring and keeping customers, with the goal of building customer loyalty and benefiting from the lifetime value of a customer.

CUSTOMER ACQUISITION COST: The amount of money it takes, in total, to secure a new customer.

CUSTOMER LIFETIME VALUE (CLV) OR LIFETIME CUSTOMER VALUE: The total income to a company, over time, that is likely to be generated by a specific customer.

DATABASE: The organized collection of information in digital form, stored on computers. Frequently used to refer to information stored relating to a company's customers and/or prospective customers.

DATABASE MARKETING: A systematic approach to using a company's customer database to communicate and sell to customers; database marketing enables companies to easily select targets within their customer list for offers, to develop and maintain loyalty/rewards programs, and to otherwise segment customers.

DATA MINING: A process of analyzing information, stored in a database, to find patterns that can be used to help predict future behavior; in marketing, this might be a software program that analyzes customer data to determine which past customers are most likely to purchase a new product.

EARLY ADOPTERS: A segment of the customer base who eagerly embrace and want to buy the newest, most innovative products and services.

INFLUENCERS: Individuals who, by their use or approval of a product or service, entice others to try it. Influencers are people whom prospects look to and look up to; they can be key product reviewers, columnists, bloggers, athletes, celebrities, or successful businesspeople.

LOSS LEADER: A steep discount given on a particular product or service to attract and acquire a new customer, often resulting in a company making no money—or even losing money.

LOYALTY/REWARDS PROGRAM: An organized program to reward customers for their continued use/purchase of a company's products or services—for example, airlines' frequent flyer programs and supermarket "club" discounts.

PROSPECTS: Individuals or businesses that could potentially become your customers.

SWITCHING COST: The time, effort, and money it takes a customer to switch from one company, product, or service to another.

CHAPTER 5

Acquiring and Retaining Customers

Without customers, you don't have a business. That's why the goal of almost all marketing campaigns is to acquire and keep customers. But it's difficult—and expensive—to get customers. In some industries, it may cost many hundreds of dollars to land each one. So once you have a customer, it's important to keep them.

Acquiring and keeping customers is the heart and soul of marketing and of all business. CRM—or customer relationship management—is the term that's been developed to describe the entire system companies set up to handle their interactions with customers. There are hundreds (if not thousands) of CRM software programs, databases, and Internet applications out there to help companies, large and small, manage and improve their customer relationships.

As you devise your marketing plan, it's important, right from the beginning, to build a CRM component into your program. You will need a thoughtful, organized way to approach acquiring customers, storing their contact information, using that information to continue to communicate and serve your existing customers, and ideally, sell to them again.

Attracting First-Time Customers

If you build it, will they come?

Just because you've created something new, something better, or something cheaper doesn't mean that customers will flock to your door. It takes a lot of work to make sure customers know about your products and services and are motivated enough to spend their money with you.

One of the first tasks as a marketer is to figure out what it's going to take to get prospective customers (prospects) to become aware of you and your offerings, give you a try, and buy.

Why Aren't Customers Coming?

- **Lack of awareness.** They just haven't heard about you or aren't knowledgeable about the features and benefits of your products or services.

- **Switching costs.** It will cost them too much, in time and money, to change to your offerings.

- **Loyalty to your competitors.** They like the company they're dealing with now or are part of a program that rewards them for repeat purchases.

- **Better offer.** Your competitors cost less or offer more than you do.

- **Inertia.** Why bother?

"If it's new, I gotta have it."

Some customers simply *must* own the newest, latest, and greatest product out there, especially when it comes to technology, electronics, and cars, but this could apply to any field, including fashion. This segment of the buying public is referred to as "early adopters," and they're a valuable market segment, especially for companies introducing innovative products or services. They can help launch a new product they embrace enthusiastically and are typically not price-sensitive—they're willing to pay more just to have a product before anybody else. Early adopters read trade websites, journals, and magazines for news of upcoming products and early reviews. They're a highly desirable target market for many companies. So if yours is an innovative product or service, you'll want to build into your marketing plan a way to target early adopters.

There are many reasons why customers don't flock to a new and better offering. Most novice marketers think they're not attracting customers because of the competition, but as you can see from the list above, competition is only part of the reason. The reality is that most of the time, it is lack of awareness and sufficient motivation to change.

That means it will take extra effort and incentives for you to get customers to try you out. Given that most customers are set in their ways and don't switch providers easily, what can you do to convince a customer to come to you in the first place? What marketing tactics can you use to get a customer to try you? Some successful methods for encouraging customers to both get to know about you and get motivated to try you out include:

- **Introductory offers.** Short-term, deeply discounted prices you offer when you first launch a product or company. They attract attention and let customers know that these prices won't last long.

- **Loss leaders/Teaser rates.** Incredibly low prices to attract a new customer, often resulting in a company making no money—or losing money—on the transaction itself. At Thanksgiving, most U.S. supermarkets deeply discount turkeys, making them a "loss leader" to attract customers to do their shopping there. Be careful, however; some laws limit loss leaders and teaser rates.

- **Free offers.** Giving customers your product or service free, at least for a while, to entice them to buy. Examples include a free month's subscription to an online dating site, free HBO and installation when you subscribe to a cable service, and one month's free rent with a year's lease.

- **Sampling.** Giving prospects a chance to try your product or service at no charge. Sampling can be something as simple as food tastings at a store or it can be a free 30-day trial version of software or a free chiropractic exam.

- **"Beta" testing.** Asking valuable prospective customers to participate in testing your product before release/sale to the general public. This is often done with technology products but could be applied in a range of industries, such as sporting goods. The testers can often become first purchasers (especially when given discounts for helping you test the product).

- **Positive reviews by influencers.** Using your public relations activities (see Chapter 17) to make sure that individuals whom others look to for purchasing advice get your product/service to review. Influencers can cause people to purchase new products they would otherwise hesitate to try.

Whichever approach you use to get first-time buyers to give you a chance, you, of course, have to let prospects know about them. That's where the marketing tactics in the rest of this book (Sections II to VII) come in. Some of the tactics you'll want to focus on when trying to get first-time customers include:

- Advertising, especially offering discounts and free offers

- Online marketing, especially reaching out to key bloggers and user review sites

- Direct mailings, including purchasing prospect lists from companies that sell lists they've compiled from various sources (such as magazine subscribers or purchasers of certain products)

■ Public relations, aimed particularly at generating positive reviews by influencers

■ Holding "grand openings" with freebies, to introduce new customers to your store, restaurant, or service

As you work through the rest of this book, keep these tactics in mind as a major part of your marketing campaign if your goal is to attract first-time buyers.

BRAINSTORMING

ATTRACTING FIRST-TIME CUSTOMERS

Use this worksheet to list ways you can attract first-time customers to your offerings.

METHOD	SPECIFICS
Introductory offers (on launch)	
Loss leaders/Teaser rates	
Free offers	
Sampling	
"Beta" testing	
Positive reviews by influencers	
Other	

Lifetime Value

An important concept to help you determine how much you can spend in your marketing campaign to acquire a customer is the *lifetime value of a customer,* also referred to as customer lifetime value (CLV). This is the amount of income you can project any single customer will be worth to your company *over time.*

What is your customer worth in actual dollar figures? Because businesses operate differently, with varying billing cycles and ways of acquiring both customers and revenue, there's no set or agreed-upon system for calculating customer value. But the basics involve:

■ Estimating the amount of time you expect your customer to continue being a loyal customer. This is the lifetime of your customer, and it's usually three to seven years, but this varies, depending on the nature of the product/service/industry.

■ Determining how much your customer is likely to spend during that period of time, through all product and service purchases.

■ Estimating the profit to you from that customer's purchases.

■ Estimating how much it costs you to acquire that customer and to retain/ serve that customer.

You need to balance the expected lifetime value of a customer with the costs of attracting and retaining them to get a sense of how profitable each customer is to you—that's their total *customer lifetime value.*

For instance, if you are an Internet service provider, hosting websites for businesses, you could estimate a customer's lifetime income to you as shown in the following sample:

SAMPLE: Estimating Customer Lifetime Value for an ISP

Expected length of time customer will keep their website hosted by my service (on average):	48 months (4 years)
Expected monthly income per customer:	$80
My estimated costs to host and service website per customer and provide ongoing communication to them:	$20
Estimated profit per month:	$60
Lifetime profit from hosting:	*$2,880 ($60 x 48 months)*
Estimated purchases they'll make of other services (for example, website design, changes):	$800
My estimated costs to provide services:	$200
Profit on other services purchases:	*$600*
Total customer lifetime income	*$3,480 ($2,880 plus $600)*
Cost to acquire that customer:	$300
Cost to retain and administer that customer's account:	$100
Total customer lifetime value:	*$3,080 ($3,480 minus $300 minus $100)*

You can do similar calculations for customers making one-time purchases. For instance, a customer using your tax preparation service may come in only once a year, but you can still estimate how many years they are likely to return to you.

Why is it important for you to know the customer lifetime value when you're starting on your marketing plan? Because that number gives you an idea of how much you can spend on acquiring a customer and still be profitable. Using the example above, for instance, if it costs you $3,500 to acquire each customer, you're never going to make any money. In reality, you'd want to spend only a fraction of that.

When you're first starting in business, your customer acquisition costs will be a much higher percentage of the lifetime value of a customer. After all, it costs a lot more to land the first client for your website hosting company than the thousandth, because you've already developed your marketing materials, tested your online marketing campaigns, and long ago paid off the graphic designer who designed your ads.

As you compute the lifetime value of a customer in the following worksheet, you may come to another realization: customers are often more valuable when you can sell them a product or service on a subscription basis rather than through a one-time purchase (because you're more likely to retain them for a longer period of time). And, of course, they're more valuable when you can sell them additional products or services besides the one they've originally come to you to buy (for instance, a maintenance agreement when they buy their new flat screen TV or the perfect necklace to go with that new blouse). And you'll want to keep that in mind as you develop your business pricing strategy.

SAMPLE: Calculating Profitability of an Ad Campaign Using CLV

Here is a very simplified way of evaluating whether it was profitable to run an ad campaign for a preschool, to attract new parents to sign up.

Cost of ad campaign, print ads (with introductory half-price discount coupon) in neighborhood newspaper:	$4,200
Number of people responding to the ad campaign:	9
Number of new customers who actually enrolled in school:	3
Campaign cost per newly enrolled customer:	$1,400
Normal cost of 1 month's school tuition:	$2,000
Loss from half-price discount on school tuition:	$1,000
Initial month customer value/return on investment:	-$400
Cost of an average school year:	8 months x $2,000 = $16,000
Lifetime customer income:	$16,000 x 3 years - $1,000 (discount) = $47,000
Customer retention costs (parent appreciation dinners; special events):	$5,000
Customer lifetime value (return on Investment):	$47,000 total customer lifetime income -$5,000 – customer retention -$1,400 – initial ad = $40,600
Customer value per year (divide by 3 years' attendance):	roughly $13,533

Retaining Customers

Successful marketing involves not just getting customers, but keeping them. Most marketing specialists agree it's far less expensive to keep a loyal customer than to attract a new one (it's estimated that it costs from two to ten times more to acquire a customer than to retain one). For instance, it costs far less to send a brochure to a customer who buys from you every year than it does to place TV advertisements to attract new customers. The longer a customer remains with you and continues to buy, the more profitable the relationship. That's why it pays to reward customer loyalty and keep customers with you as long as possible.

AVERAGE CUSTOMER LIFETIME VALUE (CLV)

Estimate the average profit your company will make on each customer. Use the appropriate portion of this worksheet, depending on whether you are selling a product/service directly or on a subscription basis. If you have different product lines or customer types, make a copy of this worksheet for each one.

TYPE OF CUSTOMER #1 – GENERAL PURCHASES

Product/service purchased: _____

Profit per purchase: _____

times customer purchases per year: _____

years they'll continue to purchase: _____

Add-on purchases/subscriptions: _____

Profit on add-ons: _____

Total lifetime income: _____

Subtract:

Customer acquisition costs: _____

Customer retention costs: _____

Result—customer lifetime value (CLV): _____

TYPE OF CUSTOMER #2 – MONTHLY SUBSCRIPTION

Product/service subscribed to: _____

Average monthly subscription fee: _____

Profit per month: _____

months they'll continue to subscribe: _____

Total lifetime income: _____

Subtract:

Customer acquisition costs: _____

Customer retention costs: _____

Result—customer lifetime value (CLV): _____

What keeps customers coming back?

The first thing is the quality of your product or service and the way the company itself is run. One of the best ways to cultivate happy, loyal, and long-term customers is to consistently give them an excellent product or service at a competitive price. Some companies stay in business for decades with virtually no advertising, customer retention programs, or other special marketing activities just by doing what they're supposed to do—being a reliable source of a product or service at a fair price and interacting with the customer in a professional manner. This isn't enough for every company, of course (especially new companies), but it is a cornerstone of customer retention. Other factors involved in customer retention include:

- **Good customer service.** Responding to customers' inquiries, showing up/delivering on time, handling complaints and concerns promptly.

- **Competitive prices.** Maintaining fair prices for what the customer is getting and against what the competition is offering.

- **Regular communication.** Staying in touch with customers on an ongoing basis, perhaps through an email newsletter.

- **Special treatment.** Going the extra mile for a customer with unexpected benefits, such as giving a diner a free dessert for their birthday or washing the customer's car after an oil change.

- **Loyalty/rewards programs.** Organized systems to retain and reward good customers (see the "Loyalty/Rewards Programs" section below).

Database Marketing: Customer Relationship Management (CRM)

To run and manage most customer reward and retention programs, you need to have a good system of keeping track of your customers, including their contact information and a record of their purchases and preferences. For this, you need a *database.* This is so important that an entire industry exists to help companies communicate and market to their customer base, with its own term: customer relationship management, or CRM.

Advanced database programs enable companies to segment, slice, and dice their customer lists to figure out which customers are likely to be most profitable, which most likely to respond to a special offer, which can be retained without special deals, and so on. CRM programs have also allowed businesses to devise sophisticated loyalty/rewards programs (see the "Loyalty/Rewards Programs" section below).

But even the smallest businesses can build a customer database by systematically keeping track of all customers and prospects, especially their contact information and purchase histories. Software and Internet applications—such as contact management programs and simple address books—are available at low prices. The key is to use the information once you compile it.

Loyalty/Rewards Programs

It pays to take care of your best customers, those who purchase frequently and/or are very profitable. Good customers want to feel that they are valued by a business, and companies want to ensure that the best customers keep coming back. As a result, over the years, many Customer Loyalty/Rewards Programs have been devised. The most obvious example of these is airline frequent flyer programs. But loyalty/rewards programs abound in businesses large and small. For instance, a punch card for a local coffee shop, where you

Myth⊘Buster

True Blue

MYTH: Once a customer loves you, they'll stay with you forever.

BUSTED: Sure, customers are busy people and if they're basically satisfied with a provider, it's hard for them to change. But they can—and do—change. Situations in their lives or businesses change. If your customers are other companies, personnel may change. Or your competitors may be wooing your customers away with special offers. And they may just plain forget about you. The truth is, it takes work to keep a customer. Don't take satisfied customers for granted.

Remember the Little Things

Many companies use database software that records customer birthdays, anniversaries, and other special occasions. Some systems automatically send customers print and online greeting cards (sometimes including discount offers) or even free gifts, in recognition of these occasions.

Stick or Carrot?

Of course, another way to hold onto customers is to make it difficult and too costly for them to leave—that is, making switching to a new provider painful (also known as keeping their "switching costs" high). This approach is more like a stick than a carrot, but it can be effective. Mobile phone companies accomplish this with binding, long-term service contracts. The price for breaking these contracts can be prohibitive. Other products or services require customers to make some kind of investment in time, training, resources, or equipment, such as learning to use a new accounting software program; once a customer has entered all their financial data, it costs too much, in both money and hassle, to easily switch programs.

While this approach may actually be very effective in keeping customers, it does little to generate goodwill, referrals, or add-on sales. And this is more a business strategy than a marketing approach.

get one free cup after purchasing ten cups is a simple, but often effective, loyalty/rewards program.

The point of all these programs is to keep customers attached to you, and they all have some basic attributes in common:

- The customer gets a reward—discount, freebie, upgrade, or special service —for being a regular or big customer.
- There is a way to keep track of customers' purchases.
- Generally, but not always, the customer gives the company their contact information, which enables the business to keep marketing to, and communicating with, them.

Structures of customer loyalty/rewards programs include:

- **Membership/clubs.** Discounts or rewards for people who agree to sign up to be a member of your club or be associated with you. These include supermarket "clubs," where customers get discounts and special offers in return for enabling the supermarket to track their purchases and continue to market to them. These work well with customers who are regularly targeted by competitors' marketing campaigns.

- **Free reward after multiple purchases.** Enticing customers to keep coming back to you by offering them something free after they make a certain number of purchases. These include punch cards at a car wash, where you get your tenth car wash free. These can be very simple, especially if the customer is motivated to keep track of purchases.

- **Buy-ahead discounts.** A significant discount or freebie for buying multiple products or services in advance. Getting 12 months' membership in a gym for the cost of only 10 when you buy the entire year at once is a buy-ahead discount. These work very well in generating advance income for a company and where there is a good chance that customers would otherwise stop purchasing.

- **Upgrades/Special services.** Many customers want special treatment (or better products) because they see themselves as valued customers. Examples include an upgrade to first or business class as a reward for achieving a certain number of frequent flyer miles or a hotel room upgrade in recognition of numerous visits. But upgrades could be as simple as giving free conditioning treatments to a regular patron of a hair salon.

- **Discounts after purchase.** Discounts given as a reward after purchase to encourage additional purchases and to thank customers. An example would be a discount coupon for the next purchase placed in an order shipped from a clothing company.

From time to time, you must evaluate the cost of your loyalty/rewards program. Are you giving free stuff to customers who would have been buying from you anyway? Are your rewards eroding away your profit margins to an untenable extent? Sophisticated customer relationship management programs help huge corporations analyze the cost-benefit ratio of reward programs—often on a customer-by-customer basis. But even a simple review will help you gain some insight into how much you are spending on rewards you're giving to customers versus the CLV (customer lifetime value) of those customers.

BRAINSTORMING

RETAINING CUSTOMERS

Use this worksheet to list ways you can retain first-time and existing customers.

METHOD	SPECIFICS
Customer service	
Competitive prices	
Discounts	
Special treatment or services	
Loyalty/rewards programs	
Communication	
Other	

BUILDING YOUR MARKETING PLAN

ACQUIRING AND RETAINING CUSTOMERS

Drawing on the Brainstorming Worksheets you filled out in this chapter, use this worksheet to outline your plans for acquiring and retaining customers.

Describe 5 methods you will use to attract first-time customers to your offerings:

1. _____

2. _____

3. _____

4. _____

5. _____

Describe 5 methods you will use to retain customers after they've made their first purchase:

1. _____

2. _____

3. _____

4. _____

5. _____

Lingo

BRAND: The complete public identity of a company, product, or service based on all the words, symbols, design, messages, and values connected with it.

BRAND EXTENSION: Taking the brand name of a product or service and using it on other, usually related, products.

BRAND IDENTITY: The representation of a brand; the elements of a company, product, or service that customers use to recognize and remember that company, product, or service. These elements can be verbal, visual, audio, or other sensory representations.

BRAND LICENSING: Allowing another company to use a brand name on their products or in conjunction with the sale of their products.

BRAND NAME: A well-known name (and other brand identity features) of a well-established product, service, or company.

BRAND PROMISE: The commitment a company is making to a customer when they put their brand on a product or service; what a customer can expect when they choose a specific brand.

UNIQUE SELLING PROPOSITION (USP): A concise description of what you are selling, why customers should buy from you, and what differentiates you from competitors.

CHAPTER 6

Your Brand and Core Message

When you meet a new person, what's the first thing you notice? Chances are, you'll first look at their face and what they're wearing. Then you'll listen to what they say and how they say it. You'll see how they behave and what they do. After a little more time with them, you'll get a sense of how they think and what they believe in. When you later recall that person, you'll just think of them as "Jessica" or "Michael" but you'll immediately associate their appearance, their behavior, and their values with that name. These are all part of their total personality or identity.

That's essentially how a brand works. A brand is the totality of the identity or personality of a company, product, or service. Branding uses words, images, design, ideas, and more to represent a company, service, or product, making that company, service, or product memorable to customers and establishing its position in the market. Developing a brand consists of defining a company's, service's, or product's:

- Promise
- Values
- Message
- Identity

Brands also affect—and reflect—how customers define themselves. Think of the kind of car you drive, the clothes you wear, the types of stores you shop in. Many of these reflect how you see yourself. A person buys a high-end luxury car like a Mercedes-Benz not merely because of quality or performance, but to show that they are successful. Another person buys a Toyota Prius not merely to save money on gas, but to show that they care about the environment.

You don't have to be a big corporation or have a huge advertising budget to develop a brand. Even a one-person company can build a reputation that is essentially their brand. For instance, you can be a carpenter who develops a reputation within the contractor community for being able to build beautiful,

> *Most people don't know what branding is, or they know what it is, but think of it as just their logo. They believe that, if they have a logo, they have a brand. But a brand is much, much more. It's your company's personality, and it's expressed in everything you do, from your print materials, to your website, to how you answer the phone and care for your customer. It's also you, and the image you present when you meet people. Your brand is who you are, what you do, and how you do it.*
>
> **Susan Schwartz**
> **Owner**
> **You Who Branding**

Ads Do It All

MYTH: You can build a brand with advertising alone.

BUSTED: A brand is much more than just a well-known name. To be at all effective, a brand has to stand for something in the customer's mind. During the early days of Internet commerce (the heady time known as the "dot-com" era), companies spent millions of dollars on advertising, trying to build brands fast. But the names, and the companies, didn't yet mean anything to customers. For instance, the public quickly got to know the name Pets.com, and the sock puppet character that represented the company was a familiar icon, easily identified. But the company itself failed to convince customers that it offered anything special in terms of value, unique products, or even convenience. A brand has to represent something, stand for something, or evoke something that consumers want, for it to be more than just a well-known name.

detailed cabinetry. Or you can be an event planner who becomes known as someone who always manages events perfectly. Within your industry, you have developed a brand name.

Brands can evolve over time. Amazon started out simply as a bookseller but now sells virtually everything. And brands can be bought, sold, and/or totally repositioned. Abercrombie & Fitch was once a staid, upscale supplier of sporting goods that could outfit adventurers for African safaris. But when it was bought by The Limited, the brand was appropriated for apparel stores for the college crowd.

Brand Promise

The most important thing to remember about branding is: *A brand is a promise.* A brand promises *consistency.* A customer choosing a brand is expecting to experience the same thing they did the last time they (or someone recommending the brand) purchased that brand. As a result, a strong brand gives customers *trust*—trust in your products, services, convenience, price, and the like—because you are consistent over time.

This doesn't mean you have to promise the highest quality or the lowest price; it just means being consistent so the customer can depend on what they'll get from the brand. Applebee's doesn't have to promise gourmet food to be a reliable brand. The company built its brand by giving customers the same experience, the same type and quality of food, and the same cleanliness at every one of its restaurants.

When a customer chooses a product or service with a brand they know, they have a certain set of expectations. They want the product or service to be very much the same as the last time they used it or the last time a person who referred them to the product or service used it. That's the *brand promise*, and the most important promise a brand makes to a customer or client is *consistency.* Some of the promises a brand can make to a customer are:

- Performance
- Reliability
- Quality
- Taste/flavor
- Cost/price
- Convenience
- Customer service
- Luxury

As you develop all your marketing materials, but especially your core marketing message, think about what promise your "brand" is making to your customers or clients.

BRAINSTORMING

YOUR BRAND PROMISE

What is your brand's promise to your customers or clients? Remember, that promise is based on consistency. What will you consistently, over time, provide to your customers/clients? (Examples include performance, reliability, convenience, luxury, price, taste/flavor, cost/price, customer service, and quality.)

_____

_____

_____

_____

Brand Name

When you build a brand name, customers will develop such a strong relationship with your company that it's difficult for others to compete. There are obviously many advantages to being a brand name, but that status is not easy to achieve. First, it is usually expensive. To become a familiar, recognized brand name, you must spend a great deal of _money_ on marketing and advertising. Next, it takes _time_. Although it seems as if some brand names develop overnight, especially with Internet-based businesses, to effectively build a name, customers must encounter you repeatedly and purchase your products or services over and over. Finally, it takes _consistency_. You have to look at the features and benefits your customers expect to receive as a result of purchasing from you, and you must deliver those benefits and features _consistently_. That means you must make certain you put company resources into supporting those features and benefits. Because you meet their expectations repeatedly, customers develop loyalty to the brand and the brand name.

Once you've developed a brand name, you have built substantial value for your company.

Brand Extension

Once you've firmly established a brand in the public's awareness, you can use that brand name to help sell other products. You can do this in at least three ways:

- **Product line extension**, in which you add the name of the brand to new variations on a similar product.

- **Brand extension**, in which you add the name of the brand to a fairly different product you own or develop.

- **Licensing**, in which you sell permission to other manufacturers (or service providers) to use your brand name in conjunction with other products they have or develop.

The Value of a Brand

Once a brand has built a large following of loyal customers, the brand itself becomes valuable. Products or services with that brand can command higher prices than the exact same products or services without that brand. That brand becomes an intangible asset (something of value that's not material) of the company. Brands are so valuable that research companies regularly evaluate the worth of a brand—how much more a product or service is worth because that brand is associated with it. Some of the brands consistently rated as the most valuable in the world, with worths in the billions of dollars, include Coca-Cola, Disney, Microsoft, Nokia, Toyota, and Louis Vuitton.

Once, the only product that carried the Oreo name was the familiar cookie with two chocolate wafers and a vanilla cream filling. Now there are all kinds of variations, including "double stuff" with twice as much vanilla cream, cookies containing colored or flavored cream for certain holidays, mini-Oreos, Oreo brownies, and even Oreo pie crust. There are also products you'd never associate with cookies—for example, Post "Oreo O's" breakfast cereal (Post is owned by Kraft, which also owns Oreo). And Kraft has licensed the Oreo name to other companies as well; you can get an Oreo Blizzard at your local Dairy Queen.

You can, however, overuse a brand until it loses the positive associations that customers have with it. Imagine how it would undermine the power of the Oreo brand if there were products such as Oreo-branded burritos or Oreo-branded floor mops.

A brand's identity can become so fixed in the public imagination that it can become part of popular culture and entertainment. Advertising images can evolve into characters. M&M's candies became characters in their ads and on their packages, and the company eventually licensed those images to toy manufacturers. The cavemen used in commercials for the auto insurance company Geico became so popular that they spawned a TV program!

Brand Management

Once a company has built a brand name, it also has to protect it. First, you have to make sure that competing companies don't use your name, especially for similar products. It would be easy, for instance, for a new nutrition bar to call itself "Weight Watchers Special" even if it had no relation to the national Weight Watchers company. So that company would have to issue a "cease and desist" letter (or eventually sue) to stop that trademark infringement.

If you have a particularly powerful brand name, you will want to make sure that other companies don't use your name for unrelated products or services. After all, if someone opened a gym named "Sony," many customers might assume it was associated with that consumer electronics giant. Sony would then have to make sure their name was not used by the gym. If you become really successful, a brand name can become a household word. If it does, you've got to take action before it loses trademark protection. *Zipper*, for instance, was once a trademarked name, but its protection was lost.

While individuals may use the term *Kleenex* to mean any facial tissue or say they're going to *Google* someone, these are trademarked names. The owners of those trademarks have to be vigilant to keep their names from becoming generic.

When using a trademarked name, be certain to indicate that the name has trademark protection, with the appropriate mark (see page 66). And insist that when others use your name, they also include the mark, indicating that you have the rights to that name.

Values

Increasingly, brands stand not only for a promise relating to their product or service (such as quality or low cost), but also for a set of values that customers can relate to. Because many consumers define themselves by the brands they buy (and wear, drive, drink), a company with enduring and strong values often engenders enduring and strong customer loyalty.

Many customers choose to spend their money with companies that reflect values they hold or aspire to hold. The Chevrolet brand has long associated itself with being American-made and patriotic, from Dinah Shore singing "See the U.S.A. in Your Chevrolet" in the 1950s to John Mellencamp singing "Our Country" in the "Our Country. Our Truck" Chevrolet ads 50 years later. Chevrolet is appealing to a segment of the market that shares their values of buying an American-made car or truck.

The founder of Chipotle built a national Mexican food chain on the concept of "food with integrity," focusing not just on the taste of the food but on the concept of food coming from "better sources, better for the environment, better for the animals, and better for the farmers . . . ." For Chipotle, this is more than just an advertising campaign: they are appealing to a segment of the market that shares their values of buying and eating sustainably grown food.

Strong values can enhance the strength of a brand. Because customers share values with a company, they feel a sense of loyalty to that brand. In some cases, that values-based brand loyalty can create an almost cult-like following. However, it is also possible that a company's strong values can alienate or turn off other segments of a market. And a company that espouses certain values had better stick to them; customers can feel betrayed (and take their business elsewhere or start complaining on the Internet) if a company with a certain set of values strays too far from their core beliefs.

Origin of a Brand: Roundup at OK Corral

The concept of brand identity literally comes from branding. Ranchers herded cows across vast plains to take them to market, and often the herds would intermingle. In order to figure whose cow was whose at the end of a cattle drive, the cows carried their ranch's identity in the form of a brand. Branding of products came into practice when artisans began to mark their work with their signatures or distinctive symbols. These symbols became identifiable to consumers. If the product was superior in the mind of the consumer, that mark or brand came to represent high quality.

BRAINSTORMING

YOUR COMPANY VALUES

Use this worksheet to list the values you want your brand to reflect/be associated with:

1. _____

2. _____

3. _____

4. _____

5. _____

6. _____

Classic Brand Marketing— Apple's "1984" Commercial

One of the most famous brand-related marketing events of all time was the "1984" television commercial from Apple Computer (as the company was then called), introducing the company's Macintosh computer. The ad ran only once, on Super Bowl Sunday, 1984.

Leveraging the public's knowledge of the novel *1984* by George Orwell, the Apple commercial first showed a group of grey, bleak followers of Big Brother, marching in lockstep then thoughtlessly listening to everything Big Brother was saying. Then one lone woman jogged in, carrying a sledge hammer. She threw it at Big Brother and broke the spell.

Apple wanted to convey the message that they were the iconoclast, challenging the staid, institutional computers of the day, especially the market leader IBM. They wanted customers who bought Apple products to feel they were special—better than the drones who bought computers from big corporations. At the time, the commercial was ground breaking. As a result, it was shown repeatedly on TV news shows, and it had a major impact:

- It played a major part in establishing Apple as a computer for the people.
- It demonstrated how one marketing or advertising event could garner substantial free publicity.
- It made Super Bowl Sunday the most important day for launching advertising campaigns.

To this day, Apple has maintained the market position that they, their products, and especially their customers are somehow cooler, hipper, and less institutional than the competition.

Core Message

What do you want your customers to remember about you? What do you want them to think when they think about your products or services? Your core message is where it all comes together. In essence, your core message is the marketing "elevator pitch" for your company and/or product or service. It is a concise summation of what you do, who your target market is, and what your competitive advantage is. Clearly, you can develop your core message only after you've evaluated those.

Your core message is *not* your tagline (although your tagline may reflect your message, see page 68). A tagline is an advertising slogan; your core message is a clear definition of your strategic position. Your core message should be based on:

- The nature of your products or services
- The key differentiators between you and your competition
- Your competitive advantages
- Your value proposition
- Your company values

Sometimes this core message is referred to as your unique selling proposition. A unique selling proposition is a clear summation of:

- What sets you apart from the competition—in other words, what makes you unique, your differentiators
- What you are offering the customer—in other words, what you are selling
- What's in it for the customer—in other words, the proposition

If yours is a large company, selling many different products, you may have a core message for each product line. In a smaller business or in a company with a narrow product line, your company's core message and your product's core message may be the same. For instance, the core message of The Planning Shop (the publisher of this book) is "We help entrepreneurs succeed by giving them practical, reality-based books and tools." This message is based on:

- Unique: a specialty in entrepreneurship (other publishers publish books on a wide range of topics and disciplines) and in being practical and true to life (other publishers may be more theoretical or abstract)
- Selling: books and other tools (such as some software products)
- Proposition: success. This is the promise The Planning Shop is making: "We'll help entrepreneurs succeed."

Message Drives Marketing

It's imperative that you understand the core message you want to send for your company, product, or service. Without articulating a core message, it's impossible to develop a consistent, meaningful marketing program. You need to keep your core message in mind when you're developing your

advertising, website, packaging, and marketing materials (brochures, catalogs) and even your company name. It must permeate every aspect of your
marketing, and it must be the foundation of all your marketing activities.

Your core message is what defines your brand. It's what you want customers to remember about you. When you have a strong, clear message,
you're much better able to develop a strong brand and a strong connection
with your customer base.

BRAINSTORMING

YOUR CORE MESSAGE

Use this worksheet to develop the core message or unique selling proposition for your company,
product, or service:

Unique: What sets you apart from competitors? What are your differentiators?

_____

Selling: What are the specific products or services, benefits or features you are selling?

_____

Proposition: What is the promise you are making to your customers? What's in it for them?

_____

BUILDING YOUR MARKETING PLAN

BRAND AND CORE MESSAGE

Drawing on the Brainstorming Worksheets you completed earlier in this chapter, use this worksheet to
summarize your plans for your company's brand identity and core message.

1. What does your brand promise to customers?

_____

2. What values will be associated with your brand?

_____

3. What is your unique selling proposition?

_____

Lingo

FONT: A specified typeface (see "*Typeface*" definition below), along with other characteristics of that typeface, such as style (for instance, **bold** or *italics*) and size (such as 10 point or 24 point)

IDENTITY: Elements of a company, product, or service that customers use to recognize and remember that company, product, or service. These elements can be verbal, visual, audio, or even sensory.

JINGLE: A melody, song, or musical phrase used to help make a company, product, or service memorable when used on radio, TV, the Web, or other audio or audiovisual devices.

LOGO: A symbol representing a company or organization. A logo can take the form of an image or words (especially the company name) designed in a specific style of type.

LOGOTYPE: A customized type style or specialized font used to form a logo.

TAGLINE/SLOGAN: A short, catchy, and memorable group of words, representing a company's message and branding.

TRADE DRESS: This is a legal term which describes the total image and appearance of a company, product, or brand. This is defined broadly and can include everything from the shape of packages, store furnishings, and graphics to what employees wear and even scents. Trade dress can be protected under trademark provisions.

TRADEMARK: An identifying mark (name, word, or symbol) that indicates which company has made a product or is providing a service. Trademarks can be legally protected, particularly through registering them with a country's trademark office.

TYPEFACE: The design of a set of characters for letters, numbers, and other symbols. Common typefaces include:

    Arial
    Times New Roman
    Courier

CHAPTER 7

Brand Identity

While a brand evokes many things for a customer—a promise, values, a message, and much more—there's a critical aspect to branding that is fundamental: the company or product's actual *identity*. After all, customers must be quickly and easily able to figure out that they're picking up a can of Red Bull, not a can of Monster, or entering a Quiznos, not a Subway.

As an entrepreneurial company, you want to distinguish yourself from the competition. Your brand identity helps you do that. By choosing colors, design, and even a company name that is very different from those of established market leaders, you will help customers immediately recognize that there's a new and different choice available.

A brand's overall identity is the sum of many parts. When you think of a company, all sorts of things come to mind—name, logo, signature colors, advertising slogans, store design, even the typeface used in ads or the music playing in the background when you walk into a retail outlet. Brand identity includes:

☐ Company name

■ Product or service name

☐ Logo (symbols created to represent the company)

☐ Colors and style (design scheme), also called "trade dress" (a legal term)

☐ Tagline (or slogan)

☐ General look and feel

☐ Packaging

☐ Audio, such as distinctive music or a special spokesperson's voice

☐ Characters (actual people, or imaginary figures like the Geico lizard)

Once you've decided on the elements of your company or product identity, use it consistently and repeatedly. After all, your identity is a major part of what customers remember when they think about you. And the components of a company *identity* enable customers to quickly identify a product or service, increasing the likelihood that they'll continue to buy from you. The brand elements—logos, taglines, and colors—come with their own set of rules (see pages 68-70).

(see pages 68-70).

Identify Your Service

It's easy to see how you can use brand identity techniques when marketing a product, but how do you use such techniques when you're delivering a service, especially when you are the sole provider?

If you're a service professional, you'll want to ensure you're a walking embodiment of your brand identity when the customer or client encounters you. Your brand is communicated through the clothes you wear, the way you act, even the vehicle you drive. That's why most nonprofessional service businesses require employees to wear some type of uniform or imprinted shirts.

Even if it's inappropriate to wear uniforms in your line of service business, you want your appearance, and your work style, to create brand expectations, such as responsiveness, reliability, friendliness, high level of skill, extensive knowledge of an area, creativity, or an up-to-date approach. For instance, a real estate office may require all employees to wear suits or dresses, and a hair salon may require all employees to wear particularly fashionable clothes.

Protecting Your Trademark

Developing and guarding your name and other aspects of your corporate identity start with understanding some basic legal protections. A trademark is a legally recognized name, image, set of words, or other branding element associated with a company, product, or service. It is subject to different levels of legal protection, depending on whether it's registered or not.

- The ® symbol signifies a trademark that has been registered with the United States Patent and Trademark Office (USPTO) and is legally protected on a nationwide basis.

- The **TM** symbol represents an unregistered trademark, which does not have the same protections as a registered trademark but is afforded some common law protections based on geography. Many companies use the **TM** symbol while in the process of officially registering their trademark.

- The **SM** symbol is used in the same way as **TM** but to identify a service rather than a product. Once it is registered, it can also be changed to an ® symbol.

Using someone else's trademarked material, whether it is registered or unregistered, can subject the user to a lawsuit.

Your Company Name

A clever business name can be an excellent marketing tool—helping make your company memorable. In small companies, *you* are the brand, and often the best name for your company is your own, perhaps with a descriptive phrase to clarify what you do. Using your own name as a business name is common for those in creative or service fields, such as architects, attorneys, graphic designers, and writers. For instance, "Carly Kwan, Caterer" or "Josh Babbitt, Attorney-at-Law."

If you plan on growing your business substantially, though, you may not want to use your own name, or any person's name. Having a name that is closely associated with the owner may later make it harder to sell your company. Also, if you hire employees, your customers might still expect service from you, even if you have perfectly capable professionals on your staff who can do the job.

For most businesses, it's better to find a name that somehow suggests the benefit your customers will get. A good business name:

- **Communicates accurate information**. A clear company name, such as "Main Street Volvo Repair" or "Des Moines Culinary Institute," immediately lets customers know what to expect. Avoid anything in your business name that could confuse potential customers about what you do or offer or that may change later. Customers will get annoyed if they find a fitness center called "24-Hour Workout" closed after 10 p.m.

- **Is memorable**. If clients or customers have an easier time remembering your name, they are likely to do business with you again. Some companies choose names that will catch attention, such as Yahoo or Yelp.

- **Conveys the appropriate concept or feeling**. Choose a name that has positive associations with your company's message. For instance, Under Armour began as a company that made performance T-shirts and other "under" wear—providing a layer of protective "armour" for athletes. A day spa named "Haven" or "Oasis" transmits the sense that customers are going to escape the stresses in their lives. Words such as "Main Street" or "Central" tell potential customers that the service is local and convenient.

- **Won't get dated quickly**. Be careful not to choose names too closely identified with recent trends or ones that are too limiting. You are likely to change the scope of your products or services over time. Look at all the e-companies that had to drop the words "dot com" from their company names once the tech boom of the late 1990s ended.

- **Is easy to spell**. If a name is too hard to spell, it becomes harder for potential customers to remember, repeat to others, or look up online. Spelling becomes even more important when you use your company's name as part of your website domain name.

- **Is easy to pronounce**. People have a harder time remembering names they can't say easily, and they feel uncomfortable doing business with companies whose names they can't pronounce.

■ **Allows the company to grow.** Consider the impact your business name will have when your company is much larger. For instance, a business called "Two Sisters Design" might imply that you're a small company and won't be a good reflection of your size when you grow to a multimillion-dollar operation with hundreds on your staff.

Sometimes, using a general name like Apple or Amazon is a way to ensure the name will last. The word *Amazon* has nothing to do with books, but it implies something BIG, like a mighty river with many tributaries, making it a nice fit for the company today. Keep in mind, though, that if you go with a general name (as opposed to one that's specific, like 24-Hour Workout), you'll probably need to spend more on marketing to communicate exactly what you do.

BRAINSTORMING

YOUR COMPANY (OR PRODUCT) NAME

Use this worksheet to list the elements you want to include in the name of your company.

Keep in mind that you should include only those aspects that are not likely to change; it's much easier to alter a tagline than a company or product name.

Your name or the name of the principals of the company:

_____

The nature of your product or service:

_____

Your location:

_____

Positive aspects of your product or service:

_____

Feelings or connotations you want associated with the name:

_____

"Off-beat" or unusual words or names you particularly want to include:

_____

Good Logos vs. Bad Logos

In general, good logos:

- Are simple
- Are memorable
- Imply something positive
- Are easy to reproduce in both color and black and white
- Can be used and repeated everywhere: on products, in advertising, on the Web, and on packaging and marketing materials
- Are not offensive (be careful of international connotations of symbols and colors)
- Are broad enough to keep using as your company grows

Bad or ineffective logos tend to be:

- Boring and unremarkable
- Unattractive and poorly designed
- Created using an unappealing typeface
- Designed with a jarring or unattractive color scheme
- Hard to reproduce in different formats and media
- Awkward: too vertical or too horizontal to be useful in a variety of settings

Memorable Taglines

FedEx

Message: reliable, fast delivery service worldwide

Tagline: *The world on time*

Subway

Message: fast food that's healthier than other fast food options

Tagline: *Eat fresh*

Logos

A logo can be an extremely powerful element of brand identity. See the golden arches and you know there's a McDonald's nearby. Spot a swoosh on a hat and you know it's made by Nike. Logos, especially strong logos advertised frequently, become another way for the public to remember you.

But even if you don't have the advertising budget to get your logo on national TV or plaster it all over the Internet, there's a good reason for you to develop a logo for your business: visual images make it easier for your customers, and potential customers, to remember you. That's because people learn and remember things in many different ways. Humans mentally process various types of information—words, images, or music—differently. So when prospective customers see your logo, as well as seeing or hearing your company's name, they're using more of their brains to process the information—both verbal and visual. You make more of an impact when people associate your company with both words and images (and, if you use music, sound).

For instance, the Target logo is simple and elegant. It tells customers that Target stores are where they'll find exactly what they want at exactly the right price. The bullseye also suggests competitiveness, accuracy, and efficiency—traits that shoppers, and shareholders, will appreciate.

Of course, your logo must also reflect your target market. A logo for products aimed at teenaged skateboarders may seem offensive, or at least jarring, to an adult market, but anything less edgy may be boring to the boarders.

Creating a good logo doesn't have to be a complicated affair. If you don't have money to have one professionally designed, use a combination of your company name and a geometric shape, or try using a logotype, which is a stylized type font that works as a logo. A well-known example is the Coca-Cola logotype.

Taglines

Many companies use a tagline or motto to better explain the nature of their business or to create a feeling about the company or product. In just a few words, it explains why customers should buy their products or use their service. A tagline helps customers remember what is unique about a business:

"Personalized service at practical prices"

"Legal services for the real estate industry"

Taglines should reflect your marketing *message*. This is the strategic position that you've carved out for yourself—how you differentiate yourself from your competitors, what makes you special, and why someone should buy from you. But your tagline has to be brief, often much more concise than your total message. And it must be much more memorable and catchy than your message.

Taglines don't have to be catchy to be memorable to your target audience. "Manufacturers of packing materials for technology products" may seem like a boring tagline, but it could be very effective if you make and sell boxes for computer products. This line tells potential customers—and reminds current ones—that you specialize in exactly what they need.

Bigger companies with more marketing dollars to devote to building their message can get away with more vague taglines, such as Mazda's "Zoom Zoom." Smaller companies are better off taking a more straightforward approach, like Danny's Drycleaners: "Good As New in 24 Hours" or LiteCase's: "We take the lug out of luggage." Keep in mind that while your tagline may be straightforward, it doesn't have to be unimaginative.

Taglines often become the basis of your advertising and marketing pieces. Use your tagline in all your advertising. You can also use a tagline on your business cards, packaging, stationery, and signs, and even as your sign-off

BRAINSTORMING

YOUR LOGO

Use this worksheet to help create an effective logo for your company, product, or service.

Describe what you want your logo to convey. What feelings, emotions, or thoughts do you want it to evoke?

_____

What images are similar to what you'd like to convey with your logo? These can be other logos or other types of images:

_____

Sketch out a preliminary idea for a logo for your company:

_____

BRAINSTORMING

YOUR TAGLINES

Use this worksheet to develop your tagline.

What are the components of your overall marketing message that you want to highlight in your tagline?

_____

What do you most want customers to remember about you?

_____

What distinguishes you from your competitors?

_____

Make a list of words that you would want associated with your company, product, or service:

_____

Using those words, craft a basic tagline you could use for your company, product, or service:

_____

I Heard It on the Radio

If you advertise on radio, recognize that there's no visual component: listeners can't see most aspects of your brand identity, such as logos and colors. So you need to have an audio component to your brand identity as well. Use the same spokesperson, so radio listeners will associate that voice with your company. Or develop a jingle or other musical or audio "signature" and use it in all your ads.

on emails. You don't have to have a tagline, and you certainly don't have to choose one before you open for business. But developing a tagline helps you clarify what makes your business special and enables you to sum up your competitive position in just a few words.

Colors

Many people start their businesses without giving colors much thought. Yet most of us intend to use some colors in our business—in our décor, on our business cards, and on our brochures, packaging, website, and so on. Coming up with a consistent use of color—your color palette—gives you another tool to help customers remember who you are and to convey a feeling about your company. Your color scheme is also one of the easiest ways for customers to quickly distinguish you from your competitors.

Use your color palette consistently throughout your marketing so your customers associate you with the same colors. The deep blue of JetBlue and—probably one of the best-known color associations—the brown of UPS, all help convey the company's brand identity. The UPS color has also become part of its tagline: "What Can Brown Do For You?"

Also be aware of feelings associated with colors and their meanings in other cultures. For example:

- Blue suggests dependability/reliability
- Red indicates power, danger, or good luck
- Purple can suggest spirituality
- Green can indicate friendliness and a connection to nature
- Pink is usually considered a feminine color

Here are a few additional points about color to keep in mind:

- Colors can date your company. Avoid trendy colors if possible. Harvest gold was popular in the 70s but looks incredibly dated now.
- Avoid using too many colors. It is confusing and can dilute your branding.
- Adhere to trade dress—your branded design and color scheme—in your color choices for all marketing material, uniforms, décor, packaging, and more.
- Colors are interpreted differently in different cultures (in India and China, for instance, white is the color for mourning). Keep in mind the color connotations of the countries you do business with.

Since you're likely to be using your color palette on your website, keep in mind that some colors don't display well on computer monitors. Check colors on several different monitors before finalizing your choice. Be careful also about how many colors you use in your business. If you use too many, it can become expensive to print your stationery, business cards, and so on.

BRAINSTORMING

YOUR COLORS

What colors do your competitors use? (You will probably want to choose colors that are different from those used by major competitors.)

_____

_____

_____

_____

What colors would you, and your customers, likely associate with the positive feelings/connotations you want to convey as part of your brand/message?

_____

_____

_____

_____

What colors would be particularly inappropriate to associate with your type of company, product, or service?

_____

_____

_____

_____

What colors do you particularly like?

_____

_____

_____

List the colors that you are considering using for your company/product/service—and check the following:

COLOR	POSITIVE CONNOTATIONS?	NEGATIVE CONNOTATIONS?	OK IN PRINT?	OK ON WEB?

Myth ⃠ Buster

**A LOGO IS
ALL YOU NEED**

MYTH: Your logo is your brand.

BUSTED: A brand isn't just a logo; it's the total connection—the relationship—a company has with its customers. A brand includes the company's promise and message to its customers and the emotional aspects of how the company relates to its customers and how the customers relate to the company. A company's logo and the rest of its *corporate identity* components are secondary and serve to support and reinforce this relationship.

Leverage the Power of Brand Identity

Your brand identity gives you power—the power to motivate people to buy from you again. The more you use and reinforce the features of your brand identity, the more familiar people will become with it and the more likely they will be to do business with you repeatedly. To safeguard and strengthen your brand identity, be sure it is:

■ **Consistent.** Decide on an appropriate design style, color scheme, and tagline and avoid changing them unless your business has significantly changed or these elements have become badly outdated.

■ **Reflective of your company's promise, message, and values.** Your identity should be consistent with and reinforce your entire brand: your promise, values, and core message.

■ **Protected.** Be sure to consult with an attorney and register key elements of your brand with the United States Patent and Trademark Office at http://www.uspto.gov/. If others use, or closely imitate, your name, logo, tagline, or other components, you will need to take action to make sure they "cease and desist." If you don't, you may lose your trademark protection.

And most important, your brand identity should be:

■ **Used frequently and repeatedly.** A brand identity works only if your audience becomes familiar with it. It's got to be seen over and over and over again to be effective. Be sure you use your brand identity components:

— **On your products, in your packaging, and on any other materials** you use to identify your products or services to your customers or clients

— **In all of your marketing materials,** both print (brochures, catalogs, letterhead, business cards, direct mail) and Web (your website, email communications, blogs, and any digital documents you circulate)

— **In all of your advertising**, especially print, Web, and TV ads

Your brand identity is extremely valuable. Especially if you're starting a new company, now is the time to recognize the value of your brand and the elements of your brand identity. Do everything in your power to build and protect it. A strong, well-regarded brand will pave the way to your goals, making just about every aspect of your business—especially marketing—infinitely easier.

BUILDING YOUR MARKETING PLAN

YOUR BRAND IDENTITY

Drawing on the worksheets you completed in this chapter, outline the components of your brand identity.

1. What is the name of your company, product, or service? _____

_____

2. What is your tagline? _____

_____

3. What colors will you use as part of your identity? _____

_____

4. Draw a draft of your logo here: _____

_____

5. What styles would you describe as part of your identity? (For example, elegant, natural, conservative/corporate, edgy/hip, beach-y)

_____

6. What furniture, décor, or other design elements will be part of your identity? _____

_____

7. What clothing or clothing style will be part of your identity? _____

_____

8. What sounds/music will you use as part of your identity? _____

_____

9. List other elements of your identity: _____

_____

10. List ways in which you plan to use your brand identity elements as part of your marketing activities:

Packaging: _____

Website: _____

Brochures/Catalogs: _____

Advertising: _____

Clothing/Employees: _____

Décor: _____

Vehicles: _____

Other: _____

Lingo

MARKETING GOALS: What you hope to achieve through your marketing as it relates to your overall business goals.

METRICS: A quantifiable means of measuring the impact of your marketing and your progress toward your goals.

MILESTONES: Achievements that help you evaluate your progress toward your goals.

QUALITATIVE GOALS: Goals based on general, often subjective and non-quantifiable, measures.

QUANTITATIVE GOALS: Goals based on numerical measures of success.

RISKS: Negative consequences of taking a certain marketing path.

TARGET DATE: The day you hope to achieve a particular milestone.

CHAPTER 8

Your Marketing Goals

You're about to plan and launch your marketing campaign. But how will you know if it's a success? You can't begin your plan unless you know what you want to achieve.

Throughout the rest of this book, you will be deciding on all the specifics and details of your marketing campaign. All of those activities must be based on—and directed toward—reaching your goals. This chapter will help you focus in on those goals, so that your actions, and those of your other team members, will all work together in a logical, well-planned fashion to reach the same desired outcome.

Set Your Marketing Goals

The first questions you need to ask yourself when nailing down your marketing goals are:

1. What do I want to achieve through marketing?

2. Why is it important in a larger business context (or in relation to the overall goals of my business)?

Your marketing goal may be to create a campaign that ultimately wins you a 60% share of your market. This will bring you the revenue you need to meet your larger business goals—for instance, to significantly expand your operations, become a multimillion-dollar corporation, and eventually go public (sell your stock on a stock exchange). Your goals don't have to be that ambitious, of course, but they need to be set in the framework of your overall business objectives.

Types of Marketing Goals

The first thing you have to determine is what exactly you want to achieve with your marketing campaign. After all, you're going to be spending a lot of time and money on it, so you should have a clear idea of what you hope the outcome will be. The major objectives of marketing campaigns fall into the following overarching categories:

■ **Awareness.** Aimed at getting customers, the public, and your industry to notice your company, products, services, website, or other offerings. This includes:

— The launch of a new company (including Web-based companies)

— Product/service/website launch

— New features, prices, versions, upgrades

■ **Action.** Aimed at getting customers (or others) to do something specific in response to your marketing activities. This includes:

— Making a purchase

— Visiting your website

— Taking advantage of a special offer

— Clicking through on an Internet ad to your website

— Coming into your place of business

■ **Brand building.** Aimed at getting the public to know and remember the name of your company and products or services. This includes:

— Continually staying in the public awareness so they know of you and your offerings

— General advertising and marketing campaigns to keep name recognition high

■ **Announcement.** Aimed at getting others (including the financial press, potential investors, your industry) to know something positive about your company. This includes:

— Key milestones, awards, other prestigious events

— Mergers and acquisitions of other companies

— New key employees

— Levels of profitability or revenue levels reached

■ **Affiliation.** Aimed at getting customers to feel they are somehow connected with you, that they're aligned with your company, belong with you. This includes:

— Joining a mailing list, signing up for a company newsletter

— Sensing you share the same values regarding social responsibility

— Having an increased sense of self-worth by owning or using your products or services

— Wanting to show others they use your products or services

— Having endorsers or celebrities that they admire or want to emulate

■ **Attitude.** Aimed at getting others to think of you in a certain, positive light. This includes:

— Confirming your place as a market share leader

— Showing that you are innovative and cutting-edge

— Demonstrating that you are committed to social values

— Indicating that your products and services are used by winners

For example, if say you were launching a new company called SleekSki, making high-fashion, high-performance skiwear for women, your marketing objectives might be as follows:

S A M P L E : Marketing Objectives for Skiwear Company

TYPE OF OBJECTIVE	SPECIFIC OBJECTIVES FOR THIS MARKETING CAMPAIGN
AWARENESS	Inform women skiers about our new company, the advantages of our skiwear, and that there's a new fashion line of skiwear
	Get sporting goods retailers to know about our new company and the advantages of our skiwear
	Get women skiers to visit our website
ACTION	Get women skiers to sign up for our email newsletter
	Get women skiers to buy our products directly from our website
	Get sporting goods retailers to carry our line in their stores
	Make the name SleekSki memorable to sporting goods retailers
BRAND BUILDING	Get positive press in ski magazines
	Get our name visible in major ski resorts
	Start creating "buzz" about SleekSki with female pro and elite-level skiers
ANNOUNCEMENT	Inform the sporting goods and ski industry when we sign major athletes as endorsers
AFFILIATION	Sponsor leading pro women skiers to wear our clothing in competition
	Get female skiers to put our decals on their cars, skis
	Form a network of SleekSki "ambassadors" to each major ski
ATTITUDE	Get female skiers to consider SleekSki the skiwear they absolutely must have to improve their skiing performance
	Get all female skiers to consider SleekSki the most fashionable new ski apparel

The first step in developing your specific marketing goals is to list what you hope to achieve as a result of your marketing efforts. Use the worksheet below to outline your marketing objectives.

BRAINSTORMING

YOUR MARKETING OBJECTIVES

In each of the following areas, list what you hope to achieve as a result of your marketing campaign.

TYPE OF OBJECTIVE	SPECIFIC OBJECTIVES FOR THIS MARKETING CAMPAIGN
AWARENESS	
ACTION	
BRAND BUILDING	
ANNOUNCEMENT	
AFFILIATION	
ATTITUDE	
OTHER	

Quantitative and Qualitative Goals

As you can see, there are many marketing goals you'll want to achieve—anything from increasing your monthly sales figures to getting customers to feel good about your company's commitment to animal rights. But as you start to set specific goals for your marketing campaign, you'll want to narrow in on your objectives, so you can later determine whether your marketing efforts have been a success. To do so, divide your goals into two main categories: quantitative and qualitative.

Quantitative goals are tied to numerical measures, such as sales figures, income, number of visitors to your website, increase in market share, and other factors you can objectively measure. Some typical quantitative goals:

■ Increase sales by $500,000 in the next quarter

■ Secure 25 new corporate customers in the next 90 days

Get 20 stories about a new product in major media outlets in the next six weeks

Achieve 40% "click through" rate on online advertising

Get 800 people to sign up for a special trial offer this month

Have 1,400 people sign up to receive our newsletter and provide contact information in the next three months

Each of these goals has a *specific number* and a *specific timeframe* attached. They are easily measurable: after a month, you've either had 800 people sign up for the special offer or you haven't. It's not very fuzzy.

Qualitative goals tend to be more subjective. They focus on objectives such as increasing customer awareness, promoting positive associations and feelings, and increasing a company's stature with investors. Some typical qualitative goals:

Introduce a new company or product to a market

Maintain brand awareness

■ Inform customers of a product's new features

Establish a product as cutting-edge in the public's mind

Build positive associations with a company or its products

Increase prestige with the financial community

Maintain positive communication with shareholders

■ Reiterate dominant market position

As you can see, these qualitative goals are difficult, if not impossible, to measure. Sure, you might be able to commission expensive market research studies, but you're only going to do that if you have a huge marketing budget. Most entrepreneurial and smaller companies aren't going to be able to measure these qualitative goals.

It's important to have both types of goals for your business. Setting quantitative goals gives you discipline: you can judge whether your marketing is effective, you can learn what is realistic to expect, you can make changes to improve your marketing. Moreover, it's essential for budgeting: you can figure out how much it costs you to achieve a certain result.

But if every marketing effort has to be easily measurable, you may not engage in some activities that are critically important to your company—and marketing—success. For instance, it may be essential to exhibit at a trade show to stay in front of your industry, even though you can't quantifiably measure results in terms of sales leads. And when you finally enter into that strategic partnership with a major corporation, you'll certainly want to advertise that prominently, even though it might not bring you any direct customers or calls.

QUANTITATIVE VS. QUALITATIVE GOALS

QUANTITATIVE	QUALITATIVE
Get 6,000 registered users for your new social networking site in the first 30 days after launch	Generate buzz on the Web about your new social networking site for young professionals
Generate traffic to your booth at the gift trade show resulting in $45,000 in at-show sales of your line of new luxury dog beds	Increase exposure for your new line of dog beds within the gift industry
Attract 10 new inquiries and sign one new corporate client monthly for your product design firm	Inform potential corporate customers of winning an award for your product design work
Get your new organic furniture line featured in 3 major magazines in the next 6 months	Build awareness of your organic furniture with environmentally conscious consumers

As the next step in your marketing plan, list your major goals—both quantitative and qualitative. You will come back to these later to remind yourself of your objectives as you choose your marketing vehicles and message and to evaluate how well your marketing campaign accomplished what you wanted to achieve.

BRAINSTORMING

YOUR MARKETING GOALS

Use this worksheet to list your major marketing goals. Remember to include timeframes and specific numbers for your quantitative goals. Be sure to list at least 3 goals in each section.

Quantitative Marketing Goals _____

Specific Goal_____

Number Associated with It_____

Timeframe _____

Goal #1 _____

Goal #2 _____

Goal #3 _____

Goal #4 _____

Qualitative Marketing Goals _____

Goal _____

Detail Specifics _____

Goal #1 _____

Goal #2 _____

Goal #3 _____

Goal #4 _____

How Much to Spend on Marketing

It's great to have marketing goals, but do you have the money to achieve those goals? As you set out to make your plan, you'll need to know: What's your marketing budget? Most companies have a general sense that they're going to have to spend money on marketing, but few companies, especially new, entrepreneurial companies, have any idea of how much money they have to set aside for their marketing efforts. Unfortunately, there just aren't any hard and fast rules about how much a company should spend on marketing.

Percentage of Sales Budget

One method some companies use to come up with a marketing allocation is to set aside a certain percentage of a company's total sales. According to this method, a company devotes a percentage of their overall sales for all marketing activities (advertising, public relations, brochures, and the like). In other words, if your solar panel manufacturing company had $2 million in sales last year and you set aside 5% for marketing this year, your total marketing budget for the year would be $100,000.

Budgeting this way is tempting—after all, it's easy. But it's arbitrary. You may be spending way too much or way too little. For instance, there are huge companies that spend only a tiny percentage of sales on marketing. Costco, the giant discount warehouse company, does virtually no advertising; it's not necessary for their success. At the other extreme, the online contact management company Salesforce.com spent $25.4 million on marketing during their first year in business, with only $5.4 million in sales. In other words, they spent 470% of their revenues!

In practice, however, the bulk of established companies spend a range of 1% to 15% of total company sales on marketing. That's a wide range: for a $2 million company, that figure could be anywhere from $20,000 to $300,000.

What factors help you determine how much to spend on marketing?

■ **Low profit margins.** Companies that, by the nature of their product or service, make very little profit per sale (low gross profit margins) can't afford to spend a high percentage of sales on marketing; they just don't have the financial ability. Examples of such companies include grocery stores, discount stores, producers of commodity products (such as raw materials and non-branded, highly discounted computer hardware). These are typically high-volume businesses. So while their marketing budget as a whole may be huge (imagine the budget for Safeway or Kroger), it still represents a very small percentage of the total amount of their sales.

■ **High profit margins.** On the other hand, companies with high profit margins have the luxury of dedicating a greater percentage of their overall expenditures to marketing. If you don't have to spend a lot on manufacturing, inventory, or high rent—if you're a software, Web-based, or service company, for instance—you can afford to spend more on marketing. Other examples include purveyors of luxury goods and automobiles.

When to Increase Your Marketing Budget

- During a new product/service/ website launch or introduction
- For a new company launch
- For extremely innovative technology or new approach
- When opening a new location
- When advertising a "sale" or specific event
- In response to a new competitive threat
- When introducing significant new features
- When introducing major price reductions
- If making a material change in company, products, services, or ownership

- **Large or hard-to-reach market.** Certain markets cost more to reach, so you're going to need a bigger marketing budget for these. If the market is very large (such as all new parents in the U.S.), your media costs are going to be high. If your market is diffuse, with many different characteristics (let's say all young adults between the ages of 22 and 35), you'll have to try to reach them in many different ways, which is costly. If you're targeting other businesses (B2B) and they're not well aggregated (for instance, not in a specific industry with a trade show or in a specific geographic location), then plan on spending more on marketing to identify and reach these customers.

- **New business.** It costs a lot of money to launch a new company, new product, or new service—more than you'll have to spend year after year once your company is up and running. And, of course, your revenues are smaller in the first years, so plan that a much bigger percentage of your overall income will go to marketing in the early years of a company or product or service.

- **Aggressive competition.** Let's face it, if your competition is spending a lot of money on marketing, there's a good chance you're going to have to spend a lot as well.

Goal-based Marketing Budget

With this type of budget, you do a complete marketing plan, determining your goals and laying out a thoughtful course of action. If your goal is to secure 1,000 new customers, what will it take to get them? How much advertising do you need to do? Which trade shows do you need to exhibit at? Will you advertise on search engines and how often?

As you can see, this type of budgeting makes the most sense. It's derived from figuring out what you want to achieve, what marketing vehicles you're going to use and how often, and how much that's all going to cost. Of course, you may have to trim back your marketing budget to meet the realities of your company's financial situation and overall expenditures, but this kind of budgeting is at least based on what it really takes to accomplish your marketing goals.

Measuring Progress

Once you've established your goals, the challenge is to stay on track and make sure your strategies are working to bring you closer to them. That means finding ways to measure your progress.

Metrics

One way that most corporations gauge the impact of their marketing efforts is through *"metrics"*—measurements evaluating the success of quantitative marketing goals and individual tactics. For instance, if your goal was to reach 1,000 new customers and only 800 responded, you've achieved only an 80% effectiveness rate. Metrics help you know whether the marketing activities you're undertaking are actually working and help you make sure you're not wasting money on ineffective strategies and tactics.

Milestones

Another key method for assessing progress is to establish milestones: a list of key events or accomplishments you hope to achieve and *the dates* by which you hope to reach those. By setting milestones as part of your marketing plan, you both clarify your specific marketing goals and give yourself a timeframe within which to achieve specific objectives. It's advisable to attach numbers to your milestones (get positive reviews in 5 technology-related magazines in 90 days), but even with more qualitative goals, you can set milestones to give yourself a sense of how well you are doing (for example, generate positive community feelings about our commitment to the environment in the next 6 months).

BRAINSTORMING

YOUR MARKETING MILESTONES

Use the worksheet below to list your major milestones. Review your goals from the previous goal-setting worksheets, select your major objectives, and assign target dates to each. These milestones will become part of your final marketing plan.

MILESTONE	TARGET DATE

The goals and milestones you've listed in this chapter will be incorporated into your final marketing plan. Those will be the touchstones to measure the effectiveness of your marketing campaign and all marketing activities.

Your Marketing Campaign

Throughout this section, you've learned what it takes to make your marketing efforts successful. You've identified your competitive advantage and your target market, crafted your message and identity, figured out ways to retain customers, and set specific marketing goals.

Now it's time to move on to the action part of your marketing plan, choosing and shaping the marketing vehicles and tactics that you're going to implement to achieve your goals and get customers and sales!

This final worksheet enables you to sum up all the decisions you've made while working through this first section. This will become the first portion of your complete marketing plan.

BUILDING YOUR MARKETING PLAN

MARKETING GOALS

Describe what you hope to achieve as a result of your marketing campaign:

_____

What are your top three specific marketing goals and what is your timeframe for achieving them?

1. _____

2. _____

3. _____

List your three most important milestones and the dates by which you plan to achieve them:

1. _____

2. _____

3. _____

BUILDING YOUR MARKETING PLAN

MARKETING ESSENTIALS

Use this worksheet to pull together the research and information you've gathered throughout Section I and begin your marketing plan.

Your company, product, or service name: _____

Your company tagline: _____

Describe the top 3 most important needs that motivate customers to buy your product or service:

1. _____

2. _____

3. _____

2. List the 3 most important reasons customers will choose you over your competitors:

1. _____

2. _____

3. _____

Describe the demographic, geographic, and psychographic characteristics of your target market:

_____

Indicate the size of your target market and describe any trends affecting your market size (is it shrinking or growing, for example?):

_____

Describe any factors or trends affecting customer purchasing decisions:

_____

BUILDING YOUR MARKETING PLAN

MARKETING ESSENTIALS (continued)

Describe how the characteristics of your target market will affect your marketing message and vehicles:

_____

List your major competitors, along with their strengths and weaknesses:

_____

Describe your own competitive advantage:

_____

Describe the marketing activities and approaches of your competitors:

_____

Explain how you will respond to your competitors' marketing efforts and highlight your own competitive advantage:

_____

Describe efforts you will undertake to attract first-time customers:

_____

Describe efforts you will undertake to retain current customers:

_____

Describe your brand's promise to your customers and the values your brand represents:

_____

State the core message or unique selling proposition your marketing efforts will deliver to current and potential customers:

_____

List ways you use your brand identity elements as part of your marketing activities (in packaging, on your website, in advertising, and so on):

_____

Describe how you will ensure that your marketing efforts are ethical:

_____

Describe how you will incorporate social responsibility into your business practices and, specifically, into your marketing practices and procedures:

_____

Indicate in which ways, if any, you intend to highlight your company's social responsibility in your marketing materials and activities:

_____

What goals do you hope to achieve through your marketing?

_____

How will you evaluate the success of your marketing efforts? What metrics and milestones will you use?

_____

SECTION II

Traditional Advertising

Lingo

CALL TO ACTION: The part of an ad that indicates how you would like the reader, viewer, or listener to respond—what you'd like them to do. "Call now," "Visit our new showroom," and "Try it today" are all calls to action.

COST PER THOUSAND (CPM): The term used to describe the cost of an ad—how much it costs to reach a thousand readers, listeners, viewers, or website visitors. ("M" is the Roman numeral for "thousand.") Using "CPM" enables you to easily compare prices across different media options.

FREQUENCY: The number of times you place an ad in a given time period; how often you run an ad.

HOOK: Something that catches the attention or interest of a reader, listener, viewer, or website visitor. An angle that entices prospective customers to pay attention to your ad or story.

MEDIA KIT: A collection of materials provided by a media outlet/venue that gives detailed information about their advertising options, including types of ads, rates, special advertising sections/opportunities, the number and demographics of their audience (readers, listeners, viewers, or website visitors). The term is also used to describe the collection of background materials a business provides to the media about the company, new products/services, or developments for public relations purposes.

MEDIA OUTLET: A term used to describe a particular newspaper, magazine, radio/TV station, website, or other member of the press/media. The *New York Times* and the Oprah Winfrey TV show are both media outlets, as are MySpace and Facebook.

MEDIA VENUE: Another term used to describe a media outlet.

RATE CARD: A card or sheet from a media outlet listing rates for ads at various sizes, placements, frequencies, and other options.

REACH: How many readers, listeners, or viewers are served by a media outlet (used mostly for radio and TV).

ROI (RETURN ON INVESTMENT): A measure of the benefits received judged against the commitment of resources made. ROI is typically measured in financial terms; in other words, how much money you made versus how much money you spent. But it can also take into consideration other benefits received; for instance, ROI on an advertising campaign may also bring benefits such as brand awareness, goodwill, and partnership opportunities.

CHAPTER 9

Advertising in Traditional Media

Even though it's only one aspect of the field, when you think of marketing, you probably first think of advertising. And when you first think of advertising, most people first think of "traditional" advertising. In other words, advertising using media such as newspapers, magazines, television, and radio.

Traditional advertising allows you to spread the word about your company, product, or service in a tried-and-true fashion. All you need to do is buy advertisements in an appropriate media outlet for a specified length of time or time slot, matching the media, frequency, and size of your ad to your product, your market, and your needs. So if you've invented a revolutionary new high-tech racing bicycle, you might decide to buy a quarter-page ad in every issue of *Bicycling* magazine for the next 12 months, because *Bicycling's* readers are cycling enthusiasts, likely to be interested in your product.

Traditional advertising gives you access to the eyes and ears of your potential customers. When traditional advertising works well—as it often does—your *return on investment* (ROI) includes direct financial benefits, such as an increase in sales, and indirect benefits, such as greater awareness among your target market and a strengthened brand identity (which translates into sales in the long run).

Advertising in traditional media can be expensive: a 30-second ad during the Superbowl can cost millions of dollars. Or it can be relatively inexpensive: an ad in a small neighborhood newspaper may cost only a few hundred dollars. But time has proven that traditional media advertising works; that's why newspapers, magazines, and radio and TV shows are all still filled with ads. For most businesses, a carefully thought-out plan to use traditional media advertising can make prospects aware of your company, product, or service and encourage them to buy. Traditional media advertising is a proven way to improve your company's revenues.

Advertising Agencies

When you're developing an advertising campaign in traditional media venues, you don't have to go it all alone. If your budget allows, you can turn to an advertising agency. Ad agencies exist to help companies plan their entire advertising presence—what ads should say, where they should appear, and how frequently they should run. Since ad agencies have been developing advertising campaigns in traditional media for many decades, they generally know which media outlets are best for which types of products and services. They may also be able to negotiate better rates or placement with some media outlets because they bring those media venues a lot of business. Of course, you'll pay for this service—often a lot. Ad agencies typically get a commission on all ads they place, as well as fees for their creative and consulting services. If you're going to be spending a lot of money on traditional advertising, you'll almost certainly want the help and guidance of an ad agency.

How to Place an Ad

Placing ads in traditional media is one of the most common ways to reach potential customers. Doing so involves these basic steps:

1. Determine what you want to say about your product or service (your message).

2. Clarify what you want people to do (your call to action).

3. Identify which media outlets your target customers are likely to read, listen to, or watch.

4. Contact publications and broadcasters to get media kits.

5. Evaluate their advertising rates and options.

6. Evaluate their reach (what types of people read/watch/listen to the media outlet).

7. Determine which media venues are the best fit for your target market and your budget.

8. Determine how frequently you can afford to advertise and what size (or time) of ads you can afford (remember, repetition is important).

9. Find out about the specifications, deadlines, and other details for submitting your advertising materials.

10. Create an appealing advertisement based on your message, your call to action, and the audience for the specific media outlet. (You'll learn more about this in the rest of this section.)

11. Buy advertising space or time in one or more media venues.

Gauge the impact of the advertising on your business and bottom line (such as an increase in sales or customers) so you can assess your ROI (return on investment).

Going Traditional: Print, Radio, and TV

Traditional advertising—that is, advertising that appears in the places you've been seeing and hearing ads for most of your life (newspapers, magazines, radio, and TV)—is effective at reaching both a large, mainstream audience and a very targeted selection of prospects. It can put your company, product, or service in front of a large group of consumers while they're reading the city's newspaper, listening to a talk show on a major radio station, or watching their favorite programs on TV. But traditional advertising can also bring your message to a select group as they read a magazine about their hobby, read a trade journal about their industry, or watch a cable TV show about their special interest.

Once you've decided to advertise in traditional media, one of the first questions you're going to face is "Where should I place my ad?" You've got the option for broadcasting: advertising to a large and diverse group of consumers. Or you can narrowcast: focusing in on a specific market niche. But isn't it always better to reach as large an audience as possible? Remember, you pay for ads based on how many people the ads reach, so you don't want to spend money reaching lots of people who are unlikely or unable to ever become your customers. You want to find the most affordable way to reach the people who have the potential to become your customers.

So to advertise effectively, you need to find out which media attract the attention of your target market—which newspapers they read, magazines they subscribe to, radio stations and programs they listen to, and channels their TVs are tuned in to. Then you'll want to find those advertising options that enable you to reach your target prospects without having to spend a lot of money communicating to nonprospects. You'll want to advertise there as frequently as your marketing budget will allow.

One way to discover what media outlets your target customers interact with is to ask them. When you do a survey of your current customers (or a survey of the type of prospects you're seeking for a new business), be sure to ask them about which media outlets they read, listen to, and watch.

Media Kits

How do you know exactly what type of audience a media outlet is reaching? The best way to evaluate your advertising options is to ask for media kits from the various publications, radio stations, and TV channels you think your target market is interested in. You can often find an outlet's media kit online: look for a link on their website with a name like "To Advertise."

Media kits are materials produced by publishers and broadcasters that not only list the specifics of their advertising options (such as costs and sizes on a rate card), but also describe the demographics of their audience—common characteristics such as income, age, gender, and educational level.

Sometimes the demographic data available from a media outlet can be quite specific, including detailed information such as percentage of audience by zip code, job title, ethnicity, or particular interests. This gives you a much clearer picture of who, exactly, is watching, listening to, or reading a particular publication. Your ads will be most effective when you make the right match between what you are promoting and who you're promoting it to. Media kits can assist you in making this match.

What to Say

One thing's for sure, traditional advertising is going to cost you money. So it's important to thoroughly think through what you want your traditional advertising campaign to accomplish, what you want your message to be, and what you want potential customers to say or do in response to your message.

Before you take out your first ad, refer back to the marketing goals and message you created in the first section of this book, Marketing Essentials. Are you trying to build a brand or do you want to drive immediate sales? Are you promoting a short-term offer or trying to develop a long-term customer base?

Keep your goals in mind as you craft your advertising message. You may be able to come up with a very creative, attention-getting ad that will help people remember your company name, but if your goal is to drive immediate sales, you might be better off with a simple message like "50% off everything in stock!"

Remember, also, the constraints of advertising in traditional media. One of the most important is that you have limited time or space to make your pitch. With any kind of traditional ad, you've got to be able to get your message across quickly and succinctly. The key elements of a traditional ad, whether in print, on radio, or on TV, are the key elements of all marketing materials:

- **Company name and identity.** These must be repeated often, to help people remember them. Make sure other aspects of your identity are included (logo, typestyle in print, music or vocals in radio or TV, and your tagline on all).

- **Hook, or attention grabber.** There are a lot of ads out there. How will you get people's attention?

- **Message.** What do you want people to remember about your company, product, or service? Emphasize benefits (what they get) rather than the features (what you do).

- **Call to action.** What do you want people to do? The most effective ads, especially for entrepreneurial companies, include a very specific, do-able, call to action, such as "Call now!", "Visit our website," or "Come to our store this Saturday."

- **Contact info.** Interested prospects need to know how to reach you.

Advertising a Service

Traditional media depends on pictures (for TV and print) and sound (for TV and radio). So advertising a service presents challenges, as services don't usually have a physical product to show. However, there are still many ways to advertise a service successfully.

Some tricks:

- Consider using radio, where there's no need to show anything and you can just describe your service.

- If you're using photos or video (in print or on TV), use pictures showing how the service is performed or delivered or photos of satisfied customers (for instance, if you have a carpet cleaning service, you can show photos of your company's trucks coming to a home or, better yet, of happy customers lying on the carpet with an infant, implying that the carpet is now squeaky clean).

- For companies where you will provide the service personally and clients need a high comfort level with you (for instance, if you are a doctor, personal trainer, or financial planner), consider putting your own picture in a print ad or featuring yourself in a TV commercial.

- Ads for services work particularly well in a problem-solution format. In other words, pose a problem in your headline, then show/explain how your service solves it. An ad for a chiropractic office might read: *Is Back Pain Sending You in the Wrong Direction?* [problem] *Jones Chiropractic Will Set You Straight!* [solution]

Myth🚫Buster

Once Is Enough

MYTH: If the offer is compelling enough, one ad will bring you customers.

BUSTED: Running just a single ad, even for a huge sale or an incredible offer, may bring you some success. But you'll still miss a huge percentage of your target market. Many prospects won't see an ad on any given day, and even those who do are likely to forget it, because they've seen it only once. It's usually far better to run many a small ad repeatedly than just one big ad.

When to Advertise

Obviously, advertising on an ongoing basis is the best way to keep your company and products in front of existing and potential customers. But let's be real: most companies can't afford to advertise all the time. So it's important to know when advertising is particularly critical. At which points in the development and growth of your business will advertising have the greatest impact?

Critical times to advertise include:

- The startup of your business
- When you launch a new product or service
- When you open a new location or change location
- When you're having a sale or offering substantial discounts
- When you upgrade or substantially improve an existing product or service
- When you want to announce a special event (such as a grand opening)
- When new competition has entered your market

Advertising Goals: Branding vs. Sales

Traditional advertising serves two primary purposes: it builds awareness of your company and it drives sales of your products or services. While a sound advertising campaign aims to achieve both, big-name companies often run ads focusing purely on brand identity. Meanwhile, smaller companies tend to run ads focusing on sales, with the goal of bringing in revenue quickly.

Think of TV commercials about cars. The ads you see from local car dealers on your cable station almost always promote a big sale, announce price breaks, and try to create a sense of urgency to draw customers to their lots for a test drive. Now consider commercials from auto manufacturers. They're more likely to lovingly linger on the contours or luxury interior of the car, show it deftly handling curvy mountain roads, and feature a memorable song or jingle. The purpose of this type of ad is to create and reinforce a brand image.

Until you reach megabudget levels and your potential customers are well aware of your brand identity and what your company offers, you'll want to stick to sales-oriented ads designed to draw people, revenue, and profits to your business.

Repetition, Repetition, Repetition

Advertising experts agree: you've got to advertise frequently—using the same message in the same media outlet—for your ad to be a success. People need to see or hear an ad many times before they remember it. While research varies on how many exposures a person has to receive before acting on an ad, all the studies are clear: hearing or seeing something just once doesn't make an impression. Various studies indicate that an ad needs to be seen or heard at least three to nine times before someone will recall it. That's just recall—it takes even longer before someone acts on an ad.

Think of it this way: say you're at a party where you meet dozens of new people. Even after you've been introduced to all of them, how many names will you remember? Who'll stand out? Chances are, unless a particular person is absolutely fascinating or drop-dead gorgeous, you probably won't remember them. On the other hand, think about the people you see over and over—at your office, at school, or around the neighborhood. You'll soon remember not only their names, but also their faces and personalities and a lot more about them. Repetition leads to remembering.

Advertising works in a similar fashion. Media venues are like big parties, and the ads are the guests. If you see or hear an ad only once, you're probably not going to remember much about it—what it said (its message), who said it (what company placed it), or what it was trying to sell. But if you see an ad every day or hear it every 10 minutes during your favorite program, you're much more likely to absorb the message (even if you don't like, agree with, or care about it).

Monitoring Effectiveness

You're going to be spending a lot of money when you advertise in traditional media, so you'd like to get your money's worth. How will you know when it's working? Unlike some other forms of marketing and advertising (such as direct mail or search engine keyword ads), traditional advertising doesn't provide an easy method by which to measure results.

Obviously, you'll judge whether your advertising is working by looking for an increase in sales, customers, and inquiries. Have revenues gone up since you began placing the ads? Are the specific products you're advertising moving off the shelves? Did a good number of people show up at your grand opening? But if you're advertising frequently, or in a number of different media outlets, how do you know which ad led to these results or whether it was the ads at all?

The truth is that monitoring the effectiveness of advertising in traditional media is more an art than an exact science. It's definitely a challenge, especially if you're advertising at the same time as you're stepping up the rest of your marketing (which is usually the case) and if the growth in your business and sales is gradual (which is also typical).

It's possible to do some tracking of specific ads. In a print ad, one way is to use clip-out coupons. Place a code specific to each publication on each coupon, and when customers bring them into the store, you'll know exactly where they found the ad. (Of course, many others may have also seen the ad but did not bring in the coupon.) You can use a similar system with radio and TV ads by asking customers to mention a particular word or phrase to get a discount on a product or service ("Call today and use coupon code TV332 to receive a special gift"), but these TV and radio codes typically have an even lower response rate, since people are less likely to remember a word than to clip out a coupon.

Another way to figure out which ads and media are most effective is to run an informal test campaign. One month, try an ad in one media outlet; the next month, try a different outlet. If you're pretty sure a particular media outlet reaches your target market, try different placement (in the print publication) or different times of day (for TV/radio) and different sizes or lengths of ads to see which is most effective, observing how these changes affect your sales and prospect inquiries.

Advertising agencies have developed complex methods of monitoring the effectiveness of ads as part of their business. They could be spending millions of dollars on their campaigns, so having sophisticated effectiveness-monitoring systems is essential.

At the very least, you'll want to start tracking your sales figures during the months (and times) you advertise versus the months (and times) you don't advertise in order to try to ascertain whether the dollars you're spending on traditional advertising are bringing you financial success.

How to Get Noticed

Whether you're advertising in print, on radio, or on TV, observing a few key principles will help your ad stand out:

1. Always include a compelling "hook," or device that grabs a reader's attention and makes them want to bother to read your ad. The most effective hook, for example, is the word "FREE"—that always gets someone to look. But anything that connects with prospects from your target market can be effective. For example, for an online dating service, the hook might be "What are you doing Saturday night?"

2. Try to tell a story in as little space or short a time as possible. A radio ad might feature a voice saying, "I spent years looking for love in all the wrong places, even the wrong Internet dating sites. That changed after I logged onto MeetYourMatch. com. It's really different." Listeners will want to find out why this service is different from all the others.

3. Include an irresistible offer ("First three months for free!" "50 percent off your first purchase") that will drive your potential customer to call you or visit your store.

4. Include a strong call to action, indicating how you would like your potential customers to respond to your ad ("Call 1-800-555-1234 now to hear more!"), and provide contact information for your business.

Lingo

ABOVE THE FOLD: The space on the top part of a page within a print publication (particularly in a newspaper that's been folded in half). Placement "above the fold" offers the most visibility for your ad.

ADVERTORIAL: A paid advertisement that contains informational content and is designed to look like regular content rather than an ad.

CIRCULATION: The number of subscribers, newsstand buyers, and others who purchase or receive a publication. The Audit Bureau of Circulations (www.accessabc.com) verifies figures for larger publications. Smaller, local publications will supply their own figures and may or may not be reliable.

CLASSIFIED: A small, print-based ad found in the back of a newspaper or magazine.

COLUMN INCH: The width and depth of a column of newspaper print, used to measure the size of an ad.

CONTROLLED CIRCULATION: Publications delivered free, only to a highly targeted list of readers (dentists, spa owners, human resources professionals), decided upon by the publication's management, rather than to individuals who choose to subscribe.

DISPLAY AD: An ad placed in the regular section of a newspaper or magazine (as opposed to a classified), often featuring artwork or a photo in addition to text.

FOUR-COLOR: Any print piece that appears in full color. The full-color image is created in print using only four colors—cyan (blue), magenta (red), yellow, and black, referred to as CMYK—which combine to create every other color.

PREFERRED PLACEMENT: A guarantee that your ad will appear in a particular spot in a publication. You'll always pay extra for preferred placement.

REMNANT SPACE: Unsold space in a publication (or other media), which may be available at substantially discounted rates at the last minute.

RUN OF PAPER (ROP)/RUN OF BOOK (ROB) ADS: An ad that can appear anywhere in a newspaper or magazine, depending on what space is left unsold. ROP ads are usually available at discount rates.

SPOT COLOR: The addition of one or more colors to a black-and-white ad, to enhance its visibility and aesthetic appeal.

STOCK PHOTO: Existing photos, purchased from stock photography suppliers, that you can use in commercial applications (such as your ads or brochures) on a royalty-free basis (in other words, you pay only once and do not have to pay for each use). Using stock photos saves you the time and expense of hiring your own photographer.

CHAPTER 10

Advertising in Print

You've been thinking about joining a gym. You open the morning paper to the Health and Fitness section, and there it is: a large, attractive ad announcing a "no initiation fee" deal at a gym that you didn't know about. You've already checked out the gym in your neighborhood but haven't made a decision to join yet, because the initiation fee was so steep. Two days later, you're working out in the new gym, having saved the $250 initiation fee.

That's the power of a good print ad. Of course, the advertisers probably had no idea *you* were in the market for a gym membership that day. They placed the ad in the Health and Fitness section every week just to be sure they'd be in the right place whenever aspiring athletes were ready to sign up.

How Print Publications Work

Even in the era of the Internet and mobile device, plenty of people still like to read, or at least flip through, print publications.

Publications are generally divided into three categories:

- Consumer (newspapers, news magazines, general interest magazines)

- Special interest (publications that deal with specific topics, such as food, fishing, or fitness)

- Trade (publications covering industry-specific topics and reaching members of a particular industry or profession, such as journals for doctors, lawyers, engineers, or other professionals).

Most people think that print publications make their money from subscriptions or newsstand purchases. The reality is that virtually all publications make most of their money from advertising. In fact, some publications are distributed free to their readers (these are called controlled circulation publications) and are completely supported by advertising, because advertisers want to reach a desirable group of readers.

ABC for the Numbers

Your ad rep promises your print ad will reach a hundred thousand potential customers. Are those numbers are accurate? To find out, first ask if the publication is a member of the Audit Bureau of Circulations (ABC). You can also find member lists on ABC's site: www.accessabc.com.

Most major publications and many regional ones will join ABC and have their numbers audited as a way of justifying their ad rates and remaining competitive. Individuals can join as associate members for a few hundred dollars, to gain access to detailed circulation and readership data. However, you can easily find general audited circulation data on the site for **free!** Here's how:

1. Go to the ABC's website (www.accessabc.com) and click the "Free Reports" button in the right-hand column.

2. Under the Circulation header, click the eCirc link, which will lead to a page where you can choose your type of media (newspapers, periodicals, and so on).

3. Use the links to select the category of the publication in question. Each link leads to a form page with search fields and pull-down menus, enabling you to easily look up the numbers for your publication.

Tip: If your chosen publication does not appear in your title search, be sure to experiment with the other search methods provided (such as geographical area and alphabetical).

Print publications base their advertising rates on their circulation numbers, which include the number of annual subscribers, as well as the number of people who buy copies from the newsstand for paid publications and, in certain cases, the number of people who receive the publication through controlled circulation. Generally, the higher the number of readers, the higher the cost of an ad.

However, ad rates are typically quoted in "CPM," or cost per thousand (M is the Roman numeral for thousand). This enables you to compare costs on an equal basis from one publication to another. *People* magazine, for example, has millions of subscribers and charges hundreds of thousands of dollars for prime advertising space. But the CPM for an ad in *People* may actually be lower than the cost to reach a thousand targeted and coveted readers in a smaller publication. For example, placing an ad in *WatchTime* magazine, which reaches upscale watch buyers, may be worth a lot more to those who sell expensive watches.

Most larger publications are structured to operate on a combination of advertising and circulation revenue. Some trade publications, and many free community publications, get their revenues completely from advertising. For instance, the magazine *CIO* (Chief Information Officer) is distributed free to corporate executives who make technology buying decisions for their companies; companies that sell hardware, software, and technology services pay to advertise in CIO so they can reach this desirable audience.

Buying advertising and getting editorial coverage (in other words, being written about in the publication) are two separate issues. Some advertisers, especially those who are new to placing ads in print publications, assume that taking out an ad entitles them to coverage in a publication. In a very few cases of specialty publications (for example, some free home design magazines), that may be true. But overwhelmingly, editors draw a strict line between editorial coverage and advertising. Otherwise, readers would lose interest in their publication.

Many publications, however, allow advertorial ads. These are ads that are written by the advertiser to promote their goods or services but contain useful informational content and are designed to look like the regular content of the newspaper or magazine. Somewhere around the edge of the ad, in fine print, you'll be able to see the words "Paid Advertisement," but you'll have to look closely to find it.

Benefits of Print

When comparing traditional advertising options, advertising in print has many advantages over advertising on radio or TV. In general, it's one of the least expensive ways to deliver your message while showing an image of your product (or service or service professional). This isn't possible on radio, and it's usually much more costly on TV. Other benefits of print advertising include:

- **Shelf life.** A radio or TV ad lasts for a minute or less and then is gone. A print publication, on the other hand, can stay around for days, weeks, even months, offering more opportunities for a customer to see its ads. A customer might respond to a print ad long after it has been published.

More info. With radio and TV, you pay for every second of time, and listeners or viewers can absorb only a very limited amount of information. Your message must be brief. With a print ad, you can offer more details and specifications.

Pass-along readership. People share print publications with others, who may also be your target customers. These "pass-along readers" expand an ad's reach and increase your exposure. Some magazines claim excessive pass-along readership. It's best to check their numbers with an industry association that's responsible for monitoring circulation claims, such as the ABC (Audit Bureau of Circulations).

Measurability. It's often easier to measure the impact of a print ad, especially if it includes a coupon with a code. When customers bring in the coupon, you know exactly where they learned about you.

More specific audience. In general, it's easier to target your customer by using print publications. This is particularly true if you advertise in magazines geared to readers with special interests (like fashion, yoga, or home improvement) or in publications with controlled circulation. Although many radio and TV programs are targeted to certain groups, these shows can often be expensive on a CPM basis, and they may reach a wider geographic audience than you are targeting.

Challenges of Print

While print offers many advantages, it can also present some challenges. One is that print ads provide a limited amount of space to present your message. This means it needs to be expressed in as few words as possible. You're also competing for a reader's attention: unless you buy a full-page, your print ad will appear with many others on the same page. If an ad is very small and tucked into a lower corner of a page, it probably won't be seen by as many people as you'd like. Radio and TV ads, on the other hand, don't compete with others during the specific time they're presenting the message. They have the stage, unless someone tunes in to another channel or leaves the room to get a snack. Other challenges of print include:

Potential customers often need to pay to see your ad. Most publications require readers to pay to read them, either by subscribing or by purchasing from a newsstand. On the other hand, your target customers don't have to shell out every time they flip the switch on the radio or TV.

Customers need to actively access your ad. Readers have to go through pages of a publication to find your ad, and they might miss it. In fact, they might never open the publication at all. A TV or radio ad, on the other hand, is much harder to miss. Unless they turn the TV or radio off, use a DVR to bypass the ad, or leave the room (or the car), potential customers are likely to hear or see it.

Print publications, particularly newspapers, have lost readership to the Internet. Many people now get their news and information online rather than in print. Although print publications are still surviving—and most will offer excellent opportunities for advertisers for years to come—

> ### Bucking the Trend: Free, Local Newspapers
>
> There's one type of newspaper that's growing in popularity even while mainstream city-wide papers have lost audience to the Internet: free, local papers that are distributed in highly trafficked spots in urban areas (such as subway or train stations, coffee houses, and bus stops). These papers have a captive audience (such as subway riders) who have time on their hands to flip through a paper. Examples include the *Express* in Washington, DC, and the *Palo Alto Daily News* in Palo Alto, CA. These publications can be an attractive option for small and local businesses.

Newsletters

Although newspapers and magazines are the print media we think of most often, print newsletters also offer excellent opportunities to reach an extremely targeted audience—often at a very low price. Newsletters are small print publications that provide news and information to a defined niche of people who share a common location, profession, or interest. A newsletter's readership is generally smaller than that of most newspapers and magazines, but because newsletters are distributed to such a specific audience, you can be sure that your advertisements will reach the eyes of those most interested in what you have to offer. For instance, if you sell industrial fruit-washing machines, a newsletter for Washington state apple growers may be a group you want to reach. Types of newsletters include:

- **Trade group/Association newsletters.** Circulated to professionals in a particular field, these newsletters allow you to place your ad before a tightly targeted group, which is particularly helpful if your goal is to serve a specific market.

- **Civic/Charity/Religious.** These newsletters are circulated to members of particular local civic or philanthropic groups, schools, churches, charities, or the like. Ads in these publications are often very affordable.

- **Professional/networking newsletters (local, regional, or national).** These are circulated to businesspeople, often in a range of industries, who are members of a particular professional organization. They're useful for reaching a broad cross-section of business professionals.

- **Community.** Some neighborhoods have their own print newsletters. Advertise in them if you are a local business wanting to reach nearby customers.

you may want to consider whether your audience is more likely to be online. This is especially true if you're targeting younger customers who may not relate to print publications much at all.

Print Ad Formats

With the wide range of ad sizes and formats offered by print publications, you're likely to find something that fits your budget and needs—particularly if you're advertising in a local or regional publication. Bigger ads almost always cost more, but bigger isn't always better. A well-placed smaller ad or even a classified ad, run frequently, can sometimes capture the interest of your target market better than a large ad placed less frequently. Placement also has a major impact. For instance, if you sell kitchen cabinets, a small weekly ad in the Home and Garden section of your newspaper is probably more effective than a large quarterly ad in the general news section.

The ad options available, and their associated costs, are outlined in a publication's rate card. This usually takes the form of a chart showing the basic ad rates by ad size, frequency (shown as 2X—two times—3X, 4X, and so on), and time advertising (such as days of the week for a newspaper or special issues for a magazine) and indicating different levels of color (generally, a price for black and white, per spot color, or four-color). Some typical ways to advertise in print formats:

- **Display Ads.** These ads usually feature both text and images. They sometimes include color. Their sizes can run the gamut from a small box to a full-page presentation. Use display ads when your target market isn't necessarily looking for your specific product or service and you need more emphasis to attract their attention.

- **Classifieds.** These are small, text-based ads, typically in the back of a publication. They often work well in local publications for smaller, service-oriented businesses (like home and office cleaners, independent computer repair people, and roofers). Classifieds are effective when your audience is already seeking what you have to offer and will sort through the listings to find it.

- **Circulars.** These are pages printed on newsprint paper, generally folded and inserted into newspapers (especially on weekends). Grocery, electronics, and office supply retailers, as well as department stores and retailers holding sales, typically use circulars as advertising vehicles. Consumers read them to see what bargains are available and to compare prices.

- **Business reply cards (BRCs).** Business reply cards are postcard-sized cards, usually found between the pages of magazines, that can be filled in and returned (postage paid) to an advertiser. The reader who returns the card may receive a special gift or offer, while the advertiser receives another address for their mailing list. Blow-in cards are slipped between pages, while bound-in or stitched-in cards are bound into the magazine and have a perforation that allows the reader to rip them out and send them in.

■ **Polybagging.** Newspapers and magazines shrink wrap, or put plastic bags around, their publications, and include free samples and other advertisements within the bags. This option, which is expensive, is particularly useful for businesses that want to get product samples out to their target markets.

Print Ad Pricing

Want to lower the cost of any individual ad? Advertise frequently. In general, the more often you advertise, the lower the cost per ad. Moreover, as a regular advertiser, you'll often be offered special promotional and advertising opportunities not generally available.

Prices for print publication ads range widely—from under $50 (for a simple ad in a small local newspaper or community newsletter) to well over $50,000 (for a full-page, full-color ad in a national magazine). Don't be put off by the numbers on a rate card. Publications will typically negotiate rates with advertisers, especially frequent advertisers. Look to see if the rate card indicates that the publication pays commissions to ad agencies or is listed as commissionable. If so, you may easily be able to negotiate a discount of at least the commission percentage (for instance, a 15% commission offered to an ad agency) if you place the ad yourself.

There are also many ways to get special pricing deals. A publication might offer special rates during a certain holiday season. Or you may get a deal on adding color to your ad if you place your ad in a particular section. Print publications offer many opportunities like these. Be sure to ask what special promotions are available.

Ad pricing is based primarily on frequency (the more ads you run, the lower the cost per ad), but other factors will also affect the cost of your ad, including:

■ **One-time ad.** This is the most expensive option, regardless of the size of the ad. If you place an ad only once, you'll pay more.

■ **Multiple-insertion ads.** The cost, on a per ad basis, is reduced when you agree, up front, to take space in a publication multiple times. This is true even if you change the wording or images, although a publication may charge you a small handling fee for making changes.

■ **Preferred placement.** Some parts of publications are more likely to be seen or read than others—for instance, the inside front cover, the back cover (inside or out), and the first pages of a newspaper or magazine. You'll pay extra to get your ad placed there. You'll also often pay extra to specify placement of your ad in a certain section of the newspaper or magazine. For instance, if you know your target market of executives reads the "Movers and Shakers" column in the Business section, you could pay extra to have your ad located on that page.

■ **Run of paper/Run of book.** Ads specified as run of paper (for newspapers) or run of book (for magazines) are ads that the publication can place anywhere they choose. This will often lower the cost of your ad, but you'll have less control over where your ad appears.

Understanding the Column Inch

In newspapers, and sometimes in magazines, display ads are measured and priced by the number of "column inches" they cover. A *column* refers to a column of newsprint, so a "3 x 20" ad would be 3 columns wide and 20 inches deep (vertical length). The actual width of each column and the dimensions of each ad vary from paper to paper, depending on their size. Ask your ad rep for the exact dimensions of your ad.

Advertisers can save money by signing up for contract rates and having annual plans or campaigns. That's when we can offer better deals and added value. Also, when remnant space does come up, we'll first offer it to our clients who advertise on a regular basis.

Veena Bhasin-Naszady
Account Executive
The Kingston Whig-Standard

Stretch Your Ad Dollars with Co-op

Co-op, or cooperative, advertising is common and an extremely good way for you to reduce how much you spend on ads. With a co-op ad, you arrange for a company that you do business with to share the cost of the ad with you. Typically, this happens with manufacturers and retailers. Say you own an electronics retail store and sell Panasonic products. If you feature Panasonic products in your print ad, you may be able to get Panasonic to pay part of the cost of the ad (perhaps 50% or more, depending on how much of the ad you dedicate to their products). The following week (or month), you might feature Sony products in your ad, getting Sony to contribute co-op dollars. In this way, you can advertise more frequently. Even service businesses can ask their suppliers to see if they have co-op advertising funds available.

■ **Color.** Publications often provide opportunities to liven up an ad by adding color. Color makes your ad stand out more and draws readers' attention, but this will increase the cost—often significantly. Options typically will be to add spot color or one or two colors to a basic black-and-white ad or to run a full-color ad. There may be one price for standard colors (such as red, blue, and brown) and a higher cost if you want a specific color—to match the color of your logo, for instance.

A number of creative ways can be used, however, to lower the cost of your print ads. These methods are used frequently by advertisers. Look into:

■ **Regional editions.** If you've ever wondered how a local business could afford to advertise in a national news magazine, here's your answer: magazines sometimes publish regional editions, opening their space up to local advertisers at a reduced cost. It makes your business look big time but doesn't entail nearly the expense of advertising nationally. After advertising, you can post your ad on the wall to impress customers or use a promotional line like "As seen in *Time* magazine."

■ **Remnant/Standby ads.** Here's another way for you to score high-profile ad placement at bargain basement prices. As they draw closer to their publication dates, newspapers and magazines often have unsold ad space they need to fill. They're willing to let a smaller advertiser take the space at a fraction of the normal cost. **Tip:** If you're looking for remnant space in newspapers beyond your local area, try http://mss-standby.com.

When considering placing a print ad, ask the ad rep or publication staff:

■ **How large is your circulation?** How is your circulation verified? You need to know how many people your ad may potentially reach, and you want to be sure those numbers are real. See if their numbers are verified by an independent audit group like ABC (Audit Bureau of Circulations).

■ **What are the demographics of your readership?** You want to make sure that the people who receive the publication you're advertising in are a good fit with your target market. Publications typically have information about the characteristics of their readership (including age, gender, income levels, and education levels).

■ **What is the "pass-along" rate?** In addition to the verified circulation numbers, publications often quote a pass-along readership rate to come up with a figure representing the total number of people who see a publication (and, possibly, your ad). The standard figure for a total readership is 2.5 readers per validated copy.

■ **Do you have controlled circulation?** Instead of relying on subscribers, some magazines or newspapers are distributed free to a targeted list of desirable readers. The publisher controls who receives a copy, usually building a list on the basis of a person's job title/industry/spending power, aiming to get information—and ads—into the right hands. For example, CIO magazine is distributed solely to corporate technology managers (Chief Information Officers), highly desirable readers for companies that sell hardware, software, and technology services.

What is the ad cost per thousand (CPM) readers? Knowing the CPM, or cost per thousand readers, helps you evaluate how much it costs to reach each reader, and this allows you to compare different advertising options easily. For instance, if one publication charges $200 for an ad and their circulation is 10,000 readers, the CPM is $20 ($200 divided by 10—remember to drop the thousand). If another publication also charges $200 but their circulation is 20,000 readers, the CPM is only $10 ($200 divided by 20).

What would be the best ad placement for my kind of business? Publications, especially larger ones, know which type of reader reads each section. They may be able to steer you to the best spot for your ad.

What are the technical specifications for my ad? You will want to know what file formats (for example, jpeg, eps, tiff) you must submit your ad in, any layout limitations, or other technical concerns that may affect whether your ad will work with that publication.

What is the deadline for placing an ad? Once you've decided to advertise, ask what the deadlines are for submitting your ad materials. If you're creating the ad, schedule all production activities to meet that deadline.

Do you do sales tracking? Any measures of ad effectiveness? Some publications collect statistics indicating how well their ads work. These can help you evaluate print ads as a part of your marketing strategy and estimate a probable return on your investment.

What are the costs of running an ad? Get a rate card or quotes for all advertising options—single insertion, multiple insertions, preferred placement, run of paper/run of book ads. Are any discounts available?

Do you offer any standby or remnant advertising? If so, what are the costs?

Are there any other discount ad opportunities? Publications often offer special deals, such as discounts on spot color for placing ads when they're running color for other reasons. Internet-also opportunities give you free or discounted ads on their websites when you advertise in the print publication.

Do you have any special advertising sections/promotions that might work well for my business? Throughout the year, publications often have special features or sections. For instance, a newspaper may run a special wedding insert in February (when many brides start planning summer weddings). This is a good time for florists, caterers, limo services, and so on to showcase their services.

Designing a Great Print Ad

Once you've figured out where to run your ad, you'll need to focus on designing the ad itself. What makes an ad work?

A catchy headline that hooks the reader. A good headline appeals to customer needs, a problem the customer wants to solve, or their desire for a good deal.

Your Sales Rep

Once you've decided on a print campaign, your most valuable source of rates and information will be the ad representative at the publication of your choice. Larger newspapers and magazines will have staff devoted to ad sales, while at smaller publications, you may find yourself dealing with the owner, publisher, editor, or another staff member who has other duties, in addition to selling ads.

Part of what makes an ad campaign successful is developing a good relationship with your ad rep. Although their job is to make money for the publication (and themselves), they also want to help you meet your business goals, because that will encourage you to continue advertising with them. Good account reps will offer a number of helpful advertising options to meet your needs.

Location, Location, Location

Where your ad appears in a magazine or newspaper can make the difference between reaching your audience and getting overlooked. Some places in a publication are known to be more likely to be viewed (such as the back cover or inside front cover), and you'll pay extra for having your ad there.

The best pages for an ad to run include:

- Inside front cover of a magazine

- Back cover of a magazine or back page of a newspaper section

- Inside back cover of a magazine

- First few pages of a newspaper or magazine

- Section of publication of most interest to your target market

- Dedicated advertising sections (magazines often have advertising sections in the back with numerous small ads)

- Occasional special interest sections, such as bridal sections, home remodeling supplements, and winter sports features

The next question is *where on a page* to locate an ad. The basic rule of thumb is that the *upper right-hand corner* of a two-page spread is where readers' eyes go first, so that's the best place for an ad.

■ **Focus on an immediate benefit to the customer.** When your target customers see your ad, they're going to want to know "What's in it for me?" The best ads let them know right away. For example, "Roof leaking? The Roofing Guys can fix that today!"

■ **What makes you unique.** How do you differ from competitors? Is that important to prospective customers? If so, explain the positive attributes of your company/product in your ad—but this takes second place to the benefits the customer receives.

■ **Crisp, concise, compelling copy.** It's tempting to say a lot in your ad—don't! Keep your text brief. Use short, clear sentences and action-oriented verbs that enliven your copy.

■ **Easy-to-read typeface (font).** Choose clearly legible typefaces (type styles). Don't use more than two or three typefaces, styles (for example, bold, italic, normal), or sizes in an ad (for headlines, body copy, and subheads or teasers).

■ **Eye-catching photos or graphics.** Images attract attention, pulling readers to your ad. Use photos of your own product or your store/restaurant/building. Or if you provide a service where personal trust is key, you can use your own photo. You can also purchase stock photos to enliven your ad. Even your company logo adds a graphic element and helps your ad stand out.

■ **A call to action.** How do you want your audience to respond to your ad? Would you like them to call you? Stop by your store? Send in a card for more information? Bring in a coupon? Make that action clear in your ad.

■ **A compelling incentive for your customer to act quickly.** Give customers an incentive to respond to your call to action. Ideally, create a sense of urgency, so customers feel they must act fast: "$100 off your roofing job if booked by Friday!" "Free gift to first 50 customers."

■ **Clear, easy-to-find contact info.** Make absolutely certain that customers can reach you and find you. Double check that you've prominently included: your business name, website address, phone number, physical location (if you have one), person to contact (if that's important), hours of operation, email address (if that's important). Double check!

■ **White space.** Resist the urge to completely fill your ad space with copy and graphics. Readers are put off by crowded ads. Allow your text and images to "breathe" by giving them some blank space (called *white space*) around them.

Some publications, especially local newspapers, will offer to design your ad for you. While this can be a great money saver, keep in mind that the graphic designers for these publications are churning out hundreds of ads, and yours may not get the attention it deserves. You may choose to produce your own ad, but you'll need to factor in the design and copywriting fees to create it. If you have these skills, you can save yourself some money by producing your own ad, but if your abilities are limited, hire professionals. It's well worth spending the money to ensure your ad presents a professional, polished image for your business.

BRAINSTORMING

YOUR PRINT AD

Develop your own ad for a print publication. Be sure to include:

1. A "hook" (a catchy headline): _____

2. Benefits to customer: _____

3. What differentiates you from the competition: _____

4. Strong, clear call to action: _____

5. Compelling incentive to act: _____

6. Contact info: _____

   Name of company: _____

   Website address: _____

   Phone number: _____

   Physical address (if appropriate): _____

   Hours of operation (if appropriate): _____

   Name of person to contact (if appropriate): _____

   Email address (if appropriate): _____

Now, combine those elements into a compelling headline, concise body text, and clear contact info:

_____

_____

_____

_____

Sketch a design for your own ad. Be sure it includes:

- Plenty of white space
- Graphics, photo, and/or logo
- Contact information

BRAINSTORMING

YOUR PRINT OUTLETS

To complete the following worksheet, *first* list the print outlets (specific newspapers, magazines, or other publications) you feel will be most effective for your company. In the *second row,* explain the reasons you feel they'll be good choices. (These could include reach to your target audience, affordability, help offered with production of the ads, and so on.) Use the *third row* to project how frequently you'd run your ads.

Depending on your business needs and budget, you may choose to place ads on a regular basis or only during certain seasons or special events. Finally, obtain rate cards from the publications you think will be most effective, and in the fourth row indicate the costs per ad or per campaign. You'll need this information to develop your print budget.

PRINT OUTLET				
REASON				
FREQUENCY				
COST				

affordability scale

Print Advertising

$	$$		$$$		$$$$
Newsletter	Community Newspaper	Small-City Newspaper	Regional Magazine	Large-City Newsaper	National Magazine

*COST KEY:
$**—Relatively Inexpensive   **$$**—Moderately Expensive   **$$$**—Fairly Expensive   **$$$$—Expensive

* These symbols represent general rate estimations. Ad rates will vary by circulation of publication, quality of publication, region, target market, and type of audience. For instance, a four-color newsletter aimed at physicians will likely command higher ad rates than a black-and-white community newsletter.

Comparing Print Media

When you think of print publications, you usually think of newspapers or magazines. But there are actually many other types of print publications where you can advertise your business as well. The challenge is finding the ad venue that works best for your business and that gives you the best results for your money. The charts below show the range of options and their relative costs.

S A M P L E : **ADVERTISEMENT**

HEADLINE

HOOK

BENEFIT-ORIENTED BODY COPY

DIFFERENTIATOR

EYE-CATCHING GRAPHIC

CALL TO ACTION

COMPELLING REASON TO ACT

CONTACT INFORMATION

COMPARING PRINT MEDIA

PUBLICATION	PRICE RANGE	DESCRIPTION	BENEFITS	CHALLENGES	BEST FOR	TIPS FOR EFFECTIVENESS
SPECIAL INTEREST PUBLICATIONS						
NEWSLETTERS	$–$$	Print publications going to a limited readership, often members of a group	Good fit to a specific target market; usually inexpensive to place an ad	Small number of readers	Targeting a particular community, group, industry	Take advantage of low price to run larger ads; repeat often
TRADE JOURNALS	$$–$$$	Publications, usually similar to magazines, aimed at members of an industry or profession	Reaches industry professionals who may not have any other media outlets in common	May be expensive; may not be well read; may have limits on the nature of the ad; may only be quarterly	Targeting a specific industry or profession	Consider also getting involved with industry trade organizations who publish these journals to stay more visible with your target market
SPECIAL-INTEREST LOCAL PUBLICATIONS	$–$$	Newspaper or magazine serving a city or region focusing on a particular interest group (e.g., Bay Area parents); typically distributed free	Good fit to a specific target market in a particular geographic area	Limited circulation; numbers may not be verified; your competitors will likely be advertising there, too	Targeting markets that are highly motivated to make purchases (e.g., new parents)	Make sure publication has been around for a while and is reliable
NEWSPAPERS						
COMMUNITY NEWSPAPERS/ FREE NEWSPAPERS	$–$$	Controlled circulation papers serving a neighborhoods or groups in urban areas (e.g., subway riders)	Reach a general group of local readers; inexpensive	Limited reach; readers may not fit your target market demographics; readers may not be motivated buyers	Targeting an audience who live in a specific area or are likely to get the paper	Feature larger, well-placed ads; appeal to local concerns; offer meaningful incentives
SMALL-CITY NEWSPAPERS	$–$$	General interest newspapers serving small cities	Reach a general group of local readers; less expensive than regional papers	May not serve enough readers; may print only a few times a week; locals may read regional papers instead	Targeting an audience who live in a specific small city, particularly those interested in local civic affairs	Experiment with ads in other newspapers as well if you need to target a wider geographic area
LARGE-CITY/ REGIONAL NEWSPAPER	$$$	General interest newspapers serving a large metropolitan area	Reach a larger group of prospective mainstream customers in your general region	More expensive than community papers; advertising here may be overkill if you're trying to attract a very local audience	Advertising to a general regional audience	If you can't afford big ads, advertise frequently in sections your target customers would read

PUBLICATION	PRICE RANGE	DESCRIPTION	BENEFITS	CHALLENGES	BEST FOR	TIPS FOR EFFECTIVENESS
NEWSPAPERS (continued)						
CITY/REGIONAL BUSINESS JOURNALS	$$	Newspapers covering business issues generally published in larger cities	Reach local and regional readers with common business interests	Limited circulation; may be costly on a CPM basis; may not reach your target audience	Targeting a regional, business-to-business market	Advertise frequently, even if your ad is small, and try for placement near editorial related to your business offering
NATIONAL-REACH NEWSPAPERS	$$$ $$$$	Newspapers reaching the entire country, such as *USA Today, Wall Street Journal, New York Times*	Reach broad national audience; and sophisticated, upscale market—often businesspeople or travelers	Expensive; many readers may not be part of your target	High-priced goods and services; advertisers with big budgets	Seek co-op dollars from major suppliers to help underwrite the cost; carefully evaluate whether this is the right fit for your market
MAGAZINES						
SPECIAL INTEREST NATIONAL MAGAZINES	$$–$$$$	Subscription based, aimed at readers who share a common interest, such as sports, fashion/beauty, hobbies	Can be very affordable or very expensive, depending on circulation; reach a clearly defined target market	Can be very expensive; many readers may not spend much time with the publication	Highly targeted goods and services that are a clear fit to the demographics of the readership	Advertise frequently—build your brand with this group over time, not just selling products or services on a one-time basis
CITY/REGIONAL MAGAZINES	$$–$$$	Subscription based, covering issues, fashion, arts, for a particular city or region	More affordable than national magazines; have higher retention—"stick around"—rates than local newspapers	Can be expensive relative to other local options	Targeting relatively upscale readers; good for arts, home design, restaurants, other upscale local companies	Make clear call to action and incentives to motivate readers to connect with you
GENERAL INTEREST NATIONAL MAGAZINES	$$$$	Subscription-based, aimed at large number of consumers (e.g., *Time, People, Parade*)	Reach the widest possible mainstream audience	Probably the most expensive print ads available	Targeting either a huge mainstream audience or a large audience of readers with particular lifestyles and interests	Unless you have a huge budget, place small, regular ads as close as possible to an editorial area that might interest your customers; ask about remnant space, regional editions, and special issues that focus on topics closely related to your product or service

Calculating Your Print Advertising ROI

The following page contains a worksheet to help you get started on your own ROI analysis. Simply choose a print media outlet in which you wish your advertising to appear on, and fill in the requested data to get an idea of the ROI you can expect from your print campaign.

Here are some tips for using the worksheets (and calculating your ROI):

■ **Be specific about your financial goals.** This means that you need to include not just the total return you'd like to receive on your advertising investment but what that translates to in terms of customers and expenditures. Thus, if you were preparing this worksheet for a dental consulting company that was considering running an ad in the American Dental Association newsletter, you might state as your financial goals that you want to secure seven new clients a year for a total of $140,000 per year.

■ **Remember non-financial goals.** While you may not be able to put a cash value on things like brand awareness and customer perception, these are important components of any marketing campaign, and as such must be considered when calculating ROI. Thus, to use the dental consultant example again, you might cite the following for your non-financial goals: increased awareness of your consultancy within the dental community, and improved credibility for your services.

■ **Get the data on the print media source you're targeting.** In other words, *know your audience:* Find out as much as you can about the readership of the source you're targeting—total circulation, demographics, open rate, and so on.

Print Return on Investment

Return on investment is a critical concept for all aspects of your business. It answers the question "What did I get for my money?" As part of your marketing planning, you'll want to get in the habit of projecting a likely ROI on the marketing dollars you're about to spend, trying to forecast what kinds of returns are realistic. Throughout this book, you'll have the opportunity to figure out an ROI on each of your marketing choices. In this section you can evaluate the ROI for advertising in print publications.

Once you've been advertising for a while, you'll be able to evaluate and compare ROIs based on actual results. If you're doing projections for a new advertising media outlet and want to get a sense of how cost effective it will be, base your ROI estimates on the following: a media outlet's total reach (provided by your ad rep or media kit), the percentage of readers who are a good fit with your target market, and how motivated buyers are likely to be.

ROI analysis enables you to compare the cost of an ad with the results. And it helps you compare various marketing options. For example, which is a better choice? Advertising once a week for a year in a local paper at a cost of $24,000 or advertising once a month for a year in a national special interest magazine for a cost of $48,000? You have to do an ROI analysis to figure that out.

Let's take the first choice: spending $2,000 a month for an ad once a week in a local city newspaper for a total of $24,000. Using your best judgment, you estimate that those ads will bring you an additional $70,000 in sales. In other words, your ROI was $46,000 ($70,000 – $24,000), or 191% ($46,000 return compared to the $24,000 investment).

That sounds great. But what if you'd made a different choice?

Let's say, instead, that you choose advertising in a monthly national special interest magazine. That costs you $4,000 per insertion, for a total of $48,000. However, you estimate that will bring you $160,000 in new business (because more of its readers fit into your target market demographics and they are more motivated buyers than those who would read the local city newspaper). That gives you a total gain of $112,000. That's an ROI of 233%

Of course, you may also meet other goals, or achieve additional benefits, from advertising, as well as getting new sales. For instance, you may be trying to increase brand name recognition within your target market; show support for an organization (by advertising in their newsletter or trade journal); or announce a new product, service, or location. So pay attention to those non-financial goals and accomplishments when trying to assess ROI.

RETURN ON INVESTMENT

YOUR PRINT ADVERTISING ROI

Your business: _____

Your target market: _____

Your media: _____

GOALS

Financial goals: _____

Non-financial goals: _____

MEDIA OUTLET, AUDIENCE, AND FIT WITH MARKET

Name: _____

Print frequency: _____

Total readership: _____

Demographics of readership: _____

% of readership that fits your target market: _____

Potential target market readership: _____

Other information (this could include things such as open rate—i.e., the percent of subscribers who actually open the newsletter): _____

PROJECTED COSTS

Cost per insertion (1/4 page ad): _____

Number of insertions: _____

Other costs (examples include color, preferred placement, and so on): _____

Cost of ad insertions: _____

Ad production: _____

Other costs: _____

Total cost of ads: _____

PROJECTED RETURNS, FINANCIAL

Expected new clients as a result of ad: _____

Expected average income per new client: _____

Increase in income from advertising: _____

Total cost of ads: _____

Total projected net financial gain (the projected increase in income minus the cost of the ad): _____

PROJECTED RETURNS, NON-FINANCIAL

_____

_____

TOTAL ROI (Total Net Financial Returns Plus Total Non-Financial Returns): _____

BUDGET

PRINT ADVERTISING BUDGET

Use this worksheet to keep track of your print publication advertising options and costs:

PROFESSIONAL ASSISTANCE

Advertising copywriters _____

Graphic design _____

Photographers _____

Illustrators _____

Other consultants _____

NEWSPAPERS

Frequency/Duration

One time only _____

Daily _____

Weekly _____

Special section _____

Circulars _____

Ad specs & rates

Display ads _____

Full page _____

Half page _____

Quarter page _____

Classifieds _____

Black & white _____

Color _____

MAGAZINES

Frequency/Rates

One time only _____

Weekly _____

Monthly _____

Ad specs & rates

    Display ads _____

    Full page _____

    Half page _____

    Quarter page _____

    Classifieds _____

    Remnant/Standby _____

    Co-op_____

    Black & white _____

    Color _____

Extras

    Preferred placement_____

    Blow-in cards_____

    Polybagging_____

    Special section _____

NEWSLETTERS

Frequency/Placement/Duration _____

    One time only _____

    Weekly_____

    Monthly_____

    Preferred placement _____

Ad specs & rates

    Display ads _____

    Full page _____

    Half page _____

    Quarter page _____

    Classifieds _____

    Remnant/Standby _____

    Co-op_____

    Black & white _____

    Color _____

OTHER PRINT MEDIA

_____

_____

PRINT ADVERTISING BUDGET (12 MONTHS)

	JAN	FEB	MARCH	APRIL	MAY
Professional Assistance					
Writers					
Graphic designers					
Photographers/Illustrators					
Other consultants					
Ad Buys					
Newspapers					
National					
Big city					
Small city					
Community					
Magazines					
National news					
National special interest/business					
National trade					
Women's/Men's					
Regional special interest/business					
Community/Regional					
Newsletters					
Community					
Local business					
Professional networking					
Trade groups/Associations					
Other print media ad buys					
Other					
TOTAL					

! **NOTE:** An electronic version of this worksheet is available as part of the Planning Shop's Marketing Budget Templates package.

JUNE	JULY	AUGUST	SEPT	OCT	NOV	DEC	TOTAL

Lingo

ARBITRON RATINGS: Data on the size and nature of radio listening audiences, collected by the research firm Arbitron. These ratings are similar to the Nielsen ratings for TV. The data collected is used to help set advertising rates based on the number of people listening to a radio station at any given time.

BILLBOARD (OR TAGS): A brief announcement (usually three to ten seconds in length) at the beginning and/or end of a program or segment, identifying the sponsors.

DAYPART: A time segment into which a radio station divides a day. Examples include breakfast time and early evening. The cost of radio advertising varies depending on the daypart selected.

DRIVE TIMES: The commute-to-work hours (early morning and late afternoon), when the most radio listeners are driving in their cars, often considered prime time for radio advertising.

FORMAT: A term used to describe the type of programming content on a radio station. Common formats are talk radio, sports, music, oldies, and all news.

INTERNET RADIO: Radio programming that is distributed via the Internet rather than over the airwaves or via satellite.

LIVE REMOTES: When radio stations broadcast live from a business or other non-station location.

ROS (RUN OF SCHEDULE): An ad that can be broadcast at any time.

SATELLITE STATION: Radio programming distributed via satellite that listeners pay a subscription fee to receive (similar to cable and satellite TV).

SPOT: The term used for a radio commercial.

TERRESTRIAL STATION (BROADCAST RADIO): Radio stations that broadcast over the airways to listeners, who tune in for free, over a limited geographic area.

TIGHTENED ROTATION: An ad that is played only during times specified by the advertiser (for example, during morning drive times). These ads are more expensive than ROS ads (see above).

CHAPTER 11

Advertising on Radio

I f you've listened to radio, you've certainly heard radio commercials. They might be ads for a concert, a new restaurant, a car dealership, or a sale on mattresses. Radio advertising is extremely popular because it can be surprisingly affordable, even for small businesses. It enables you to target a very specific audience, and it often reaches a captive audience.

In an age when people can get their news and entertainment from myriad sources, radio still maintains strong appeal and reaches a large number of people. Moreover, each radio station has a fairly clearly defined demographic group that listens to its programming, which makes it easy to determine whether a station's audience represents the right target market for your business.

Benefits of Radio Advertising

Radio offers a number of advantages over other types of traditional advertising—the primary one being that messages are broadcast to a captive or semi-captive audience, primarily people in cars. When someone is driving, they're focused on getting to their destination and less likely to change stations when commercials come on. Likewise when someone has the radio on in the background at work or at home, they're not likely to be listening with a remote in their hands, ready to change channels quickly. In contrast, TV watchers channel-surf, wander to the kitchen during the commercials, and even record shows and skip the commercials entirely on playback. Print suffers from a similar downside in that people generally only read the ads that interest them, skipping over the rest. Other benefits of advertising on radio:

■ **Radio is targeted and segmented.** Because each station's format is clearly defined, you know exactly whom you're reaching. Young urban listeners will tune in to very different stations than people over 60. Sure it's possible that a grandmother will tune in to a hip-hop station, but it's likely that the overwhelming majority of listeners will be good prospects for your urban-oriented clothing store.

■ **Radio is typically a customer's last media contact before purchasing.** This is because radio ads often reach them while they're driving— meaning there's a good chance a prospect will be on the way to a mall or

---

Make It Memorable

When advertising on the radio, remember that many listeners won't be able to write anything down, because they're riding in a car, cooking, or are otherwise occupied. Increase your chances of success by using an easy-to-remember name, phone number, or website address. Ideally, choose names, numbers, and URLs that are simple to recall and closely affiliated with your business. For instance, if you're selling gear for serious cycling enthusiasts, a website named www.CompetitiveCyclist.com or a phone number like 1-888-555-BIKE will be easy for listeners to remember, even if they can't write it down.

> *If you have a business that can be illustrated by sound, you have a great opportunity to create a vivid picture in people's minds. The ideal use of radio is to paint pictures with sound, using sound and verbal imagery. Don't just take it literally, saying 'Hey, there's 10% off this weekend at Zap Electronics,' but think about what Zap Electronics might sound like. How about if we put a ZAPPP in it! Now you've got a memorable signature. There's a reason Intel has its own audio logo. It's a sound everyone knows. That's how you establish your branding on the radio—with sound.*

Mark Ramsey
Author
Fresh Air: Marketing Gurus in Radio

not far from your office, where they can buy your products or services as soon as they get out of their car.

■ **Radio listeners are often fiercely loyal.** Since radio audience members often keep their dials locked on a single station, you will have plenty of opportunities to reach them if you find a station that appeals to your target market.

■ **Terrestrial radio broadcasts have a limited geographical range.** This makes it an ideal medium for reaching potential customers if your company relies on business from your local area.

■ **Radio offers an effective way of promoting a product or service that doesn't require too much description.** Everyone understands what dentists, print shops, and restaurants provide. These kinds of businesses can use radio time to build name recognition, focusing on the benefits they offer and the things that distinguish them from the competition.

■ **People often remember things they hear.** Word-of-mouth advertising (see Chapter 15) is very powerful. And people who hear your ad on the radio often remember hearing about you but forget that it was in an ad.

■ **Radio can be affordable even to small businesses.** Especially on smaller stations or in smaller cities, radio can represent a relatively cheap advertising option—particularly when compared to TV advertising or advertising in a big-city newspaper.

■ **Radio ads are often inexpensive to create.** Most stations will help advertisers prepare a script that one of their announcers reads over the air.

■ **Radio ads can incorporate music or a jingle.** Music is very memorable, making it a good way to get your name and message into prospects' heads.

■ **Radio stations are ready to help advertisers.** Because radio stations depend on ads for their survival, they have ad representatives ready to help you. In fact, once you're in any kind of retail or hospitality business, it's likely that a radio ad rep will find you.

■ **Radio hosts or personalities will often read your ad or actually endorse your product or service.** This provides a terrific means of reaching listeners loyal to a radio personality.

7 Challenges of Radio Advertising

While advertising on radio offers many benefits, it also imposes a number of limitations. Thus, choosing to advertise a product or service on the radio takes careful consideration and some creativity. The biggest obstacle is that radio is an *aural,* or heard, medium. Prospects can neither see your product nor read about your service. You can't show your product to an audience or demonstrate how it works. If your product or service absolutely has to be seen to be understood or if your advantage over your competition is primarily visual, then radio is probably not the medium for you. Other limitations of advertising on radio include the following:

■ **Listeners are distracted.** Almost no one is sitting around doing nothing but listening to a radio station. They're either driving in their car, working in an office, puttering around the house, or engaged in another activity. This isn't entirely bad—it's what keeps them from changing stations when your ad comes on. But when a person stops to read an ad in print or sits through a commercial on TV, they're often giving that ad more attention than a radio spot.

■ **Listeners often have to rely on their memories to follow up, since they are frequently not in a position to write down information they hear.** You may make a compelling offer to a receptive listener who's busy driving or cooking only to have them forget your address, phone number, or website address before they can make a note of it.

■ **There are usually many ads on any one radio station or program.** This makes it more difficult to be memorable or stand out.

■ **You have only a very short period of time to get your message out.** For this reason, radio is not a good medium for businesses that are advertising complicated or difficult-to-explain products or services.

■ **You're reaching people through only one sense—their hearing.** In most other media, prospects use more of their brains to interact with an ad (for example, reading words, seeing images, listening, and clicking on websites). That's why many radio ads use both words and music to more deeply engage a listener.

■ **You must advertise frequently on the same station in a short period of time.** This is the only way to ensure that your message is noticed and remembered.

■ **Radio is a more challenging medium for businesses advertising to other businesses (B2B) than for those trying to reach consumers (B2C).** This is because fewer business customers are listening to radio, and even when they do, they may not be thinking about their business needs.

Types of Stations

With ads appearing on radio as far back as 1923, radio advertising has been around a long time—and it's come a long way since then. While radio programming was once limited to broadcast stations, listeners now have a number of ways to tune in. There are currently three basic types of radio: terrestrial (or broadcast), satellite, and Internet.

The overwhelming majority of radio advertising, however, is placed on terrestrial, or broadcast, radio stations, which offers a number of advertising choices. For starters, you can advertise locally by dealing with a locally owned radio station. Or you can place radio ads nationally—either on shows created by a national network or on stations owned by a national company that owns a string of stations. Some of your options include:

■ **Local commercial broadcast.** Generally, these take the form of music stations (FM) or news/talk radio stations (AM). In general, they reach a large audience. The most popular stations are particularly good for getting a message to a large, diverse consumer market (when advertising with

---

Land, Air, or Net?

Ever wonder where that radio signal is coming from? Read on to find out.

■ **Terrestrial, or broadcast, radio,** as the name suggests, is based right here on Earth. Using broadcast transmitters, radio programming is sent over the public airwaves. Broadcast radio stations serve limited geographic areas, and a limited number of stations can exist within any geographic area. However, these very limitations mean that broadcast radio often presents good, targeted opportunities for advertisers wishing to reach a local audience.

■ **Satellite radio** transmits programming via a satellite from space and typically reaches a national audience. Satellite stations offer a much broader range of programming than broadcast stations and often target much narrower audiences (for instance, a satellite station might broadcast not just oldies but oldies from the 1940s, 1950s, or 1960s). Primarily listener-supported, satellite radio also supports advertising—in fact, an increasingly large portion of satellite radio revenue now comes from ads.

■ **Internet radio** is just what its name implies: radio programming transmitted over the Internet. However, keep in mind that the radio you're hearing over the Internet could be terrestrial radio that's being "streamed" over the Web but programmed for broadcast stations, or it could be true Internet-based radio programming—a station created especially for the Web, aimed at audiences listening through their computers.

National Advertising on Local Stations

Your local radio station may not be local at all. In addition to possibly not being owned by a local company, the station's "local" disc jockey, newsperson, and even weather announcer may be located across the country. Yes, Boston weather can be announced from San Diego. Changes in U.S. law in 1996 made it possible for corporations to own an unlimited number of broadcast radio stations. Now a few major companies— Clear Channel Communications, Cumulus, Citadel, and Infinity— own a vast number. While this means less diversity in radio programming, it also means that advertisers have the opportunity to place ads with one company and have their ads heard on "local" stations nationally.

general interest programming such as news and sports). Stations with a more narrow programming focus (including music genres) enable you to reach a large number of those in your target market. These stations may be independent or they may be affiliated with a national network.

- **Local affiliates of national networks.** In years past, a few major national radio broadcast networks, such as CBS, ABC, and NBC (the precursors of the national TV networks), owned stations in major markets and supplied programming to other stations, known as *affiliates*. Today, there are many more national networks, most of which get many, if not most, of their programs from a national source. And many stations are owned by a few national companies that control most of the programming— even for local stations.

- **Local public radio.** Public radio is noncommercial and nonprofit. Local public radio stations offer regional news, community affairs, local talk shows, and, in most markets, music that appeals to a narrower audience than most commercial radio stations. Since public radio is noncommercial, you don't have opportunities to advertise. Instead, you can become a sponsor for a program or the station as a whole. Under this arrangement, your name and contact information are briefly mentioned on air during a particular show. Sponsorships on local public radio stations are relatively reasonably priced, give you a positive association with a well-respected nonprofit group, and give you access to a well-educated, affluent audience. However, they provide a limited format to deliver your message. You cannot, for example, broadcast a commercial complete with sound effects and pricing information for your product or service.

- **National networks.** National radio advertising is available through national networks, either on specific programs produced by these networks or across a number of stations owned by one company. By choosing to advertise on a national level, you can use radio to reach beyond your limited geographic area. You can reach a large consumer audience on programs that appeal to a general audience (such as news on CBS or music on popular music stations) or to a fairly clearly defined target audience (for instance, programming produced by networks such as Performance Racing Network or American Blues Network). Fees are, in general, higher than advertising on local stations because of the larger audience and are naturally highest for the most popular networks and programs.

- **National public radio networks.** You can reach a national audience of local public radio station listeners by supporting national public radio networks such as NPR (National Public Radio), APM (American Public Media), and PRI (Public Radio International). These networks create programming that is syndicated to local public radio affiliates. You will not be "advertising"; instead, you'll be sponsoring programs and you will receive a limited mention (generally your company name, the nature of your company, and limited contact information) usually before and/or after a show. Sponsorship fees will depend on how many markets you want the announcement to cover.

- **College stations.** These are effective for reaching a younger, educated audience, often with money to spend on food and entertainment, within a very limited geographic area, because the signals for these stations do not usually reach far beyond the campus. Many receive their funding through their affiliate schools but supplement their budgets with advertising. College DJs can be an eclectic group, and their music and programming choices can be unpredictable. If you decide to advertise on a college station, check that its content positively reflects on your company's image.

Key Considerations for Radio Advertising

When choosing to advertise on radio as part of your overall marketing plan, these are the key considerations to keep in mind:

- Content and message
- Type of ad
- Length of ad
- Time, or *daypart,* when an ad is run
- Station/program where an ad is run
- Frequency
- Continuity

Effective Content and Message

No matter how many times you run your ads on radio, the message and content of your ad must get viewers to remember your name and motivate them to purchase, or you're wasting your money. (For more on what makes an effective radio ad, see page 124.)

Types of Radio Ads

Radio commercials are commonly referred to as *spots*. But that is just the generic term for any kind of radio ad. In fact, you can choose from among many different styles of radio ads:

- **Live read/Live script.** The most common and least expensive type of ad consists of a single announcer describing a product or service. You come up with a simple script (the station's radio ad rep can often help you write it), and a radio station personality (disc jockey or talk show host) reads the ad. This is not only relatively inexpensive, but it also gives your commercial the added value of having a popular personality associated with your company.

- **Combination live/taped.** In this form of radio ad, the announcer (or other radio personality) still reads a script live, but the advertiser also provides a tape to go along with the live read. The tape typically has music and is often used as a beginning and end to the live read, helping to identify the product or company.

Radio Formats

Every radio station has a specific *format,* or program genre—defined narrowly enough to easily identify the demographics of the listening audience. The following are just a few of the formats identified by Arbitron:

- Active Rock
- Adult Contemporary
- Adult Hits
- Adult Standards
- Album Adult Alternative
- Album Oriented Rock
- Latino Urban
- Mexican Regional
- Spanish Adult Hits
- Spanish Contemporary
- Spanish Oldies
- Spanish Religious
- Spanish Traditional
- Tejano
- Urban Adult Contemporary
- Urban Contemporary
- Urban Oldies
- All News
- News/Talk/Information
- Educational
- Talk/Personality

Arbitron: Can You Hear Me Now?

Founded in 1949 as the American Ratings Bureau, Arbitron is a for-profit research firm that collects data on radio listenership, similar to Nielsen ratings for TV. Stations use Arbitron data to set their rates, market their ad space, and determine which programs stay or go, based on the number of people that tune in to them.

Arbitron gathers its data four times a year from a random sample of the population in hundreds of metropolitan areas nationwide. The data provides advertisers with a range of information, such as the average number of people listening to a station, how much time they spend listening, and to what demographic group they belong. Advertisers used to have to flip through huge quarterly print books to access the data, but it is now available online to subscribers of Arbitron's eBook.

Costs for subscribing to Arbitron services vary, depending on the market and the reports needed. However, you can access free general listener (called *topline*) info at Arbitron's site (www.arbitron. com). On the home page, click "Topline Ratings." When you reach the page, select your market (city or region) to retrieve data for a variety of stations and formats in the area. You'll find lots of other free reports on the site, along with contact information for further info on the company's services.

■ **Advertiser produced.** This is any commercial you produce, at your own expense. You supply it as a finished tape for the radio station to run. The advantage of this type of ad is that it gives you control over exactly what is said and how it is said, and you can work with a wider variety of commercial styles (as opposed to working with announcer-read copy). Some of the formats you can use when producing your own radio ads:

—**Testimonial.** With a satisfied customer, well-known personality, or celebrity talking about the qualities of your product or service.

—**Dialogue.** An ad usually featuring two voices. Often the first voice relates a problem or need your potential customers have: "My teeth are killing me, but I'm scared to go to a dentist," for instance, and the second suggests a remedy: "You should try No-Pain Dentistry. They have gentle dentists, and they're conveniently located at the Laurel Street Mall. No-Pain Dentistry is perfect for people like you."

—**Vignette.** With this type of advertising, you tell a mini-story that engages the listener. This kind of commercial is challenging to produce since you have to craft in such a way that your company name comes up repeatedly and listeners are convinced of the benefit of your product or service. When done right, though, a vignette can evoke emotions as well as convey information.

■ **Billboards/Tags.** Shorter and less expensive than regular commercials, tags consist of one or two lines of copy about your business, either pre-recorded or spoken live by the on-air announcer. These are heard before or after a radio segment—perhaps the news, weather, or some other regular feature, such as a daily top-20 countdown or the stock market report. When used to introduce a piece ("... and now the weather, brought to you by Citywide Snow Removal"), they are called *intros*. Used at the end of a piece ("... this hourly market report brought to you by Smith and Wilson Accounting. Call us when it has to add up"), they are referred to as "*extros*." Tags are an inexpensive way to get your name and positioning statement into the ears of an audience.

■ **Endorsements.** When you hear a radio announcer talking about their personal experience with a product or service, either in a commercial or live on air, that's an endorsement. Endorsements come at a cost—either cash or the product itself (which you'll pay or give directly to the announcer). So if you've started a travel company and are packaging trips to Cabo San Lucas, an announcer may endorse your business in return for a free trip. Most announcers will only endorse a product or service they like or believe in.

■ **Sponsorships.** In many communities, the local public radio station can be a good, and relatively inexpensive, choice for reaching a particular segment of the community (businesspeople, well-educated, or high-income). These stations do not accept ads, but they do accept program sponsorships. With a sponsorship, you can get the name of your company, and often the location, website, or other identifying information, mentioned at the time of the program. Although the nature and content of your "ad" is very limited with a sponsorship, if you sponsor a popular program over a long period of time, your business name can become very familiar to this target audience.

Length of Ad

One nice thing about radio is that you can convey a fair amount of information in very little time. The basic rule of thumb: plan on a bit more than two words for each second of radio time. That may not seem like a lot, but you may need only 15 seconds to get your message across and even repeat it. "Huge blow-out sale on new trucks! Saturday and Sunday at Willis Ford, Third and Central. Come get a great truck bargain at Willis Ford Saturday and Sunday. Willis Ford, Third and Central." This is only 32 words.

Common radio spot lengths are 15, 30, 45, and 60 seconds—though in some programming formats, there may be longer ads, especially on smaller stations or late at night. Some of these ads may even seem like programming, similar to TV infomercials (see page 139).

You may not have your choice of all lengths on every radio station—and generally, the longer the spot, the more expensive it is (because you're paying for airtime). Some stations may have a minimum amount of time (perhaps 60 seconds) for an ad, and many may have a maximum length (not more than 60 seconds).

Timing

Unlike TV, where the largest audience is at night, radio audiences are the largest during the day. There are some exceptions, of course—a sports station may get a larger audience for a major league baseball night game than they will during the day. But generally, you'll reach more listeners, and pay a higher advertising rate, during daytime hours.

In particular, there are two times of day when the radio audience is the largest: early in the morning and at the end of the workday. These "drive times" are when commuters are in their cars heading to and from work. Even though there are now many other distractions while you're in your car (iPods, and car phones, to name a few), a huge percentage of auto commuters still tune in to radio stations.

The radio day is divided into "dayparts"—specific times that the industry uses to refer to segments of the programming day. Because most stations have much smaller audiences on weekends, they may change their programming significantly on those days. Thus, you might be able to find targeted programs (such as "FlyFishing Report") on Saturdays and Sundays that reach your exact audience, and commercials played during those shows may be fairly inexpensive. Generally, other than weekends, overnight is the least expensive time to advertise on radio.

Station/Program

Clearly, the most important consideration when deciding whether to advertise on radio is whether you can identify a radio station (and program) that reaches your target customers. Fortunately, radio makes this fairly easy to determine. In fact, this is where radio shines as an advertising medium.

Arbitron, the company that measures the audience of radio stations and programs, characterizes radio stations by different *formats*, based on the nature of that station's programming. It lists more than 50 different formats,

---

Music Makes Memories

A *jingle* is the term used for a musical radio commercial, or the musical part of a commercial, which is designed to convey a message and make the advertiser's name more memorable. Associating music with your brand or name makes it more memorable to the listener, especially if you run your ad frequently. While big companies often license popular songs to use as their jingles, they pay large sums of money for the right to do so. You should not use any copyrighted musical material in your ad. However, there are numerous jingle-producing services that can create a radio-ready jingle for you for as little as a few hundred dollars (enter "jingle producers" in an Internet search engine). There are also stock music services available, where you can purchase royalty-free sounds to include in your ad.

"Place your ads Wednesday or Thursday, 8 a.m. to 8:30 a.m., to get the biggest bang for your buck. More people are stuck in traffic listening to their radios at that time than any other!"

Adryenn Ashley
Media Strategist, Entrepreneur, and Filmmaker

<table>
<tr><td>

Best Times to Advertise on Radio

Choose your advertising spots to coincide with the times your target market is likely to be listening. Simply advertising at the most popular times may not be the best way to reach your target audience. If you're targeting students or independent professionals, for instance, who tend to work late into the evening, a late-night spot might be a better choice. Understanding where your customers will be at key times of day will show you the best times to reach them.

</td></tr>
</table>

and some stations and radio markets break down the formats even more specifically: country is not only country, for example; it may be young country or hit country or classical country or ranchera/country.

Because differing radio formats appeal to very specific listeners, it is easy to focus in on the listeners you think will be most receptive to your products and services. Moreover, many stations, regardless of their regular programming, switch to even more narrowly defined audiences at certain times of the week or day when they have low listenership levels. At these times they may run programs that are dedicated to a very narrow group of listeners (for example, a show on new technology or one that appeals to a specific ethnic group or to skiers). If that group fits your target market, advertising on a show directed to them may be an extremely effective and inexpensive way to reach good prospects.

Ask the ad rep for any station you're considering to give you information about the demographics of their listeners, not just during weekdays, but also at any time on weekends or overnight when they have special programming.

And be sure to listen to any station and program on which you are considering advertising. Some stations may have disc jockeys, content, or a tone you'd rather not have associated with your business. Before signing a contract to advertise on any station, make sure it's right for your audience.

Frequency

Frequency is critical in radio. Radio ads are there and gone, usually in a minute or less. While experts disagree on the number of exposures a listener must have to be able to recall the name or message, it is clear that someone must hear your message a minimum of three times to remember it. The actual number is probably much higher. Since listeners won't hear your ad every time it's run, you must run your ads frequently to reach your target customer. For this reason, radio ad representatives will always sell you an ad schedule, or campaign, placing your ad numerous times, either at different times of day with different programs or for a long period of time with a single program. Running an ad only once or twice is ineffective.

It's important to know not only when your target market is listening to a radio station, but also how they are listening. Depending on the type of station they're tuned in to, listeners might give the radio their full attention for short periods of time—when listening to the weather or stock market reports, for example—or they might keep their favorite station on for hours at a time as when listening to a soft rock station at work. In the first instance, you may wish to repeat your ad frequently, as listeners will be tuning in and out often. In the second, your ad may get enough exposure with less frequent repetition.

One of the problems is that people get into radio, but then they don't buy enough advertising, not enough frequency. If you buy a very small amount of anything in mass marketing, it's going to have a very small amount of impact.

Mark Ramsey
Author
Fresh Air: Marketing Gurus in Radio

Continuity

Another thing you need to consider is the *duration* (number of days, weeks, months) on your advertising campaign. You may need to run a campaign for only a short period of time. Let's say you've got a big sale on a holiday weekend, so you may want to run your ads for only the week or two before it happens. More typically, you'll have identified a program that has a very good fit with your target audience—perhaps the nightly stock market report on the all-news channel when you want business customers to listen to ads for your insurance company. In that case, you'll want to run your ads continually for a long period of time. This not only makes your prospects familiar with your company name and products/services, but it can create the impression that you're a much larger or more established business, since they become so familiar with you over time.

Non-advertising Radio Options

Many radio stations make other marketing opportunities available to companies that advertise with them. Once you decide to advertise, you should inquire about the possibility of any of the following:

- **Promotions.** Radio stations run a variety of promotional campaigns to raise their own visibility in the community. You can get your name mentioned frequently if you sponsor such an event or supply products or services as giveaways or prizes. For instance, your electronics store could sponsor a radio station's Oscar party or your grocery store could supply food for a radio station's barbecue. Depending on the complexity of the promotion, you may be offered promotional opportunities as part of the cost of your ad campaign or you may have to pay for them separately.

- **Live remotes.** If there's a reason for a radio station to broadcast from your place of business, you can get a great deal of recognition. This is an excellent way to generate buzz and get people to visit you. Live remotes work well for businesses that have high consumer interest (like a club or sporting event venue) or for a company giving away big prizes or offering huge discounts (like a car dealership giving away a new car). Events like these give a station a reason, or "hook," for the live remote.

- **Sponsor profiles.** Some stations will offer you the option of producing a brief segment in which you discuss your business with an announcer, especially in times when they are not running popular programs (such as weekends). Being profiled like this is a good way to get added exposure. Consider such an option if your product or service ties in closely with particular station content—say, profiling your garden supply company after a show on landscaping—or if it has more interesting options and benefits than you can describe in a 30-second spot.

- **Websites.** Most larger radio stations have websites, featuring additional news, information, and downloads, which are often promoted on air. Ask your ad rep about featuring or linking to your company website from their home page. This provides an excellent opportunity to put your business in front of the eyes, as well as the ears, of their listeners.

Creating a Great Radio Ad

A great ad, heard frequently, will remain in the minds of your prospective customers. It doesn't take a huge advertising budget and high-end production resources to create an effective ad. In fact, some of the best commercials are the ones that find a simple, effective way to communicate their message to their prospective customers.

Effective Radio Scheduling Strategies

- **Run the same ad on different stations at the same time.** So even if your listener changes channels (and people do!), they'll be likely to hear your ad. This strategy works best if you're trying to reach a general audience.

- **Run a spot on the same station at different times.** If you've chosen a radio station that reaches your target audience, make sure you reach them by being there at different times of day.

- **Run a spot on the same station at the same time for a long period of time.** If you know your target market is listening to a particular show, keep advertising on that one show for a long period of time to make sure they remember you.

- **Run an ad repeatedly within a short timeframe.** Experts suggest a minimum of 18 to 24 ad buys during one week to be most effective.

- **If you own a retail store or other type of business where customers come to your location or call to order, run the ad when your business is open** or telephone operators are on hand to take orders.

What *Not* to Include in Your Radio Ad

When crafting your radio ad, *don't* include the following:

- **Derogatory comments** about your competition. Instead, focus on your positive attributes.

- **Tongue twisters.** Make sure your ad copy is easy for the announcer to read and for a listener to understand.

- **Inappropriate humor.** Humor can be effective when done well, but jokes often fall flat—especially when heard repeatedly. And do not under any circumstances use racist, sexist, or off-color humor.

- **Too much information.** Remember, people usually can't write anything down and are also distracted by other things when listening to the radio.

Speak Their Language

If you're noticing that many of your patrons speak a language other than English, it may be time to change your advertising venue. Depending on the market you're in, you might be able to find a non-English-language station that could help you target a particular customer demographic. Take advantage of the way that radio caters to market segments by airing your ads where you know your customers will be listening.

An effective radio ad:

- **Mentions the name of your company, product, or service repeatedly**—at least at the beginning and end of the ad but more frequently if possible. Remember, people aren't likely writing anything down.

- **Grabs the listener's attention in the first five seconds.** Since radio listeners are often distracted (driving, for instance), you have to do something to get them to listen to your commercial.

- **Is tailored and appropriate for the station where it's played.** You may not want to include the same content, tone, or delivery for an ad played on a rock station as you would for one played on a classical musical station. Make sure your ad fits the audience.

- **Uses common, one- or two-syllable words.** Listeners can't go back and re-listen to your ad. They have to understand it completely the first time.

- **Makes clear "what's in it" for the listener, focusing on benefits, not features.** For example, if you own a mattress retail company, indicate that you're offering a better night's sleep, one-stop shopping with the best selection in the area, and convenience with same-day delivery—and that you'll take their old mattress away.

- **Features an announcer with a compelling voice** or features a variety of voices, to keep the listener interested.

- **Includes a call to action** to get your listeners, ideally, to respond quickly. "Visit our store for 50% off all merchandise today only!"

- **Gives your contact information clearly, succinctly, and frequently.** It is usually advisable to use landmarks or street intersections ("at Valley Fair Mall" or "At Main and Central") rather than street numbers ("123 Main Street"), since listeners usually can't write details down.

- **Uses music.** Music helps people remember information. Use other sound effects if appropriate.

- **Is punchy.** Use short sentences and eliminate unnecessary words (instead of "Willis Ford is located at Third and Central," say "Willis Ford, Third and Central.") Use contractions; they not only shorten sentences (and make better use of your limited advertising time), but they also make your ad sound friendlier (instead of "You cannot miss," say "You can't miss.")

Once you've written a script for your radio ad, be sure to tape yourself (or someone else) reading it a number of times to hear how it sounds. Ask others to listen to see if they quickly grasp the key parts of your message.

Pricing

Fees for advertising on the radio vary widely and depend on a station's total audience, a program's audience, the nature of the demographics, and the *daypart* (or time of day) selected. Generally, you'll pay the least for the smallest stations and for spots played late at night or, at some stations, on weekends. Commercials on smaller stations range from $10 to $250 per commercial, depending on time of day and program. On larger stations,

BRAINSTORMING

YOUR RADIO AD

Write the script for a 15-, 30-, or 60-second radio spot for your business, product, or service. You can make it a script for an announcer to read, a dialogue between two people, or a vignette. Remember length considerations (generally a bit more than two on-air words per second).

Make sure it includes:

- **Attention grabber**
- **Company name (several times)**
- **Customer benefit**
- **Call to action**
- **Contact information, perhaps more than once**

_____

_____

_____

_____

prime spots (such as morning drive times), may be as low as $400 per commercial (when bought as part of a package), but it's not uncommon for them to cost more than $1,000 per commercial.

But rather than buying just one spot, you'll want to work out a total package or campaign with your ad rep; this will give you room to negotiate better prices and times of day. You can also negotiate for other mentions (such as billboards before or after segments or breaks in programs), participation in promotions, and even live remotes.

One of the best ways to lower the cost of your radio advertising is to purchase ROS (run of schedule) spots. This is advertising that the station can play at any time during their broadcasting hours. Because ROS advertising gives the station a lot more control over when it runs your ad (it can put the ad in prime drive times it hasn't sold or late at night if its ad schedule is full), these types of ads are available at a much-reduced rate. If you feel your ad must be heard at a particular time, opt for the more expensive "tightened rotation" option, which will allow you to specify exactly when you want your ad to be broadcast.

In addition to the cost for your advertising campaign, you need to factor in fees for creating your commercial. This includes the cost of studio time, talent, copywriting, sound editing, and other fees. However, you can negotiate with many stations to include the cost of creating and producing your ad in the total campaign price. This is particularly true when you're preparing scripts for a radio station personality to read. Unless you're a veteran at creating radio ads, take advantage of this and put their experienced creative and production departments to work for your business.

More for Your Money

Radio stations understand that they compete with many different media (print, TV, and the Internet) for companies' advertising dollars, so they usually offer plenty of promotional opportunities for advertisers. This is especially true for stations in smaller markets.

Always ask what special promotions are available. For example, you could get a couple of evening spots thrown in if you advertise at a certain frequency during prime time. Alternatively, you may get extra commercials if you partner with the station in some other promotional endeavor, such as co-sponsoring a concert, a party, or a listener contest.

Comparing Radio Broadcast Media

A number of different options are available for advertising on radio as part of your overall marketing campaign. The challenge is finding the venue that works best for your business—that reaches the right target audience and the largest number of listeners—and gives you the best results for your money. The chart below shows the typical relative cost of many of the available options. The actual costs will vary dramatically, depending on your market and the nature of the station or network chosen. For instance, advertising on a small national network may be less expensive than advertising on a public radio station in a major market. Remember, these are costs relative to other radio options, not costs relative to other advertising or marketing choices.

Radio Return on Investment

The effectiveness of radio advertising can be difficult to measure. Unlike print, or even TV, it is difficult to use coupon codes on the radio (since customers may not be in a position to write anything down). And physical coupons are clearly out of the question! That means you should assess what your baseline of income or sales is *before* you begin a radio ad campaign and then measure the increase in sales, if any, you see as a result of running radio ads. This type of analysis, of course, has its limitations. If you're advertising on a number of radio stations or programs, you can't really determine which one has worked for you. And if you're advertising in other media at the same time, it won't be easy to figure out how much of your new income was attributable to radio sales.

affordability scale

Radio Advertising

$	$$	$$$	$$$$

| College | Local Public Radio | Local Independent Station | Local Affiliate of Major Nat'l Network | National Public Radio | Major National Network |

*COST KEY:

$—Relatively Inexpensive $$—Moderately Expensive $$$—Fairly Expensive $$$$—Expensive

* These symbols represent general rate estimates. Ad rates will vary widely by station reach, region, and time of day.

COMPARING RADIO OUTLETS

MEDIA VENUE	COST	BENEFITS	DRAWBACKS	BEST FOR	TIPS FOR EFFECTIVENESS
COLLEGE	$	Young audience; inexpensive	Content can be edgy; very small geographic reach	Targeting a young, educated demographic	Produce ads in a voice that mirrors the tone of the station
LOCAL PUBLIC RADIO	$–$$	Moderate fees; educated audience; good community image	Sponsorship spots (as opposed to ads) limit format for message	Building positive brand associations; targeting educated, often financially secure listeners	Create a tagline demonstrating your philanthropic nature while still delivering your message
LOCAL COMMERCIAL RADIO	$$–$$$	Medium to large listener base; can target audience; small stations can be inexpensive	Nat'l affiliate & popular stations can be pricey; ads could get lost if not well placed and frequent	Targeting a large segment of your regional customer demographic	Carefully check stations' demographics; see where your competitors are
NATIONAL PUBLIC RADIO	$$$–$$$$	Can reach a large national, educated audience and create a positive image of brand on a national scale	Expensive; limited message format	Enhancing brand image nationally	Same as local public radio above
NATIONAL NETWORK PROGRAMMING	$$$—$$$$	Reaches a national audience of targeted listeners; small networks may be affordable	Expensive for best networks; competition with the big guns may preclude smaller companies from getting good spots	National brand building and sales	Make sure station programming is appropriate; ask about ROS or remnant space (unsold spots you can get at a discount)

Nevertheless, it's useful to try, as much as possible, to determine how well your radio advertising dollars are working for you by doing an ROI, or return on investment, analysis. An ROI analysis shows you whether your radio ad dollars are being well spent. It compares the cost of a radio ad campaign with the results. For example, if you're spending $5,000 per month on ads on a local radio station, and it has resulted in a monthly bump in sales of $7,500, your ROI would be $2,500 (the cost of advertising subtracted from the increased revenue). Based on the ROI analysis, you'll probably choose to continue running your ad.

If you're just starting to advertise on radio and want to get a sense of how cost effective it will be, you'll start by doing an ROI based on estimates of the station's or program's audience (provided by your ad rep or media kit). Keep in mind, however, that you'll need to significantly discount these numbers to figure out your own ROI—just because a radio program has a large audience doesn't mean *you'll* get a large response!

Of course, there are other, non-financial, goals you may want to achieve with your radio advertising. These could include being associated with a station or program or raising your visibility with your target market. Be sure to figure these into your ROI analysis as well.

BRAINSTORMING

YOUR RADIO OUTLETS

To complete the following worksheet, first list the media outlets (specific programs or stations) you feel will be most effective for your company, then detail why you feel they're good matches, project the frequency of your ads, and finally, obtain those stations' rate cards so that you can fill in the costs per ad or per campaign. You'll also need this information to develop your final radio budget.

MEDIA	WHY	FREQUENCY	COST

Calculating Your Radio Advertising ROI

The following page contains a worksheet to help you get started on your own ROI analysis. Simply choose a station you wish your advertising to appear on, and fill in the requested data to get an idea of the ROI you can expect from your radio campaign.

Here are some tips for using the worksheets (and calculating your ROI):

- **Be specific about your financial goals.** This means that you need to include not just the total return you'd like to receive on your advertising investment but what that translates to in terms of customers and expenditures. Thus, if you were preparing this worksheet for a luxury day spa, for example, you'd specify that you wanted to secure five new clients per week for the duration of the 12-week ad campaign. Do the math for that, and it comes out to 60 new customers, paying $1,800 per year each for a total annual return of $108,000 (60 clients x $1,800).

- **Remember non-financial goals.** While you may not be able to put a cash value on things like brand awareness and customer perception, these are important components of any marketing campaign, and as such must be considered when calculating return on investment. Thus, to use the day spa example again, you might cite the following for your non-financial goals: heightened awareness of the brand and association of the spa with a prestigious destination (enabling you to command higher prices for spa services because of the spa's perceived increase in value).

- **Get the data on the station you're targeting.** In other words, *know your audience:* It's not enough to be aware of the size of a station's audience, you also want to know how that audience breaks down demographically so that you can see how well it matches up against your target customers. It's also worth noting whether those demographics shift significantly between day and evening, weekdays and weekend, or during particular shows.

RETURN ON INVESTMENT

YOUR RADIO ADVERTISING ROI

Your business: _____

Your target market: _____

Media (local radio station): _____

GOALS

Financial: _____

Non-financial: _____

MEDIA OUTLET, AUDIENCE, AND FIT WITH MARKET

Station name and format (e.g., soft rock, classical, etc.): _____

Audience size: _____

Listener demographics: _____

Percentage of listeners who fit your target market: _____

Other information (this might include more detailed listener demographics, such as whether the

audience make-up changes from day to evening or during particular shows): _____

PROJECTED COSTS

Cost per spot: _____

Frequency (number of times per day and number of days per week the spot appears): _____

Spot production (some stations offer free production): _____

Total cost (cost per week multiplied by the number of weeks the ad is set to appear): _____

PROJECTED RETURNS, FINANCIAL

Expected new clients as a result of ads: _____

Expected average income per new client per year: _____

Increase in income from advertising: _____

Total cost of ads: _____

Total projected net financial gain (the projected increase in income minus the cost of the ad): _____

PROJECTED RETURNS, NON-FINANCIAL

_____

_____

TOTAL ROI (Total Net Financial Returns Plus Total Non-Financial Returns): _____

RADIO ADVERTISING BUDGET (12 MONTHS)

	JAN	FEB	MARCH	APRIL	MAY
Professional Assistance					
Writers					
Vocal talent					
Studio time					
Technical production					
Radio station production					
Other consultants					
Ad Buys					
Satellite					
National affiliate					
National public radio					
Local commercial					
Local public radio					
College radio					
Other Radio Ad Buys					
Other					
TOTAL					

! **NOTE:** An electronic version of this worksheet is available as part of the Planning Shop's Marketing Budget Templates package.

JUNE	JULY	AUGUST	SEPT	OCT	NOV	DEC	TOTAL

Lingo

AVERAGE AUDIENCE: The estimated audience for a particular TV program during a specified period of time.

BROADCAST TV: Television programming delivered over the public airwaves, which viewers receive free.

CABLE TV: Paid, subscription-based TV programming delivered to viewers through fixed wires (coaxial or fixed optical cables).

DESIGNATED MARKET AREA (DMA): A geographic area, used by Nielsen and others in the TV ad world, to identify a specific local TV market.

DIGITAL VIDEO RECORDER (DVR): A device that enables a viewer to record television programs to watch at a later time, and which also typically enables a viewer to skip ads.

DIRECT RESPONSE (DR) TV: TV commercials designed to get viewers to respond immediately, by placing an order, requesting information, or calling a phone number. DR TV usually includes tracking codes, making it easy to gauge the effectiveness of a commercial.

INDEPENDENT STATION: A television station that is not affiliated with any national television network; typically serving a local market.

INFOMERCIAL: A TV commercial that resembles a TV program. It is usually as long as a TV show (often 30 minutes or more) and often uses sets or personalities that mimic regular TV programs.

NETWORK: A company that creates or acquires programs to be distributed to many TV stations nationally. Some networks (such as ABC, CBS, NBC, and Fox) also own television stations, while others (such as MTV, Food Network, and the Golf Channel) simply provide programming.

NIELSEN RATINGS: A measure of how many viewers a TV station reaches, based on research data from the Nielsen Media Research company.

PRIME TIME: The time most viewers are likely to be watching TV; the main evening TV viewing hours.

RATING: A measure of a show's viewership; each rating point represents 1% of either the total population or a specific demographic group owning TVs who are watching a specific show at a specific time. For example, if a show has a 3 rating with males 18–49, it means that 3% of all males aged 18 to 49 with TVs in that market are watching that program.

REACH: The total number of households receiving a program or TV station.

SATELLITE TV: Paid, subscription-based TV programming delivered to viewers via satellite; viewers must have a satellite dish to receive the signals.

SUBSCRIPTION TV: Television that viewers must pay to receive, generally meaning cable or satellite.

SYNDICATED SHOW: A program that is produced by a national company and then sold, or syndicated, to local stations throughout the country.

CHAPTER 12

Advertising on TV

Have you ever found yourself repeating the words of a TV commercial verbatim? Or perhaps you've gone shopping with a child who, upon seeing a toy advertised on TV, cried, "I want that!" If so, you've experienced the power of TV advertising.

TV is everywhere. In spite of the rise of the Internet, recent studies indicate that television remains the dominant medium in the U.S. and Canada, with close to 99% of all households in the U.S. and 98% of all Canadian households having television sets. The average American watches four hours of TV a day; Canadians watch about three hours. TVs can be found just about everywhere, and people spend significant chunks of time in front of them.

And where there are TVs, there are TV commercials. Commercials have been part of TV since the beginning. These ads are powerful and persuasive, and study after study has shown them to be effective motivators to get customers to buy. Thus, if you have the budget, you should consider TV advertising as part of your marketing plan. TV advertising, however, represents one of the more expensive marketing options, placing it out of reach for many smaller or newer companies. So for many companies, the only way to afford TV as part of their marketing mix is to find creative ways to create and place their commercials.

Benefits of TV Advertising

Television is a powerful advertising medium. In fact, studies indicate that the public considers television to be the most persuasive, authoritative, and influential advertising medium they encounter. There are many reasons for this. One of the most important, however, is that TV taps into two senses: sight and hearing. By so doing, it allows you to be much more creative with your ads, giving you the opportunity to create an emotional connection with a prospect that goes far beyond what other traditional advertising media can offer. Moreover, with a TV ad, your message comes right into a prospect's home via their TV set—typically when they're relaxed and thus likely to be more receptive to messages.

> *One of the biggest mistakes TV advertisers make is not building in any frequency to their ad campaigns. You can't do an ad just once. By advertising frequently, you stay in [people's] heads. If you don't have the budget to be on every week, try every other week. It will give you the appearance of always being there.*
>
> **Loni Amato**
> **President**
> **Ingenious Solutions**

Other benefits of advertising on television:

- **You can reach a large, diverse audience.** TV reaches a "mass market." No other medium reaches as many people at one time. Major programs appeal to wide demographic groups. No other advertising option allows you to reach as many people, or as diverse an audience, as some TV shows.

- **You can target a narrow audience.** If you choose to advertise on smaller stations or cable stations geared to a specific interest or demographic (such as the Golf, Food, Home and Garden, or Outdoor channels), you can find a large audience that is an appropriate fit for your products or services.

- **TV is authoritative.** People believe what they "see" and "hear." Your message becomes more believable when someone gets it from TV, because the viewer often experiences it as real life. That's why many TV ads feature an authoritative-seeming spokesperson talking straight to the viewer.

- **People see only one TV ad at a time**, so you've got the audience to yourself. As long as a viewer stays in front of the TV set without channel surfing or fast-forwarding through your ad using a DVR, you've got the prospect to yourself. Unlike print advertising in newspapers or magazines, your ad isn't competing with others on the same page.

- **You can show how your product or service works.** You can show people using—and enjoying—your product. You can create a positive image associated with your product that they have "seen" for themselves.

- **It's emotional.** You can tell a story, create a feeling, and associate images with your company or product. These positive associations help motivate customers to buy.

- **It's credible.** Appearing on TV gives your business stature and credibility. TV advertising is viewed as expensive, and therefore companies that advertise on TV are seen as mainstream.

- **TV ads show how products are packaged.** This means that even if a person isn't looking for your product, it will likely look familiar when they see it on the shelf.

- **TV advertising reaches customers when they're relaxed.** When their defenses are down, prospects are going to be less skeptical about messages.

- **Your audience is less likely to be distracted.** This is because they aren't paying attention to driving or some other activity, as they often are with radio.

- **TV ads enable you to target a range of geographic audiences.** This runs the gamut from small local populations to a national audience.

- **You have twice the opportunity to get your message across**. Because you engage two senses, sight and hearing, potential customers can hear your message even when they're not directly watching the TV, and they can see your ad even when the volume is turned off.

Challenges of TV Advertising

One of the key challenges of the current TV advertising landscape can be summarized in one word: *DVR*. Digital video recorders, or DVRs, have changed how viewers watch TV commercials. Many of today's viewers don't want to look at ads, so they record programs on a DVR and then fast-forward through the ads—making the money spent on producing and placing them wasted.

Some other challenges TV advertisers face:

- **It's expensive to run a TV ad.** TV is the most expensive advertising medium. A 15-second TV ad on a popular program can cost more than a full-page ad in a major newspaper.

- **It's expensive to create a TV ad.** TV ads are far more expensive to produce than radio or print ads.

- **You pay for eyeballs you never reach.** Rates for TV ads are set based on total viewership—but that doesn't mean all of those people will see your ad. In addition to fast-forwarding through ads, viewers can (and do) channel-surf, leave the room, take phone calls, and otherwise ignore what's on their screens.

- **You reach—and pay for—people who aren't in your target audience.** Unless your target market is broadly defined, TV shows generally reach many more people than are likely to be your customers.

- **Your ROI may not be good for smaller, more targeted stations.** Even when you find affordable TV advertising options on smaller local stations or narrowly targeted cable stations, the response you get may not justify the costs.

- **Results are not very trackable.** It's often very difficult to determine whether your TV ads are leading to actual sales.

- **Major national television programs and larger cable stations have limited airtime available for local programming.** Thus, it can be difficult to buy these spots.

Types of Stations and Programming

Technology has expanded the ways television is delivered to an audience. The major TV delivery systems are:

- **Broadcast.** Traditional television, delivered over the public airwaves to viewers free of charge. Only a limited number of broadcast television stations that can be received, and due to the limitations of transmitting signals over airwaves, broadcast stations are restricted to serving a specific geographic area (though they can carry national programming). Some broadcast stations are owned by national television networks (such as ABC, CBS, NBC, and Fox); others are owned locally and run primarily local or syndicated TV programs (programs produced by national companies but licensed by local stations).

Nielsen Media: Watching the Watchers

Just as print advertisers turn to the Audit Bureau of Circulations and radio advertisers look to Arbitron ratings to find their audiences, TV advertisers depend on Nielsen ratings to figure out how to get the biggest bang for their broadcast ad buck. Nielsen Media Research tracks viewership to determine the size and nature of audiences for television programs. When someone refers to the size of a TV audience, they usually talk about a show's "Nielsen rating."

Advertisers use Nielsen ratings not only to figure out the number of viewers in a particular market, but also to learn about their demographics, such as age, gender, race, education, and income level. That way, they can determine whether enough of their target customers are watching particular shows to make advertising during those programs worthwhile.

Nielsen data is available to you through station ad reps. You can also find some Nielsen data available on its website (www.nielsenmedia.com).

- **Cable.** Programming delivered via coaxial or fiber optic wires. Viewers pay a subscription fee to receive the signals and must install a box to receive and decode the signals. A large number of television stations can be delivered over cable systems, and these systems include both national and local programs and stations. They also tend to offer stations devoted to specific ethnic groups, as well as to specific interests and demographics.

- **Satellite.** Programming delivered via satellite. Viewers pay a subscription fee to receive the signals and must install a satellite dish to receive the television signal. Satellite TV typically delivers an extremely large number of television stations.

- **Internet.** Television programming delivered over the Internet. This can take the form of existing broadcast or cable stations being streamed over the Internet or video content developed specifically for the Web. Internet TV is still in its early days.

Within these delivery systems, there exist many types of TV stations, programming companies, and options for advertisers. The main options for TV advertising include:

- **Local network TV affiliate broadcast stations.** Local stations that carry national programming provided by one of the major television networks, such as ABC, CBS, NBC, or Fox. The stations may be locally owned or owned by the network itself. They usually have very large local audiences—they are often the most-watched stations in any local market. Advertising on these TV stations gives you access to a broad, geographically based mainstream audience during prime time or during well-watched programs such as news and sports. However, advertising on larger local stations can be expensive, and audiences tend to be less targeted than those of cable stations.

- **Local independent broadcast stations.** Local stations that are not affiliated with any national network. These stations usually have somewhat smaller audiences than network affiliates, and their advertising rates are somewhat lower. The programming tends to include many syndicated shows, as well as some locally originated shows. Advertising on these locally produced shows may be the most affordable. Stations that run these programs tend to reach a larger audience than most local cable stations. The programs may be aimed at a general mass audience, or they may be more targeted to specific audiences.

- **Local public television broadcast stations.** As with public radio stations, public TV stations are noncommercial and nonprofit. They are supported by donations from viewers and sponsors who don't advertise but donate funds to sponsor the station or specific programs. Most local public stations produce a number of community affairs shows. Due to the nature of their programming, the audience for public television tends to be limited, but in general, it is well-educated, socially aware, and from higher-income groups. If this is your target audience, you can gain visibility by paying for short sponsorship announcements accompanying specific programs. Remember, however, that your airtime will be limited as will the format for delivering your message.

■ **National broadcast networks.** A broadcast network providing content such as sitcoms, reality TV, movies, newscasts, and sports events to its affiliated local stations. (Some local affiliates may actually be owned by the national network.) National network TV shows are seen nationwide at the same time, attracting millions of viewers, especially in prime time. These are the most expensive shows on which to advertise, because of their large reach and diverse consumer audience. While most advertising time on these national broadcast shows is purchased by ad agencies for major national advertisers, many such shows offer a limited number of slots for local advertisers.

■ **National public television programs.** These are programs produced or distributed by the Public Broadcasting Service (PBS) or produced by other major local public television stations (such as WGBH in Boston) and distributed throughout the national public television stations. These programs are designed to be noncommercial and are supported by charitable foundations, viewers, and corporate sponsors—who receive recognition for their support. Sponsorship of national public TV programs can be expensive but provides access to a large audience of educated, financially secure individuals. The nature of the recognition you will receive is limited in time and format, but you receive the positive connection of being associated with a program highly valued and respected by its audience.

■ **National commercial cable (or satellite).** These are stations that produce programs designed for a national audience and delivered nationally over stations on cable or satellite systems—meaning they're only available to those who pay a subscription fee. If you're trying to access a large, highly targeted audience, these stations offer a promising venue. However, cable TV ad opportunities can be difficult to buy. Some of the bigger national stations, like ESPN, allow limited time per hour for local advertisers (usually two to three minutes), making competition tough for these pricey spots. Other stations, though, are highly specialized and not as coveted by a large group of advertisers.

■ **Local commercial cable.** Every cable operator has a number of stations that are owned and operated by local companies. These stations carry a wide variety of TV programming, targeted largely to very specific demographic groups, including ethnic or religious communities. These shows offer relatively low-cost opportunities to reach a highly targeted audience with your message. Local commercial cable stations also run programming such as older movies, syndicated TV shows, and reruns of old shows, appealing to a wider audience. Advertising on these local cable stations is among the least expensive options for getting your message out through television. In addition, many of these stations offer the chance to buy time for paid programming, such as infomercials, especially late at night.

■ **Local community cable/Public access stations.** Cable operators are generally required to dedicate a certain number of stations to the public good. In addition to stations covering local community government (transmitting city council meetings, for instance), there are certain *public access* and community stations that carry locally produced programs. These stations target a very local audience, which means their reach is limited to the community's geographic area. Just about anyone with a programming idea can get airtime. This programming isn't technically advertising, but rather an opportunity to present yourself as an expert (on a local talk show, for example). The atmosphere is informal, and production quality is on the low end. These stations generally have low audience numbers and reach, but if you're looking for local customers, they can provide inexpensive exposure for you and your business.

Key Considerations for Advertising on TV

When choosing to place an ad on television as part of your overall marketing plan, these are the key considerations to keep in mind:

- Effective content and message
- Type of ad
- Length of ad
- Time—or daypart—when an ad is run
- Station/program where an ad is run
- Frequency
- Continuity

Effective Content and Message

No matter how many times you run a spot, the message and content of your ad must get viewers to remember your name and motivate them to purchase. If not you'll be wasting your money. (For more about what makes an effective TV ad, see page 141.)

Type of Ad

Television, like radio, offers a number of advertising options:

- **Spot.** A "spot" can mean many things in connection with TV advertising. It can be used colloquially to refer to any commercial ("I'm running a TV spot now to promote our new golf clubs"), but the more precise meaning of the term is: *purchasing an ad on a specific channel at a specific time in specific markets.* In other words, you choose which program/station you want to run your ad on and at which time in which markets. ("I want a 15-second ad on the Golf Channel, four times during the PGA tournament, every half hour, in Atlanta, Phoenix, San Diego, and Dallas.") This gives you the best chance of reaching exactly the market you are targeting. It is also the most expensive form of TV advertising.

- **Remnant.** Unsold advertising space or time is referred to as *remnant,* or *remainder,* ads. After a TV station has sold all the ads for a particular program, there may be some time left over. As an advertiser, you can purchase this remnant ad space at a significant discount. Of course, your audience will not be as targeted and it may be smaller, and the programs and times when your ad runs may be far less desirable. Instead of appearing on the Golf Channel during the PGA tournament, your ad for golf clubs may run on a late-night rerun of an old movie about golf. But remnants offer a far less expensive way to get your ads on TV.

■ **Sponsorship.** Instead of advertising on a show, you can "sponsor" a program. This is typically used with public television but can also be used with independent TV stations, both broadcast and cable. Sponsorships get your name mentioned ("Brought to you by ...") at least twice during a specific program (at the beginning and end). They also enable you to target a specific audience and become positively associated with a show that appeals to your market. While sponsoring a national TV show is extremely expensive, companies with smaller advertising budgets can sponsor specific shows in small markets or on local cable TV channels. For instance, your knitting shop could sponsor a knitting program on Sunday afternoons on a local cable channel.

■ **Billboards/Tags.** Just as with radio, TV programs can mention your company or product name as a lead-in or follow-up to a program (or commercial break). This is often done with sponsorships, but you might be able to negotiate a mention, especially with local stations. For instance, before the weather segment on the local news channel, the announcer might say, "The weather is brought to you by Austin Optometry, helping you see clearly on even the cloudiest day." These ads can be cost effective because they don't cost anything for you to produce and viewers do not fast-forward through or skip these mentions.

■ **Product placement.** Having your product shown on part of a TV program, often prominently. One way to prevent viewers from skipping over your ads using DVRs is to have your product shown on the program itself. On national programs, major advertisers work with production companies to get their cars, clothes, furniture, soft drinks, and much more used and seen on TV shows (and in movies). They may pay substantial sums for this opportunity, as well as providing product. However, you can approach producers of local programs that appeal to your target audience to see if you can provide product in return for the station including it in a show. For instance, you could offer your line of pet care products to a local TV show about animals.

■ **Infomercial.** An ad that is the same length and style as a TV program. Typically, it calls on viewers to immediately purchase a product or otherwise take action—known as *DR (direct response)* programming. Infomercials can be relatively inexpensive to produce, and they're usually shown during the least expensive times to advertise on TV (overnight). Infomercials are good for products or services that appeal to a broad segment of a consumer audience and where there is an immediate incentive to buy.

Length of Ad

TV stations sell "air time," so the price of TV ads is based on the duration of the commercial. Generally, most TV ads are sold in 15-second increments. The most common length for commercials on most popular stations is either 15 or 30 seconds. But it is possible to get longer ads (for instance, 60 seconds) or even purchase 30-minute (or longer) segments for infomercials.

Research has shown viewers are better able to remember shorter commercials (15 seconds) ; however, research has also shown that shorter ads, while being more memorable, are less persuasive in getting customers to buy.

Ticking Away the Hours

Like radio, television is divided into *dayparts*; you can choose to run your ads during certain dayparts as well as during specific programs.

TV dayparts are divided into:

■ Early morning: 6:00 a.m.–9:00 a.m.

■ Daytime: 9:00 a.m.–3:30 p.m.

■ Early fringe: 3:30 p.m.–5:30 p.m.

■ Early news: 5:30 p.m.–7:00 p.m.

■ Prime access: 7:00 p.m.–8:00 p.m.

■ Prime time: 8:00 p.m.–11:00 p.m. (Mon–Sat); 7:00 p.m.–11:00 p.m. (Sun)

■ Late news: 11:00 p.m.–11:30 p.m.

■ Late fringe: 11:30 p.m.–1:00 a.m.

■ Late night: 1:00 a.m.–6:00 a.m.

If you don't have the budget to run many short ads, you may actually want to run fewer, longer ads, like 30-minute infomercials late at night. While these may reach only a small number of viewers, the viewers who stick with your ad are more likely to be persuaded to purchase.

Time

When choosing what time of day to run your ad, the three most important considerations are:

1. **Fit with your target market.** If you're trying to reach housewives or seniors, morning or afternoon will be a good choice; if you're trying to reach college-age males, late fringe will be a good time.

2. **Size of market.** If you want to reach a large market, you need to choose times when the most viewers are tuning in.

3 **Budget.** Advertising rates vary dramatically, depending on the daypart. Prime time is the most expensive time to advertise, and overnight is typically the least expensive time to advertise.

Station/Program

If you're running spot ads or sponsorships, you'll have the opportunity to choose a specific program that you want your ad to run with. If you're using remnant or other, less expensive choices of ads, you may only have a choice of station.

The critical consideration in choosing a program or station is determining how well its viewers fit the demographics and characteristics of your prospective customers. TV stations will usually have a media kit describing the demographic make-up of their viewers, and you will want to read and evaluate it very carefully.

Cable TV gives you the opportunity to choose a station that aligns with the interests of your target market. A Home and Garden station is perfect for advertising your garden supply company; a Health and Fitness station will attract viewers interested in your new gym.

Frequency

How often will you run your ad? As with all forms of advertising, repetition is key. The more often you run an ad, the greater the likelihood that a viewer will be exposed to your message.

There are two main ways to plan frequency for TV advertising:

■ **Many times of day on the same station.** If you know a station reaches your target market (for example, the Golf Channel for your golf clubs), you may want to run your ad throughout the day.

■ **Many different stations at the same time of day.** If your product or service is aimed at a broader audience and you know a time when *your* audience is most likely to tune in (for instance, seniors for the early evening news), you may want to try to advertise at the same time on many different stations. This increases the chances that your target market will see your ad.

Continuity

Another way to increase the repetition of your advertising is not only to run it frequently over a short period of time, but also to run your ad continually over a long period of time. By continuing to run an ad for many weeks or months, viewers become familiar with you and have a greater chance of remembering your name and message.

Sponsorships may represent a relatively affordable way to establish continuity with a particular target audience. By sponsoring a specific show, your name becomes associated with that program throughout the season or throughout its lifetime. For instance, if your restaurant sponsors (via a "billboard" ad) the local movie review segment of the evening news every Thursday night, the audience will become familiar with your restaurant and be more likely to give it a try.

Creating a Great TV Ad

You're probably most familiar with the ads run by major companies during popular TV shows. Most often, these ads are all about building and reinforcing a brand. They're intended to get viewers to remember the name of the product or company and associate that name with a certain feeling, rather than leading customers to making an immediate purchase or taking an immediate action. For example, "The Ultimate Driving Machine" (BMW) or "Zoom-Zoom" (Mazda) commercials are designed to establish an association with the brand (a great, fun driving experience) rather than focusing on the specific benefits and features, let alone price, of the autos advertised.

Entrepreneurial companies, which tend to be newer and smaller, typically don't have the budgets to run ads just to create brand image. Instead, their ads have to pay off—show a direct return on investment—with increased sales as a result of the ads. This means that when you craft your TV ad, you have to build it around motivating the audience to purchase your product or service. It can be a relatively soft sell ("Come visit us at our new location at Main and Grand"), or it can direct viewers to take a specific action (such as going to your website, coming to your store, or calling a phone number). A great TV ad:

- ■ **Mentions the name of the product or company repeatedly and shows it on screen.** Remember, an ad cannot be effective in increasing sales if viewers do not remember your name.

- ■ **Has a clear, memorable message.** You must clearly tell the audience what you want them to think or do. This is often conveyed by the use of a tagline that's repeated in a jingle or song.

- ■ **Conveys benefit(s) to the user/purchaser.** Viewers should be able to visualize how they will benefit by using your product or service or by patronizing your company.

- ■ **Engages both hearing and sight, using visuals, words, music, and sounds**. Take advantage of the benefits of television to involve the viewer's eyes and ears. In fact, make sure your message and name can be heard even when the viewer isn't watching the screen or seen even when a person isn't listening.

Don't Forget Co-op

Just as with other forms of traditional advertising (print and radio), manufacturers and vendors make funds available to their retail partners to help offset the cost of TV ads. Check with your vendors to see what co-op money they have available for you to use. Some vendors may even have video that you can use as part of your TV commercial.

Working with an Ad Agency

If your company has a budget large enough to allow you to advertise on TV regularly and repeatedly (especially on major national channels), you may want to consider working with an advertising agency. An agency will help you determine what to put in your ad and where, when, and how frequently to advertise. They can also help you create and produce your ad. Because ad agencies work with TV programmers all the time, they may be able to help you find or negotiate better prices. Agencies generally get a commission from the TV channels/stations on the ads you place, as well as charging you for their creative services directly.

"Video" on the Cheap

If you're working with a very small ad budget and can't afford to produce your own decent-quality video, you can make an inexpensive commercial that still uses images and sound effectively by pursuing any of the following options:

■ **Photo slide montage.** One method is to use a voice-over announcer with a montage of photo slides that take the place of video. Done well, this can look almost like video. It's a very inexpensive way to produce a TV ad and can be used for late-night ads on local cable or independent stations. It's especially good for local restaurants, hotels, retail outlets, and such.

■ **Get the station running your ad to help you produce it.** You may be able to negotiate some services in return for signing a contract.

■ **Do-it-yourself digital video.** Software makes it easy to edit your own video, and if you're capable, you may be able to produce fairly decent-quality video if you are not overly ambitious—for instance, if you stick to a very simple set and people just sitting or talking.

■ **Stock video.** Just as with still photos, stock video is available from agencies that sell pre-produced, high-quality video that you can buy inexpensively on a "royalty-free" basis. In other words, you pay for it one time and can use it as many times as you wish. You can find a wide variety of stock video at relatively little cost. Just do an Internet search on "stock video."

■ **Attracts attention quickly.** People are exposed to so many ads that it's hard to get noticed. As much as possible, you want to capture the audience's attention quickly so they can notice your name and message.

■ **Uses people.** Research has shown that customers relate better to ads that show people, not just places or things.

■ **Evokes feelings, associations, and images.** You're trying to create a connection with the viewer. By calling on their emotions, you help the audience connect with your product or company.

■ **Aligns with your brand.** An ad should extend and reinforce your brand, so make sure that the message, quality, look, and content of your ad is aligned with your brand.

■ **Has good production quality.** Poorly produced ads reduce your credibility.

■ **Avoids hyperbole.** Viewers are suspicious of marketing hype. Make positive statements about the benefits and features of your product or service, but be careful not to overpromise or oversell.

■ **Includes a clear call to action.** If you want viewers to do something specific as a result of seeing your ad ("Come on down this Saturday"), be very clear in your call to action.

■ **Is truthful.** Be careful not to make claims or comparisons that stretch or alter the truth. Not only is this unethical; it may also be illegal.

■ **Provides clear, easy-to-remember contact info.** This could be a website address, phone number, address, or other way to reach you.

■ **Includes a way to track responses (if doing DR advertising).** This could be a special coupon code, website, phone number, or other unique identifier for each commercial, program, or TV station.

TV Advertising Costs

Generally more expensive than other forms of advertising, TV ads are often out of reach of smaller or newer companies. Just as with print and radio, pricing is done on a CPM, or cost-per-thousand, basis. The more viewers a program or station has, the more money you pay. Having rates quoted to you on a CPM basis gives you a baseline to compare how much it costs to reach a thousand prospects in print versus radio versus TV.

Certain times of day, or dayparts, will cost less, not just because there are fewer viewers, but also on a CPM basis. That's because viewers at those times may be deemed less desirable; they may be less likely to make purchases, have lower household income, or be demographic groups less in demand by major advertisers.

Spot advertising is the most expensive option, as you choose a specific time, program, and market in which to advertise. In other words, if you want to be sure that your ad is shown during "American Idol" in Chicago in the month of March, you're going to pay a very high price for that time and space.

Remnant advertising, in contrast, can save you a lot of money—anywhere from 60% to 75% of the cost of a spot ad (and sometimes more).

BRAINSTORMING

YOUR TV AD

Use this worksheet to create an outline of a sample TV ad for your product, business, or service.

First, indicate how you will include:

Company name (several times): _____

Message: _____

Customer benefit: _____

Visuals: _____

Sound: _____

Attention grabber: _____

People: _____

Emotional triggers: _____

Brand reinforcements: _____

Call to action: _____

Company contact information: _____

Then specify what format your ad will take: _____

Commercial (indicate length: 15-, 30-, 60-second): _____

Simple announcement with visuals, or story? _____

Sponsorship/Billboard/Tag: _____

Infomercial: _____

Next, write a draft of your ad: _____

_____

_____

_____

_____

_____

_____

_____

_____

_____

_____

_____

_____

However, when purchasing remnant advertising, you're not guaranteed specific times or programs (or geographic markets, if buying remnants on national channels). You may be able to purchase remnant space for as little as $500 to $2,000 a spot, even on national cable, if you purchase a large number of ads and give up all control over when the ad will run.

The least expensive options for using TV as part of your overall marketing plan include:

- **Local cable stations.** They may reach a small audience, but if you choose the outlet well, they may give you a very targeted audience (for instance, advertising your restaurant on a local show devoted to food).

- **Late night.** Running ads overnight is definitely the cheapest option. You may reach a smaller audience, but you'll be able to advertise more frequently. This is a good option for infomercials.

- **Product placement.** This is the most affordable option if you can get your products used—and seen—on TV in return for giving the show products or services.

- **Local commercial stations.** These are more expensive than local cable stations but generally reach a larger audience and may be very affordable, especially in smaller cities or late at night.

TV stations have standard rate cards and specific advertising schedules to choose from. And just like print and radio, they offer deals to customers who buy more frequently.

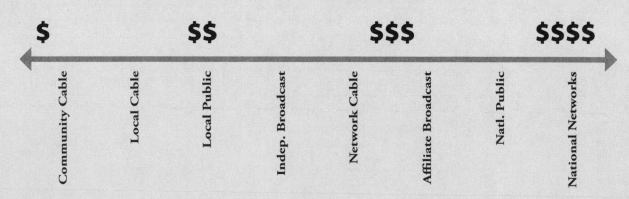

*These symbols represent general rate estimates and are based on comparing one type of TV ad to another, not to other forms of advertising (for instance, print). Ad rates will vary widely by station, reach, region, and time of day.

COMPARING TV OUTLETS

VENUE	COST	BENEFITS	DRAWBACKS	BEST FOR	TIPS FOR EFFECTIVENESS
LOCAL NETWORK-AFFILIATE STATION (BROADCAST)	$$–$$$$	Reaches large numbers of a mass consumer audience in a specific geographic area	Expensive, especially for popular shows; audience not targeted	Broadcasting to a large, regional, less-targeted base of potential customers	Work with the station to find ad deals; look for co-op ad opportunities; choose time slots/ programs carefully
LOCAL INDEPENDENT STATION (BROADCAST)	$–$$$	Reaches relatively large numbers of mass audience; may have specially targeted programs	Can be costly in larger markets; audiences may not be targeted; smaller viewership than network affiliates	Less expensive option for reaching mass audience in a locality than affiliate stations; late-night options may be very affordable	Seek out less expensive shows and time slots; may have opportunities for paid programming and infomercials; ask for help producing ads
LOCAL PUBLIC TV (BROADCAST)	$–$$$	Can be affordable, especially in smaller markets	Offers sponsorships, not ads, with limited formats and time lengths for your message	Building positive brand image with local community; reaching an affluent market; helping support local community affairs programs	Include an effective tagline, as well as your company name, in your announcement; ask to include your website address
NATIONAL BROADCAST NETWORKS	$$$$	Provides access to the largest viewing audience	Very expensive; harder to target audience; big corporations buy up the best spots on multiple stations	Launching or promoting a very well-funded consumer product aimed at a mass market	Ask about "remnant" or unsold space: you won't be able to target your programs, but it will be much less expensive
NATIONAL PUBLIC TV (BROADCAST)	$$$–$$$$	Reaches a national audience of often educated, financially stable listeners	Offers sponsorships, not ads, with limited formats and time lengths for your message; can be expensive	Reaching large audience; providing positive association with a respected national entity	Include an effective tagline, as well as your company name in your announcement; ask to include your website address
NATIONAL COMMERCIAL CABLE	$$$–$$$$	Reaches a targeted audience of national subscribers	Expensive, especially for most popular networks; limited space for local ads	Targeting a specific national TV audience	Find stations that are an excellent fit to your customer base; look for "remnant" or unsold ad space to get deals
LOCAL COMMERCIAL CABLE	$–$$	Can be very affordable; can reach a targeted, local audience; larger audience than many print or radio options at similar price	Reaches small audience relative to other TV options; audience may not be motivated buyers	Reaching ethnic or other specific demographic groups; reaching a target group in your community	Late-night ads will be cheapest; consider running "paid programming," or infomercials, on these stations; ask for help in producing ads
LOCAL COMMUNITY CABLE/PUBLIC ACCESS STATIONS	$	Provides inexpensive access to a very local audience	Limited reach; limited credibility; low production values; have to create "program" rather than ad	Targeting neighbourhood and local customers; getting your first TV ad made	Create your first TV video at little expense; gain some credibility as an expert

BRAINSTORMING

YOUR TV OUTLETS

To complete the following worksheet, first list the media outlets (specific programs or stations) you believe will be most effective for your company, then delineate the reason these stations/programs represent good choices. Next, project how frequently you'll run your ads and finally, use your chosen stations' rate cards to calculate the costs per ad or per campaign. You'll need this information to develop your TV budget.

MEDIA	REASON	FREQUENCY	COST

Costs of Producing an Ad

In addition to what you'll spend on advertisement time slots, you will have to allocate funds for the creation of the ad itself. In most cases, you'll pay to have your ad created and produced. This may mean hiring a creative team: a writer, director, actors, videographer, and lighting and sound technicians. Or you may decide to hire an advertising agency or other creative team to create and produce the ad for you. These costs can add up. A top-of-the line TV commercial for a major national advertiser can easily cost more than a million dollars. Smaller companies, of course, can find less expensive video or TV ad producers. You may be able to produce a custom commercial for as little as $20,000 to $50,000.

For many entrepreneurial companies, that amount is still way out of reach. So look for some more creative, less expensive options (see sidebar on page 142).

Comparing TV Broadcast Media

There are a number of different options for advertising on television as part of your overall marketing campaign. The challenge is finding the venue that works best for your business—that reaches the right target audience and the largest number of viewers and gives you the best results for your money. The chart above shows the typical relative cost of many of the available options. The actual costs will vary dramatically, depending on your market and the nature of the station or network chosen. For instance, advertising on a small national network may be less expensive than advertising on a public television station in a major market. Remember, these are costs relative to other TV options, not to other advertising or marketing choices.

Television Return on Investment

Television is costly in comparison to most other forms of advertising. So if you decide to use TV advertising as part of your marketing mix, you'll want to make sure you're getting your money's worth. Unfortunately, the effectiveness of TV ads is notoriously hard to measure. Sure, large advertising agencies have methods of tracking the response to TV ads, including hiring market research firms to interview viewers of the shows they advertise on. But those methods are out of reach of most entrepreneurial companies.

That's why most smaller and newer companies that advertise on TV choose to do DR—or direct response—advertising. In DR ads, the viewer is called on to take an immediate action ("Call now. Our operators are standing by.") and is typically given a special code to use for a discount ("Just mention TV25 to get free shipping!"), a special phone number, or a special website URL. By including a special code (and an incentive to get viewers to use the code) for each TV outlet you advertise on, you can track which TV programs or stations are bringing you the best results. In other words, when you advertise on the Home and Garden Network, you can prompt viewers to "Use Code TV HGTV to get free shipping" and when you advertise on the Food Network, you can have a voice-over announcer say, "Use Code FoodTV to get free shipping." You can then easily see which station brings you the most calls. All of this enables a company to track where customers are coming from and to determine whether they are getting a positive return on their financial investment.

Even if you don't use DR advertising, you should try to determine how much new business a TV ad campaign will bring in. One way to do this is to measure, as accurately as you can, your sales volume before you begin your ad campaign and then monitor the amount your sales increase once your TV advertising has begun.

You'll then need to do a return on investment (ROI) analysis to determine whether your ad dollars are or will be well spent, comparing the costs of an ad with the results. For example, if you're spending $10,000 per month on ads on a local TV station and have seen a monthly $40,000 bump in sales, your ROI would be $30,000 (the increased return minus the cost of advertising). Based on that ROI analysis, you'll probably choose to continue running your ad. But you will want to continue to do an ongoing ROI, because your results may lessen over time.

If you're just starting advertising on TV and want to get a sense of how cost effective it will be, you'll start by doing an ROI based on estimates of the station's or program's audience (provided by your ad rep or media kit). But these numbers must be significantly discounted to figure out your own ROI! Remember, many viewers will be skipping the ads entirely, and many will never respond to your advertising message. Even if you advertise on a TV program with a large audience, you may not get a large response.

Of course, there are other, non-financial, goals you may want to achieve with your TV advertising: being associated with a particular program, raising your visibility, getting professional-quality video you can use repeatedly in other marketing efforts (for example, on your website). So you will want to figure these into your ROI analysis as well.

Calculating Your TV ROI

The following page contains a worksheet to help you get started on your own ROI analysis. Simply choose a station you wish your advertising to appear on, and fill in the requested data to get an idea of the ROI you can expect from your TV ad campaign.

Here are some tips for using the worksheets (and calculating your ROI):

■ **Be specific about your financial goals.** This means that you need to include not just the total return you'd like to receive on your advertising investment but what that translates to in terms of customers and expenditures. Thus, if you were preparing this worksheet for, say, a boat dealership looking to increase its sales within a community surrounding a large lake, you might specify that you would like to make one sale per week for the duration of your six-week TV ad campaign. You would then figure out the average price of that sale and multiply it by six to get your target number.

■ **Remember non-financial goals.** While you may not be able to put a cash value on things like brand awareness and customer perception, these are important components of any marketing campaign, and as such must be considered when calculating return on investment. Thus, to use the boat dealership example again, you might cite the following for your non-financial goals: increased awareness of your new boat line and heightened visibility of your brand.

■ **Get the data on the station you're targeting.** In other words, *know your audience:* It's not enough to be aware of the size of a station's audience, you also want to know how that audience breaks down demographically so that you can see how well it matches up against your target customers. It's also worth noting whether those demographics shift significantly between day and evening, weekdays and weekend, or during particular shows.

RETURN ON INVESTMENT

YOUR TV ADVERTISING ROI

Your business: _____

Your target market: _____

Media (TV station): _____

GOALS

Financial goals: _____

Non-financial goals: _____

MEDIA OUTLET, AUDIENCE, AND FIT WITH TARGET MARKET

Station name: _____

Audience size: _____

Viewer demographics: _____

Percentage of viewers that fit target market: _____

Other information (this might include anything else that makes the station significant, such as viewer income levels, the fact that its evening news is the consistent market leader, etc.): _____

PROJECTED COSTS

Ad production: _____

Cost per spot: _____

Spots per week: _____

Number of weeks in campaign: _____

Total number of spots: _____

Total costs for spots: _____

Total costs for advertising campaign: _____

PROJECTED RETURNS, FINANCIAL

Expected new sales as a result of ads: _____

Expected average income per sale: _____

Increase in income from advertising: _____

Total cost of ads: _____

Total projected net financial gain (the projected increase in income minus the cost of the ad): _____

PROJECTED RETURNS, NON-FINANCIAL

_____

_____

TOTAL ROI (Total Net Financial Returns Plus Total Non-Financial Returns): _____

TV ADVERTISING BUDGET (12 MONTHS)

	JAN	FEB	MARCH	APRIL	MAY
Professional Assistance					
Writing					
Talent					
Wardrobe					
Hair and makeup artists					
Set design					
Location rental					
Video crew					
Studio time					
Location travel					
Food for crew					
Ad agency					
Technical production					
TV station production					
Other consultants					
Ad Buys					
Local community/Public					
Local public TV stations					
Local network TV affiliates					
National public television					
Commercial stations					
National broadcast networks					
Other TV ad buys					
Other					
TOTAL					

NOTE: An electronic version of this worksheet is available as part of the Planning Shop's Marketing Budget Templates package.

JUNE	JULY	AUGUST	SEPT	OCT	NOV	DEC	TOTAL

BUILDING YOUR MARKETING PLAN

TRADITIONAL ADVERTISING

Drawing from the worksheets in this section, plan the traditional tactics you will use in your campaign.

1. Will you include traditional advertising (print, radio, or TV advertising) in your marketing plan? If so, which of the traditional advertising channels described in this section will you use?

_____

_____

_____

_____

_____

2. What is the message you will focus on in your traditional advertising campaign? After seeing or hearing your ad, what do you want people to remember about your company, product, or service, and what action would you like them to take?

_____

_____

_____

_____

_____

3. What is the goal of your traditional advertising campaign? Is it to build your brand (company and/ or products/services), to directly drive sales, to promote a specific offering or event, or other?

_____

_____

_____

_____

4. Which specific media outlets will you use to advertise your company, product, or services? (Use the names of the publications and stations you collected in the worksheets for choosing your media outlets that you filled out for print, radio, and TV.)

_____

_____

_____

_____

Print outlets:

_____

_____

Radio outlets:

_____

_____

TV outlets:

_____

_____

5. Why did you choose these specific outlets? How well do these outlets reach your target demographic market? What other aspects of these outlets make them an appropriate fit for your marketing plan?

_____

_____

_____

_____

6. Describe the timing and frequency of your traditional advertising campaign. When will you run your ads (time of year, time of day), and how frequently will you run them?

_____

_____

_____

_____

7. How will advertising in traditional media—and the specific traditional media outlets you've chosen—bring you closer to your marketing goals?

_____

_____

_____

_____

_____

_____

_____

SECTION III

Person-to-Person Marketing

Lingo

INFLUENCER: A person whose opinion affects other people's buying decisions. An influencer can be another person in the same company, someone in the media (such as a columnist who does product reviews), an industry leader, or a celebrity.

LEADS: Individuals or businesses that are potential customers for your business. One of the primary goals of all marketing activities is to generate leads for future sales.

NETWORKING: Any activity where you interact with people to build your business. This can be done in a formal situation (such as at a networking event or trade show) or in an informal situation (such as business entertaining). Your list of connections with other businesspeople, referral sources, and prospects is referred to as your *network*.

PERSON-TO-PERSON MARKETING: Any activity that involves building your business by interacting directly with other people, generally on a one-to-one basis. Now includes person-to-person marketing done over the Internet. Also referred to as *peer-based* marketing or *contact-based* marketing.

PUBLIC RELATIONS (PR): Activities that generate a positive public opinion of your company, products, or services, primarily by interacting with the media to generate stories, reviews, product mentions, or other coverage. Leveraging this unpaid media coverage to increase public awareness of your company, products, or services.

TESTIMONIAL: A statement from a past or current customer (or others in a position to know), testifying to the qualities of a company, product, or service. Testimonials serve as evidence that a company can deliver on its promises and can be powerful in persuading others to purchase.

TRADE SHOW: Events, usually held on an annual basis, that attract members of a common industry who come to network, purchase, make sales, and view the latest products, services, and developments.

WORD-OF-MOUTH: A type of marketing that occurs when people (usually other customers) provide recommendations, testimonials, and product and service information to prospects.

CHAPTER 13

The Power of Person-to-Person

When it comes to marketing, nothing beats the power of other people. Human interaction is the strongest motivator to get someone to buy. Whether it's sitting down to lunch with a referral source, a former customer recommending your company to a friend, or a staff person meeting a prospect at a trade show, when you can engage someone on the person-to-person level, you have a much better chance of increasing your business.

Consider the power of person-to-person marketing from the customer's point of view. If you're a business owner looking for a website developer, you're likely to trust the recommendation of another business owner who contracted and had a good experience with a specific Web development company. That's a lot stronger motivator than seeing an ad somewhere. You may even be more comfortable hiring a Web developer you've met at a business event or a trade show, because at least you've met them face to face.

That's the power of person-to-person marketing. And that's why you'll want to make person-to-person marketing a major part of your marketing plan, regardless of what type of business or industry you're in.

> **"** *Networking is a reciprocal exchange of people sharing contacts, leads, resources, information, and business. It's the art of giving, not the art of getting. Real networking comes when you can help someone who can perhaps never pay you back.* **"**
>
> **Sandra Yancey**
> **Founder and CEO**
> **eWomenNetwork**

What Is Person-to-Person Marketing?

Broadly defined, person-to-person marketing is any activity that involves building your business by interacting directly with other people. Anyone you meet can serve as a promotional agent for your business. There are several activities associated with this type of marketing. They include:

- **Networking.** These are activities where you interact directly with other people with the aim of building your business.

- **Word-of-mouth marketing.** These are marketing activities designed to get people (usually customers) to provide recommendations, testimonials, and product and service information to prospects.

- **Trade shows.** These are events that bring together people and companies in an industry to show off the latest products or services, get acquainted, and make sales.
- **Public relations.** These are tactics aimed at generating positive public awareness of your company, primarily through the media.

Your Message

In any form of marketing, it's important to know what you want people to remember—that is, your *message*. But in person-to-person marketing, it's even more critical that you focus on your message. In other forms of marketing (such as in an ad), you have a limited amount of space to get your message out, so you're likely to be thoughtful and efficient. But in person-to-person situations, you may feel like you can ramble on forever, meaning you might never get to the point—which would not be good marketing!

Lead Generation

One of the primary goals of person-to-person marketing is to generate *leads* for your business. Leads represent the names and contact information of potential customers, and person-to-person marketing provides a particularly effective means of generating them. Here's how it works: Let's say your company makes solar panels for commercial buildings. You decide to attend an industry event for architects, and the event includes a "networking hour," during which you meet a number of architects who build large corporate buildings. During the networking time, you don't try to corner an architect and make a sale. Instead, you "work the room," meeting a number of architects, telling them what your company does and exchanging business cards.

Testimonials

Since people trust other people when making purchasing decisions, one effective extension of person-to-person marketing is the testimonial—or statement—from a past or current customer (or other) saying how great your company, product, or service is. Place testimonials in your marketing materials, ads, and website—even on your packaging.

Influencers

While most of your person-to-person marketing will be directed to potential customers, another target may be *influencers,* or those people who will affect prospects' buying decisions. Influencers can take the form of someone in the media, a well-known person in an industry, or a popular leader in a consumer niche. For instance, when Walter Mossberg, the *Wall Street Journal* technology columnist, reviews a technology product, he has a great deal of influence on businesspeople considering buying the product.

It Won't Work for Wallflowers

MYTH: I'm too shy to do person-to-person marketing

BUSTED: You don't have to be the most gregarious person you know or a salesperson at heart to be effective at person-to-person marketing. By selecting the right type of person-to-person marketing, learning a few simple techniques, and preparing before meeting with people, even the shy can shine. And don't forget the Internet! Online person-to-person marketing can be effective for even the shiest businessperson.

The Internet Multiplier Effect

Person-to-person marketing doesn't just happen in person. The power of recommendations, reviews, and word-of-mouth has been greatly enhanced by the Internet. People share opinions online in many ways—through product review sites (such as TripAdvisor, Yelp, or Angie's List), social networking sites (such as Facebook and industry-specific sites), blogs, company email lists, and a range of other methods. As part of your person-to-person marketing, you'll want to do everything you can to encourage satisfied customers to share their thoughts in these online forums.

It's Free, Right?

You might think of person-to-person marketing as a free form of marketing, but it usually comes with its own associated costs, from the fees to join and attend networking organizations to the price of entertaining clients and exhibiting at trade shows. However, even though person-to-person marketing may not be completely free, it does represent one of the most affordable forms of marketing for entrepreneurial companies. Even if you're spending funds to exhibit at costly trade shows across the country, the price of person-to-person marketing is likely to be a fraction of what it would cost to reach the same number of qualified leads through traditional advertising media, such as major newspapers or TV.

The chart below compares the costs of the forms of person-to-person marketing covered in this section. Keep in mind that this chart is based on rough estimates. Costs vary widely, depending on the specifics of any option.

Over time, you'll learn to identify what type of person-to-person marketing best suits your business and provides the healthiest return on your investment.

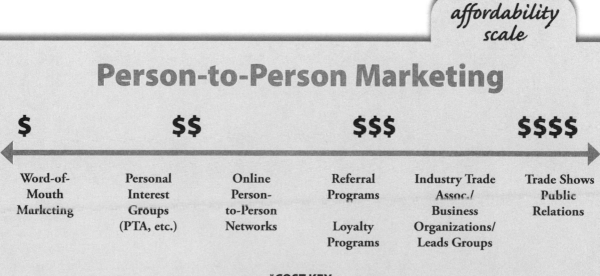

affordability scale

Person-to-Person Marketing

$	$$	$$$	$$$$
Word-of-Mouth Marketing	Personal Interest Groups (PTA, etc.)	Online Person-to-Person Networks	Referral Programs Loyalty Programs	Industry Trade Assoc./ Business Organizations/ Leads Groups	Trade Shows Public Relations

*COST KEY:

$**—Relatively Inexpensive   **$$**—Moderately Expensive   **$$$**—Fairly Expensive   **$$$$—Expensive

* These symbols represent general rate estimates.

Lingo

BUZZ: Positive promotional momentum, primarily generated by word of mouth, focusing on you and your business.

ELEVATOR PITCH: A brief description of your company, product, or service that could be given in the time it takes for a short elevator ride, summing up what you do, how you differ from your competitors, and other key attributes.

INDUSTRY OR TRADE ASSOCIATION: An organization made up of members from the same industry or trade. There are tens of thousands of trade associations in the U.S. and Canada.

LEADS GROUP: An organization formed to help members share leads, or prospects. Typically, only one or two members from any given industry can join each group.

NETWORKING GROUP: An organization formed to help members expand their personal lists of business contacts.

SERVICE ORGANIZATION: A community group focused on providing service to the community. Examples include the Rotary and Kiwanis clubs.

SOCIAL NETWORKING: The term for online communities such as MySpace, Facebook, and LinkedIn.

CHAPTER 14

Networking

The term *person-to-person marketing* is very broad, covering any type of personal interaction that helps build your business. In the widest sense, the word *networking* is often used to mean the same thing.

But when someone talks about building a business through *networking*, they're referring to something a bit more specific. They're referring to the process of intentionally developing and maintaining personal contacts for the primary purpose of gaining customers and sales, and using those contacts to help make introductions to others. In other words, they are referring to the process of building a web—a network—of people who can help drive business. Such people could be potential customers, other business people, people in your industry, or just the guy you meet at your kids' soccer game who might be able to help you meet the gal at the company you've hoped to land as a customer.

For many people, networking means joining and attending organizations and events designed to help them meet prospects, referral sources, and business contacts. Most often, these are business-centered organizations and events, such as chambers of commerce, industry associations, trade shows, and local entrepreneurship groups. But you could join any type of organization that attracts people who might be your customers or who know people who could help you build your business, such as a golf or health club, a religious institution, or a cultural or community group.

At events held by business organizations, networking is generally expected. After all, most people join business groups with at least some intention of meeting people who can help them grow or run their businesses. That's why at such events time is typically set aside for socializing—in fact, you're likely to see "Networking time" listed on their schedules. Take advantage of that time!

Networking Groups

In every community, there are dozens, if not hundreds, of organizations you can join that will help you build your network and your business. Some of the major types include:

- **Entrepreneurs'/General business associations.** These are groups of business professionals and entrepreneurs from different industries who come together to discuss general business topics, learn business skills, and make business contacts. They may be community-based groups,

---

What Goes Around Comes Around

The entrepreneurs who are the most successful networkers understand that networking is a reciprocal system. They are not only doing it to find business for themselves, but to help others succeed as well. When they meet someone, they try to learn what the other person's business is all about and what they need, and they try to see if there's a way to help. This is a great way of opening a door to a conversation and ultimately building a strong relationship with another entrepreneur or professional—much stronger than one you'd create just by shoving a business card in somebody's hand.

Seminars and Workshops

In addition to joining ongoing groups, you can build your business network by attending one-time seminars and workshops. In every community, there are numerous opportunities to learn new skills and improve your business education while meeting other businesspeople. Examples include taking courses at university extension programs—typically one-day or weekend business events that include educational sessions and industry-sponsored training seminars. The advantage of these is that you learn a lot, they take a limited amount of time, and you can meet a targeted group of other businesspeople. Going to a weekend event for "green business" entrepreneurs can help you learn how your business can be more environmentally sensitive while at the same time giving you opportunities to network with other businesspeople who share that concern.

Network Marketing

Want to be confused? You may run into the term *network marketing*, which sounds a lot like marketing your business through building your personal network. In fact, *network marketing* is a term used for *multi-level marketing* (MLM) businesses (sometimes considered pyramid schemes). In MLM or network marketing plans, people are rewarded for bringing other people in to also become "business owners" or "distributors," who then purchase goods and services from the parent company.

such as the Better Business Bureau or chamber of commerce, or they may be more specifically for entrepreneurs, such as EO (Entrepreneurs' Organization) or NASE (the National Association for the Self-Employed).

- **Industry/Trade/Professional associations.** There are tens of thousands of industry associations in the U.S. and Canada. Every industry has a trade association; many have local or state chapters. Professions have associations as well, such as the American Bar Association for lawyers and the American Medical Association for doctors. These organizations are particularly useful for both meeting people in your own industry and networking with people in industries you might target as a customer base. In other words, if you're a website designer, you might join the local chapter of the International Association of Business Communicators (IABC) or American Marketing Association to meet individuals in the marketing departments of major corporations who might hire you for projects.

  Industry associations tend to offer a great deal of education for their members. You may need to be from that industry to join, but some industry associations are open to everyone (sometimes as an "auxiliary" member). To find a trade group, do a search on the Web, using the name of your industry and the words *trade association* or visit www. PlanningShop.com/tradeassociations.asp for a list.

- **Ethnic or gender-based business groups.** Many business groups are created to help members of a particular group improve their business and networking skills. These groups generally include individuals from diverse industries who share a gender or an ethnic, national, or religious heritage. Examples include the Hispanic Chamber of Commerce, National Black MBA Association, Women in Technology (WIT), The Indus Entrepreneurs (TiE, for Indian entrepreneurs), National Association of Women Business Owners, and the Asian Business Association. These groups help strengthen the business ties and skills of their members. In most cases, you do not need to be a member of that ethnic group or gender to join, and if you are targeting that particular group or gender for business purposes, you may consider joining.

- **Networking organizations.** Some business groups form solely so that their members can do business with one another and develop referral sources. Most such organizations—though not all—are not-for-profit associations of businesspeople. Generally, members come from diverse industries, and meetings tend to focus on finding ways to help members secure customers and referrals. There may also be an educational portion to the meetings, but most often one or a few members will discuss their businesses. You may have a chance to be the featured speaker at a meeting, or you might be able to showcase your business on their website or newsletter. Look for business networking groups in your community; they often meet at breakfast or lunchtime. The advantages they offer are that their goal is to help members increase their income and they're structured to support that goal. The downside: There may be a number of members from your industry, and many of the members may not necessarily be good prospects for your business.

■ **Leads groups.** Leads groups are a subset of networking organizations. As the name suggests, these are organizations formed to help members develop sales leads. They tend to maintain very specific group structures and formats, usually allowing only one or two members from each industry so that leads don't become diluted. Generally, at meetings, members give brief statements about what they do and what they need. If you get a customer lead that would be of interest to the group member who represents a particular industry, you're expected to refer that person to your leads group member. Some of these organizations are for-profit enterprises and may, in fact, be part of a franchised operation. One example is Le Tip International, a for-profit business with hundreds of chapters throughout the U.S. and Canada.

■ **Non-business groups.** Networking isn't always about business. You'll find plenty of social networks based on a wide range of communities and shared interests. These include nonprofit and community organizations, service associations, religious organizations, environmental organizations, sports and hobby groups, social clubs, school and alumni groups, and on and on. While these groups are not specifically designed to help you build your business, your active involvement in them could lead to many local clients, as well as to referrals throughout your community. However, you'll want to take a far less aggressive approach to networking within these groups because people don't generally join them to do business. Build trust first, wait till your business comes up in conversation, and present your card only if someone asks for it.

Choosing the Right Groups

You know you have to build your business network, but how do you choose the right groups to join? First, of course, you have to find lists of organizations in your community. You can usually do this by looking at the business section of your newspaper or local business journal or by searching online. You can also contact your local Small Business Development Center. (SBDCs are located in virtually every community in the U.S.) Then you will want to evaluate the following:

■ **Types of businesses represented and fit for your target market.** Since you'll be looking for clients or referral sources, you'll want to make sure members are the types of people who have a need for or can use your products or services. For instance, if your target market is small businesses, you might join a chamber of commerce, since their members are mostly small businesses. If you're hoping to gather with professional colleagues for mutual benefit (like trade education, resources, influence, and discounts on services), choose an association that serves your industry.

■ **Number of members.** Bigger groups work well when you want to find as many potential clients, or leads, as possible and your products or services can serve many types of people. Smaller groups are better when you're targeting a specific industry or need only a few big clients, whom you'll have a better chance of meeting and landing in a close-knit environment.

Social Networking Online

Everyone's familiar with social networking sites like MySpace, Facebook, and YouTube. (*Social networking* is the term for online communities.) Some of these online networks can be powerful resources for entrepreneurs, helping you connect with others who may help you build your business. They feature a range of resources for displaying information and interacting with other members. On these sites, you'll be able to post your profile and photo, and add a link to your blog (Web log). You can join chat rooms, email newsletter lists, and much more.

The leading social networking site designed especially for business is LinkedIn (www.linkedin.com). But popular social networking sites are also being used for businesses. Some industries have launched their own social networking sites or at least Listservs (email contact lists) or bulletin boards to help people in that industry connect. (See Chapter 26 for more information on using social networking sites for your business.)

❝ *It's important that you participate in a network that is representative of people who can either afford your products or service or refer you to others who can afford your products or services.* ❞
Sandra Yancey
Founder and CEO
eWomenNetwork

- **Convenience.** Check to see when the group meets, where, and how often to ensure that you can be a regular participant.

- **Networking opportunities.** Do the meetings and events allow time for you to easily meet and get to know other members, or is the time structured solely for educational sessions? Will you have other opportunities to tell members about your business (for example, by making presentations, giving your elevator pitch, or being featured in emails or newsletters)?

- **Cost.** Some organizations can be extremely expensive, particularly for-profit networking and leads groups. Check the prices not just of membership but also of attending events (including meals and parking) and compare them with those for other groups you might join. Also find out how many meetings you can attend as a guest before joining.

When deciding whether to join a group and when evaluating it after you've joined, be sure your goals are realistic. What do you hope to achieve by joining? How much business do you expect to attract?

Make sure you'll be able to attend any group you join frequently. If you can get to the meetings only once or twice year, the group probably won't provide much in the way of results. As with any form of marketing, you need repeat exposures to make an impact.

On the following worksheet, make a list of organizations you could consider joining to help build your business network. Check the websites of these organizations and email or call to find out what types of people are members and the cost of joining and attending meetings (making a note of other costs, such as parking or tolls). Also ask about the potential business opportunities you will gain if you join.

BRAINSTORMING

YOUR NETWORKING GROUP LIST

Make a list of organizations you're considering joining in the next year. Include the name of the group, the types of members (industries, size of businesses), membership fees, cost of events (including other costs such as parking), when and where meetings are held, contact info/website, and the reasons you believe joining would be good for business.

Group _____

Types of members_____

Membership fee _____

Event costs _____

Time/Place of mtgs. _____

Contact info _____

Reasons for joining _____

Employing Effective Networking Techniques

Even the most successful businesspeople can be daunted by having to "work the room" at a meeting or talk to strangers to make business contacts. But anyone can become proficient at meeting and greeting people at business events and making a positive impression by adopting a few key networking techniques:

Develop and practice your *elevator pitch*. Have at the ready a clear, concise description of your company, products, or services and what makes you unique and memorable. (See the Elevator Pitch worksheet on page 166.)

Listen and ask questions. When you meet someone who interests you, ask the person what they do—*take an interest in them*. Ask what they're looking for to build their business and how you can help.

Approach people who are standing alone. A person standing alone is likely to be eager to talk and happy to be rescued from having to make the first move.

Don't interrupt. When you do join a group already in conversation, listen for a while before speaking.

Don't pounce, don't pressure. When the time is right—that is, *after* you've had a meaningful conversation and that person has asked about your business—give your elevator pitch.

Exchange business cards. After you have had a conversation, ask for the other person's business card and offer yours so that you can follow up in the future. Make a note on the back of that person's card to remind yourself of who they are or what they need.

Bring marketing materials. Have a few brochures describing your product or service in your briefcase, purse, or car in case a potential customer wants additional information. However, don't bring them out until asked.

Wear the appropriate clothes. Dress neatly, cleanly, and appropriately for the group and the event (business meeting versus barbecue). Check with the event organizer about the accepted mode of dress.

Show up early, stay late. You have the best chance to talk with people before and after the business portion of the event. You'll get the most for your money by meeting as many members as possible.

Arrange a follow-up. If you've had an especially meaningful conversation with someone who is clearly a prospect or referral source, indicate how and when you'll follow up with them.

Move on. Once you've had a good conversation with someone, conclude by exchanging business cards and then move on. Avoid sticking with one person. Both of you could miss an opportunity to meet other important contacts.

Circle back. At the end of the event, try to find your most promising contacts, say goodbye, and reiterate that you will touch base with them soon.

Over time, you will become more comfortable and relaxed with this process and get better at it.

Bring a Friend

It's hard to sing your own praises at an event. Even if you really are the most talented architect in your city, it's going to sound boastful (and not necessarily believable) coming from you. If, however, someone else is standing there when you're introduced to a prospect, your friend can easily say, "You should see the buildings she designs. She's the most talented architect in the city. In fact, she was given the Architect of the Year Award last year."

Make It Fast!

Providing a concise summary of your company, products, or services, an *elevator pitch* is based on the premise that sometimes the only place you can catch an influential or powerful person is in an elevator. Thus, your pitch must be deliverable in the time it takes for an elevator to move from one floor to another. Since the typical elevator ride ranges between 30 and 60 seconds, you should keep your pitch to 60 to 120 words.

The best elevator pitches incorporate five key pieces of information:

- The name of your company
- The products or services you sell
- The target market you serve
- What makes you unique, what differentiates you from the competition, your niche
- What you'd like (if anything) from the person receiving the pitch

SAMPLE: **ELEVATOR PITCH**

❝ *Hi, I'm Sam Sears. I write marketing collateral, and I've specialized in the food service and hospitality industries for the past ten years. I've had a great deal of successful marketing experience with hotels and restaurants, and I've written collateral for Hilton Hotels. Over the years, I've become known for developing collateral that truly connects with the hospitality customers of today. Here's my card. Give me a call if you need marketing materials.* ❞

BRAINSTORMING

YOUR ELEVATOR PITCH

Develop your elevator pitch. First, provide the information requested below. Then write a brief statement (no more than about 100 words).

- **Your name:**
- **The products or services you sell:**
- **The market you serve:**
- **What makes your business/products/services unique:**
- **Desired response:**

Now incorporate this information into one clear, concise statement:

_____

_____

_____

_____

_____

_____

_____

_____

_____

_____

_____

_____

_____

_____

Following Up ...

Once you say farewell to your new contacts, tuck the cards you've gathered into your briefcase, and walk out of the meeting room, you're done, right? On the contrary: your work has just begun! Now you need to follow up. Follow-up activities can include emails, phone calls, and setting up appointments or sending catalogs, merchandise, or samples.

The follow-up strategies described below will help you make the most of your networking efforts and turn your leads into effective and lucrative business relationships:

■ As soon as possible, enter the business cards you've collected into a database or contact management program.

■ Send personal emails to the people you met. Include:
  — A line stating what a pleasure it was to meet them
  — A brief review of your conversation
  — An offer of your services
  — A suggestion to meet for lunch or for coffee

If someone you met indicated they could use services like yours and you made a good connection, follow up with a phone call. If you have an email newsletter, send them a link that would make it easy for them to subscribe or sign them up for your newsletter yourself. (Under U.S. anti-spam laws, if someone gives you their business card, it is legal to sign them up to receive emails from you.)

Although networking takes time and energy, it doesn't have to be a chore if you follow a few simple rules. The most important rule: Show up! By attending networking events frequently, you greatly increase the chance that you'll be in the right place at the right time—when somebody needs what you have to offer.

Don't Just Show Up

To get the most from your organization membership—including the largest number of referrals and customers—don't just attend meetings. Join committees, take on a leadership role, or volunteer to help out. Raise your visibility within a group and you'll raise your rewards.

Stay on Your Contact's Radar

If you've made a contact during networking whom you're especially interested in establishing a relationship with but who has no immediate need for your services, find ways to stay in touch. One great strategy is to occasionally forward articles and contacts that might interest that person. Usually, they'll appreciate that you're thinking about them and remembering what they do. Generating this kind of goodwill works wonders in getting referrals and keeping you in contacts' minds when they're ready to do business.

Entertaining Clients and Referral Sources

People do business with people they like. While many networking activities take place at group events, the most important person-to-person marketing occurs when entertaining clients, prospects, and referral sources. In fact, for most entrepreneurial companies, "entertaining" represents their primary form of marketing. Social events—taking your client out for a business lunch or a round of golf, attending a baseball game together, or throwing a holiday party—are an important part of your business.

Social events and business lunches (or breakfasts or dinners) allow you and your prospect, client, supplier, or employee to get to know each other. They also cement ongoing relationships, making it likely that a customer will continue to purchase from you in the future.

Often looked at as expendable, entertaining is frequently the first item cut when expenses are being reduced. But the truth is business entertaining is typically one of the most affordable marketing approaches you can employ. While it may seem expensive to take a client out to the best restaurant in town, enhancing a relationship with an important customer who makes large orders every year is far less costly than buying ads, exhibiting at trade shows, or using most other forms of marketing to find and secure customers.

How to Have a Business Lunch

Knowing how to have lunch (or breakfast or dinner) is an essential business skill. Don't feel embarrassed if you're uncomfortable with the idea of sitting over a grilled chicken breast while talking to a client, prospect, or referral source. Mastering the business lunch is a skill that can be developed just like any other.

First, you must understand the purpose of the business lunch, which is to build a relationship. However, this is not a two-way street. You should be more interested in your client than they are in you. Therefore, the single most important thing you can do at a business lunch is *listen*. Ask questions about your guest as a person, not just about their work or business—but don't make it seem like an interview. Three good questions: *Where did you grow up? How did you like living in a small town/ big city? Tell me about your family.*

You don't need a particular reason or occasion to ask someone to lunch. Instead, try the straightforward approach: "We've been doing business together for almost a year. I'd like to take you to lunch and get to know you a little better."

Once you've made your lunch (or breakfast or dinner) date, here are some general rules to follow:

- Let your client suggest the venue.

- Don't be in a rush—linger over the meal, and don't finish before your guest.

- Avoid messy food.

- Turn off your cell phone.

- Pay for lunch—but don't fight over the check.

- Don't bring any reports, presentations, or samples (unless requested).

- Don't drink alcohol unless your guest does, and limit your consumption.

Calculating Your Networking Membership ROI

To evaluate whether joining a specific group is worth your money and time, do a simple return on investment (ROI) breakdown on it just as you would for any other marketing activity. The following page contains a worksheet to help you get started. Simply choose a networking group and then estimate the costs associated with joining, the value of the time you devote to the group, and your projected results.

Here are some tips for using the worksheet (and calculating your ROI):

- **Be realistic about your financial goals.** If you have no other information about potential returns, assume that you will—at most—land one new referral per three meetings and one new client for every three referrals. In other words, *be realistic*: if, say, you were joining the Software Developers' Alliance to land an early-stage software company as a client for your business plan development and management consulting business, securing just one new client in return for a year's membership is a reasonable goal—especially when you consider that this one new client could generate thousands of dollars in annual revenue.

- **Remember to include non-financial goals.** It's easy to assign a dollar value to customers retained as a direct result of your involvement in networking groups, it's important to remember that you're there to raise visibility for your organization and to gain a better understanding of your customers' needs as well. What goes around comes around—and nowhere is this more evident than in the world of business networking. Thus, to use the example of that management consulting business again, you would do well to include among your non-financial goals things like building recognition within the software industry, assembling a network of industry leaders, and helping current and future clients find employees, partners, and funding sources.

- **Be sure to include travel time and time spent *outside* of meetings on work for the group when you calculate your time commitment.** Time is money; thus, it's important to consider how many hours you're likely to put into the group—and then assign a price tag (in other words, your billable rate) to those hours. Often times the cost of joining and participating in such groups is relatively low; however, if a big time commitment is required on your part, those costs could pale in comparison to the value of the time you put in.

RETURN ON INVESTMENT

YOUR NETWORKING MEMBERSHIP ROI

Your business: _____

Your target market: _____

Networking group you plan to join: _____

Description of that group's members: _____

GOALS

Financial: _____

Non-financial: _____

PROJECTED COSTS

Initiation fee (if any): _____

Annual membership fee: _____

Annual costs of meeting attendance: _____

Annual cost of meals (if any): _____

Annual incidental costs (parking, donations, raffle tickets, etc.): _____

Total annual direct financial cost: _____

Time commitment: _____

Value of time: _____

Total cost (list both your out-of-pocket cost and the cost for your time): ___

PROJECTED RETURNS, FINANCIAL

Number of referrals received: _____

Number of new clients from referrals: _____

Annual revenue generated from new clients: _____

Total cost (include the cost of your time as a separate item in parentheses): ___

Total projected net financial gain (annual revenue minus total cost): _____

PROJECTED RETURNS, NON-FINANCIAL

_____

_____

TOTAL ROI (Total Net Financial Returns Plus Total Non-Financial Returns): _____

NETWORKING BUDGET (12 MONTHS)

	JAN	FEB	MARCH	APRIL	MAY
Professional Assistance					
Writers					
Graphic designers					
Photographers/Illustrators					
Other consultants					
Printing/Reproduction					
Shipping and Postage					
Membership/Subscription Fees					
Industry/Trade associations					
Business/Entrepreneur associations					
Professional associations					
Personal interest groups					
School groups					
Social groups					
Non-Profits/Charities					
Other membership/subscription fees					
Travel					
Travel (airfare/car expenses)					
Hotel					
Meals					
Other travel expenses					
Entertainment					
Other					
TOTAL					

! **NOTE:** An electronic version of this worksheet is available as part of the Planning Shop's Marketing Budget Templates package.

JUNE	JULY	AUGUST	SEPT	OCT	NOV	DEC	TOTAL

Lingo

AFFILIATE PROGRAM: A form of online referral program where the referring website receives a payment for driving new customers to a website.

ASTRO-TURFING: A false word-of-mouth campaign initiated by a company (or politician or others) to make it look as if it's coming spontaneously from the public. The term refers to generating fake grassroots support.

BLOG: An online journal or other type of specialized website that allows an individual or group of individuals to share insights on a particular topic. Blogs, short for "Web logs," exist on a wide range of topics, from business strategies to baldness.

BLOGGER: An individual who writes a blog. Key bloggers can be major influencers and spread the word about your product or service.

CUSTOMER COMMUNICATION: Methods of staying in touch with current and former customers so they remember your name and can help spread the word to potential customers.

LOYALTY PROGRAM: An organized plan to retain customers by using rewards, discounts, or other incentives for repeat purchases. Examples would be frequent flyer programs or punch cards at a coffee house.

REFERRAL PROGRAM: A program that provides incentives for your existing customers to tell others about you. Usually, it offers discounts on services, free products, or other perks when customers bring in their friends or colleagues.

STEALTH/UNDERCOVER MARKETING: A campaign where consumers do not realize they are being approached by a marketing professional or other type of marketing effort. (This form of marketing is viewed as unethical.)

TEXT MESSAGING: A form of mobile phone communication to generate word-of-mouth campaigns, generally around the subjects of entertainment and politics.

VIRAL MARKETING: Occasionally synonymous with word-of-mouth marketing, the term originates in online communications, where, due to the ease and speed of communications, spreading the word has a viral effect.

CHAPTER 15

Word-of-Mouth Marketing

A sk successful business owners how most customers learn about their company, and you're likely to get one answer repeatedly: *word-of-mouth.*

The term *word-of-mouth* refers to the process of one person telling another person about something he or she likes. When you're thinking about buying something, you're likely to ask your friends what they use and like. Similarly, if you're hiring someone to do work for your home or business, you're likely to ask a friend or fellow entrepreneur for a recommendation. Overwhelmingly, that's what people do. People trust referrals and reviews they get from other people far more than they trust ads or company websites. That's what makes word-of-mouth marketing (WOMM) so powerful.

What's more, word-of-mouth marketing represents one of the most affordable marketing activities. In fact, one way to develop strong word-of-mouth marketing is to simply run a terrific business for many years. After a decade or so, you're sure to have a large number of former (and current) clients who think you're terrific. That's great, but what do you do when you're a new or small company—when you can't wait a decade to build your business?

It takes work and planning to build a word-of-mouth marketing campaign. And that takes *a bit* of time and *a bit* of money—but the good news is that word-of-mouth can be generated, and enhanced, by planned marketing efforts.

What Is Word-of-Mouth Marketing?

Quite simply, word-of-mouth marketing happens when one person tells another person about your company, products, or services. Rosa asks Janice where she gets her haircut; Janice tells her the name of her hair salon; and Rosa calls and makes an appointment. That's the most basic form of word-of-mouth marketing. But it relies a lot on luck and chance. What happens if Janice doesn't remember the name of the salon, for instance?

> **"** *It's all about word-of-mouth. Your satisfied customer is your best spokesperson. Reach out to them and ask their permission to use their words as a testimonial. Usually, they're flattered and will say yes. Always do what you can to turn your best customer into your top PR person.* **"**
>
> **Julie McHenry**
> **President**
> **Communications Insight**

The Contagion

The term *viral marketing* is often used to refer to word-of-mouth marketing. Originating in the online world, the term was coined because of the lightning speed at which information could be disseminated in that environment—in other words, like a *virus*. Today, however, the term is frequently used to describe the offline spread of information as well.

People Trust People

According to the Word of Mouth Marketing Association (WOMMA), 76% of consumers don't believe information they see in advertisements. At the same time, 68% *do* trust product advice from their peers. Does this mean you shouldn't advertise? Not at all. Ads provide valuable exposure that builds awareness of your company, attracts customers, and keeps your name in front of satisfied customers. What these statistics do show, however, is the power of word-of-mouth communications. People trust other people—so you have to help them get the word out.

In fact, there are marketing tactics that will significantly increase the chances that Janice *will* pass the name of her hair salon along to others. That's where planned word-of-mouth marketing campaigns come in.

You can plan a word-of-mouth marketing campaign just as you would any other marketing campaign (for example, an advertising campaign). In fact, consciously working to develop and maintain word-of-mouth marketing can be one of the most effective ways to build your business and increase sales.

Who Spreads the Word?

When planning your word-of-mouth marketing campaign, keep in mind that you can target many types of people (in addition to current customers), including:

- **Current customers**

- **Past customers**

- **Referral sources.** These are individuals who know about your business and are in a position to tell others with a need about you (for example, a real estate agent alerting new homeowners to a local gardening service).

- **Industry contacts.** These people can help spread the word about opportunities such as business prospects, subcontracting, and other referrals.

- **Employees**

- **Other businesspeople**

- **Influencers.** These are people whom others look to for advice or insight (for example, industry leaders, media figures, product reviewers, and influential bloggers).

- **Friends and family**

Word-of-Mouth Tactics

Word-of-mouth begins when you not only satisfy your customers; you *delight* them. Providing high-quality products and services consistently helps compel current customers to talk about you. But even if customers love you, they can forget about you. Word-of-mouth doesn't just happen—you need to find ways to get people to remember you, talk about you, and consciously refer others to you.

The key components of a word-of-mouth marketing campaign are:

- Customer communication

- Formalized programs, such as loyalty and referral programs

- Generation of "buzz"

Customer Communication

Word-of-mouth marketing campaigns rely primarily on customer communication programs. Customers can refer others only if they remember you and your contact information. So the key to a successful word-of-mouth marketing program is to keep your name in front of current customers, past customers, referral sources, and others. This requires regular and repeated communication and, perhaps, a formal program to encourage customers to return or refer business to you. Some ways to accomplish this:

Email newsletters. The Internet makes staying in touch with your current and past customers easy. One of the most effective ways to communicate is through digital newsletters sent via email. Individuals sign up to get regular information from you, often monthly. Examples include a veterinarian providing pet care tips and a nutritionist providing health tips. Maintaining a regular newsletter takes some work, but it keeps your name in people's inboxes and reinforces your standing as an expert or authority. (For more about email newsletters, see Section V, Online Marketing.)

Print newsletters. Just as with online newsletters, print newsletters provide valuable information to customers, keeping your name in front of them and reinforcing your company's standing in its field. Print newsletters have the added advantage that recipients are likely to keep them around for a while; however, they're also considerably more costly than email newsletters.

Notices of sales and discounts. Everyone loves a bargain, so if you're providing a product or service that customers can use repeatedly, your customer may appreciate getting notices of frequent sales or discounts. By changing these discounts regularly, you keep customers looking for your notices and your name in front of them. This not only drives new purchases but also makes it easier for customers to refer others to you. Make it simple for them to forward email notices of such sales to friends by including a "Forward to a Friend" button in the email notice.

Catalogs and product announcements. Catalogs and other product descriptions also serve to keep your name and product information in front of customers. Even if customers don't immediately make a purchase, they are reminded of what you have to offer so they're better able to recommend you to others.

Specialty advertising products. One way to keep your name (and phone number and website address) in front of customers is by giving them something valuable they want to keep. Specialty advertising products (also known as promotional advertising products) such as pens, mugs, calendars, key chains, and the like keep your name in front of a customer for a long time.

Company or employee blogs. Blogs, or Web logs, written by company personnel can be an effective way to share inside information and keep customers up to date on what's going on in your company.

Entertaining clients. One of the most time-honored ways of keeping your name in front of customers is by keeping your face in front of them,

> *Everyone in your business needs to commit to this one concept: 'From this point on, every one of our customers is going to be so thrilled with what we have to offer, they're going to refer their friends and neighbors. And we're going to put in a system that makes it easy for them to do that.'*
>
> **John Jantsch**
> **Author**
> *Duct Tape Marketing*

Where'd I Put That Name?

The backbone of any word-of-mouth marketing program is a useful, up-to-date contact list of current and past customers and other referral sources. Ideally, this is maintained in an electronic database, such as a contact manager or customer relationship manager (CRM) program. It doesn't have to be complicated, but you need a good, reliable list to be able to contact your customers and referral sources regularly.

When Do You Become a Pest?

How often should you contact current and past customers? If you get in touch less than twice a year, they're going to forget you. But if you contact them too frequently (say, weekly), you could become a pest (and they could block you from their email). For most companies, staying in touch monthly by email or every other month with a printed mailer (such as a catalog or flyer) is a good course of action.

too. If you have a relatively small base of customers or referral sources, then regularly getting together with them—whether one on one or at small get-togethers—keeps them thinking about you. Entertaining serves as an important way of staying visible and improving word-of-mouth marketing for virtually all businesses.

- **Touching base.** If you don't have time to entertain or if you have a larger base of customers and referral sources, you may want to find other ways to stay in touch. Some possibilities: forwarding items of interest (such as newspaper articles) to customers and referral sources via email or regular mail, becoming friends with them on social networking sites, or just picking up the phone and giving them a call.

BRAINSTORMING

YOUR CUSTOMER COMMUNICATION TACTICS

Describe the ways you plan to stay in communication with current and past customers so they'll remember your name and contact information and thus be able to refer others to you.

Email newsletters:_____

Print newsletters: _____

Notices of sales: _____

Catalogs, product announcements: _____

Specialty advertising products: _____

Company, employee blogs:_____

Entertaining: _____

Touching base: _____

Other: _____

_____

Formalized Word-of-Mouth Marketing Programs

In addition to the ongoing customer communication tactics that should be part of every business, many companies may want to establish more formalized programs to help generate word-of-mouth referrals. Referral, affiliate, and loyalty programs can be very effective in keeping your name visible and in driving new and repeat business.

■ **Referral programs.** One way to encourage current and past customers to send business your way is to reward them for doing just that. Thus, you should definitely consider a referral program as part of your overall word-of-mouth marketing campaign.

In many types of businesses, referral bonuses can be stated up front. A hairdresser, for instance, could put up a sign stating, "$25 off your next haircut when you refer a new client" or a website hosting company could send out a notice to clients offering "Two months of free hosting for every new customer you refer to us." This kind of inducement motivates some people to tell others about your services.

In other businesses, however, an upfront reward might appear unseemly. Thus, a doctor or CPA might instead send a thank you gift after a client refers new business to them—for instance, a gift basket or a gift certificate. This type of soft referral program rewards customers for sending referrals your way and (ideally) encourages them to continue doing so. However, it won't encourage customers to make referrals if they hadn't thought of doing so already. One caution: in a few industries, paid referrals may be illegal (for example, in relation to some real estate transactions).

Be sure to include employees in your referral programs—they're in a good position to tell others about the features and benefits of your products or services.

■ **Affiliate programs.** An online affiliate program is another type of referral program. With affiliate programs, other websites agree to add a link or links to your website, typically with some graphics and descriptions of your products or services. In return, they get paid a fee for driving new customers to you—often a small percentage of whatever the new customer purchases. While the main purpose of affiliate programs is sales, they also spread your company and/or product name across more websites, improving word-of-mouth marketing.

■ **Loyalty programs.** Loyalty programs provide an excellent way of keeping your name in front of customers, encouraging them to come back and to spread the word about your business. Any established process of rewarding customers for repeat business constitutes a loyalty program. The best-known such programs are frequent flyer programs; however, loyalty programs exist in every type of business and can be as simple as a punch card at a coffee house. If your customer loyalty program encourages customers to keep something with your name on it (such as a frequent-buyer card), that object can also be a handy tool in your word-of-mouth marketing campaign.

Influencer Marketing on Campus

Seth Hill is a well-known competitive snowboarder on the University of Colorado snowboard team and a popular, well-connected student on campus. When team sponsor Red Bull was looking for University of Colorado students to promote its products on campus, Seth was the perfect candidate. He kept his dorm refrigerator stocked with Red Bull and had a backpack stocked with cans of the drink.

Seth's friends and acquaintances were always pretty happy when he offered them free cans of Red Bull at his home or at the parties or events he attended. He also helped organize events to promote the product, such as a "Ski Bums and Snow Bunnies" party at a campus fraternity, where he kept the Red Bull flowing. It wasn't a stealth marketing campaign. Students knew that Seth was working for, or at least was affiliated with, the company. "But usually they don't care," says Hill. "They're getting free Red Bull, and they feel okay about it because they're getting it from me."

Seth made sure there was plenty of Red Bull around, especially during exam time and at sports events, when students need extra energy. Red Bull knew that if the other students liked the product and got used to drinking it, and if they associated it positively with a popular snowboarder like Seth, it would probably lead them to buy Red Bull the next time they needed an energy drink.

BRAINSTORMING

YOUR REFERRAL, AFFILIATE, AND LOYALTY PROGRAMS

Use this worksheet to describe the types and specifics of the referral, affiliate, and loyalty programs you plan to use to generate word-of-mouth marketing and drive new sales.

REFERRAL PROGRAMS: How will you encourage current customers and others to refer new business to you? How will you reward them for referrals?

_____

_____

_____

AFFILIATE PROGRAMS: Will you institute an affiliate program to enable other websites to add a link to your website, drive traffic, and get a reward for purchases made from those who link from their website to yours? If so, what percentage will affiliates receive from new sales, or what other payment amount will they receive?

_____

_____

_____

LOYALTY PROGRAMS: How will you reward customers for repeat or frequent purchases?

_____

_____

_____

Other "Buzz"

How else can you get people talking about your company, products, or services? One of the most effective means is through public relations—generating unpaid coverage and mention of your company, products, or services in the media or online. (For more on PR, see Chapter 17.) Most helpful are:

- **Online mentions.** Whether in social networking sites, product review sites, or popular blogs on topics related to your products or services, you can create online word-of-mouth by working to be mentioned and reviewed (ideally favorably) in these online venues. This is classic public relations behavior directed at the online world.

- **Events.** Hosting events, whether at your place of business or at outside venues, reminds customers and referral sources about you.

■ **Product placement/Associative marketing.** Everyone's seen celebrities using brand name products such as computers, soft drinks, and cars in movies or on TV. While such high-profile product placements are typically time-consuming and expensive to produce, you can accomplish the same thing at much less cost by getting your products placed in well-respected venues where your customers will see them. A florist, for example, could put a beautiful bouquet in a hotel lobby with a "Flowers provided by …" placard or business cards nearby. In some cases, you'd pay to get your goods in these venues. In others, you'd donate your products and services in exchange for the exposure.

■ **Influencers.** This form of marketing involves seeding products among well-respected members of a particular demographic, group, or network (whether social or business) as a means of influencing others to try the product.

■ **Text messaging.** This form of buzz generation is used occasionally for young markets (teenagers and 20-somethings). The best text message campaigns are often associated with events such as a concert or a prize giveaway. The idea is to get people attending the event to text their friends, tell them what's going on, and get them to act.

BRAINSTORMING

GENERATING BUZZ

Describe some of the methods you will use to generate "buzz" and increase word-of-mouth marketing for your product or service.

Online mentions: _____

Events: _____

Product placement: _____

Influencers: _____

Text messaging: _____

Other: _____

Play It Straight

The best and most effective word-of-mouth marketing efforts are (a) subtle and (b) propagated by customers, not by company owners, employees, or PR people. If a person attends a party, loudly praises the food, and then starts handing out cards for the catering company, the recipients are going to get suspicious about why that person is *really* there. If that person is being paid by the caterer and doesn't mention his or her involvement, it's called *stealth marketing*, or *astro-turfing*, which means trying to initiate a false word-of-mouth campaign, often by misrepresenting oneself as a happy customer.

Good word-of-mouth marketing takes a degree of tact. Existing customers don't want to feel bombarded by you or manipulated into saying nice things about you. And prospective customers don't want to feel as if they're just getting hype. There's nothing wrong, however, with asking clients who value your products and services to recommend your company to friends and colleagues. Treat your customers well, and they'll be more than happy to tell others about their positive experience with your company.

Calculating Your Word-of-Mouth Marketing ROI

As with every type of marketing tactic you employ, you'll need to project your potential return on investment for the money you spend generating word-of-mouth marketing. While many of your activities, such as calling current customers or taking them to lunch, may not have a substantial financial cost, you still need to assess how much time you'll spend on such tactics and figure that into your "investment" equation.

The following page contains a worksheet to help you get started on your ROI analysis for word-of-mouth marketing. Simply define your target market, set some goals, and fill in the requested data to get an idea of the ROI you can expect from your word-of-mouth marketing efforts.

Here are some tips for using the worksheets (and calculating your ROI):

■ **Be specific about your financial goals.** This means that you need to include not just the total return you'd like to receive on your advertising investment but what that translates to in terms of customers and expenditures. Thus, if your business is, say, a health care consulting company and your goal is to secure 10 new clients a year, you would need to figure the average income you could expect per client and multiply that by the number of clients to come up with your total ROI.

■ **Remember to include non-financial goals.** While you may not be able to put a cash value on things like brand awareness and customer perception, these are important components of any marketing campaign, and as such, must be considered when calculating return on investment. Thus, to use the health care consulting company example again, your non-financial goals might include increased awareness of your consulting service within the medical community, increased demand for services, and heightened brand visibility.

■ **Be sure to include *all* of your word-of-mouth tactics.** Golf dates, business lunches, gifts for referrals, even holiday greetings—they all add up, especially when delivered in volume over the course of a year. Consider that health care consulting company example again, and you may be shocked to find that it projected to pay $38,600 to retain those 10 new clients. But break it down, and it begins to make sense: $10,000 on golf and entertaining, $15,000 to send out a regular email newsletter to the medical community, $3,000 for holiday cards and gifts, and so on. The lesson: Add it all up; include *all* of your word-of-mouth expenses, even those that may seem inconsequential.

RETURN ON INVESTMENT

YOUR WORD-OF-MOUTH MARKETING ROI

Your business:_____

Your target market:_____

GOALS

Financial: _____

Non-financial: _____

Word-of-mouth marketing tactics and projected costs (yearly):_____

PROJECTED RETURNS, FINANCIAL

Expected new customers/clients: _____

Expected average income per client/customer: _____

Increase in income:_____

Total cost of word-of-mouth marketing tactics: _____

Total projected net financial gain (increase in income minus the total cost of word-of-mouth marketing):_____

PROJECTED RETURNS, NON-FINANCIAL

_____

_____

TOTAL ROI (Total Net Financial Returns Plus Total Non-Financial Returns): _____

WORD-OF-MOUTH MARKETING BUDGET (12 MONTHS)

	JAN	FEB	MARCH	APRIL	MAY
Professional Assistance					
Writers					
Graphic designers					
Photographers/Illustrators					
Event planners					
PR consultants					
Marketing consultants					
Other consultants					
Printing/Reproduction					
Shipping and Postage					
Membership/Subscription Fees					
Business/Entrepreneur associations					
Industry/Trade associations					
Professional associations					
Personal interest groups					
Non-profits/Charities					
School groups					
Social groups					
Other membership/subscription fees					
Travel					
Travel (airfare/car expenses)					
Hotel					
Meals					
Other travel expenses					
Entertainment					
Referral & Loyalty Programs					
Supplies/Cost of Goods/Manufacturing					
Promotional items					
Product samples					
Other supplies/goods/manufacturing costs					
Other					
TOTAL					

! **NOTE:** An electronic version of this worksheet is available as part of the Planning Shop's Marketing Budget Templates package.

JUNE	JULY	AUGUST	SEPT	OCT	NOV	DEC	TOTAL

Lingo

BOOTH: An exhibit space at a trade show, meaning the empty space (standard size: 10' x 10') the exhibitor rents. But the term *booth* can also refer to the physical structure installed in the booth space or purchased to display materials at a trade show.

BREAK-OUT SESSION: A small educational seminar or panel discussion conducted as part of a conference or trade show. Only a portion of show attendees participates in each break-out session because many run simultaneously.

CONFERENCE/CONVENTION: An event that gathers industry or association professionals together for educational or policy-setting purposes. Many also include a trade show floor with exhibitor booths.

DISPLAY: The visible materials used to promote your company within your exhibit space at a trade show.

EXHIBIT SPACE: The area you rent at a trade show to promote your company.

EXPO: Another name for a trade show, often meaning a trade show without an educational component or a trade show open to the public (as opposed to one limited to members of an industry).

KEYNOTE SPEECH: An educational session, usually delivered by a prominent member of an industry or a celebrity, where all attendees are invited. No other educational sessions are conducted at the same time.

SHOW SERVICES: The full range of services offered to exhibitors by show organizers, all of which are paid for. Show services include everything from rental of carpeting, furniture, and electronics to exhibit installation and dismantling, electricity, Internet connections, and even wastebaskets.

SPONSOR: A company or organization that pays additional funds to have its name more prominently associated within the trade show (on banners and programs, for example) and that helps underwrite the show's costs.

SWAG, OR GIVEAWAYS: Trinkets, toys, tools, knickknacks, and other items that feature your company name and logo and are used to promote your business (at a trade show or to the press).

CHAPTER 16

Trade Shows

Trade shows represent one of the most important marketing options for entrepreneurial companies. That's because they bring together large numbers of target customers with potential suppliers and provide them with opportunities to meet face to face. As a result, they can expose entrepreneurial companies to an enormous number of prospects, industry leaders, influencers, and even members of the media in a very short period of time.

Trade shows attract members of an industry, who come together to see what's new. Virtually every industry conducts at least one trade show a year. One of the largest trade shows is the Consumer Electronics Show, which features all the latest and greatest gadgets, but there are literally tens of thousands of trade shows featuring all kinds of wares.

Benefits of Trade Show Marketing

Trade shows offer a lot of bang for your marketing buck. They provide:

☐ Opportunities for meeting potential customers and partners

☐ Opportunities for collecting sales leads and building lists—that is, collecting names, contact information, and business cards to identify hot prospects and build your company's mailing list

☐ Exposure—the chance to show potential customers (and competitors) that your business is a player in its industry

☐ Splashy launch vehicles for new products or services

☐ A forum for learning about new products, services, technologies, and other resources

☐ A venue for sharing ideas and strategies

☐ A way to stay current in your field

☐ A glimpse into what competitors are doing

Myth◯Buster

No Sale, No Show?

MYTH: If I don't make a sale at a trade show, it hasn't been a success.

BUSTED: Years ago the primary purpose of trade shows was to make sales. For many shows, that's still an important purpose. But over the years, exhibiting at trade shows has generally become more of a marketing technique for a company than a direct sales activity. Sales are often made afterwards, by following up with leads collected at the shows.

Types of Shows

Although the term *trade show* is used widely, there are actually many different types of shows attended by industry professionals, with slightly different formats and goals. The most common:

■ **Industry trade show or expo/exposition.** These shows' primary purpose is to display products and services and bring vendors together with prospects and industry professionals. The focus is the exhibition hall, where booths showcase products and services.

■ **Conference, symposium, or seminar.** The primary purpose of these types of shows is to provide a forum for industry education and information, networking, and policy setting. The focus is on the educational sessions—keynote speeches, workshops, and break-out sessions. There may be exhibits, but they are not central to the event.

■ **Convention.** Typically, conventions are very large gatherings combining a trade show, industry conference, and educational sessions.

■ **Consumer expos.** These are events aimed at the public (rather than members of an industry) and designed to showcase the latest products and make sales. Typical expo types include home and garden, bridal, and boat.

Choosing the Best Show

Trade shows are expensive, so you want to make careful choices about where you exhibit. Some of the biggest or best-known trade shows may not necessarily be the best ones for you, so do your homework to find the best fit. To start:

■ **Identify your goals.** What do you hope to achieve by exhibiting at a trade show? Do you want to make sales? Launch a new product? Find strategic partners in your industry or distribution channels?

When you start by clearly identifying your goals, you have a much better chance of finding a venue that's appropriate for you. A large convention attracting thousands of people may mean that more people walk by your booth, but a smaller show with a more carefully targeted audience might provide you with more qualified sales leads. If you have a very complicated or technology-based product, a show that allows you to be a speaker in a break-out session or to make a presentation to the entire group may enable you to better explain the nature of your products or services.

■ **Ask your customers.** An excellent way to select your show is to learn which ones your potential customers and competitors attend. Talk to others in your industry; request lists of past attendees and exhibitors from show organizers; and ask customers directly to identify potential shows.

■ **Identify a number of potential shows.** While there's usually one giant convention for most industries, there are also typically dozens of smaller gatherings serving subsets of those industries, and they may be a better fit for you. For instance, even if the American Medical Association has a giant national convention, if you sell medical supplies, you may be better off exhibiting at the annual conference of plastic surgeons or cardiologists.

■ **Search the Internet for trade shows serving your industry.** To start finding shows, identify the associations serving your industry (or the industry of your target customer). Virtually every industry association holds annual conventions or conferences.

A few good Internet resources:

— www.tsnn.com (Trade Show News Network)

— www.TradeshowWeek.com

— www.PlanningShop.com/tradeassociations.asp (for a list of associations)

— General search engines can also help. (Just type in your industry name and "trade show" or "conference.")

■ **Consider state or local shows.** Most associations have state and/or local chapters that hold annual meetings which often include exhibits. These are generally more affordable to exhibit at, and the cost of travel is usually far less than for a show with a wider catchment area. These can be excellent choices if your market is limited to a particular geographic region, if your business is new and budget is limited, or if you just want to get a feel for trade show marketing.

BRAINSTORMING

YOUR TRADE SHOW LIST

Make a list of the trade shows at which you are considering exhibiting. Include show names, dates, cost, contact info/website, and the reasons each show may be good for your business.

SHOW		
Attendees		
Exhibitors		
Dates		
Location		
Contact/Web Address		
Cost of Booth Space		
Reasons for Choosing this Show		

**Trade Show
In A Day**

Looking for more information on trade shows? You'll find valuable information on choosing your show, booking your space, designing your booth, making travel arrangements, finding and qualifying leads, and doing post-show follow-up, plus dozens of other ways to make the most of your trade show investment in *Trade Show In A Day*, available in bookstores or online at *www. planningshop.com*.

How Trade Shows Work

Industry associations typically sponsor trade shows; however, some shows and conventions are put on by for-profit companies. Even when sponsored by a trade association, though, the largest shows are generally managed by a professional exhibition management company, such as Reed Exhibitions. These companies market the show to exhibitors and attendees, coordinate educational and promotional activities, and take your reservations.

Companies that exhibit at trade shows pay for floor space where they can put up booths or rent tables to demonstrate and display their goods or pitch their services and interact with prospects and other attendees. Typical booth space is 10' x 10', and you can rent more than one space to create larger or more elaborate booths.

For the larger shows, a separate management company will provide and manage show services, such as installing and building your booth, providing tables and chairs and electricity, and placing carpeting. You will pay extra for any and all such services, even getting a wastebasket. Expect very strict limits on what you can do or bring yourself. For instance, you may not be allowed to install your booth if it takes more than an hour or any tools.

Once you have narrowed down which trade shows might be appropriate for your business, contact the show registration office and request an exhibitor packet, which will provide a menu of exhibitor options and trade show prices.

Increase Your Visibility

One way to increase your visibility at a trade show is through *sponsorships*, which provide additional opportunities for you to put your name, logo, and other contact info on show-related advertising, marketing material, and events. If you've ever been to a trade show or even received an invitation to one, you've seen evidence of these sponsorships. A sponsor's name may be on a show's website or printed brochure; its logo may be on the free tote bag given to attendees; or it may be named as sponsor of a lunch, dinner, or even coffee break.

Trade show sponsorships give a company the opportunity to increase its name recognition with attendees. Depending on the size of the show and the nature of your sponsorship, costs range from about $1,000 to more than $100,000. For smaller or newer companies, if the trade show attracts exactly your targeted audience and the cost is affordable, trade show sponsorships can be a good way to make a big marketing impact. Sponsorships don't drive direct sales, but they do make your company seem important—and they get your name out there.

Pre-show Promotion

Much of your important marketing should be done long before the trade show starts. Studies indicate that pre-show promotion can increase traffic to your booth by 33%. Here are some of the ways that you can facilitate pre-show promotion:

■ **Send emails.** Many trade show organizers will provide you with a list of registered attendees, including their email addresses: Use it to send emails inviting attendees to visit your booth.

■ **Make appointments.** The time-honored method of getting the most from trade shows is to make appointments with people in the industry. Your booth then becomes your office, and you're sure to see the people most important to you.

■ **Place ads in industry publications and on industry websites.** Announce your upcoming presence and invite visitors by advertising your plans to exhibit.

Marketing at the Booth

Once a show is under way, you want to do all you can to attract attendees, give them your message, and turn browsers into buyers. Hundreds of people will pass by your trade show exhibit, so it's important that you have a plan for approaching them and determining whether they might now, or in the future, bring business your way. Use the following five-step approach to engage and qualify show goers:

1. **Make contact.** Many attendees will approach you by coming up to check out your booth. If they don't, the best way to start up a conversation with a passing show attendee is to make eye contact and begin speaking to them. Another option is to offer a brochure or a giveaway.

2. **Initiate the conversation.** Introduce yourself, shake hands, and start off with an open-ended question that allows the person to share something abut themselves: "How are you enjoying the show?" or "Tell me why you're here today." People love to talk about themselves. Engaging the other person is more important than the specific content of your questions. Be frank and open, rather than contrived or salesy.

3. **Direct the conversation.** Once you're past the ice breaker, talk business as soon as possible. Ask questions that will help you determine whether the person you're speaking to fits your target customer profile. Practice your elevator pitch (see page 166) before the show, so you know what you want to say to attendees and prospects and what you want them to remember.

4. **Agree on a next step.** If the attendee is a good prospect and is interested, they will become a serious lead only when the two of you agree on a next step to take after the show. The best time to transition into next step mode is after you've explained how your product or service can help meet their needs. Assuming the person responds positively, suggest a follow-up: "I'd appreciate the opportunity to explain this in more detail. Can I call you next week?"

5. **End the conversation.** If the person you're talking to is a strong potential customer, summarize the next steps you have agreed to take: "I'll send you our catalog tomorrow and give you a call next Thursday." Then shake their hand and wish them a successful show. If, however, the person is not likely to become a customer, bring the conversation to a close as quickly and gracefully as possible.

> ## Look Before You Leap
>
> The best way to find out whether a trade show is a good fit for your business is to go first as an attendee. You'll discover what the atmosphere is like, who attends and exhibits, and how business is done at the event—and you'll still be able to take advantage of the large number of industry contacts assembled in one place.

Selling *Yourself* at a Trade Show

If you have a service-oriented business, you won't have products to demonstrate or give away at a trade show, so you'll need other ways to showcase your accomplishments. Use these strategies to sell yourself:

- Put together a binder, Power-Point presentation, or report on past projects. Include lists of clients, especially big-name companies. Some businesses use images of their client lists as the background walls of their booths. One way to present your completed projects is in a problem-solution format. Clearly indicate what your customer's problem or task was and then show how you solved or accomplished it.

- Use photos of yourself or your service professionals in action at your booth.

- Consider using before-and-after photos. These work well for businesses whose services make a visible difference, such as cosmetic professionals or home/office space remodeling companies.

- Present customer testimonials on posters or in PowerPoint presentations.

Marketing Materials and Handouts

Many of the marketing materials you'll distribute at a trade show may be the same as those you've developed for other uses in your company, such as company brochures, product sales sheets, catalogs, and order forms. However, you may also want to develop special materials and giveaways just for the trade show—especially since your other materials may be too costly to give away in large numbers. Consider creating:

- Brochures about your company
- Product sales sheets (with specific products and prices)
- Special offers with discounts
- Order forms
- Lead gathering forms
- Catalogs (to be given only to serious prospects because of the expense)

Demonstrations and Videos

Anything interactive gets people's attention and attracts more visitors to your booth. If appropriate, do a live demonstration of your product or service. If it's impractical to demonstrate your product or service live, create a video or computer slide promo showing its features and benefits. If it's fun and engaging, it will attract and keep attendees at your booth, leading them to ask questions and learn more. Make sure to test your product and demo ahead of time—and practice, practice, practice. If you're using PowerPoint, back up your presentation on a DVD or portable drive in case anything happens to the computer in transit.

Free Stuff

People love to get something free—and they'll trek across a crowded trade show floor if they see an attractive giveaway on the other side. Thus, giving away free stuff—sometimes called swag—is a great way of attracting visitors to your booth.

The best giveaways are samples of your own products—if they're inexpensive and small enough to fit into your booth. If your product or service doesn't meet these requirements, you may want to consider giving away a trinket or knickknack that includes your name, logo, website, and/or other contact info.

After the Show

This is where you make your trade show efforts pay off. If you walk off the trade show floor thinking your work is finished, you're not getting all you can from your trade show dollars. After the show, you need to follow up on all the leads you've captured.

Once you return from the show, organize the information you collected. Within a week or two of the show, contact any potential customers you met there; wait any longer, and they're likely to have forgotten you. You can follow up your customer leads in any of the following ways:

■ **By email or letter.** Send your message as soon as possible after the show. Be sure to attach or enclose relevant promotional materials and to thank your prospect for stopping by your booth.

■ **By phone.** Make a call about a week after the show. If your prospect is truly interested, try setting up a meeting.

■ **With a meeting.** Set one up as soon as your prospect's schedule allows. Plan to use the meeting to make a sale.

■ **With products and services.** For customers who ordered products at the show, ship products right away, along with catalogs showcasing your company's other offerings. For service providers, immediately schedule time for your service professionals to meet with and assist potential new clients.

Trade Show Costs

The cost of exhibiting at a trade show varies substantially, depending on the show you choose, the number and nature of attendees, how targeted the market is, and who the other exhibitors are likely to be. For many of the biggest shows and the ones with the most desirable audiences (such as some technology conferences), booth space alone can start at close to $10,000. In contrast, smaller local shows may cost only a few hundred dollars. *Trade Show Week* estimated the average price of exhibit space at $23 per square foot in 2006. (The standard-size booth is 10' x 10', or 100 square feet, or $2,300.)

On top of the cost of the space, of course, you must factor in the cost of a custom booth (if you choose to have one), displays, furniture, materials, traveling expenses, samples, catalogs and brochures, and other fees. Expect to spend only about 30 percent of your total show budget on your space—the rest will go to these other costs. In other words, if you spend $3,000 for a booth space, you can estimate that your total trade show costs will be around $10,000 (not including the cost of your time or staff time).

But a good show can be well worth the price, bringing you great client leads, partnership opportunities, and a host of resources to help better your business. The chart on the next page will help you determine how much to estimate for trade show expenses.

TRADE SHOW BUDGET

TYPE OF EXPENSE	ESTIMATED PERCENTAGE OF TRADE SHOW BUDGET
Exhibit space	25%–35%
Booth construction	12%–18%
Show services	12%–20%
Shipping/Transportation	10%
Promotion	6%–10%
Travel/Accommodation	18%–21%

Calculating Your Trade Show ROI

As with all marketing activities, you'll want to determine whether you're getting a good return on your trade show dollars—a complicated task, since the return on much of your investment won't necessarily be financial. Instead, that return could take the form of increased exposure to your target audience or some other non-financial result. If this is the case, you'll need to emphasize these non-financial benefits in your ROI analysis.

To begin your analysis, do a rough estimate of the sales you expect to generate from the new leads you procure at the show. If this is your first show (or your first show of this type), assume that you'll convert no more than 10% of your leads into actual sales—a reasonable goal, especially if you do good follow-up. For non-financial gains, go back to your list of trade show goals. Did you accomplish what you hoped to in terms of exposure, identification of strategic partners, participation in panels and/or break-out sessions, and so on? All of these things can be vital to your long-term success.

The following page contains a worksheet to help you get started on your own ROI analysis. Simply choose a trade show that you think will be a good fit for your company, and fill in the requested data to get an idea of the ROI you can expect from your trade show marketing.

Here are some tips for using the worksheets (and calculating your ROI):

■ **Be specific about your financial goals.** This means that you need to include not just the total return you'd like to receive on your advertising investment but what that translates to in terms of customers and expenditures.

■ **Remember non-financial goals.** While you may not be able to put a cash value on things like brand awareness and customer perception, these are important components of any marketing campaign, and as such must be considered when calculating return on investment. Thus, if you were preparing this worksheet for your organic cosmetics company appearing at a spa and salon regional show, you might list the following as your non-financial goals: to procure a new sales rep for the region, to identify potential strategic partners to carry your line, and to increase customers' awareness and improve brand visibility for your cosmetics line.

RETURN ON INVESTMENT

YOUR TRADE SHOW ROI

Your business: _____

Your target market: _____

Your trade show: _____

GOALS

Financial: _____

Non-financial: _____

SHOW AND FIT TO TARGET MARKET

Show name: _____

Attendees: _____

Attendee demographics: _____

Percentage of attendees that fit target market: _____

Other information (if any): _____

PROJECTED COSTS

Booth space: _____

Cost of booth shipping and set-up: _____

Other show services: _____

Cost of materials: _____

Cost of samples to give away: _____

Travel, hotel, meals, and other costs: _____

Pre- and post-show promotion costs: _____

Total direct show costs: _____

PROJECTED RETURNS, FINANCIAL

Expected new customers: _____

Expected average sale per customer at show: _____

Expected lifetime average income from each customer signed at show: _____

Increase in income: _____

Total cost of show: _____

Total projected net financial gain (increase in income minus cost of show): _____

PROJECTED RETURNS, NON-FINANCIAL

_____

_____

TOTAL ROI (Total Net Financial Returns Plus Total Non-Financial Returns): _____

TRADE SHOW BUDGET (12 MONTHS)

	JAN	FEB	MARCH	APRIL	MAY
Professional Assistance					
Writers					
Graphic designers					
Photographers/Illustrators					
Booth design firm					
Other consultants					
Printing/Reproduction					
Shipping and Postage					
Trade Show Fees					
Exhibit space					
Booth construction/setup					
Meeting room fees					
Other trade show fees					
Travel					
Travel (airfare/car expenses)					
Hotel					
Meals					
Other travel expenses					
Entertainment					
Supplies/Cost of Goods/Manufacturing					
Booth					
Banners/Signs					
Promotional items					
Product samples					
Other supplies/goods/manufacturing costs					
Other					
TOTAL					

NOTE: An electronic version of this worksheet is available as part of the Planning Shop's Marketing Budget Templates package.

JUNE	JULY	AUGUST	SEPT	OCT	NOV	DEC	TOTAL

Lingo

BEAT: The topic a reporter or columnist regularly covers. Rhonda Abrams' "beat" is entrepreneurship and small business.

CLIPPING SERVICE: A service that monitors the media (newspapers, magazines, online sites); finds mentions of your company, product, or service; and forwards those to you, thus enabling you to track the effectiveness of your PR activities.

EMBARGO: A restriction on the publication of a press release or story until a certain date. Embargoes allow you to time press coverage so that it comes out simultaneously or in time for another event, such as the release of a new product.

HOOK: An angle to a press release or story that makes the reader or media target interested, motivating them to run your story. Often a hook is a way to tie a story to a current event or holiday.

LEAD: The most important point of the story, typically the first paragraph.

MEDIA DATABASE: A collection of contact information on members of the media, including the topics they cover, the media outlets they work for, circulation or reach of each outlet, contact information, and more. These are typically developed and maintained by for-profit companies, and you can subscribe to these services and/or buy media lists targeted to your media efforts from them.

NEWSWIRE (OR WIRE SERVICE): A service that transmits news, press releases, and other information to members of the media. Some newswires (such as PR newswires) exist specifically to transmit press releases to the media.

PR AGENCY: A company that specializes in garnering and coordinating public relations activities for other businesses.

PRESS KIT: A collection of information, including your press release, background information, clippings, and photos, that is sent to members of the media to provide greater detail than could be included in a press release alone.

PRESS RELEASE: An announcement to the media of news or other information made with the hope of generating media coverage about your company, products, or services. Press releases can be distributed in print, via email, or through wire services.

PUBLICITY STUNT: A promotional event that attracts media coverage, particularly one that has a strong visual component, to appeal to TV or Internet media contacts.

CHAPTER 17

Public Relations

If you want to reach a lot of potential customers, what better way than to get people in the media talking about your company, product, or services? Think about what a great impact it makes when a well-known TV personality mentions a company or a well-respected columnist gives a glowing review of a product. This kind of coverage has two major benefits: it's more believable and persuasive than ads and other kinds of marketing that originate from a company, *and* you don't (directly) pay for it.

Public relations (PR) is a way of making yourself known to potential customers by leveraging *unpaid* media, as opposed to paying for ad space. This most often takes the form of mentions in magazines and newspapers and on websites, radio, and TV and using other forums to spread the good word about your company. (Public relations appears in this section of the book, because successful PR requires extensive person-to-person interaction with media professionals.)

Good press is essentially free advertising for your business. An article in the press, especially if it's favorable, is equivalent to thousands of dollars' worth of free ad space. An objective article that speaks well of your company and/or your products or services is actually worth far more than advertising, because press coverage, unlike ads, is viewed as an unbiased take on what you have to offer. Typical public relations activities include:

- Convincing journalists to cover your product or service in stories they do for their print, TV, radio, or Internet media outlet. You could send samples of your organic tamales to a local morning TV talk show and contact the show's producers to encourage them to include your product in their Cinco de Mayo coverage.

- Working to get your product or service reviewed in media outlets that influence customers' purchases. Explaining to a well-known print and online reviewer why she should evaluate your company's new mobile service for wireless devices in her upcoming story about high-tech gadgets would be part of a public relations campaign.

- Coordinating a special event aimed at the media, such as a new product launch or demonstration, press conference, or other publicity stunt that will attract news coverage. Hosting a male beauty contest to launch your new line of swimwear could draw a lot of attention to your products.

> *Look for the few most important people in the segment you're in and become friendly with them. Send them real news, not just press releases; make sure they get the news first. Ask them out to lunch once in a while. If they have a question, make sure they get an answer quickly. Offer an embargoed press release to them before it hits the newswire, giving them an exclusive.*
>
> **Adeena Babbitt**
> **Manager of Media Relations**
> **American Society for Aesthetic**
> **Plastic Surgery**

■ Hosting a special Investor Day, where investors can preview your upcoming products and learn about your prospects for future growth. This builds their confidence in your company and may attract additional investment dollars.

Keep in mind, however, that even though you won't have to pay for media coverage, PR is not really free. You will need to dedicate time and resources to nurturing media contacts, coordinating media events, and putting together media material. And unless you have staff to manage your PR efforts, you are likely to want to hire a PR agency or consultant to do this. But PR, when done well, can be one of the most effective marketing techniques available. In fact, most large corporations have inside PR staff and also retain outside PR firms, because PR is such an important tool in a company's marketing plan.

Why PR?

The purpose of PR, like all marketing efforts, is to increase sales. To achieve that, of course, people need to be aware of you and to think favorably about your company, product, or service. PR is an extremely useful method for accomplishing that. It helps make your company, product, or service look attractive to the public, potential customers, and other interested parties (like investors and potential partners).

PR has a range of specific goals, including to:

■ Get your company noticed and increase name and brand recognition

■ Establish and/or improve your company's image

■ Keep your company name, brand, product, service, and leadership team in the public eye

■ Educate the public, media, investors, and others about what you do or produce

■ Convince prospects that your company's products or services are worth buying and that others think highly of them

■ Introduce a new product, service, or member of your management team

■ Correct a falsehood about your company

■ Influence public policy in a way that benefits your company

PR Versus Customer-Oriented Marketing

The key difference between PR activities and your other marketing activities is that PR activities are *aimed at generating media coverage*. Basically, any activity that targets members of the media (including online media such as bloggers) comes under the PR umbrella. In addition, a subset of marketing activities aimed at investors is typically included in PR. Yet while the field of PR has traditionally focused on influencing the media, the term has broadened to include a wide range of activities that capture the public attention. For this reason, you may find PR firms today specializing in offbeat events aimed at consumers or in spreading viral marketing to consumers through online social networking sites.

But while PR activities are directed toward the media, their ultimate goal is to reach your target customer. This means that the type of customers you're trying to reach will dictate your PR approach. Choose the right PR vehicle for your target market:

- **Consumer.** Use media aimed at the general public (such as general-circulation newspapers, popular magazines, TV, radio, and websites) to make consumers aware of a company and its products/services and the benefits of those products or services. This can include specialty media (such as *PC Week* or *Cat Fancy* magazines) aimed at consumers.

- **Business-to-business.** Use the trade media (industry-specific publications such as *Nation's Restaurant News* or *Aviation Week*) or business events, like trade shows and conferences, to promote a company, product, or service to other businesses, in order to generate new clients or find partners.

- **Investor.** Educate existing or potential investors and attract funding using investor-oriented media (such as the *Wall Street Journal* or *Investor's Business Daily*) or events.

When to Do PR

Consistent PR keeps your company's name and products in front of existing and potential customers—which is why big corporations maintain year-round PR efforts. Most companies, however, can't afford to do PR all the time, nor do they necessarily have anything new or interesting to attract media attention on an ongoing basis. Given your limited resources, it's important to know when PR is most useful and effective. Key times to initiate active PR efforts include when you are:

- Introducing a new company, product, or service

- Upgrading or changing an existing product or service

- Announcing new executive staff or other members of your leadership team

- Announcing a strategic partnership with another company (especially a large or well-known one)

- Celebrating a significant company milestone, such as achievement of revenue or investment goals, venturing into new markets, or winning an award from an outside agency

- Announcing major funding or mergers/acquisitions

- Announcing public appearances of a company executive (for example, as a keynote speaker for an upcoming conference)

- Developing a specific campaign to get coverage in the consumer, business, or trade press

- Announcing changes in a company stock/investment situation

- Doing damage control for a company crisis

The Usual Suspects

One way to keep your company name in the news on an ongoing basis without a large PR budget is to develop relationships with key journalists so they'll turn to your company or executives as reliable sources of information. By positioning your company owner or key team members as experts in their field, especially if they can offer useful data or lively quotes, you may be able to get them quoted frequently in relevant articles.

Your PR Arsenal

When developing your PR campaign and ongoing PR activities, you'll utilize a number of key PR tools to capture media attention and find the right media members to contact. These typically include:

- **Press release.** A written notice to the press announcing a company development (such as the launch of a new product), which can be distributed in print or online or both to members of the media. A press release is the backbone of all media efforts and must grab the attention of the media. You'll learn more about what makes a good press release and how to develop your own on pages 201–205.

- **Press kit.** A collection of material supporting your press release—typically including photos, background material on the company, pictures, samples, and other press clippings—which is distributed to members of the media. (For more about press kits, see pages 206–207.)

- **Visuals.** Photos, videos, product covers or boxes, or other graphic elements. Most media want or need visual elements when telling a story. By including these, you increase your chance of getting coverage.

- **Media list.** A list of reporters and members of the media (including their contact information) who are likely to cover stories relating to your industry, product, or service. Such lists can be purchased from media list database services. (For more about developing your media list later in this chapter see pages 207–208.)

- **Your Rolodex.** The media contacts with whom you've developed ongoing relationships. These are your key targets when developing stories for the press as well as the people most likely to give you coverage.

- **Wire services, or newswires.** These are services that distribute press releases to members of the media, getting the word out to hundreds or thousands of journalists and editors.

- **PR agencies.** Companies that provide public relations management, planning, and services. Because managing and developing public relations is such a time-consuming marketing activity, most large corporations, and many small companies, hire outside PR agencies to manage this part of their marketing efforts. If PR is important to your company, you'll either want staff dedicated to PR or you'll want to hire a PR agency or consultant.

- **The "hook."** The angle used to tie coverage of your company, product, or service to external events, news, and trends. (For more about hooks, see pages 202–203.)

- **Your pitch.** The words you will use to convince a member of the media to do a story about you or include you in a story they have planned. Your pitch can be used in a cover letter or email when you send your press release or in a follow-up phone call you'll make after sending a press release. Prepare and practice a pitch before you start making calls to reporters, focusing quickly on what's in your story for the reporter and their audience—that is, why your press release is the basis for an interesting, informative, or amusing story.

The Press Release

The backbone of all PR activities is the press release—and getting good media coverage starts with a great press release. A press release is a written piece, distributed via email, print, or both, containing all the details of your story. A good press release should give a journalist everything they need to write a story—traditionally the five w's: who, what, where, when, why—as well as explaining how to reach you or someone who can speak for your company. Of course, if a journalist decides to cover your story, they are likely to contact you for more information, but be aware that many online news sites will run press releases exactly as they are received. So it's important that your press release reads like a complete story.

Keep in mind that most members of the media get dozens, if not hundreds, of press releases each and every day! That means it is *very* hard to break through the clutter and capture their attention. (And that's why personal relationships are so important.)

Make your press release catchy enough to entice a member of the media to open their email or pick up the printed press release and start reading. Once a journalist, editor, or producer starts reading, it's got to be compelling enough to hold their attention. To move your release to the top of the pile:

- Find a compelling news hook or angle (see page 202–203).
- Write a catchy headline, connected to the hook
- Create a strong opening paragraph (lead) connecting a holiday, trend, or newsworthy item to your company's activities
- Keep it short—one page is best; two pages at most
- Demonstrate benefits to the public or customers rather than singing the praises of the company or products
- Use simple, clear language
- ■ Include quotations from customers, company management, or industry experts
- Offer visuals— graphics, photos, videos—to make your story more appealing for TV, print, or Internet
- Offer interviews with members of the public, customers, key executives
- Place an "About the Company" section at the end of the release and include clear, easy-to-locate contact information
- Typical press release components include:
- Contact name, phone, email address
- ■ Date the information can be reported and/or indication that it is to be *embargoed* (that is, not to be publicized) until a certain date
- Headline
- Subhead
- Dateline (location and date of publication)
- Hook (in first paragraph, ideally in first line)

Myth🚫Buster

Techies Love Buzzwords

MYTH: To interest the technology press, you have to speak their language.

BUSTED: PR people often try to impress tech journalists, showing they can "talk the talk" by filling their releases and pitches with buzzwords and jargon. However, this is not always necessary, especially for the vast majority of technology journalists. Even if journalists are tech savvy, they still have to know how to communicate to their readers. Sure, include specifications and details, but make sure the gist of your story—what makes your product or service unique or better—can be clearly understood. Bridge the gap between industry jargon and plain English, and show why your message matters to their readers—and your potential customers.

> *One of the key things for small businesses to remember is to make their stories as local as possible. Find a satisfied local customer and get approval to use their experience. If you're a national business or a franchise, you still need to find local customers to appeal to the local media. Tell your story through their voices.*
>
> **Julie McHenry**
> **President**
> **Communications Insight**

- Key facts: Who, what, where, when, why
- Quotation (from someone in your company, a customer, or an affected party)
- The reason people should care about the information therein
- Background information about the company
- Additional resources available to the media (such as graphics, video, interview subjects)

Get Them "Hooked"

If you want *your* request—your press release—to stand out from the crowd, you have to grab a journalists' attention quickly and effectively. To do this, you need a "hook."

A hook is a compelling story angle that makes journalists want to write or produce a story about your company, because they believe it will interest their readers, listeners, or viewers.

One effective hook is to find a newsworthy trend or development relevant to your business. For example, if you own an electronics recycling service, your hook could be to tie the story of your business into news stories about overflowing landfills or about a new survey revealing the amount of chemicals leaking into groundwater. In the headline of your press release, immediately link the issue to your company, then show how your company is helping solve this serious community problem. Your press release has given the journalist a timely story with a newsworthy angle. And you'll get positive coverage!

Effective PR hooks:

- **Holidays or special months.** Every media outlet looks for stories tied to holidays and events that capture the public's attention (back-to-school, New Year's resolutions). Link coverage of your company or product to these holidays, and you're far more likely to get mentioned. There is also a huge range of specially designated months like National Weddings Month, National Candy Month, National Small Business Week, and so on.

- **Local angle on national story or trend.** Local media outlets are always interested in finding ways to cover national trends with local examples. If you can provide that example, you're more likely to get coverage. If your business mirrors a national trend, use that as a hook. For instance, "Local Girls Form Knitting Groups, Reflecting National Trend," demonstrates how the national popularity of knitting among young females is showing up locally.

- **Surveys, statistics, data.** Journalists love numbers, and new surveys are news. So conducting a survey gives you an excuse to send out a press release. If you can't do your own survey, find ways to include statistics compiled by others to increase the effectiveness of your press release. For instance, a gourmet chocolate maker could use the hook: "Chocolate contains up to four times the anti-oxidants found in green tea, according to Holland's National Institute of Public Health and the Environment."

■ **Lists/Tips.** Journalists also love lists of tips and checklists. These make good reading and TV, and they establish your company as an expert in an area. A local home insulation company, for instance, could send out a press release explaining the "Top Seven Steps to Cut Heating Costs."

■ **Innovation.** If you've created something truly new, then you're definitely newsworthy and a good target for media coverage. But this depends on being really innovative. An inventor could say, for example: "Entrepreneur creates lightweight, foldable, portable treadmill—perfect for frequent travelers."

■ **Awards, national recognition.** Local and industry press may be interested if you win national awards or receive major recognition.

Finding a hook is an important part of getting coverage. Once you find your hook, carefully weave it into a compelling headline and *lead,* or first paragraph, of your press release, tying it to your business. Build the rest of your release around your hook, using any additional information and quotations you can find to support it.

BRAINSTORMING

WHAT'S THE HOOK?

Identify potential hooks for your story:

■ **Holiday/Special month:**

■ **Local angle on national trend:**

■ **Surveys, statistics:**

■ **Lists/Tips:**

■ **Innovation:**

■ **Awards, recognition:**

■ **Other:**

Write a sentence tying the hook to your company, product, or service:

_____

_____

_____

_____

_____

_____

_____

_____

_____

SAMPLE: **PRESS RELEASE**

the**Planning**shop

FOR IMMEDIATE RELEASE

Contact: Maggie Smith

The Planning Shop

Tel: 650-289-9120

Email: msmith@planningshop.com

Three Million New Entrepreneurs in Search of Business Numbers (HEADLINE)

New How-to Guide Solves Perennial Business Challenge (SUBHEAD)

(DATELINE) PALO ALTO, CA, September 6, 2006 – More than three million new businesses are launched every year—and most entrepreneurs face the same problem: Where do I find the information I need to make smart decisions? (HOOK)

Recognizing the need for businesspeople to find data on customers, markets, and competition, The Planning Shop today launched ***Successful Business Research: Straight to the Numbers You Need—Fast!***, the first simple, step-by-step guide to gathering critical business data. (WHY, WHAT, WHO, WHEN)

"Finding reliable business data is a challenging task," explains author Rhonda Abrams. "There's either too little information—or too much. Entrepreneurs are hungry for information. In a competitive market, they need immediate help finding this vital data that exists, and often for free."
(QUOTATION FROM COMPANY EXECUTIVE)

Successful Business Research: Straight to the Numbers You Need—Fast! provides a step-by-step guided tour of all the major business resources. It focuses on providing tools to find *free information*, whether for starting a new business or for expanding an existing one. (MORE DETAILS)

Molly Lavik, Practitioner Faculty of Marketing, Pepperdine University's Graziadio School of Business and Management, has this to say about the new book: "At last, a straightforward book that demystifies business research. The Planning Shop has given business practitioners and students an incredibly useful tool."
(QUOTE FROM REPUTABLE SOURCE)

About The Planning Shop: (BACKGROUND INFO)

The Planning Shop, located in Palo Alto, California, specializes in business resources for entrepreneurs and is the leading publisher of books on small business.

Screen shots of the book are available at the following link: www.planningshop.com/screenshots
(ADDITIONAL RESOURCES)

EDITORS: If you would like more information about this topic or to schedule an interview with Rhonda Abrams, please contact Maggie Smith at 650-289-9120 or msmith@planningshop.com. (CONTACT INFORMATION)

BRAINSTORMING

YOUR PRESS RELEASE

Use this worksheet to draft a press release for your company, product, or service. Be sure to include:

- Contact name, phone, email address
- Date the information can be reported (if it's to be embargoed) or indication that the information is for immediate release
- Headline (to catch attention)
- Subhead (to provide explanation)
- Dateline (location and date) of press release
- Hook (what makes this newsworthy) in first paragraph, ideally in first line
- Key facts:
  - What is happening
  - When it is happening
  - Who is behind it (your company)
  - Why it is happening (what is motivating the development, why people should care)
  - Where it is happening
- Quotation (from someone in your company, a customer, an affected party)
- Background information about the company
- Additional resources available to the media (such as graphics, video, interview subjects)

_____

_____

_____

_____

_____

_____

_____

_____

_____

_____

_____

_____

_____

_____

_____

_____

Press Kits

A press release can be sent to a large number of people in the media, but you'll often want or need to provide more information to key media targets. To do so, you'll create a *press kit*. A press kit gives journalists more resources to help them craft their stories and provide coverage of your announcement. Once again, the goal is not just to convince them that yours is a story worth covering but to *help them do their work*. The easier it is for an overworked journalist to produce your story, the more likely you are to get coverage. Your media kit can include anything that motivates and helps journalists in relation to your story, such as:

- Your press release
- Visuals (photos, charts, videos, illustrations)
- Samples of your product (if practical and affordable)
- Positive articles about your company
- Studies or surveys (journalists love numbers)
- Names of potential interview subjects and their contact info
- Company background information

But don't overwhelm your recipients! If your media kit is too large, it will be intimidating, and busy journalists won't want to take the time to look through it.

BRAINSTORMING

YOUR PRESS KIT

Use this worksheet to identify the items you could include in your press kit:

Your press release:_____

Visuals (photos, charts, videos, illustrations):_____

Samples of your product: _____

Articles about the company: _____

Studies or surveys: _____

List of potential interview subjects and contact info: _____

Company background materials:_____

Other: _____

You can assemble a media kit in print and send it to journalists, or you can create a digital media kit to send via email—or both. One advantage of a print media kit is that it has a certain importance and staying power. When a physical kit shows up in someone's mail, they're likely to at least look at it, but a kit attached to an email may never be opened. If you send a physical kit, you may want to include your visuals on a CD as well, since journalists will need digital versions for their own use. Of course, the cost of putting together a physical media kit can be high. Digital media kits are far less expensive to produce and distribute.

If you decide to send a press package to journalists, put it in a presentation folder with your company name and logo on the front cover. For your online media kit, create a special section of your website or add it as an attachment to your email (this is less desirable, as many people will not open attachments from unknown senders).

Finding the Media

Once you've developed your press release and press kit, you need to pinpoint the right media members to contact—that is, those who are most likely to do stories on topics related to your company and to be receptive to your approach.

There are companies devoted to developing and maintaining databases of media contact information, letting you know which journalist, producer, or researcher covers which topics for which media outlets and how you can best reach them. Using one of these media database services, you can build a media list specifically for your business. You can specify the beat/assignment/topic area (for example, business, book reviews, fashion, or technology), the type of media (newspaper, magazine, TV, website), how large a circulation or reach you're aiming for, and more.

Media lists, however, are only a starting point: you'll also want to do your own research to find the reporters and producers most likely to be receptive to your story. Start by identifying the media outlets you already know you'd like to reach. Then check the publication's or station's websites, which often list the names, email addresses, and/or phone numbers for section editors and key journalists. This information is also listed in newspapers and magazines within their first few pages. If you can't find who edits or writes for a particular section, call the publication and ask. Do the same for radio and TV programs and websites.

Get the Editorial Calendar

Print publications, especially magazines, maintain an editorial calendar, which shows when they are going to focus on certain topics (such as an annual summer travel issue, a special New Year's resolution section, or a guide to summer camps). Some radio and TV programs may also have editorial calendars. These calendars provide a preview of the kinds of stories, themes, and special sections to be featured in upcoming issues or shows. Request a media or advertiser kit, study the topics planned for each week or month, and plan your PR according to the schedule. For instance, if you're launching a new health club, time your PR so that journalists will have information in time for their magazine's special health and fitness issue.

Making Contact

Need to know which members of the media to contact about your product or services? The following are good sources for media lists, which you can then use to build a list specific to your business:

- **Bacon's (Cision):** www.us.cision.com
- **Media Atlas:** www.mediatlas.prnewswire.com
- **Vocus:** www.vocus.com
- **BurrellesLuce:** www.burrelles.com

One of the advantages of using these databases is that you'll discover there are more media outlets covering your type of story than you'd ever imagined—and you'll have the names and numbers of the journalists working for those outlets in front of you.

BRAINSTORMING

YOUR MEDIA CONTACTS

Researching media outlets that serve your target market or using PR sources such as Bacon's or Media Atlas, make a list of some of the individuals who cover topics related to your company, products, or services. Use this list to develop and nurture relationships that can lead to increased media coverage.

CONTACT NAME:			
Media Outlet			
Beat/Assignment			
Email			
Phone			
Notes			

Send Out Releases and Kits

Once you've compiled a list of key media contacts, it's time to actually reach out and get your message to those contacts. How will you get in touch with members of the media?

■ **Newswires.** By far the most efficient way to send out a press release is to use a wire service, or newswire. Wire services send members of the media information that may be of interest to them. Well-known wire services that send out "hard" news include the Associated Press and Reuters. However, you're not likely to get your press releases on those wires. Instead, you can pay to have your press release distributed on a PR wire service, which will distribute (via email) notices of press releases to the media. Some PR wire services:

— PR Newswire (www.prnewswire.com)

— Business Wire (www.businesswire.com)

— Marketwire (www.marketwire.com)

— Internet News Bureau (www.internetnewsbureau.com)

These services charge for submitting releases (usually a few hundred dollars per release), or you can subscribe to the service if you plan to submit releases regularly. Many of these services also provide media list database services, which you may have access to as a subscriber. Members of the media do look at these wire services, but remember that thousands of stories move on these wires every week, so don't depend on wire services to do the full job for you.

■ **Mass emails.** Once you have a media list, you can send your press releases directly to your media contacts. Assuming you have the technical skills to send mass emails without showing individual addresses, this can save you the cost of using a wire service. Although you'll reach far fewer members of the media, if you have a good list, it may be as effective as using a wire service. Keep in mind, however, that many members of the media use email filters, so they may never open your email. And because they're unlikely to open attachments or click on links in an unsolicited email, remember to include the text of your press release in the email itself.

■ **Personal contact.** Regardless of how you send out mass press releases, you should still personally contact the members of the media who are your most likely targets. Over time, you'll have developed personal relationships with your most important media contacts; give these people a call or send an email when you have something to announce. But even before you've had a chance to establish these long-standing personal relationships, your PR efforts should include:

— Personal emails to your most important targets that include a short (one-paragraph) intro that's been personalized for them and that relates directly to their beat/assignment and the media outlet they work for, followed by your press release (included in the body of the email, not as an attachment)

— Phone calls to your most important targets, to make sure they've received the press release and to find out whether they want additional information or a press kit

---

Not So Fast!

Just because you've sent out the press release and personally contacted your key media targets doesn't mean you're finished getting the word out to the media. You now need to *follow up* with these key contacts. If they've run a story, call to thank them. If they haven't run your story, contact them to see what types of stories they're interested in running in the future.

Leverage the Investment Press

Want to attract funding for your business? Consider pitching stories to the investment press. That's how many investors learn about new companies or innovations in the market—and many base investment decisions on what they read, hear, or see. Some venues to consider:

■ http://bankrate.com

■ CNNMoney.com

■ Investor's Business Daily

■ http://kiplinger.com

■ *MarketWatch*

■ *Money*

■ Morningstar.com

■ TheStreet.com

■ *The Wall Street Journal*

■ Zacks.com

You'll find a more comprehensive list of investment and general business press on Yahoo's finance site at http://biz.yahoo.com/apf/.

— Events and press conferences if you have something very important, visual, or exciting to announce that might entice the media to attend

Because all of this takes so much work, you may want to consider hiring a PR agency or a PR consultant to manage your media activities. Ideally, you'll find one that already has contacts with members of the media who cover topics related to your business. Often, PR agencies are hired on a year-round monthly retainer basis, but it's also possible to hire an agency or consultant for just one PR campaign. You'll usually pay for these services regardless of whether the agency succeeds in getting you press coverage. However, a few agencies offer a "pay for placement" cost structure.

Calculating Your Public Relations ROI

As with every part of your marketing plan, you'll want to estimate a potential return on investment (ROI) for your public relations expenditures. The good news: when your PR efforts are successful, your ROI will be fairly high—at least in terms of providing exposure you'd otherwise have had to pay much more for through advertising and/or other marketing methods. Unfortunately, however, you can't control the outcome of your PR efforts, which means that even well-planned and well-executed PR campaigns can sometimes result in little media interest and even less customer response. In such cases your ROI will be very low.

Moreover, it is often difficult to measure the real ROI for PR. Even if you get a lot of good press coverage, it's hard to know whether that will necessarily convert to sales. That's why PR is frequently done in conjunction with other marketing efforts, such as advertising.

On the following page you'll find a worksheet to help you get started on your own ROI analysis. Simply describe the aspect of your business you're trying to publicize, identify your target market, detail the public relations activities you plan to undertake, and fill in the requested data.

Here are some tips for using the worksheets (and calculating your ROI):

■ **Be specific about your financial goals.** This means that you need to include not just the total return you'd like to receive on your public relations investment but what that translates to in terms of customers and expenditures.

Thus, if you were preparing this worksheet for a restaurant looking to increase sales by introducing an all-local menu, you might state as your financial goal that you wanted to raise your average sales per square foot by achieving full bookings on weekends and 80% bookings on weeknights and weekday lunches. Then you'd figure out what this translates to in terms of expected new diners annually and the average annual income per diner to get your total projected income from your PR efforts.

■ **Remember non-financial goals.** While you may not be able to put a cash value on things like brand awareness and customer perception, these are important components of any marketing campaign, and as such must be considered when calculating return on investment. Thus, to use the restaurant example again, you might cite the following as your non-financial goals: four positive print reviews of the restaurant (and its new menu) in major local papers, coverage by at least one TV station, three stories in local magazines aimed at the environmental community, and reviews on local restaurant review websites.

■ **Be sure to include *all* of your PR activities in support of your financial and non-financial goals.** In the case of the above-mentioned restaurant focused on sustainable dining, your PR activities might include throwing a press party to showcase the new menu items as well as hiring a PR consultant, preparing and sending out press releases, and preparing a media kit.

RETURN ON INVESTMENT

YOUR PUBLIC RELATIONS ROI

Your business: _____

Your target market: _____

Your public relations activities: _____

GOALS
Financial goals: _____

Non-financial goals: _____

PROJECTED COSTS
Cost of PR consultant/agency/staff: _____

Cost of event(s): _____

Cost of printing/reproduction of materials: _____

Other costs: _____

Total costs for PR campaign: _____

PROJECTED RETURNS, FINANCIAL
Expected new sales as a result of PR: _____

Expected average annual income per sale: _____

Increase in annual income from PR: _____

Total cost of PR: _____

Total projected net financial gain: _____

PROJECTED RETURNS, NON-FINANCIAL

_____

_____

TOTAL ROI (Total Net Financial Returns Plus Total Non-Financial Returns): _____

PUBLIC RELATIONS BUDGET (12 MONTHS)

	JAN	FEB	MARCH	APRIL	MAY
Professional Assistance					
Writers					
Graphic designers					
Photographers/Illustrators/Videographers					
Internal PR staff					
PR consultant/Agency					
Other consultants					
Printing/Reproduction					
Press releases					
Media kits					
Graphics/Photos					
Other printing/reproduction costs					
Shipping and Postage					
Media Services					
Media database services					
Newswire fees					
Survey/Poll design/Implementation					
Other media service fees					
Travel					
Airfare, car expense, etc.					
Hotel					
Meals					
Other travel expenses					
Entertainment					
Supplies/Cost of Goods/Manufacturing					
Promotional items					
Product samples					
Other supplies/goods/manufacturing costs					
Other					
TOTAL					

! **NOTE:** An electronic version of this worksheet is available as part of the Planning Shop's Marketing Budget Templates package.

JUNE	JULY	AUGUST	SEPT	OCT	NOV	DEC	TOTAL

BUILDING YOUR MARKETING PLAN

PERSON-TO-PERSON MARKETING

Drawing from the worksheets you completed in this section, outline the person-to-person marketing tactics you will use in your Marketing Plan.

1. Will you use person-to-person marketing techniques (networking, word-of-mouth, trade shows, public relations) in your overall marketing plan? If so, which of the person-to-person marketing techniques described in this section will you use?

_____

_____

_____

2. Which groups, if any, do you plan to join (business, industry, professional, community) in order to network to increase your business? How can the members of these groups help your business?

_____

_____

_____

3. Reiterate your elevator pitch (short description of your company and products or services, to use when networking and meeting prospects).

_____

_____

_____

4. How much, and what types of, entertaining of clients and referral sources will you do, if any, to help market your company?

_____

_____

_____

_____

5. What customer communication efforts (such as email or print newsletters, specialty advertising products, or blogs) will you put in place to make sure you keep your name in front of current and past customers?

_____

_____

_____

6. Will you establish formalized customer loyalty, referral, or affiliate programs to help retain customers and drive new prospects? If so, what is the nature of those programs?

_____

_____

_____

_____

7. What other activities, if any, will you engage in to encourage word-of-mouth marketing about your business?

_____

_____

_____

_____

8. Which trade shows will you attend and why? What will be the nature of the products/services you feature at these trade shows? How will you follow up with contacts you meet at trade shows?

_____

_____

_____

_____

9. Will you use public relations as part of your marketing plan? If so, describe the timing and frequency of your PR efforts (when will you use PR, and for what products, services, or company events?). Will you manage PR internally or hire outside consultants/agencies? What types of PR will you utilize and which media outlets will be the target of most of your PR efforts?

_____

_____

_____

_____

10. How will the person-to-person tactics you have chosen bring you closer to your marketing goals?

_____

_____

_____

_____

SECTION IV

Print Marketing

Lingo

BUSINESS CARDS: A small card that fits in a wallet, featuring your name, business name, corporate identity, and contact info.

BROCHURES: Print pieces designed to give an overview of your company, products, or services.

CATALOG: A printed booklet listing a company's products (including descriptions, photos, and often, prices and specifications).

DIRECT MAIL: Print marketing pieces sent to customers through the postal service. Typically designed to generate immediate sales, they include a strong call to action.

HARD COPY: A digital document printed on paper (as opposed to a soft copy, which is the digital document).

MARKETING COLLATERAL: Print materials used to support a company's marketing efforts—includes brochures, catalogs, newsletters, and even non-print materials (such as website content and slide demonstrations).

PDF: Short for Portable Document Format, this type of document can be viewed on the computer (on the Web and using Adobe Reader software) and still retain the design of the original print piece.

PULL QUOTES: Excerpts or quotes from text enlarged to serve as graphic elements; these are often seen first by readers.

SUBHEADS: Text—usually set in larger type and/or a different font—indicating the topic of the text that follows and serving to break up the text in a document.

WHITE SPACE: Areas in your print marketing pieces without text or images. By including ample white space in your print marketing pieces, you make them more attractive, easier to read, and more sophisticated in appearance.

CHAPTER 18

Marketing in Print

Your print marketing materials are the face of your business on paper. Thus, even in a day and age when everyone depends on electronic information, printed materials continue to play an important role in your marketing plans and efforts. You'll give business cards to people you meet at networking events, catalogs to clients during sales calls, and brochures to prospects at trade shows. You may send direct mail marketing pieces to leads, hoping to persuade them to buy what you're selling. However you use them, print marketing materials provide an important tool for delivering or reinforcing your marketing message, attracting prospects, and ultimately, making sales.

Often referred to as *marketing collateral*, print marketing materials include just about any piece of ink-on-paper material you use to promote your business. These include brochures, catalogs, print newsletters, flyers, and sales sheets and price lists. They also include direct mail pieces—letters, postcards, and other materials you send to customers and prospects to drive sales. (For information on print advertising, see Chapter 10; for information on printed signs and banners, see Chapter 29.)

In many cases, your print materials serve as your representatives when you're not there to sell your business or offer information in person. Because of this, your print marketing materials must be clear and compelling enough to lure customers in without them hearing your elevator pitch.

When done right, print marketing materials can be very powerful. That's because they're *tangible*. Unlike their radio, TV, or Web counterparts, print marketing materials represent something prospects can hold in their hands and interact with, forming a personal connection with your company which is why perhaps people tend to assign more weight to information they've gleaned in print.

Myth ⃠ Buster

R.I.P. Print?

MYTH: In the Internet age, print marketing materials are no longer necessary.

BUSTED: Print marketing is alive and well, though businesses and consumers must approach the task differently than they did before the dawn of the Internet. Long gone are the days when print marketing pieces represented the sole source of company, product, and service information. Today, customers expect to get most of their information from a company's website—and indeed many companies use their print materials to direct people there. For example, executives at L.L.Bean—which mailed a quarter-billion catalogs in 2006 (fifty million more than they'd sent two years earlier)—say they use their catalogs to direct consumers to the company website, as well as to drive sales. Thus, it's wise to have both print and online marketing tools—they complement each other.

Working with Designers and Writers

How do you determine whether you need to hire a designer or writer to help you with your print materials? That will depend on your skill set. If you have a good eye for print layout and can use design software, you might be able to design your own print marketing collateral. And if you're a great writer, you might be able to create sizzling marketing copy. But these skills rarely converge in one person—people with design talents often can't write, and writers aren't usually the best designers. Be honest with yourself and seek feedback. You may be able to collaborate with someone within your company. If the skills aren't there, however, and the materials are important to your marketing plan, hire a professional.

The key to working with designers and writers is making sure they understand your marketing message and goals when creating a piece.

Writers

Here are some things you can do to improve your chances of getting what you need from a copywriter:

- Prepare a document outlining the marketing piece's goals and intended audience.

- Supply the writer with corporate identity material such as logos, colors (Pantone Matching System—or PMS—numbers, if you know them), taglines, previous brochures, and press releases to ensure consistency with your brand identity.

- Supply the writer with a concise list of your offering's features and benefits. Jot down key phrases and ideas you consider critical to attracting your market and selling your product or service. Think benefits, not features.

- Gather testimonials from satisfied clients to be used as part of your copy.

Effective Print Marketing Techniques

Whether you're creating business cards, a catalog, or a direct mail piece, to be effective, all print materials must share a set of common principles. A successful marketing piece catches a prospect's eye and delivers your marketing message concisely. It tells your potential customer what you offer, why they need it, and how to get it. Each marketing piece may serve a slightly different purpose, but together they establish and reinforce your brand and identity through consistent use of logos, taglines, colors, and images. The most successful marketing pieces urge the customer to do something that will get them to try or buy your product or services.

Keys to Effective Print Marketing

Regardless of what type of print marketing collateral you're creating, there are a few key things you need to keep in mind if you're to get your marketing message across and convert prospective customers into purchasers of your products or service:

- **Capture attention.** People suffer from information overload. You've got to hook them with something that will grab their attention.

- **Focus on your marketing message.** You're spending time and money to get a message to your readers—focus on that message clearly. It may appear in copy, headlines, taglines, or images.

- **Reflect your corporate identity**. All of your marketing materials should encompass and be consistent with your overall company identity. Use the same colors and typeface you've chosen for your company's look and feel. Include your name, logo, and tagline. And always reinforce your brand.

- **Remember your target audience.** Use language and images your target market and industry understand and appreciate—but avoid jargon.

- **Keep it simple.** Avoid including too much detail in your print marketing materials, especially technical information. Instead, focus on your core message and use simple, direct language.

- **Include a call to action.** A reader should understand exactly what you're offering and what you want them to do. Whether that's "Use this coupon for a 20% discount" or "Stop by our booth at the trade show," make sure to state your call to action clearly and often.

- **Prominently feature your contact information in multiple places.** Make it easy for customers to contact you and take the next step. Include your company name, phone number, address, contact person, website URL, and email address. Feature your contact information in as many easy-to-spot areas as possible, ideally on every page.

Keys to Effective Design

Print is, after all, a visual medium—so take advantage of that fact. Eye-catching, well-designed print marketing pieces will go a long way toward getting your message across. Keep in mind the following as you design your print marketing collateral:

Design it. Assemble your marketing pieces with an eye to how appealing they will be visually, not just what information you want them to convey. If you or your staff has design skills, or you're working on a simple piece (such as a price list), you may be able to design your material in house. If not, use a preformatted template from an online service or hire a graphic designer.

Embrace white space. The term *white space* refers to areas in your marketing materials that contain no text or images. In most cases, including white space makes your marketing pieces easier to read, more attractive, and often, more sophisticated looking. It also compels you to minimize text, forcing you to choose your words carefully and get to the point quickly. Brochures or flyers crammed with words and images are confusing, making them appear to involve too much effort to read.

Use colors. Careful use of colored ink makes your material pop and reinforces your brand identity. Your use of color, however, doesn't have to be fancy or expensive: choosing just one color in addition to black can liven up a piece considerably.

Use graphics and images wisely. Many marketing pieces include photos, graphs, charts, or illustrations. Choose photos that illustrate the product or service you're offering or reflect your target customer base. You can find many inexpensive, even free stock photos through stock photo services; however, avoid cheesy "clip art."

Break it up. If you have a lot of text, make it more appealing by breaking it into sections. Emphasize important aspects of your message by using subheads (bold, large, or distinctive type that indicates a new topic) or pull quotes (excerpts or quotes enlarged to serve as graphic elements).

Use decent-quality paper. Many of your readers will "touch" your company for the first time through the paper in your marketing materials. Make sure it conveys a feeling of quality.

Designers

Here are some things you can do to improve your chances of getting what you want from a designer:

- Give the designer the document outlining the goals and audience of the marketing piece.

- Finalize and proofread all text before handing off the marketing piece to your designer. Although text changes, cuts, and/or additions are often inevitable, try to keep them at a minimum. Changing text after layout will drive up your costs.

- If you've hired a designer based on the recommendations of others in your field, or on an impressive work portfolio, trust that they will create an effective layout and structure for your marketing piece and don't constantly second-guess them. The design needs to appeal to your target audience, not you.

- When viewing your designer's work, be sure the text is highly visible and flows logically through the piece.

Go Green

One major drawback of print marketing materials is their potential for waste and negative environmental impacts. After all, you not only consume a lot of paper in producing such materials, you also consume a great deal of energy—in producing them, in shipping them from the printer, and in mailing or distributing them to your prospects. And when it's over and done, you're likely to have extra copies.

With this in mind, here are some things you can do to reduce waste while still achieving your marketing goals:

Design "print" materials that never see ink. Produce PDF—or Portable Document Format—versions of your print materials and distribute them electronically. PDFs retain their graphical design and can be viewed on the computer (though not modified) using Adobe Acrobat Reader. Anyone who wants a *hard copy*, meaning a paper version, of the marketing piece can simply print it out on their own printer.

■ **Order lower quantities or print on demand.** Yes, it's cheaper to print large quantities, but this is also likely to result in more overage and waste. You'll also pay more in shipping and storage. Instead, be as realistic as possible about the number of copies you expect to distribute and only order what you truly need. This will also make it easier for you to update materials if details (such as prices or specifications) change.

■ **Print smaller pieces and send readers to your website.** Do you really need a 32-page catalog? Could you accomplish the same thing in 16 or even 8 pages by sending customers to your website for more information? Can you use a postcard-size handout instead of a full-page one? You'll save money and trees by thinking smaller.

■ **Use environmentally sensitive materials.** Choose recycled paper and soy-based inks.

■ **Recycle.** It's inevitable that you'll have leftovers. Don't throw them in the trash; recycle.

■ **Update your lists.** Reduce waste in both printing and distribution by making sure you mail materials only to real prospects. Check the names and addresses to make sure they're current. Eliminate duplicates and remove old names. There are services that will check mailing lists to eliminate outdated contact info.

Distributing Your Marketing Materials

How do you get your marketing pieces into the hands of customers? In many cases, this will depend on the type of piece. For example:

■ **Business cards** are usually handed out or exchanged during person-to-person marketing encounters, including networking and trade shows. Some entrepreneurs also keep a stack of them in a cardholder on their retail countertops or desks.

■ **Brochures** are usually distributed fairly freely. You can make them available at your place of business, hand them out at networking events, send them through the mail to prospects, pass them out at events (like trade shows) that attract prospects, and, of course, give them to prospects in one-on-one meetings.

■ **Catalogs** are more expensive to produce than brochures and are thus distributed more carefully. They're usually given to prospects/customers during sales calls, mailed to targeted prospects, and made available at events like trade shows—though on a more selective basis than, say, brochures.

■ **Sales sheets, product specification sheets, and price lists** help support the sale of a particular product. They're often placed near a product in a retail environment for customers to pick up. They can be sent to prospects interested in a specific product (rather than your entire product line). And they can be brought to trade shows to be given to prospects in place of your entire catalog.

■ **Flyers** are often distributed by hand directly to consumers at events, posted in public locations such as colleges and schools, and dropped off at partner businesses or public places.

■ **Newsletters** can be mailed, handed out at your place of business, or made available to customers on promotional tables at events likely to draw a target market.

Try to match the distribution method to your target market, keeping in mind the expense of producing a particular marketing piece. Postcard-size pieces are usually pretty cheap, even printed in color, so you can distribute a large number of them. Catalogs, in contrast, are typically very expensive to produce, so you need to be more selective in who you send them to.

When determining how and where you'll distribute a particular marketing piece, consider what kind of piece it is, who it's designed to attract, and where and how you plan to reach that target market. Put yourself in your customer's shoes, and ask whether that individual (or business) would be receptive to receiving your materials in the way you plan to distribute them.

Adding It Up

Costs for print marketing vary widely, depending on many factors. First and foremost is how you create the materials: do you write and design them yourself, use preformatted templates, or hire outside specialists? Then there's the matter of printing—do you run them off on your laser printer, use an online print source, or employ a local printing company? What kind of paper and ink do you use? And how many copies will you make? Finally comes the matter of how you plan to distribute these print materials—for example, it's a lot cheaper to hand out flyers on a street corner than to do an expensive mailing through the postal service.

In general, the affordability scale below shows the range of costs for your print materials options.

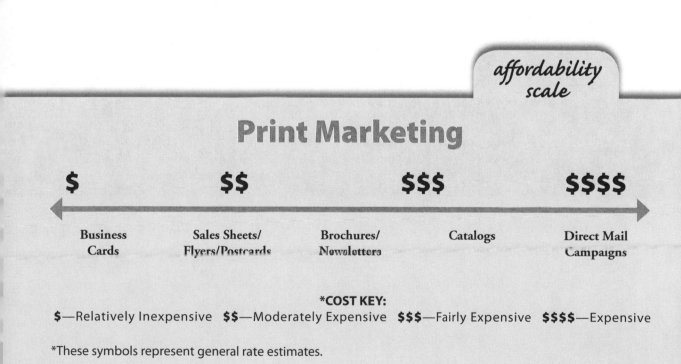

affordability scale

Print Marketing

$	$$	$$$	$$$$
Business Cards	Sales Sheets/ Flyers/Postcards	Brochures/ Newsletters	Catalogs	Direct Mail Campaigns

*COST KEY:

$—Relatively Inexpensive $$—Moderately Expensive $$$—Fairly Expensive $$$$—Expensive

*These symbols represent general rate estimates.

Lingo

CARD STOCK/COVER STOCK: Paper that is thicker than regular paper, such as that used for stationery. Card/cover stock is typically used for postcards, report covers, and high-quality marketing pieces.

CLUB CARD FLYERS: Marketing pieces printed on card stock, designed to be distributed in clubs, restaurants, and other venues.

EVERGREEN: Material or content that does not get outdated quickly (and thus can be used for a long time).

FLYERS: One-page, inexpensive sheets of printed paper containing advertisements or announcements for an event, sale, new company, or other timely information.

GLOSSY/COATED PAPER: Printing paper (or card stock) with a smooth, shiny surface, useful for showcasing photos and graphics, often making a printed piece seem more impressive.

LEAVE-BEHIND: A print marketing piece (like a brochure, folder, or catalog) meant to be left with a client after a meeting.

NEWSLETTERS: Printed informational material, usually four pages or more, with news and tips useful to the recipient mixed with (generally subtle) promotional pitches for products and services.

POINT-OF-SALE (POS): The store or other location where a customer purchases your product. A POS can be the shelf where a product is located or a display near the cash register.

POSTCARDS: Marketing pieces in standard or enlarged postcard formats containing concise, compelling messages sent to prospects by postal mail.

PRINT BROKER: An individual or company that finds appropriate companies to print your materials and negotiates prices.

PRODUCT SPECIFICATION SHEET: A sheet delineating product specifics—particularly useful for technical or industrial products.

SALES SHEET: A single-sheet document that presents the major features (and often pricing) of a product in an easy-to-read format. Sales sheets usually offer more detailed product information than you would find in brochures.

CHAPTER 19

Print Collateral

Y ou may have a flashy website, a killer sales pitch, and a winning conversational manner, but sooner or later, you're probably going to need something more to convince prospects to buy from you. You're going to need *marketing collateral*, or printed pieces that support your marketing and sales efforts.

Definitions of *collateral* include *serving to support, running side by side, parallel, accompanying,* and *additional*—all of which precisely describe the function of marketing collateral: it supports and accompanies your other marketing and sales efforts. Going on a sales call? Better bring a brochure, business card, and catalog. Speaking at a community event? You'll make a bigger impact if you have some flyers to hand out. Is your product a bit complicated? Help explain it to your customers (and salespeople!) by supplying them with product sales sheets.

Print materials represent an important part of your marketing plan because they provide an affordable way of communicating and connecting with customers and prospects. The following are some of their most important features:

- They're tangible: they give prospects something they can touch and feel.

- They're long lasting: they give prospects something to remember you by.

- They indicate commitment: a high-quality printed piece shows that you've put time and money into building your relationship with customers.

- They demonstrate that you're prepared—that you didn't just breeze into an appointment.

- They create connections: by giving prospects something, you begin to build relationships.

- They help make sales by providing information, visuals, and incentives to support your sales pitch.

- They serve as an inexpensive way to promote your business, events, or sales.

Print materials are easy to carry with you and relatively inexpensive to give to potential customers. And it's always good to have something to help prospects remember you by—that's why a casual term for a printed marketing piece is a *leave-behind*, something you can leave behind when you meet with someone.

> **"***Most often, your business card is all somebody gets. It's all they know you by. Everything it is, you are. The money you put into the design of your business card is the best money you can spend on your print collateral. If I had to choose only one thing to promote myself, it would be a business card. And it wouldn't be boring and cheap.***"**
> **Alan Luckow**
> **Luckow Designs**

What's *Not* Required on Your Business Card

When it comes to business cards, there *is* such a thing as too much information. Only include the information you know your prospects and referral sources need most. For example, do prospective customers really need your fax number? If not, leave it off. You might even be able to eliminate your address if customers rarely visit or send you anything. Here's the information that's optional:

- Your job title
- Your mailing address
- A secondary phone number (such as a cell phone)
- Your fax number
- Your instant messaging (IM) address

Remember the Back!

When you begin thinking of your business card as a marketing tool, you'll realize that the reverse side is wildly underutilized! While it's true that many people may want to scribble down info on the reverse side of your business card, this doesn't mean it has to remain blank. You can use this space to print more information about your business or even offer a discount ("Bring in this card for a free consultation").

The most essential print marketing pieces include:

- **Business cards.** Wallet-size cards featuring your corporate identity (company name, logo, tagline, company colors) and contact info.

- **Brochures.** Print pieces of one to ten pages, typically folded over or stapled together, designed to introduce your company and offerings through information that does not change quickly.

- **Sales support materials.** Print pieces—including catalogs, sales/product specification sheets, and price lists—that detail your product and/or service offerings. Catalogs are generally many pages in length, while sales/product specification sheets are usually one to two pages.

- **Flyers, postcards, rack cards.** Inexpensive pieces designed to be distributed in large quantities to announce events, sales, or special offers.

- **Stationery and other miscellaneous printed marketing material.** Letterhead, envelopes, and presentation folders that reinforce your corporate identity, as well as other printed pieces such as calendars, door hangers, posters, announcements, and the like.

- **Direct mail pieces.** Print pieces with a strong call to action, such as an enticement to buy or an announcement of a special offer or sale. (For more on direct mail, see Chapter 20.)

Some of these print marketing materials are also advertisements (particularly flyers, club cards, and rack cards): they're designed to get people to take action—that is, to come to your event, take advantage of your discount, and so on.

Business Cards

Your business card may be your smallest and least expensive marketing piece, but it's also the one you'll give out most, that customers and prospects will hold on to longest, and that will most often serve as the first physical representation of your company. Make your business card work for you by using it to communicate what you do and to convey a feeling about the nature and quality of your company.

It's also good marketing practice to get everyone in the company into the habit of carrying their business cards with them at all times. You never know when you'll meet a potential customer or referral source.

What to Include

Once upon a time, business cards were simple. Then came cell phones, faxes, email addresses, websites, and more. However, not all of that information is absolutely necessary. Too much information forces you to use tiny type, which makes the card difficult to read. Moreover, in trying to include all of that data, you'll likely omit information that's actually more important—such as what you do and, ideally, who your target market is. Remember to think of your business card as a marketing piece. Add one brief line describing your business, especially if the company you work for is not well known or you have a specialty or serve a particular market: "Green Travel Agency, Focusing Exclusively on Eco-tourism."

Here's the essential information to include on your business card:

- Your company name
- Your company logo (if you have one)
- Your name
- Your primary phone number
- Your email address
- Your website URL
- Your tagline (describing what you do, such as "Specializing in corporate gift services")

Color

Adding color makes a big impact—and it's not very expensive. In a stack of colorful cards, black-and-white ones can seem flat and unimpressive. Color is particularly important for your logo and brand identity elements.

Graphics

A graphic element can make your business card stand out. The very best graphic element—and the only one you really need—is your company's logo. Adding a graphic element such as a bold line, triangle, or circle can also make your card more interesting—and thus more memorable.

Design

As is the case with all of your marketing pieces, good, clean design is vital to the effectiveness of a business card. Even though you're only working with a small space, you need to incorporate white space, choose an appealing layout of text and graphics, and remember *not* to attempt to cram everything in. If you don't have the resources to lay out your business card in house, use a template from an online printing service or hire a graphic designer.

SAMPLE: Business Card

Business Card Design "Don'ts!"

Here are some things to avoid in your business card design:

- **Tiny or illegible type.** No matter how minimalist and sophisticated it may appear, difficult-to-read text will only frustrate people.

- **Colors that make the text difficult to read.** Sure, it may look cool to have pale beige ink on a light brown card, but can anyone actually read that? Make sure there's enough contrast between ink color and paper color. Dark ink against a light background is the most legible. Also, choose colors that are appropriate to your line of business—for example, a lawyer wouldn't want dark pink on their card, but a florist or child-care center might.

- **Photos.** In a few select industries (such as residential real estate), including photos on business cards has become commonplace. In general, however, photos are to be avoided.

- **Shapes that don't fit into wallets.** No matter how dazzling your card looks, if it's hard to slip in a wallet, your prospect will probably end up tossing it. For business cards, more than for other marketing pieces, using a standard size is important. In the United States and Canada, that size is 3.5" x 2".

YOUR BUSINESS CARD DESIGN

Sketch a design for your 3.5" x 2" business card. Include your company name and logo, along with your name, key contact information, and a tagline describing what you do.

Brochures

Brochures likely represent the second most common type of printed marketing, with most companies making use of them in one form or another. Designed to provide an overview of your company, products, or services, brochure content is best when it's *evergreen*—in other words, when the information is likely to remain accurate for a long time and thus won't need to be updated frequently. Brochures are particularly useful because they're generally inexpensive to design and produce, so you can be generous in distributing them.

Producing effective brochures isn't difficult, but it does require careful consideration. Before you begin creating your brochure, think about the information your prospects will be looking for and expecting. And consider what headlines will capture their attention and which content will motivate them to take action. Which images, colors, and paper size, shape, and format will engage them? What design will best convey your desired image?

The most commonly used brochure format is a single 8.5" x 11" page, printed on both sides and folded twice to form three panels. Sometimes (inaccurately) referred to as *trifold* brochures, brochures in this format are popular because they fit easily in a standard-size North American business envelope (No. 10).

Brochures, however, can come in virtually any size, length, and format (folded, stapled, or even bound). If you offer an expensive product, such as a car, you might create an oversized, four-color brochure on glossy paper. A brochure for a very complicated and expensive product line, such as major industrial equipment, might even be the size and shape of a book.

Many brochures are designed to be distributed in a point-of-sale display rack—a holder placed in a store or other retail location near the place a customer makes a purchase (such as on the shelf next to the product or near the cash register). Since brochures are often placed where customers and prospects pick them up without interacting with someone from your company, your brochure serves to make a positive impression of your company, provide critical information, and motivate a sale—all on its own. P.O.S. marketing materials have great importance because they are immediately available when a prospect is at their final decision-making point.

What to Include

Brochures exist to give readers information, motivate them to take action or make a purchase, and tell them how to contact you. Make sure anyone who picks up your brochure can easily find your contact information. Put your key contact details, such as phone number, email address, and website URL, in more than one place.

Here's the essential information to put in a brochure:

Your company name, logo, and tagline

Contact information: phone number, address, website, email address (ideally, in more than one place)

■ Description of your products, services, or other offerings

Reasons why readers would take action/make a purchase

In your brochures, always be sure to:

Reinforce your brand. Prominently feature your company's name, logo, and tagline, and use the same colors, typeface, and look and feel that inform your brand image.

■ **List your products/services.** If your brochure introduces your company, list the range of products and services you offer, with *brief* descriptions (if there's room). Do *not* go into great detail—that's the catalog's job.

Make your text sales oriented. Provide the information and marketing messages your readers need to get them to take action. Think of the questions they'll need answered to become motivated to buy.

Limit the amount of text. Brochures are meant to provide an introduction or overview—*not* to provide every last detail about your products or services. Leave the reader wanting more (you can always direct them to your website), and remember to embrace white space!

Include a client list. A list of past and current clients can serve as an extremely effective marketing device, showing prospects that you have solid experience and reassuring them that others have chosen you. If your client list is impressive and/or long, it's particularly motivating. Of course, do not include such a list if it would violate your clients' privacy or without first receiving appropriate permission.

Use visuals. All-text brochures are not very inviting. Photos, especially of people, can liven things up. Preformatted templates from online printers and preprinted brochure paper (to use with your in-house printer) from office supply stores often come with graphic elements that will help make your brochure come alive.

Free Business Cards?

Some online printing services will print your business cards free—but there's a catch. You have to let the print service include its name and logo on the back of the card. Unless you're just starting your business and expect to change information very soon or truly can't afford business cards, avoid this. You card should feature information about your business, not somebody else's.

3-Panel Brochure

Below is a sample three-panel brochure. Remember the page gets folded twice (bi-fold) so make sure you design it so that the information is where you want it to be when finished and folded.

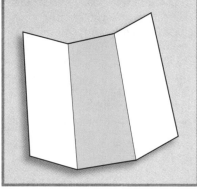

■ **Use benefits/features charts.** Charts listing your features/benefits are extremely effective marketing devices, providing a quick at-a-glance view of how a customer benefits from purchasing your product or service. If appropriate, use these to compare your offerings with the competition (without mentioning names) or to compare the features and benefits of your different offerings (for instance, a chart comparing the three different levels of memberships in a health club).

■ **Take special care with your front-panel message.** If your brochure is going to sit out where people can see it (even if they don't pick it up or read it), it's going to serve more as an ad than an informational piece. For this reason, make sure the front panel or cover contains a message you want them to remember, as well as your company name and logo.

■ **Reassure potential customers.** Include testimonials or success stories from past customers. If you have room, illustrate how your products or services have helped others. Even one recommendation from a satisfied customer can be a powerful influencer.

BRAINSTORMING

YOUR BROCHURE DESIGN

In the spaces below, sketch out a rough design for the front and back of a three-panel brochure. Be sure to include:

■ Your company name, logo, and tagline

■ Contact information: phone number, address, website, and email address

■ Description of your products/services

■ Reasons why readers should take action/purchase

■ Call to action

_____

_____

_____

_____

_____

_____

_____

_____

_____

_____

Sales Support Materials

Some of the most important print marketing materials you'll produce are those that support your sales efforts. The key difference between these materials and other marketing pieces is that these are *directly* and *immediately* related to the sales process (while other marketing collateral may be used to provide information about your company, build your brand, or increase customer interest).

Sales support materials are used primarily at the time or point of sale, often given by a salesperson to a prospect. As such, their primary purpose is to provide the information and details prospects need to make purchasing decisions, as well as to motivate them to choose *your* offering over a competitor's.

Catalogs will be used by salespeople when making in-person sales calls or given to interested prospects at trade shows. You'll also hand out product sales sheets to prospective customers considering purchasing complicated or technical products or services, and you might put a stack of product specification sheets in a display rack near your products in a retail store to give customers more detailed data. Individual product sales sheets represent an inexpensive item you can mail to prospects that need a bit more info to prompt them to buy. And if part of your business is based on direct sales, you may even send your catalog to thousands or tens of thousands of prospects.

As you craft these sales materials, make sure you're developing useful tools for your sales team. Get input from the sales personnel who interact directly with customers to find out what questions prospects ask most. You'll especially want to know which selling points seem to be the most important in "closing the deal."

Catalogs

A catalog provides a complete listing of your products or services, along with descriptions, photos or illustrations (if appropriate), and instructions on how to place an order. Catalogs often include marketing text delineating the benefits of the products or services and providing more details about them. Catalogs are particularly useful for companies that have many product offerings, including auto parts manufacturers, restaurant supply companies, industrial supplies wholesalers, and clothing manufacturers. Catalogs can be many pages long—some, in fact, are the size of a phone book—and they're often printed in color.

As a result, catalogs are often the most expensive print marketing piece a company produces and can be costly to distribute. For this reason, they're usually sent only to highly qualified prospects—that is, customers who've requested them or ordered from your company in the past, or people who've made similar purchases from companies like yours.

Although some people believe (and hope, for environmental reasons) that online catalogs and websites will ultimately replace print catalogs, many marketers believe print catalogs are here to stay—at least for the foreseeable future. In many industries (such as auto repair), customers would rather have a print catalog handy than be forced to access the information via computer. And some companies don't want consumers to be able to access their

Understanding Print-Speak

Printing techniques change rapidly, and you may not need to know a lot of technical terms. Still, you might find it useful to learn the following ones, which are used frequently in relation to print materials:

- ◼ **4-color process.** A process for reproducing full-color photographic images using four colors of ink: cyan (blue), magenta (red), yellow, and black (represented by the letters *CMYK*, respectively). The inks are placed on paper in layers of dots; when viewed, the dots combine to create the illusion of many more colors.

- ◼ **Bleed.** Ink color that extends to the edge of the paper (without any white space).

- ◼ **Glossy/Coated paper.** Paper with a smooth, shiny surface that's good for printing photos and high-quality marketing pieces.

- ◼ **GIF, JPEG, TIFF.** Common electronic file formats for images. GIF and JPEG formats compress the images, making them smaller and often easier to use on the Web. TIFF files do not compress the images, making them better for printing.

- ◼ **Matte.** Paper with a nonreflective, non-textured surface.

- ◼ **Offset printer.** A machine that prints pages and documents, using plates created via a photographic process.

- ◼ **PMS colors.** Pantone Matching System, or PMS, is a process for matching desired colors. PMS colors are standard, numbered shades.

- ◼ **Press check.** The final check—which occurs when a job is already on the press (and entails examining the first few printed pages)—for color, sharpness, and overall print quality.

- ◼ **Print run.** The number (or volume) of pieces you plan to print at a particular time.

wholesale prices, believing they can more easily control the distribution of that information through printed catalogs than on the Web.

Many companies, however, use printed and mailed catalogs for direct sales or mail order business—which can make up a huge percentage, if not a majority, of their revenues. In fact, you likely receive catalogs from a number of such well-known companies—for example, Pottery Barn, Lands' End, R.E.I., PC Connection, Ikea, Dell Computer, Crate & Barrel, and so on.

These print catalogs typically complement and support Web and retail store sales, as well as generate direct sales. Some customers who receive a catalog will order by calling the number on the catalog, while those who prefer to shop online or go to a store will be prompted to do so by what they see in the catalog.

Sales Sheets and Product Specification Sheets

Because many customers want to see detailed information about a product or service before making a buying decision, and catalogs are so expensive to produce, it's useful to have something relatively inexpensive to give them that provides that info. Sales sheets—sometimes referred to as product specification sheets for more technical or complex products—serve that function.

Typically composed of one-page handouts with detailed information about a particular product or service, sales sheets differ from brochures in that they usually focus on just one product or service and present more in-depth information about features and benefits. They also often include pricing information. Sales sheets can be printed in color or black-and-white, and the data they provide often mirrors the in-depth information you find on product Web pages.

It's also important to keep in mind that because sales sheets are inexpensive to produce, they serve as a good way to present information that's likely to change over time, such as pricing or features, since you can update them at relatively little cost.

Price Lists

Separate price lists provide a good way of saving money on your sales materials. By omitting prices from your more expensive materials (such as catalogs, full-color brochures, and sales sheets), you can continue to use these costly marketing collateral pieces even when prices change. Use a separate sheet—which can be as simple as a one-page black-and-white piece of paper copied in house—to list prices. You can then distribute the price list with your sales materials by inserting it in your catalog or sending it along with a sales sheet.

What to Include

When creating your sales support marketing pieces, it's critical that you:

- ◼ Include your company name, logo, and identity on every piece—even on a black-and-white one-page price list

- ◼ Make certain any colors you use reinforce your company's signature colors

- Place how-to-order information on every page of your catalog and feature it prominently on your sales sheets, perhaps more than once

- Include a pre-addressed order card or form in catalogs—especially those sent for direct marketing purposes

- Use both sides of a sales or product specification sheet

- Prominently highlight your offering's key benefits and features

As you choose the text and design the layout of your sales piece, make sure the most important information jumps off the page. Use pull quotes, bold type, or visual elements to emphasize these critical selling points. For instance, if you make portable video players and customers are particularly interested in (and impressed by) how long your battery lasts, you can use a pull quote that states, "Longer battery life than the competition."

Flyers, Postcards, and More

In addition to the key collateral pieces already discussed, there's an arsenal of other print pieces you can use as part of your marketing plan. These include (but are not limited to) flyers, postcards, newsletters, and letterhead.

Flyers

Flyer is a general term that's often used to describe any inexpensive marketing piece. Typically, however, flyers are one-sheet marketing pieces, unfolded, used primarily to announce an event, discount, sale, or special. Although the most common size for flyers is 8.5" x 11", they can take the form of any size one-page announcement. (Printing half-page flyers is particularly affordable.) They're generally printed on regular paper, as opposed to on cards.

One of the great advantages of flyers is that they're inexpensive and fast to produce—you can often print them yourself. As such, they make great marketing tools for organizations with limited marketing budgets: You can print a lot of them at very little cost; there are many places to post them; and they are particularly effective for businesses or events targeting students or young adults.

Flyers can also be used as handouts in many business settings, such as at trade shows and networking events. And they can be distributed door-to-door to consumers by restaurants, clothing stores, and home service providers (such as painters, handymen, and movers). They're good for announcing grand openings, seminars, special sales, and other events. A chiropractor might hand out flyers at a street fair announcing free consultations, or a real estate developer might hire someone to distribute flyers advertising a model home showing at a new residential development.

Due to their temporary nature, you don't need to get too fancy with flyers. Just make your message ("Grand Opening This Saturday!") highly visible and your business identity (name, logo, contact information) crystal clear. Images always attract attention so try to find one to include on your flyer.

Getting Your Flyers Out

Club cards, rack cards, and flyers can be effective advertising pieces, but how do you get them out to the public? An industry has developed to do just that. You can now pay companies to get your club cards out to clubs, parties, and restaurants; your rack cards to hotels; and your door hangers hung on doors. They can post your flyers on signs in grocery stores, laundromats, and other appropriate businesses, and they can even distribute flyers to businesses, not just consumers. Use the terms "flyer distribution," "rack card distribution," and "brochure distribution" when searching the Web to find distributors in your area.

Club Card Flyers/Postcards/Rack Cards

Club card flyers, which were originally distributed in clubs and restaurants, have become a popular marketing tool for promoting parties, nightclubs, concerts, events, and other businesses, products, and services aimed at younger adults. Similar to postcards, they're printed on card stock and are typically about the same size as a postcard (around 4" x 6"), though they can come in any size. Club card flyers are printed in full color (on both sides) and often come with a gloss coating; they also sometimes come in special shapes.

Club card flyers are relatively inexpensive to print (many online printers offer low prices)—which means that if you have a way to distribute a large number of marketing cards to the public (or at an industry event), they can serve as an extremely economical marketing tool. You can use them for many purposes, such as tickets, handouts, announcements, and invitations. And, of course, you'll often find racks for card club flyers in clubs and popular restaurants. This can be a good way to market your event, product, or service in a venue that attracts customers who go out frequently.

Also printed on card stock, *postcards* are basically the same as club card flyers. The only significant difference is that they're designed to be sent through the mail (rather than handed out). As such, they may be printed on slightly heavier card stock. And you must leave room on the back for the recipient's address and postage. Postcards are particularly good for direct mail campaigns, thank you cards for new customers, sale announcements, invitations, and appointment reminders (for dentists, doctors, and veterinarians).

Rack cards—which are also printed on card stock—are ads designed to be placed in the display racks often seen in the front lobbies of hotels, tourist locations, restaurants, and other public places. Their standard size is 4" x 9," and they're typically printed in full color on both sides of a single card. Rack cards are best suited for businesses appealing to a tourist market or advertising local attractions.

Newsletters

Print newsletters are informational pieces sent to existing and prospective customers, containing news, tips, and resources. Their content is usually based on a single, company-related topic or theme, such as health, home improvement, or finances—mixed with subtle promotional pitches for products and services, and company contact info.

Newsletters work well for a wide variety of businesses, especially those that can offer their prospects and customers some news or useful advice. An accountant might send a newsletter with tips for reducing your taxes. A newsletter sent by a staffing company to human resource departments might feature updates on employment laws. Newsletters can contain brief descriptions of new products and services, but they should primarily feature news and helpful information that will be of interest to your customers.

The primary benefit of newsletters is that recipients typically view them as a welcome source of information rather than an advertisement. And recipients are likely to keep them around for a while.

With the advent of inexpensive email newsletters (see Section V), many businesses have switched to online-only newsletters. However, many have also continued (or started) to send out print newsletters—even though they're much more expensive to produce and distribute. The reason for this is that there's a greater chance a recipient will actually open a print newsletter than an email version—and the printed newsletter is likely to stick around longer, reminding customers of your name.

Stationery, Letterhead, Folders, Envelopes, and Labels

With most people now using email for basic business correspondence, corporate letterhead (stationery and envelopes) no longer plays the essential role it once did in company communications. However, *stationery*—which refers not only to letterhead but also to thank you notes, invoices, purchase orders, receipts, fax covers, and forms—still represents an important marketing tool, since it plays a part in the overall impression you make with customers and prospects.

For this reason, you should use stationery, envelopes, and labels printed with your corporate identity for any correspondence you send out by postal mail. For example, if you met a promising prospect at a networking event who requested a detailed brochure or product catalog, you'd mail it accompanied by a cover letter on your letterhead, in an envelope with your letterhead or with a letterhead label attached. You might also put a few brochures and a cover letter in a *presentation folder,* a folded piece of heavy card stock about the size and shape of a physical file folder with pockets for you to put your material in, imprinted with your company name and logo. When all of these items reflect a consistent identity, you look more professional and better established, and you reinforce your brand.

In addition to including contact information, the design of your stationery should support your company's branding efforts with a consistent corporate identity (name, logo, tagline). As with business cards, keep stationery simple and coherent. If you've hired a graphic designer to create your corporate identity, designing a selection of basic stationery (letterhead, envelopes, labels) is generally a standard part of that service.

Miscellaneous Print Marketing Pieces

You can use virtually anything with ink on paper as a print marketing piece. Some of your many choices include:

- **Door hangers.** Inexpensive marketing pieces placed on prospects' front doorknobs, often used by food delivery services, home services, contractors, and restaurants.

- **Posters.** Large printed pieces that you can put up to attract attention in public places, retail stores, trade show booths, and so on.

- **Calendars.** These can be given as New Year's gifts to customers to remind them of your business all year long.

- **Stickers, decals, and bumper stickers.** Anything you can attach to something else can be used to advertise products or services appealing to the youth market.

BRAINSTORMING

YOUR PRINT MARKETING MATERIALS

Use this worksheet to plan which print collateral pieces to use as part of your marketing plan, and when and how you'll use them (such as for specific promotions or events).

Piece	Do you intend to use these?	Will they be company- or product/service-specific?	What is their primary purpose?	What are the main messages and key elements?
Business cards				
Brochures				
Catalogs				
Sales sheets				
Price lists				
Flyers				
Cards: club, post rack				
Newsletters				
Stationery				
Other				

Print Marketing Materials Return on Investment

It can be difficult to accurately measure the return on your investment for print marketing materials—especially in the case of materials that are not designed expressly to support other sales and marketing efforts. For instance, if a salesperson brings an impressive brochure on a sales call and the prospect makes a purchase, how much of that was due to the brochure and how much to the salesperson? These things are difficult to measure.

Instead, much of the ROI in your print materials will likely be non-financial. For instance, in the case of the above-described brochure, it supported the sales effort, answered the most common questions prospects raised, and left a good impression—all positive results, even if you can't pin a dollar amount on them.

Calculating Your Print Marketing Collateral ROI

Use the following worksheet to get started on your own print marketing collateral ROI analysis. Simply select the print marketing materials you intend to use and then fill in the requested data about projected costs, checking in with designers and printers to get a better idea of what those costs might be.

Here are some tips for using the worksheets (and calculating your ROI):

- **Be specific about your financial goals.** This means that you need to include not just the total return you'd like to receive on your advertising investment but what that translates to in terms of customers and expenditures. Thus, if you were preparing this worksheet for a company that provided college test preparation services, you might specify that you wanted to get at least 300 students per year through counselor referrals and 600 registrants per year from orientation sessions for a total of 900 customers.

- **Don't overlook non-financial goals.** While you may not be able to put a cash value on things like brand awareness and customer perception, these are important components of any marketing campaign, and as such must be considered when calculating return on investment. Thus, to use the college test prep company example again, you might cite the following for your non-financial goals: increased attendance at orientation sessions, heightened awareness of services among counselors and parents, and increased name recognition.

RETURN ON INVESTMENT

YOUR PRINT MARKETING COLLATERAL ROI

Your business:_____

Your target market:_____

Your print marketing collateral activities (printing and posting flyers, designing and printing

brochures, and so on): _____

GOALS

Financial: _____

Non-financial: _____

PROJECTED MARKETING COLLATERAL COSTS (BREAKDOWN BY TYPE, TASK)

Projected returns, financial:_____

Increase in income from print marketing collateral:_____

Total cost of print marketing collateral: _____

Total projected net financial gain (projected increase in income minus the cost of the collateral): _____

PROJECTED RETURNS, NON-FINANCIAL

_____

_____

TOTAL ROI (Total Net Financial Returns Plus Total Non-financial Returns):_____

Where to Get It Printed?

When you're preparing print collateral, you have a variety of printing options:

▪ **In-house, on your own printer.** Depending on the quality of your printer and the print quality you need, you may be able to produce some of your marketing materials in house. Small quantities of price lists, flyers, and even sales sheets and product spec sheets can probably be produced in high enough quality to serve your needs. If you go this route, you'll save money, be able to tailor information for specific recipients or situations, print materials at the last minute, and reduce waste by printing just enough for your needs. For your more important pieces, however, you'll want to use an outside print company. And if you need large quantities, it's usually less expensive to have an outside vendor print your materials. Do *not*, however, use your own printer to produce your business cards. Home printers require thinner paper stock than commercial printing presses, and even after you print your cards, you'll have to cut them apart, adding to their flimsy, amateur feel.

▪ **Local copy shops.** Encompassing places like Kinko's and FedEx, local copy shops represent a fast and relatively inexpensive way to produce many of your print materials. They can produce higher-quality and larger-quantity materials than you can on your own printer, and they may offer much faster service than an online print company. You simply email or bring them your electronic file, choose the paper stock and any other services you want (collating, folding, stapling), and they can do it all for you, often in the same day. If you need help designing your material, some of these copy shops may have staff members who can assist. If so, ask them to give you the electronic file of your project so that you can make changes in the future. Office superstores also have printing services; however, their selection of paper and options may be more limited than what you'd find at a copy shop.

▪ **Online print companies.** Internet-based print services abound—and they're typically less expensive than copy shops. With an online printer, you either upload digital files containing your *camera-ready* design or, in most cases, choose from a selection of their preformatted templates and drop in your copy. This is a way to get a variety of print marketing materials (business cards, brochures, flyers) at very reasonable prices. The downside, however, is that the quality of online printers can vary: they offer limited choices of card stock, colors, and such, and you'll have less control over the final product than if you had worked with a local printer.

Some of the many online print companies include:

—vistaprint.com

—psprint.com

—123print.com

—gotprint.com

—overnightprints.com

▪ **Commercial printers.** For the highest-quality printed materials, and the greatest selection and control over your design and finished product, you'll want to turn to a professional print company. These are businesses that have their own printing presses. Generally, you'll work with a local printer so you (or your designer) can do a press check (that is, be at the location when your project is coming off their machines to make sure the colors and printing are exactly as you intended). For large quantities of expensive four-color marketing materials, you may choose an internationally based printer (typically in China) to reduce costs. You can use a print broker—an individual or company that knows print companies—to help you find the right print company for your local and international print projects.

PRINT COLLATERAL BUDGET (12 MONTHS)

	JAN	FEB	MARCH	APRIL	MAY
Professional Assistance					
Writers					
Graphic designers					
Photographers/Illustrators					
Other consultants					
Printing/Reproduction					
Business cards					
Brochures					
Catalogs					
Club card flyers					
Flyers					
Newsletters					
Postcards					
Sales/Product datasheets					
Stationery					
Other printing/reproduction costs					
Shipping and Postage					
Other					
TOTAL					

! **NOTE:** An electronic version of this worksheet is available as part of the Planning Shop's Marketing Budget Templates package.

JUNE	JULY	AUGUST	SEPT	OCT	NOV	DEC	TOTAL

Lingo

BULK MAIL/PRESORTED MAIL: Terms used interchangeably by the U.S. Postal Service to describe presorted mail sent in large quantities (usually more than 200 pieces) and qualifying for discounted rates. The term *bulk mail* has also come to mean any mass mailing.

DIMENSIONAL MAIL: Any type of mailing that involves more than just a flat letter or postcard—for example, cardboard boxes or tubes as well as thicker paper packages.

DIRECT MAIL: Marketing materials—including postcards, brochures, and catalogs—sent to prospective customers by mail, with the purpose of getting them to respond to a call to action.

DIRECT RESPONSE MARKETING: Any type of marketing done to get a prospect to respond immediately and directly to a call to action.

JUNK MAIL: Unsolicited direct mail. Although the term is often used to refer to any direct mail, it's most appropriately applied to mail received by prospects who are not good targets for the offer.

LIST BROKER: A person or company who sells mailing lists (usually after tailoring them to the needs of those using the mailing lists).

MAILING LIST: A list of prospect names and addresses.

RESPONSE RATE: The percentage of prospects who respond to a direct mailing. Response rates of 1%–2% of a total mailing are considered good.

SELECTS OR SELECTORS: The terms you use to define the characteristics of your direct mail list, such as zip or postal code, industry code, income or revenue level, years in business, and gender.

CHAPTER 20

Direct Mail

There's a reason why people open their mailboxes every day and find stacks of offers for products and services. It's because *direct mail*—marketing pieces printed and sent to potential and existing clients by postal mail—works. It attracts new customers to a business, keeps existing customers coming back, and increases sales quickly.

Direct mail can take many forms, including postcards, letters, catalogs, coupons, and even product samples and gifts. Regardless of form, the purpose is the same: to get a *direct response* from the recipient. In other words, direct mail is designed to get a prospect to take an immediate action—such as making a purchase, sending in an information request card, or calling a phone number. All of these actions are solicitations, and all are quantifiable and measurable. That makes direct mail one of the best marketing methods for driving immediate results—getting those orders to come in—while at the same time giving you a clear and measurable picture of whether your marketing efforts are paying off.

Of course, there are downsides to direct mail as well. The most obvious is that it's expensive. Designing, writing, and printing your marketing pieces can be costly. On top of that, you've got to add the cost of stuffing and mailing those pieces. In many cases, you'll also purchase a mailing list of potential customers. Then there's the environmental impact of all that printed matter, often tossed in the trash or recycle bin, plus the energy used to send those pieces. That's a lot of waste. But in comparison to some other forms of marketing, especially traditional advertising such as on TV or radio, direct mail can be much less expensive and can result in a more immediate uptick in sales.

To achieve success in your direct mail campaigns, you must understand direct mail *response rates*—or the percentage of recipients who are likely to act on your offer. Direct mail response rates are very low. According to the Direct Marketing Association, the group representing the direct mail industry, typical response rates to order-generating direct mail campaigns are a bit over 2%, but even a well planned and executed direct mail campaign may get only get a 1-2% response rate. That means that if you send a mailing to 10,000 people, you might get 100 responses. So you'd better be very realistic about the likely return on your investment on direct mail.

Even so, your mailbox is still stuffed with catalogs, letters, and postcards urging you to buy something. Why? Because marketers know that a 1%-2% response rate can add up to substantial, immediate income—especially when

> ## Testing
> ## One, Two, Three
>
> If you're going to make direct mail an ongoing part of your marketing plan, you'll want to test the various elements of your direct mail campaigns to see which generate the best results. Modify only one factor at a time—your offer, the nature of the package, the wording in your letter, or the type of mailing list you use—and experiment to determine what works best.

they've got a good list, are selling the right product or service, and have put together a good direct mail campaign.

The components of a direct mail campaign include:

- The offer/call to action
- The physical mailing piece(s), or "package"
- The mailing list
- The logistics of your campaign

Your Offer and Call to Action

Key to the success of any direct mail campaign is the offer you make to the prospect—in other words, what's in it for *them*. Remember, the prospect hasn't walked into your store or clicked onto your website looking for something; instead, they're a passive recipient of your message—which means you'll need to provide them with something extremely compelling to overcome that passivity.

Every direct mail piece, then, must offer an immediate and obvious benefit for taking action, especially quick action. Direct mail is no place for the soft sell. Your message must have a clear *call to action* and a clear benefit—for example, "Order today and receive a free travel tote" or "Call today and get $100 back." And you've got to repeat that call to action many times—even in the course of a one-page direct mail letter.

---

10 Tips for Effective Direct Mail

There's a reason direct mail is often called "junk mail": much of it gets thrown away. There are, however, ways to keep yours out of the circular file:

1. **Think like your customer.** Think about the reasons you throw direct mail pieces away. Usually, it's because the piece doesn't appeal to your needs or desires—either because it didn't make its point or because you weren't the true target customer. When conceptualizing your piece, put yourself in your customers' shoes and think about what they want.

2. **Narrow the list.** It makes little financial sense to do a huge mass mailing that's not well targeted. Keep costs down with a rented list or one you've carefully compiled. If you're a local business, narrow your list down to key zip codes or streets.

3. **Experiment.** Try different offers, pieces, and mailing lists. Since it's easy to track responses, you can determine which works best.

4. **Start with the envelope.** Put an irresistible offer, question, or solution on the outside that will entice the prospect to open your mailing. Consider using an odd-size envelope that stands out in the mail pile.

5. **Educate your recipients**. Engage your readers with information, statistics, or a story that acknowledges a need or desire and promises to lead to a solution.

6. **Hint at the *deal* before you state the offer.** Entice readers throughout with little promises and offers of a great deal. *"For just a few pennies a day, Sam was able to solve his weight problem for life."*

7. **Repeat the call to action frequently.** State your all-important call to action many times, in many ways, and in many places.

8. **Offer or send free stuff.** Everyone loves free stuff. Offer a free gift with purchase or enclose a sample.

9. **Create a low-risk proposition.** Show customers they have nothing to lose by giving you a chance. Offer reassurances like "Satisfaction guaranteed or your money back" and "Cancel at any time."

10. **Make sure your contact information stands out.** Whether it's an order card, a website, or a phone number, make sure your contact info is highly visible—and repeat it.

Some of the enticements you can offer include:

- **Money savings.** These can take the form of either dollars or a percentage off or cash back. Remember, you can make the same offer in many different ways: "Half off" is the same as "50% off" is the same as "Buy one, get one free." You can test wordings on different mailings to see which gets the best response.

- **Gifts.** Everyone likes getting something free, so gifts are always tempting. The gift can be for making a purchase, sending in a response card, or signing up on a website. "Buy one, get one free" is often perceived as a gift rather than a discount.

- **Added features, bonuses, or upgrades.** These can be the offer itself ("2 nights free at our luxury resort when you book 4 nights") or an incentive for acting fast ("Extra night free if you book by March 15").

Reassure your prospects—many of whom have never done business with you before—by guaranteeing their purchases with phrases like "Money-back guarantee" and "100% satisfaction guaranteed."

It's also a good idea to make your offer time-sensitive. By citing an expiration date, you create a sense of urgency and force readers to take action *soon.* Be certain, however, to add a clear and direct *call to action* that prospects can respond to by that deadline, such as "Phone today" or "Order today from our website."

BRAINSTORMING

YOUR DIRECT MAIL OFFER

In the box below, indicate what you plan to offer prospects—that is, what you're selling and what discounts, gifts, or bonuses they'll receive. Also list exactly what you want prospects to do—that is, your *call to action.*

YOUR OFFER	YOUR CALL TO ACTION

<table>
<tr><td>

Give Yourself a Lift

Many direct mail packages also include a *lift letter*—a short, small extra piece of mail in the same package/envelope to help increase, or *lift*, the number of replies. The lift letter usually offers the reader an additional bonus such as, "Reply in the next 24 hours and get six free issues!" Because it's smaller in size, the lift letter gets read even in instances when the primary letter doesn't.

Other direct mail package options include:

- **Postcard.** A simple one-page piece that doesn't need to be opened. Best for compelling offers or offers from companies the prospect already knows and likes.

- **Self-mailer.** A one-page letter folded so that it can be mailed without an envelope. Cheaper than an envelope package, the self-mailer gives you the feel of a letter (unlike a postcard) and can be designed so that one panel allows space for the prospect to reply (as a postage-paid mailer).

- **Dimensional mail.** Anything that is not a flat envelope or postcard—that is, something that has dimensions and an element of surprise, such as a cardboard box or tube. Advantages are that dimensional mail is almost certain to be opened. Disadvantages are that it can be expensive to produce and send, and that it can disappoint the prospect when opened. Best for very expensive products or services.

- **FedEx, UPS, USPS, or other express mailings.** These are likely to be opened, but they're also going to cost considerably more than other types of mailings.

</td></tr>
</table>

Your Mailing Piece

When you start to design and write your direct mail piece, you must figure out how to get people to open your mailing piece, *read* the offer, and respond positively. Knowing, as you do, that a good response rate is only 1%–2%, you must understand that everything you do has an effect on your results.

The purpose of the mailing piece is, first and foremost, to get the prospect to read your offer. It's not to look great or to win a design award, it's to engage the reader enough so that they'll want to know what you're selling.

Before you begin to plan your mailing piece, check the postal regulations in your country for size and weight. Oversize or overweight pieces will cost more, and undersized pieces may not be accepted at all.

The classic direct mail package consists of five elements:

- **Envelope,** usually a white No. 10 envelope. To increase the chances your envelope will be opened, print *teaser* text—questions, statements, or amazing offers—on the outside of the envelope. Another way to attract attention is to give no indication of what's inside. Most people will at least open the envelope to see if it's something important.

- **Letter,** typically signed by the company CEO or other prominent person, and often personalized in the address line. This is your sales pitch and should be written as if you were talking directly to the prospect. It should include all of the benefits and reasons why a person would want to accept the offer, the offer itself (repeated a few times), and the call to action. Be sure to include a P.S. Most people read postscripts before anything else.

- **Brochure,** describing the offer in more detail. This gives you the opportunity to provide specifics for a prospect motivated to go beyond the letter.

- **Response card/piece,** describing how a prospect places an order. Your order form should be short and easy.

- **Response envelope,** if the response card is not a self-mailer.

Your Mailing List

Most experienced direct mail marketers believe that the most important factor in a direct mail campaign's success is the quality of the mailing list. In other words, have you gathered names of people who are likely to respond positively to your offer? Are they people who will be interested in your product or service and who will be likely to respond to a direct mail offer?

One of the great advantages of direct mail advertising is that you can target recipients with great precision. For instance, if you were selling season ski passes, you could get a mailing list of people in zip codes or postal codes within driving distance of your mountain resort who make over $75,000 a year and subscribe to ski magazines. Likewise, if you're selling a business-to-business product, say, packaging supplies for the electronics industry, you could get a list of purchasing officers for companies in that industry.

There are two main ways of developing a mailing list: compiling your own list or renting one from a mailing list company.

Compiling Your Own List

Putting together your own mailing list is less expensive than purchasing one from a mailing list company. And although it may not yield as many names as you'd get by paying—since you're primarily reaching people who've already interacted with your company—the lists you create from your own database will likely have a fairly good response rate.

To assemble your mailing list, pull together names you've gathered from:

- Current and past customers
- Trade shows
- Organizations you belong to
- Contacts from industry and community associations
- Sweepstakes, contests, free drawings, and other giveaways (though be sure you're in compliance with the rules governing contests)
- Website visitors (whom you've enticed into providing mailing information by offering something in exchange—for example, a free downloadable report)
- Mailing list sign-up sheets in your place of business

Renting a List

A sizable industry has evolved around compiling and renting direct mail lists. You'd be surprised, in fact, how specific you can get when it comes to choosing mailing lists. These lists let you carefully target your direct mail recipients by choosing the *selects* or *selectors* offered by the mailing list company that best define the characteristics of your prospects.

Keep in mind, though, that broker-provided mailing lists are *rented,* not bought. This means you can only use the names and addresses for a specified number of mailings (typically just one at a time). If prospects contact you, you can reuse their names; if they don't, you may not contact them names again. And just to make sure renters are staying honest, brokers "seed" their lists with stealth names and addresses so they can track their reuse.

To give you an idea of the diversity of available lists, you can rent lists of:

- **Consumers** who buy books, go clubbing, own stocks, visit theme parks, own horses, wear eyeglasses, or make donations (by charity type or political party). You can get a list of college-bound high school seniors by choice of majors, or people who have life insurance by the amount of coverage, or even people who have a vegetable garden versus a flower garden.
- **Businesspeople** who own hot air balloon companies, sell scientific instruments, or are partners in accounting firms, female bank executives, farmers (by acres owned and/or by crops farmed), personnel training or purchasing directors (by industry), or tire wholesalers or dealers.

Finding Direct Mail Lists

It's best to get recommendations from businesses that have already conducted direct mail campaigns. However, if you're looking online, here are a few sites to get you started:

- The Direct Marketing Association Vendor Search, www.thedirectmarketingsearch.com.
- InfoUSA, www.InfoUSA.com
- Hoovers, www.hoovers.com (for business-to-business prospects)

Mind Your Mailing Costs

Check with your country's postal service on how to receive discount or "bulk mail" services. In the U.S., for instance, sending out your marketing pieces by regular first class rates could cost four times as much as sending it by bulk mail rates.

For a rundown of bulk mail costs, U.S. businesses can find information from the U.S. Postal Service at www.usps.com/businessmail101. Alternatively, you can go to the U.S.P.S. site (www.usps.com) and search for "Discount Mail" or "Business Mail." Canadian businesses can find similar resources at the Canada Post site (www.canadapost.ca). Search for "business" or "direct mail," or look for related links on the home page.

Brokers compile their lists from a wide variety of sources, some of which include other mail order companies, magazine subscription databases, lists of charitable donors, and public records. If you've made a direct mail or online purchase from a sporting goods company, for example, it's likely that company "sold" your name and information to a company compiling lists of people who've bought sporting goods through direct mail or online.

BRAINSTORMING

YOUR MAILING LIST

Creating a list: What sources will you use to create your mailing list? Consider past and current customers, people you've met at networking events or trade shows, lists of members of organizations to which you belong, and so on.

_____

_____

_____

_____

_____

_____

_____

_____

_____

_____

Renting a list: What types of people/names will you target for your direct mailing? Consider what types of products they already buy and the roles they have at companies (if doing business-to-business marketing) or demographics of consumers, including which magazines they subscribe to.

_____

_____

_____

_____

_____

_____

_____

_____

_____

_____

_____

Direct Mail Logistics

Once you've got your mailing piece and mailing list together, it's time to get the package in the mail. You have three options:

- **Send it yourself.** This may be a less expensive option than using an outside service—especially if you're doing a small mailing (less than a few thousand names) or have sufficient staff. Remember, however, that you'll not only have to prepare the piece for mailing (putting on address labels and stuffing envelopes), you'll also have to presort and bundle the mail (by zip or postal codes) following your postal service's rules if you want to qualify for discount postage. You'll also need to get a mailing permit.

- **Use a mailing house/mailing service.** Mailing houses can coordinate all aspects of your direct mail logistics. If you choose to go this route, you can send your marketing pieces directly to the mailing service, and it will put everything in the mail for you—even obtaining any necessary permits. If you have a large mailing, you'll definitely want to use an outside service.

- **Use your online printer.** If you're using an online printer to produce your mailing piece, that printer may also be able to handle the logistics of sending out the mailing. This can provide an affordable, integrated solution—especially for a smaller company.

Why Am I Still Getting This?

As with every other form of marketing, a key rule in direct mail is *repetition, repetition, repetition.* It may take many mailings before a prospect even opens your mail, let alone responds. When you realize that only 1%–2% of people respond to a direct mail piece, you'll realize why so many people consider direct mail to be "junk." They've gotten the same mailing at least three or four times.

Your Direct Mail ROI

As with every aspect of your marketing plan, you'll want to carefully monitor the return on investment of your direct mail campaigns. Fortunately, direct mail is one of the easiest marketing methods to measure. That's because direct mail elicits a direct response, typically a purchase or serious inquiry, so you can easily track whether or not a campaign has paid off.

For instance, if you spend $10,000 (including designing and producing your piece, buying a list, and sending it out) and get a 2% response, with new orders amounting to $13,500, you have a net gain of $3,500.

When projecting potential ROI, keep in mind that a 2%–3% response rate signifies a successful campaign. If you're new to direct mail, with an untested marketing piece, your response rates are likely to be considerably lower. Nevertheless, you will still be helping to spread the word about, and increasing the name recognition of, your company.

Understanding Mailing List Costs

Mailing lists are generally priced based on the cost per thousand contact names, or CPM. Therefore, a consumer list with a CPM of $100 is charging 10 cents per name (.10 x 1,000 names = $100). The CPM for a business-to-business list is typically higher than prices for consumer lists. Most lists are rented with a minimum of 5,000 names.

All Lists Are Not Created Equal

When ordering a list, be sure to ask the following questions:

- **When was the list compiled?** Make sure both the list and the contacts it contains are very recent.

- **How was the list compiled?** What sources were used, and are they a good fit to your market? Look for lists composed of people who have recently purchased (ideally by direct mail) similar products or services.

- **How much does it cost?** Typically, business-to-business lists cost more than consumer lists, and the more targeted the list, the more expensive the names. (For example, you'll pay a higher fee for a list as specific as one that contains Hispanic females who own homes worth more than $400,000 with children living at home.)

- **What are typical response rates from others using the list?** Ask about the results experienced by companies with products and services similar to yours.

- **In what form is the list provided?** Will you receive the electronic data to print your own labels and envelopes, or will you get peel-off labels?

Calculating Your Direct Mail ROI

The following worksheet can help you get started on your own ROI analysis. Simply describe what your direct mail campaign will entail, and fill in the requested data to get an idea of the ROI you can expect from your direct mail campaign.

Here are some tips for using the worksheets (and calculating your ROI):

- **Be specific about your financial goals.** This means that you need to include not just the total return you'd like to receive on your direct mail advertising investment but what that translates to in terms of response and purchase rates—that is, how big a list will it take to generate the kind of results you're seeking.

- **Remember non-financial goals.** While you may not be able to put a cash value on things like brand awareness and customer perception, these are important components of any marketing campaign, and as such must be considered when calculating return on investment. Thus, even if your direct mail campaign is only seeing a 1–2% response rate, it's reaching the eyeballs of a much wider audience, imprinting your company and brand in the process—even if they're not responding to your direct call to action.

- **Get the data on the recipients you're targeting.** In other words, *know your audience:* The more targeted your campaign, the more likely it is to bring the desired results.

RETURN ON INVESTMENT

YOUR DIRECT MAIL ROI

Your business: _____

Your target market: _____

Your direct mail campaign: _____

Number of contacts you plan to send your direct mail piece to: _____

GOALS

Financial: _____

Non-financial: _____

PROJECTED DIRECT MAIL COSTS

Writing/designing piece: _____

Printing/producing piece: _____

Buying mailing list: _____

Mailing house costs: _____

Postage: _____

PROJECTED RETURNS, FINANCIAL

Number of contacts sent to multiplied by percentage of contacts responding = _____

Number of contacts responding: _____

Average sale per contact responding: _____

Total amount of new revenue from this mailing (number of contacts multiplied by average sale): _____

PROJECTED RETURNS, NON-FINANCIAL

_____

_____

TOTAL ROI (Total Net Financial Returns Plus Total Non-financial Returns): _____

DIRECT MAIL BUDGET (12 MONTHS)

	JAN	FEB	MARCH	APRIL	MAY
Professional Assistance					
Writers					
Graphic designers					
Photographers/Illustrators					
Other consultants					
Printing/Reproduction					
Shipping and Postage					
Postage/shipping					
Mailing house services					
Other shipping and postage costs					
Supplies/ Cost of Goods/Manufacturing					
Mailing list rental					
Other supplies/goods/manufacturing costs					
Others					
TOTAL					

NOTE: An electronic version of this worksheet is available as part of the Planning Shop's Marketing Budget Templates package.

JUNE	JULY	AUGUST	SEPT	OCT	NOV	DEC	TOTAL

BUILDING YOUR MARKETING PLAN

PRINT MARKETING

Drawing from the worksheets in this section, plan the print marketing tactics you will use in your marketing campaign.

1. How will you use print-based marketing techniques (marketing collateral, direct mail) in your overall marketing plan? Which of the print marketing techniques described in this section will you use?

_____

_____

_____

_____

_____

2. Which print marketing collateral pieces do you plan to use, if any? How do you plan on using and distributing them? How can they help your business?

_____

_____

_____

_____

_____

3. How will your corporate identity and marketing message be incorporated in your print marketing materials?

_____

_____

_____

_____

_____

4. Do you plan on doing any direct mail marketing? If so, what will be the nature of your offer? How often do you plan on sending your piece?

_____

_____

_____

_____

_____

5. If doing a direct mail piece, what type of prospects do you plan on targeting? Where will you get your mailing list?

_____

_____

_____

_____

_____

6. How do you plan on designing, writing, and producing your print marketing materials? Will you create this in house, use an outside company, or employ a combination of both?

_____

_____

_____

_____

_____

7. How will you handle the direct mail pieces? Will you stuff and stamp them in house or use an outside service?

_____

_____

_____

_____

_____

8. How will the print marketing tactics you choose bring you closer to your marketing goals?

_____

_____

_____

_____

_____

_____

_____

_____

SECTION V

Online Marketing

Lingo

BLOG: Short for *Web log*, a blog is an online journal created and maintained by one or two people to share their views, thoughts, and activities. Users tend to update their blogs frequently and invite commentary from others.

EMAIL MARKETING: Communicating with customers by email, in the form of newsletters, company updates, announcements of sales or discounts, and other messages that are not routine business.

INTERNET ADVERTISING: Paying for ad placement on a website other than your own.

KEYWORD(S): A word or words used when performing a search on a search engine to describe what the searcher hopes to find.

ONLINE MARKETING: Finding and attracting customers by leveraging Web technologies such as websites, email, search engines, blogs, social networking sites, and the like.

SEARCH ENGINE: Software, or the website based on such software, that looks at—or searches—the contents of Internet sites to find information for users. The best-known search engines are Google, Yahoo, and Microsoft Live Search.

SEARCH ENGINE MARKETING (SEM): Marketing that involves paying for prominent placement on a search engine's results page, based on the keyword used to search.

SEARCH ENGINE OPTIMIZATION (SEO): Improving your search engine result rankings through a variety of measures, such as strategically placing keywords on your site and encouraging other sites to link to you.

SOCIAL NETWORKING SITES: Internet sites aimed at building online "communities" around user-generated content and information, offering members a place to share personal and professional information and interact with each other regularly.

CHAPTER 21

Get Online

No marketing plan is complete without an online component. That's because, increasingly, this is where customers are—online, on the Internet. Both consumers and businesses use the Web to research products and services before making purchases—shopping for the best price, looking for reviews, seeking work samples and client lists, and ascertaining business locations and hours. And it doesn't end there: millions of people also go online every day to socialize, seek entertainment, and find out the news of the day—all of which also present marketing opportunities.

Any one of the millions of people on the Internet could be your next customer; you just have to find the best ways to reach them. Luckily for you, there are a wide variety of ways: you can create websites, buy ads on others' websites, pay for placement on search engines, write a blog, send email newsletters, get your products reviewed in online forums, create buzz on social networking sites, put up a video on a video sharing site, and more.

Marketing on the Web also gives you a chance to broaden your customer universe geographically. Without having to travel farther than your computer, you can suddenly reach a global market. If, for instance, you manufacture high-quality culinary knives but live in a small community, you might find a few local chefs interested in buying your $500 product; however, if you extend your presence to the Web, chefs the world over will learn about—and possibly purchase—your knives, expanding your market exponentially.

At the same time, Web-based marketing also lets you target very specific customer sets, allowing you to extend your marketing dollars by using them more effectively. If you can clearly identify the best customers for your product or service, the Web provides a number of relatively inexpensive ways of reaching them. For example, you could place ads for those culinary knives on blogs that chefs read, or you could purchase ads on search engines, designating that they be displayed on the results pages that come up when people search on keywords for chefs' tools and equipment. This last method is called *search engine marketing*.

One of the most important benefits of online marketing is that it's measurable and immediate. You can find out almost instantaneously if an online ad program is working. Unlike TV, radio, and magazine advertising (where response rates are difficult to measure with any accuracy) and person-to-person networking (which can take months to produce results), online

> **❝** *The Web changed the way the world does business. What's surprising is the number of businesses that have little or no Web presence, or that don't do any online marketing. This is what happened to the dinosaurs—except in this case, no bones will be left behind.* **❞**
>
> **Alan Luckow**
> **President**
> **Luckow Communications**

marketing provides immediate feedback: you can see just how frequently your ads are getting clicked, and thus determine whether the search engine key words you purchased are increasing visitors to your site. This also means you can test online ad campaigns much more easily and quickly than traditional ones. If your Web-based ads aren't working, you can change their message in minutes—something that's simply not possible with newspaper or television ads.

In addition to being targeted, immediate, and measurable, online marketing offers one other major advantage over other forms of marketing—it's *affordable.* While companies can (and do) spend millions of dollars on Internet marketing, it's also possible to effectively market a business on the Web for relatively little money.

No matter what type of business you're in, you will devote a portion of your promotional budget and efforts to the Internet. Methods of online marketing you can choose from include:

- **Websites.** Consumers and businesses alike turn to the Internet to check out products, services, and potential vendors. You can use your site for a wide variety of marketing (and sales) functions, ranging from simply describing what your company does to providing in-depth product information, building a community of customers, and operating a full-fledged shopping venue. (The focus of this book, however, is on using your website for marketing purposes; thus, it does not explore in depth how to build and run a shopping, or e-commerce, site. For more about websites, see Chapter 22, Websites.)

- **Search engine optimization and search engine marketing.** Most people looking for information on the Web start by using a search engine such as Google, Yahoo, or Live Search. To help these Web searchers find *you,* you need to rank high in their search results. Two ways you can do this are through search engine optimization (SEO) and search engine marketing (SEM). Both are based on choosing words—or *keywords*—that your target customers are likely to use in their searches. (For more about SEO and SEM see Chapter 23, Search Engine Optimization and Search Engine Marketing.)

- **Email.** Virtually everyone checks their email regularly, so communicating with customers and prospects through email represents an effective, efficient, and inexpensive way of reaching them. One of the most successful forms of email marketing is the email newsletter, a succinct, easily read collection of useful information. Other effective uses of email include announcements of sales, discounts, product launches, and positive press coverage. You can even set up personalized, individual emails to go out when customers or prospects take a certain action, such as making an inquiry or placing an order. (For more about email marketing see page 295.)

- **Internet advertising.** As is the case with advertising in more traditional venues, such as newspapers, TV, and radio, online advertising helps prospects become aware of your company, builds your brand, motivates people to buy, and reinforces your company message. Moreover, advertising on the Web enables prospects to act immediately. Once they see your ad, they can click over to your website and place an order, make an inquiry, or find out more about what you sell or do. Internet advertising takes a number of different forms (in addition to search engine marketing), including purchasing ads on others' websites, sponsoring sites, and paying to be listed in online directories. (For more about Internet advertising, see page 311.)

■ **Social networking, blogs, podcasting, YouTube, and more.** A significant portion of your customers and prospects are spending a lot of time connected to the Internet. This gives you the chance to build an ongoing, even daily, relationship with them. Social networking communities such as MySpace, Facebook, and YouTube can generate powerful viral marketing campaigns as well as enhance one-on-one relationships. And tools such as blogs, podcasts, and video logs enable you to give information and advice or just stay in touch with customers and prospects regularly. (For more on these types of online marketing tools, see page 327.)

Online marketing is effective, affordable, and immediate. However, just like every other form of marketing, it must be planned and executed properly to be effective. To develop and manage an online marketing program, you'll need to devote time, energy, and resources to it. If you're managing a search engine marketing program, you'll have to monitor results and continually make changes in your choice of keywords. If you're sending monthly email newsletters, you'll need someone to write the newsletter. Even if you have an information-only website, you'll need to update it from time to time. Nevertheless, online marketing is a critical component of any marketing plan.

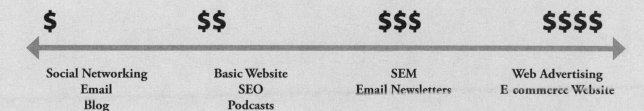

affordability scale

Other Online Marketing

| $ | $$ | $$$ | $$$$ |

Social Networking	Basic Website	SEM	Web Advertising
Email	SEO	Email Newsletters	E commerce Website
Blog	Podcasts		

*COST KEY:

$—Relatively Inexpensive $$—Moderately Expensive $$$—Fairly Expensive $$$$—Expensive

* These symbols represent general rate estimates.

Lingo

DOMAIN NAME: A name that identifies your website to users and which, when they type it in their Web browsers, takes them to your home page. For example, www.planningshop.com is the domain name of the publisher of this book.

E-COMMERCE: Doing direct sales from an Internet site, as opposed to using a website for other purposes, including marketing. The primary purpose of an e-commerce site is to sell products or services directly to customers online.

FAQS, OR FREQUENTLY ASKED QUESTIONS: A list of questions and answers that many users have asked or are likely to ask. Including a list of FAQs on your website helps users find what they need and reduces technical and customer service calls.

HOME PAGE: The first, or primary, landing page for a website—usually where users enter a website.

HTML (HYPERTEXT MARKUP LANGUAGE): A basic programming language used to build Web pages.

NAVIGATION: The term used to describe how a user moves around a site.

SHOPPING CART: Software programmed into a website enabling customers to make purchases online.

URL (UNIFORM RESOURCE LOCATOR): The unique text typed into a Web browser that takes users to a specific web page. A URL, technically, contains the entire string of characters for a specific page that can be anywhere within a website, such as http://www.planningshop.com/products.

CHAPTER 22

Websites

Every business needs a website. Your website serves as the public face of your company online. It provides customers and prospects with a way to interact with and learn about your company. And it helps determine whether they'll trust you enough to take the next step and actually do business with you.

Prospects and customers expect to find you on the Internet. They want to check out your company's background, clients/customers, location, and hours of service. They also want to make sure you're legitimate and learn a bit more about the people behind your organization. Even if you run a one-person consulting firm and get most of your clients from word-of-mouth referrals, you still need a website—after all, the first thing someone's likely to do after being referred to you is check you out online.

A website:

- Builds your brand

- Provides credibility

- Motivates and encourages prospects to buy

- Provides basic information about your company and business

- Allows you to present detailed information about your products and/or services

A particularly good website can also give you an edge over your competitors, making you look more professional, established, and capable than others.

Many companies use their websites to actually make sales: these are referred to as *e-commerce sites*. The focus of this chapter, however, is on using your website for marketing purposes (rather than direct sales).

Types of Websites

Websites can take many forms and serve a multitude of purposes. In fact, most sites combine a number of functions, such as informing the public about the company *and* selling products or providing customer service. From a marketing point of view, however, you'll want to concentrate on how your website attracts, retains, and motivates customers to do business with you.

Myth🚫Buster

The More the Merrier?

MYTH: More visitors mean more sales.

BUSTED: It's great to get a lot of people coming to your website. But high traffic alone doesn't guarantee high sales or lots of inquiries. You have to design a website that will motivate visitors to take the action you desire. And you must offer products or services customers want to buy. Fortunately, a wide range of website software exists, making it easy to analyze things like where visitors go on your site, which pages they linger on, which pages they leave, how much time they spend on your site, and more. With this information at your fingertips, you can figure out what's stopping people from buying and then revise your site to change that.

Websites can be categorized generally along the following lines:

- **Brochure sites.** Like a print brochure, a good brochure website includes an overview of a company's products or services, basic information about the company (such as location and hours of operation), and background on the company's history and the people who run it. Brochure sites serve as the face of a company for anyone interested in learning more. Brochure sites are *not* generally used for e-commerce, though some such sites provide links to purchase products.

- **E-commerce sites.** The primary purpose of e-commerce sites is to sell products and services directly to customers. Although this type of site may well include information about a company and its products or services, its primary function is to promote and process sales.

- **Content sites.** These are websites whose primary function is to provide information, advice, or entertainment to users. The content of such sites may be created especially for the sites, adapted from other media (such as magazines), or brought together (*aggregated*) from other sources (such as websites, blogs, and videos). In most cases, these sites are supported by advertising and are free to users. In other cases, companies offer content related to their products or services as a way to draw in and retain visitors.

- **Lead generation sites.** One of the primary purposes of such sites is collecting leads for salespeople to call upon. Such sites often require that visitors provide contact info if they're to access the sites' content, videos, and/or downloads. The company then uses this contact info to follow up with users.

- **Portal sites.** These are sites whose basic function is to attract users who share a common interest and send them to related sites and show them relevant advertisements. For example, a portal site for a vacation spot such as Hawaii might have nothing more than ads from people who own condos and beach homes in Hawaii that they want to rent out.

- **Social networking sites.** These sites are designed to let users develop communities, interact with one another, create connections, make referrals, and have fun. Some of the best known are MySpace, Facebook, and LinkedIn.

- **Customer service sites.** Customers often need support for the products and services they purchase. These sites provide it. Providing everything from technical advice to shipping information, such sites—whether they're devoted exclusively to customer service or represent a portion of an existing site devoted to the topic—enable companies to reduce costs and increase customer satisfaction.

What to Put on Your Website

Remember, your website is a, if not *the*, primary marketing tool for your company. As you choose what to put on your website and how it should look, keep your marketing goals and message uppermost in your mind. Just because you know how to add trendy features doesn't mean they'll help you achieve your marketing goals.

The site sections and features you choose to include will depend largely on your business and the nature of your prospects and customers. If you know your customers are likely to need lots of information before deciding to do business with you, offer plenty of background details about your company, products, and/or services. Include media articles about your company, testimonials, and lists of clients. If you run a consulting firm, prospects are going to want to know as much about you as possible. If, on the other hand, your customers simply want to know some basics, such as where you're located or your hours of operation, you can put up a much simpler site with less detailed info.

No matter what type of site you decide will best serve your business, there are certain standard sections that every website should provide. These include:

Home page. The home page of your website is the front door to your company's online presence. It's where people land after they type in a website address or link to your site from a search engine or another site. Your home page should reflect your company identity and branding, including name, logo, and colors; tagline; and marketing message. If your website consists of many pages, you should include navigation bars or buttons on your home page to provide easy, graphical ways for people to find what they're looking for and to move around your site.

Overview of products or services. Visitors want to know what you sell or do. That information, at least in brief, should be easily available either on your home page or just one page away. And remember, when describing your offerings, focus on their *benefits* rather than on the features or the process by which you supply them. If you sell many products or services, you'll want to provide links to detailed descriptions (including photos and specifications) on other pages. If you have an e-commerce site and are selling directly to customers from the web, you'll want to link to pages where users can place their orders.

About the company. Background information on your company—including marketing message, business philosophy, and history, as well as the biographies of key executives—is a must for your website. Many visitors will read this page early in their visit to see if you seem credible and established. Include information that will show them you're legitimate and capable, such as number of years in business, names of members of the board or advisory committee, key customers (especially well-known companies), awards, and so on.

Contact info. How will people reach you? Typical contact page information includes street address (if appropriate), phone number(s), and at least one email address (either a general company email or specific addresses for reaching key personnel).

Privacy policy. Be clear about how you'll treat customers' private information, including their addresses, phone numbers, and credit card information. Some users will check out your privacy policy before doing business with you or signing up for a company newsletter. Many sites guarantee not to sell or use customer information—a practice that can encourage people to do business with you. Never share or sell your visitors' or customers' personal information without their express consent.

Other marketing materials you may want to include on your website include:

■ **Relevant content.** By adding articles, information, and links that relate to your products or services and will be of interest to your visitors, you increase the chances that visitors will return to your site and recommend it to others. What's more, search engines place sites containing lots of relevant material higher on the results page. And if you have particularly valuable content, you can require users to register to download that content, using the content for lead generation.

■ **Media section.** If you've been mentioned the media, don't be shy about including articles, podcasts, and videos on your website—they add credibility and luster to you and your business. The media section is also the place to post any press releases you create as well as information about how the media can contact your company.

■ **Testimonials.** Praise for your company and its offerings from satisfied customers is particularly helpful, assuming your customers believe it's coming from credible sources. The opinions of other customers tend to be much more powerful than a company's marketing claims.

■ **Client list.** If current and past customers or clients are comfortable with you revealing them to the public, such a list greatly enhances prospects' sense of confidence in doing business with you. This is particularly true if you have well-known clients or big corporate customers.

■ **Awards.** If your company or products have received any awards, be sure to list them.

■ **Newsletter sign-up.** If you've decided to create a newsletter to develop a stronger bond between you and your customers (see pages 300–302), be sure to prominently display a link where visitors can sign up for it.

■ **Samples/Portfolio.** If you run a business (such as an architecture firm, graphic design studio, or even a writing service) that has examples or visuals to show, include a few selections of your work on your site. Many clients decide whether to contact a company based on reviewing an online portfolio.

■ **Demos.** These comprise downloadable videos or a series of Web pages that show how a product or service works. Demos are often used for software products; however, you can use them for any product or service that customers would like to see demonstrated before buying. Demos can also serve as a great way to generate sales leads if users are required to provide contact information before receiving the demo.

Other features you can add to your website include:

■ **Catalog.** Since a website's space is virtually limitless, you can put up an entire catalog of your products or services. If you're selling from your site, you'll definitely want to provide this, along with links enabling users to make purchases. However, even if you're not selling from your site, you may want to display a range of your offerings along with in-depth descriptions. Just make sure you update the contents as necessary.

◀ **Customer service.** Do you want to make it easy for customers to reach you for help or support? If so, provide a fill-out form, phone number, or an email address. Offering customer service is particularly helpful if you run an e-commerce site, since this assures customers that you're with them through all stages of their purchases.

User-generated content. In some cases, you may want to foster a sense of community among your customers or prospects, or encourage them to share information—for example, letting them explain how they've used your product or solved problems or issues with it (particularly if you have a complicated product, such as software). Online communities can sometimes increase traffic as well as the amount of time visitors spend on your site. Be aware, however, that if you open an area for user-generated content (such as a bulletin board) or create an online community (through social networking), you run the risk of having a relatively low response. If this turns out to be the case, it can give users the impression that your site is not well visited. You also may encounter individuals posting negative comments about your company or products.

Frequently asked questions (FAQs). Many sites include a document that answers commonly asked questions from customers. This cuts down on support costs and makes it easy and efficient for customers to get answers to basic inquiries about your site or offerings.

◀ **Search box.** If your site is going to include lots of content or products or is news oriented, consider including a search box so that visitors can easily find what they're looking for.

◀ **Site map/Index.** If you don't want to go to the expense of adding search functionality to your site, you can create a simple site map. This is a high-level outline of your website with links to the various pages. Site maps are most often used for sites that have a lot of pages. Visitors use site maps to find the information they're looking for quickly.

◀ **Investor-related information.** If yours is a company whose stock is publicly traded on a stock exchange, it's likely you'll want to include information for investors and stockholders, such as annual reports, recent earnings reports, and historic stock prices.

■ **Enhanced visuals or sound.** If you have the budget, you can add user interest to your site by adding sounds, video, or Flash animations (based on Adobe's Flash software to create moving images). Keep in mind that some or all of the content of these may not be able to be identified by search engines.

Other features are determined by the function of the site. Naturally, an e-commerce site will have a shopping cart programmed to allow customers to make purchases online. And a customer service site will likely include an online form where a customer can identify a product used and submit a problem.

BRAINSTORMING

YOUR WEBSITE CHECKLIST

Check off and describe the elements you plan to include on your business website, noting what you want each section to include or say:

○ **Home page:** _____

○ **Overview of products/services:** _____

○ **About your company:** _____

○ **Contact info:** _____

○ **Privacy policy:** _____

○ **Relevant content:** _____

○ **Media/Press section:** _____

○ **Testimonials/Awards/Client lists:** _____

○ **Newsletter sign-up:** _____

○ **Samples/Demos:** _____

○ **Catalog:** _____

○ **User-generated content:** _____

○ **Customer service info and/or forms:** _____

○ **FAQs:** _____

○ **Site map/Search box:** _____

○ **Investor information:** _____

○ **Enhanced visuals or sound:** _____

○ **Other:** _____

12 Tips for Selling on the Web

While this chapter is devoted to employing your website for marketing—not sales—you may want to devote at least a section of your site to e-commerce. Here are some tips for improving your sales:

1. **Make sure your site is easy to find.** Include your website address on all of your marketing material and in your ads, and work to make it easy to find your business online through search engines (see pages 279–293).

2. **Keep your site's design clean and simple.** Figure out what things your users are most commonly looking for—such as product and/or service lists—and make those items highly visible.

3. **Make your site easy to navigate.** Make sure that users don't have to click through more than one or two pages to find what they're looking for and make a purchase.

4. **Provide an easy-to-use navigation bar on the home page and, ideally, on all subsequent pages.**

5. *Sell* **your products; don't just list them.** Highlight the benefits and features customers are likely to be looking for. Include terms such as *Best Seller* and *Award Winner* (when appropriate), and post customer testimonials.

6. **Match or beat competing sites' prices.** Offer Special Deals, discounts, specials of the day, "Buy one, get one free" offers, and other incentives.

7. **Provide clear and accurate information on your products and services.** Offer customers links to additional product specs.

8. **Add a "Tell a friend" feature to encourage viral marketing.**

9 **Find ways to make customers feel secure on your site.** You can achieve this by posting "seals of approval" and implementing online transaction security programs. You can also do so simply by building a trusted brand.

10. **Clearly identify all charges as well as your return and exchange policy.** This includes shipping and handling as well as product costs.

11. **Insure shopper privacy.** Ask customers to opt-in on receiving emails and other marketing communications from your company, partners, and associates. Avoid making opt-in the default.

12. **Provide great customer service.** Make it a pleasure to shop on your site, and your customers will come back.

Website Essentials

Getting a website up and running can be either an easy task, involving just a little time and money, or an enormous undertaking, requiring months of work and many thousands of dollars. It all depends on how big and complicated a site you want and, more importantly, whether you create a custom site using internal resources and outside contractors, or instead use preformatted templates and services that provide turnkey solutions (see sidebar on page 272). Keep in mind that if you develop a custom site, you'll need people skilled in graphic design, basic website programming, and HTML, or HyperText Markup Language, the basic computer language for website backend programming.

BRAINSTORMING

YOUR WEBSITE

Drawing from the worksheets you completed in this section, outline your website marketing plan.

What are your goals for the website? (Providing company information? Sharing product information? Creating deeper connections with current customers? Reaching a new market? Making sales? Generating leads?)

_____

_____

_____

_____

_____

Who is the target market for your website?

_____

_____

_____

Describe your website's primary content:

_____

_____

_____

What functions will your website need to provide (for example, e-commerce, customer service forms, newsletter sign-up, search box, and so on)?

_____

_____

_____

List the primary sections you plan to include in your website.

_____

_____

_____

Describe the basic feeling of your website's design. This should be consistent with your overall branding (professional, corporate, friendly, or cutting edge).

_____

_____

_____

In the remaining space, sketch out a basic design for your home page.

Hosts with the Most

Many companies provide turnkey solutions for websites that include everything from domain registration to hosting, design templates, a menu of website services (for example, e-commerce/shopping carts), standard forms, and customized programming. These make launching a website relatively easy and inexpensive.

To find a Web hosting firm that's right for you, start by looking at ones that serve your industry. There are companies like this specializing in websites for lawyers, real estate agents, doctors, dentists, and more. In a search engine, type in "website design companies for…" and the name of your industry.

Many companies offer simple website templates and hosting services aimed at smaller companies or retailers. A couple of the bigger ones are Yahoo Small Business (http://smallbusiness.yahoo.com) and Homestead (www.homestead.com). For a broader range of preformatted website designs, check out one of the many companies offering plug-and-play templates that you can upload to a hosting company. They include:

- www.templatemonster.com
- www.freewebtemplates.com
- www.freewebsitetemplates.com
- www.webtemplatebiz.com
- www.templatesfactory.net

Note: most of these companies allow you to start with a template and will offer to customize it for an additional fee. Be careful: this extra service can translate to big bucks, since it's where most of these companies make their real money. If you decide to go for the customization, be sure to ask for estimates for the total cost of building the website.

Domain Name

Every website has a domain name, which identifies the site to users, taking them to the home page of that website. For example, www.planningshop.com is the domain name of the publisher of this book. Every Web page also has a unique URL, or *uniform resource locator,* a string of text that identifies specific page, such as www.planningshop.com/products. However, the term URL is often used as a synonym for domain name.

Your domain name not only helps your potential customers locate your business; it also serves as a marketing tool. Like your business name, it tells online customers who you are and what you do. That's why it's important to find a good one. The best domain name is the exact name of your company. If that name is already taken with a ".com" suffix (the most common suffix for business websites, especially in the U.S.), you can use a suffix for the country you're in (.ca for Canada, .uk for the United Kingdom, .us for the United States, .mx for Mexico) or some of the other suffixes that are available (for example, .biz).

If you can't use the exact name of your company, choose a name that reflects your branding/identity or that conveys something you want prospects to associate you with, and (ideally) is also easy to remember and spell. For example, if you want to call your mortgage broker service Karensmortgage.com but that name is taken, you could instead choose something like GetYourLoan.com.

After you've decided on a few domain names that make sense for your business, you'll have to register. First, check to see which are available. Many online companies, or *registrars,* enable you to do this. One site that lists registrars and does a basic search of domain name availability, is Internic (www.internic.net/). On the Internic site, click the "Search Whois" link to see if the domain name is available, then select a registrar to register your name. If you're using a website hosting company (see the following section), it can usually perform all of these functions for you.

Website Hosting

To eliminate the cost and hassle of maintaining a website on your own computer servers (for which you'd need both the computers and the technical staff to provide reliable, secure, round-the-clock access on a year-round basis), most companies choose to use outside Web hosting providers.

These Web hosting services offer a range of services—from complete turnkey services, where they manage all of your website's software and programming (and perhaps offer website design and templates as well; see "Hosts with the Most" sidebar) to nothing more than provision of space on their computers for your technical staff to manage your website. Your choice of website hosting company and services will depend on whether you're designing a custom site and have the technical staff to provide ongoing maintenance and programming services, or want the ease of having an outside company handle all of that for you.

Other Considerations

Here are some other things to keep in mind as you design and develop your website:

Design for search engine optimization. Make sure you do whatever's necessary to help your site appear high in relevant search engine results—and if you can't manage that, at least make sure that search engines can find you. (For more on this topic, see pages 279–293.) For instance, before you decide that it would be cool to use only video to describe your products or company, consider the fact that video and graphics are harder for search engines to locate and identify than plain text. Read more about ways to optimize your website for search engines in the next chapter.

Plan for ongoing maintenance. Most websites need to be updated from time to time. Whether it's adding or deleting products, changing your location or hours of operation, or adding new features or content, all such tweaks require that somebody be able to upload the information or add the new features. Do you have such a person on your staff, or will you have to hire someone? Moreover, computers have technical glitches. Who will deal with these? As you decide on how to design and program your site, and where to host it, keep in mind the ease and cost of making changes and providing maintenance.

Inspire customer confidence. Once your site is up and running, you'll need to convince potential customers that they can feel secure visiting and doing businesses on your site—especially if it's an e-commerce site. Businesses often use online seals of approval to accomplish this. Generally, you have to apply for these and pay a fee to have the certifying companies review your site. Two of the best-known seals are the Better Business Bureau's *OnLine* Reliability mark (www.bbbonline.org) and TRUSTe (www.truste.org).

Website Costs

Website costs vary tremendously depending on the type of site, how the site is developed, and what functions it performs. Generally, websites based on templates are far less expensive than custom-designed and programmed ones. Keep in mind that a simple, template-based site can cost less than $100, and a complicated e-commerce site for a major retailer can cost more than $1 million to design and maintain.

Website Return on Investment

Determining a website's return on investment (ROI) can be difficult, since most serve many purposes—a majority of which are not directly financial, such as enhancing company branding and awareness, answering customer questions, and providing in-depth product and company information. And if you're making sales from your website but are also making sales in other channels (such as in retail shops or through other sellers), you'll have a hard time figuring out whether sales in those channels resulted from visits to your website.

For the overwhelming majority of companies—especially those not engaged in e-commerce—a website's ROI comes from leads generated and enhanced relationships with current and prospective customers. Thus, you'll likely have to provide "guesstimates" of these amounts when calculating your website ROI.

Still it's worth your while to try, since it will get you thinking (again) about your marketing goals for the website—and how much you want to spend to achieve those goals (both financial and non-financial).

Calculating Your Website ROI

The following worksheet can help you get started on your own ROI analysis. Simply describe what your website marketing will entail, and fill in the requested data to get an idea of the ROI you can expect from your website.

Here are some tips for using the worksheets (and calculating your ROI):

- **Be sure to break out all of your costs.** Thus, for example, if you're using a website hosting company's templates to create your site, make sure you include the costs of any customizations you'll require to those templates—since these are likely to cost far more than the hosting service itself and can add up to big bucks if they're extensive.

- **Remember non-financial goals.** While you may not be able to put a cash value on things like brand awareness and customer perception, these are important components of any marketing campaign, and as such must be considered when calculating return on investment—especially for an item like websites where the financial results are so nebulous and difficult to calculate.

---

affordability scale

Website

$	$$	$$$	$$$$
Simple, template-based site from turnkey provider	Small e-commerce site from turnkey provider	Simple custom brochure site	Simple custom e-commerce site	Major e-commerce site

*COST KEY:

$—Relatively Inexpensive $$—Moderately Expensive $$$—Fairly Expensive $$$$—Expensive

* These symbols represent general rate estimates.

RETURN ON INVESTMENT

YOUR WEBSITE ROI

Your business: _____

Your target market: _____

Description of website: _____

GOALS

Financial: _____

Non-financial: _____

PROJECTED COSTS

Design: _____

Hosting: _____

Writing: _____

Programming: _____

Maintenance: _____

Total cost: _____

PROJECTED RETURNS, FINANCIAL

Number of leads generated: _____

Number of leads converted: _____

Annual revenue generated from conversions: _____

Annual direct sales from website (if applicable): _____

Total cost: _____

Total projected net financial gain (annual revenue and sales minus total cost): _____

PROJECTED RETURNS, NON-FINANCIAL

_____

_____

TOTAL ROI (Total Net Financial Returns Plus Total Non-financial Returns):_____

WEBSITE BUDGET (12 MONTHS)

	JAN	FEB	MARCH	APRIL	MAY
Professional Assistance					
Web writers					
Web designers					
Photographers/Illustrators					
Ongoing content management					
HTML programmers					
Customization/Special programming					
Other programmers					
Network/Systems administrator					
Ongoing web management/Webmaster					
Community master					
Website user support					
Other consultants					
Website Hosting					
Annual domain registration fee					
Monthly hosting fee					
Backup service					
E-commerce shopping cart service					
Other hosting-related expenses					
Supplies/Cost of Goods/Manufacturing					
Computers/Services					
Software					
Backup equipment and supplies					
Other supplies/goods/manufacturing costs					
Other					
TOTAL					

NOTE: An electronic version of this worksheet is available as part of the Planning Shop's Marketing Budget Templates package.

JUNE	JULY	AUGUST	SEPT	OCT	NOV	DEC	TOTAL

Lingo

ADWORDS: Google's search engine marketing program devised around keywords (see definition below).

ALGORITHM: A formula and process search engines use to rank (or order) websites on search results pages.

CLICK THROUGH RATE (CTR): The ratio of the number of times a searcher has clicked on your ad to the total number of times your ad was displayed.

CONVERSION RATE: The rate at which someone who clicks through to your site takes an action you desire, such as making a purchase.

COST PER CLICK (CPC): The rate you pay per click through from an ad to your website on any given search engine. Looking at the CPC helps you determine the return on investment and efficiency of your search engine marketing efforts.

CRAWLER: Software used by search engines (or others) to go through websites looking for information, keywords, and the like.

ORGANIC SEARCH: Search results that are returned to users naturally, rather than as a result of paid placement by website advertisers.

PAID/SPONSORED SEARCH: Results that are returned to users as a result of website advertisers paying search engine companies for higher placement in result rankings.

PAY PER CLICK (PPC): A Web advertising system whereby advertisers pay each time their ad is clicked (rather than each time their ad is displayed).

RANK OR PAGE RANK: Where the site listing is ranked in the search engine results (that is, its proximity to the top of the page).

TRAFFIC: The volume of visitors to a website.

WEB ANALYTICS: Software programs used to quantify website traffic and actions of website visitors.

CHAPTER 23

Search Engine Optimization and Marketing

Build your website, and they will come, right? Not necessarily. For starters, how will people know you've got a website and that it has something they're interested in? Sure, you'll do everything possible *offline* to direct people to your website—putting its address on your business cards, brochures, ads, and so on—but the people in the best position to visit your website immediately are already online. So how do you get them to notice you? One of the best ways is by making sure your site is easy to find via *search engines*—websites, such as Google, Yahoo, and Microsoft Live Search, which help people locate things online.

For the vast majority of online users, search engines serve as the main gateway to Internet information. This means that if your website is highly visible in the results that appear when someone types in a keyword or phrase associated with your type of business, there's a decent chance that person will click on over to your website.

There are two primary ways to insure that your website is highly visible on search engines:

- **Employ search engine optimization (SEO).** *Search engine optimization* refers to the steps you can take to place your website high in search results—ideally on the first page—*without* paying search engine companies directly for that placement. This is also called *organic search* because the results appear to come naturally, or organically.

- **Engage in search engine marketing (SEM).** This refers to the process of paying search engine companies to insure that your website (or specific pages of your website) appears in users' search engine results—typically either at the top or in a column that appears beside other, non-paid results. This is also referred to as *search engine advertising, paid placement, paid search,* or *sponsored listings.*

> **"** *Your rankings on search engines are like brick-and-mortar real estate. A Page 1 ranking is like being located in a busy shopping district. A ranking somewhere on Page 5 is like being located on a small side street with no traffic.* **"**
>
> **Rick Allen**
> **Vice President**
> **CaboVillas.com**

If drawing people to your website is an important component of your marketing plan, you'll want to employ either SEO or SEM (or both).

Understanding How Search Engines Work

If you want your website to appear high in search engine results—as a result of either unpaid (SEO) or paid (SEM) marketing activities—you need to understand something about how search engines work (in other words, how they determine a page's rankings within their results). Even if you intend to hire others to take care of your SEM or SEO, you should have at least a basic understanding of search engine operation when you're choosing what to put on your website and where.

Keywords

When a user wants to find something on the Internet, they type a word or series of words into a search engine's "Search" box. The search engine software then uses these *keywords* to search the Internet and return listings of relevant websites. A keyword can be one word—for instance, *business*—or a series of words—for example, *business plan* or *business plan book.* Users may also type in keywords that narrow their search but are seemingly unrelated—for instance, "Mexican restaurant" and "Chicago Highland Park."

Any steps you take (whether paid or unpaid) to move your website to the top of search engine results will be based on choosing the right keywords.

Crawlers (or Spiders)

When someone types keywords into a search engine, the search engine instantaneously sends out software to search the Internet for Web pages related to those keywords. These applications—called crawlers, because they crawl through the web—analyze Web pages to see which pages they should include in the search results and how high those pages should rank.

Here's something to keep in mind, though: crawlers don't necessarily scour the entire Internet but rather a stored, or *cached,* version of it that the search engine has previously crawled through—a practice established so that search results can be returned faster. This means that it often takes a while—anywhere from days to weeks—for a search engine to include a new website in its results.

Results

Once a user has typed in keywords, a search engine generally returns two types of results:

■ **Listings of related websites found by their own software.** Website owners do not pay search engines to return these results, which generally appear in the main body of the results pages.

■ **Listings of websites that people have paid to associate with specific keywords.** Generally, these results appear at the top or side of the results page, with some visual indicator (such as a shaded background) showing that they represent a different type of result.

Algorithms

When choosing which websites to show in search results—and how high to place, or rank, those pages in results—search engine software uses a set of formulas, or *algorithms*. These formulas look for certain factors, such as the number of times a keyword appears in a website, and apply mathematical weighting to them to determine how closely aligned a website is to a Web searcher's likely intent. (See page 283 for more on what the algorithms of search engines generally look for).

The algorithms employed by search engines are heavily guarded secrets, continually changed and updated because search engine programmers want to make it difficult for people to "game the system" to make sure their websites rank high.

Search engines particularly want to avoid returning results that include websites put up for the sole purpose of drawing Web traffic to generate advertising revenue for the website owner. Such sites have little or no value to Web users—which is why search engines essentially blackball any they discover.

These constantly changing algorithms make it difficult to determine exactly how to make your website most visible in search engine results. Moreover, you need to make sure you're not inadvertently doing things that will make search engine crawlers believe you're *not* a legitimate site (and thus lower your rankings or get you blackballed). Thus, it's important to know what *not* to do as well as what to do when trying to appear high in search engine results.

Search Engine Optimization

To employ search engine optimization to make your website appear high in search engine results, the first thing you need to do is figure out which words your target customers are most likely to use when searching for the types of products or services (or content) you offer. Once you've made that determination, you'll need to repeat those keywords throughout your site—in your content, headlines, page names, additional Web pages, and more. In other words, you must *optimize* your site so that search engine crawlers are likely to associate your website (or certain pages within your website) with those keywords.

Finding the right keywords—and using them over and over—can be critical to a Web-based company's success and significant to any business trying to build market share through the Web. Imagine, for instance, that you own a company that creates and sells educational software that parents use to help teach their kids math. There are lots of terms you'd expect searchers to use when looking for products like yours—and these are the terms you'd use when developing your site's content regardless of whether you were considering SEO: terms such as *software, educational software, math software,* and even *kids software.*

These, however, are all very broad terms—that is, lots of companies sell math software or educational software. This means your site is unlikely to show up high in natural search results based on those keywords because

Search Engine Watch

If you want to learn a great deal about how search engines work—and how to keep up on changes to search engine policies, algorithms, and more, an excellent place to turn is Search Engine Watch, www.searchenginewatch.com.

Choosing Keywords

Critical to success in both search engine optimization and search engine marketing is choosing the right keywords—the ones most likely to be searched on by the largest number of users (who also happen to be the most likely buyers). Here are two tools to help you with the task:

Wordtracker (www.wordtracker.com/). The site offers a free trial.

Google's Keyword Tool (https://adwords.google.com/select/KeywordToolExternal). You can either enter keywords or have the tool evaluate your site's content and suggest keywords.

millions of other sites are also using them. Instead, you'd be better off focusing on keywords that are more specific to *your* products—so in the case of that educational software company, something like *kids math software* would yield better results.

And since these keywords need to be peppered throughout your site if a search engine is to list it high in its results, you need to have SEO in mind right from the start as you develop and update your site. In fact, the best time to work on SEO is when you're designing, writing, and coding your website. Thus, if you plan to hire someone to help with search engine optimization, you should do so as early as possible in your site's development or redesign.

Be aware, however, that SEO is as much art as science. Since search engines—especially the top ones, like Google and Yahoo—frequently change their search algorithms, the optimization rules that kept a company in the top spot one month might not apply the following month. For example, you might have done everything you could to get your kids' math software site ranked in the No. 2 spot for months, only to suddenly see it disappear from the first page of search results simply due to a change in the search engine's ranking system.

SEO Costs

Just because you don't pay search engines for your ranking doesn't mean SEO won't cost you anything. Because effective SEO requires staying on top of the algorithms and knowing exactly how to optimize a website (in terms of design, language, and coding), an entire industry has grown up around that task, and SEO consultants can cost anywhere from a few hundred to many thousands of dollars per month. Large corporations—and nimble smaller businesses—have staff members devoted to managing their SEO and Web ranking presence.

Whether you hire an SEO specialist or devote internal resources to keeping track of SEO will depend on your marketing goals. The first thing you need to determine is how important a high search results ranking is to your business. Do you get most of your customers through the Web? Is it critical for your overall marketing plan that you drive a large number of new visitors to your website? If so, you might consider hiring an employee or contractor who specializes in SEO. If, on the other hand, your customers are local and more likely to find your site through your advertising and networking efforts, simply educating yourself on a few site optimization techniques should suffice.

Search Engine Alchemy

Given that search engine optimization is at best an imprecise science, here's a quick primer on what works and what doesn't (that is, what's sure to get you blackballed) when it comes to getting your website listed high in search engine results.

What Works

- **Carefully chosen keywords.** Strive to make the words on your page match the keywords searchers are most likely to use.

- **High keyword density.** Make sure that the keywords searchers are likely to be looking for appear frequently on your Web page.

- **Well-placed keywords.** Keywords near the top of a page generally fare the best in search results.

- **Keywords placed in page titles, headlines, and bold text.** Sites on which keywords appear frequently in display type (such as titles, headlines, and bold text) will generally rank higher in search results.

- **Meta tags.** These content descriptions programmed into the code of a website are one of the places search engines look for keywords—which means placing key words in meta tags will help improve your site's ranking in search results.

- **Long-established sites.** Stick around long enough, and search engines are bound to rank your website higher: it's standard search engine practice to attach higher relevance to older sites, because they assume such sites are legitimate—that is, they're not just trying to "game" the ranking system.

- **Lots of links in.** If many sites link to a page, search engines assume you have a good site worthy of a higher ranking.

- **High-quality links in.** If the links in to a page come from highly ranked or heavily trafficked sites, those links are even more valuable in determining rankings.

- **Lots of links out.** Likewise, if a page links out to a lot of other sites, search engines assume the page contains genuine content.

- **Fresh content.** Search engines look to see how recently a website's content has been updated, assuming that newer content is of more interest to users.

What *Doesn't* Work

- **Keyword stuffing.** Although you want to use keywords repeatedly to get noticed by search engines, you must do so in context: when crawlers spot a keyword over and over without content or context, they assume the website is a spammer.

- **Keywords in graphics, animation, sounds, and videos.** Crawlers generally have a difficult time recognizing keywords in anything other than text or coding, so while it's great to use plenty of visual and audio effects on your site, make sure that you include lots of relevant keywords in your page's text and coding.

- **Duplicate content.** While search engine sites are interested in returning unique content, spam sites typically reuse the same big chunks of content on myriad different sites and pages. Thus, to avoid being tagged as a spammer, don't repeat large blocks of text on many pages.

- **"Invisible" text.** Because readers tire of seeing long strings of unnecessary keywords, some spammers make these keyword strings the same color as the background, hoping that search engines will see them (and that users won't be annoyed by them); search engine algorithms, however, are set to detect this.

- **Meaningless keywords.** Only use popular keywords in your site's coding if they actually relate to your content.

- **Broken links.** Crawlers rate sites with lots of bogus or broken links lower.

- **Incompatible site structure.** Avoid website structures—such as frames (a page-within-a-page structure)—that are known to trip up crawlers.

- **Misspellings.** If your website's keywords are misspelled, the site is less likely to turn up in users' search results.

- **Unsavory website hosting companies.** If the company that hosts your website has hosted a lot of websites that have used search engine spamming techniques, every website from that hosting company will suffer.

BRAINSTORMING

YOUR SEARCH ENGINE KEYWORDS

Use this worksheet to begin thinking about the keywords that are likely to bring the highest search result rankings for your site.

What keywords are your customers likely to use when searching for a business similar to yours? Choose at least ten keywords (words and/or phrases) that your target customers might use to search for your company, products, services, or content.

_____

_____

_____

_____

Now, use a search engine's keyword search tool to see what similar words and phrases people are using when they search for those keywords, and then generate some synonyms. A good such tool is the one from Google (https://adwords.google.com/select/KeywordToolExternal).

_____

_____

_____

Which keywords have the least amount of competition from other sites?

_____

_____

_____

Which keywords have a high volume of searchers?

_____

_____

_____

Which keywords are most distinctive to your website?

_____

_____

_____

List any other keywords you can use to narrow a search and make it more likely that your site will rank high—for example, location, industry, unique features, and so on:

_____

_____

_____

Search Engine Marketing

Search engine marketing (SEM) is a broad term that could apply to any type of marketing activity aimed at associating your company's name and website with search engine results; however, to distinguish it from search engine optimization, the term *SEM* has come to mean those activities in which you *pay* to have your site appear high within search results. SEM can also be called *search engine advertising.*

Here's how SEM works: Advertisers choose the keywords they want to be associated with—that is, the ones they think searchers are most likely to use when looking for products, services, and content similar to theirs. Then, when the customer enters into a search engine one of the keywords an advertiser has purchased, a small ad appears either above or near the list of naturally generated search results. Most such ads consist of just simple text, often indistinguishable from the actual search results except for their placement on the page or a faint background color. These ads are very small—usually just a headline, followed by about ten words or so, and a link to a website or a page within a website.

SEM has proven to be an extremely effective advertising medium for two primary reasons:

■ **Highly qualified prospects.** Searchers are often highly qualified prospects—especially for the most narrowly defined terms. For instance, if someone types in the term "bike repair San Francisco," there's a good chance they're in Northern California with an immediate need to get their bicycle fixed.

■ **Effectiveness of pay per click (PPC).** Another—extremely compelling—reason that SEM is so popular is that advertisers are charged *only* when a searcher clicks on their ads. Although advertisers pay each and every time a searcher clicks on their listings (called a *click through)*, they do not pay just for the ad being displayed—and this fact distinguishes PPC advertising from virtually every other type. If you run an ad for your bike repair shop in the newspaper or the Yellow Pages, for example, you'll pay the same amount for that ad no matter how many people actually see it. You may get zero response, but you'll still have to pay.

The combination of highly qualified, or motivated, prospects and PPC financing makes SEM an extremely powerful marketing tool—and one that's important to consider as part of your marketing plan.

Advertising on Content Pages

In addition to paying to have your website ad appear on search engine results, you can use some of the same search engine marketing programs to have your ad appear on websites with content closely aligned to your keywords. For instance, if you sell gymnastics equipment, you can bid to have your ad appear on sites (even blogs) having to do with gymnastics. These sites have to agree to accept these ads, but many do. This is another way to get your ad in front of highly qualified prospects on the Web. Two of the leading programs are Google's AdSense (www.google.com/adsense) and Yahoo's Publisher Network (http://publisher.yahoo.com).

Search Engine Marketing Basics

As with search engine optimization, search engine companies continually update their SEM offerings and practices. As a result, if SEM is a significant component of your marketing plan, you'll probably want to hire an SEM consultant, SEM firm, or in-house SEM specialists to manage this part of your marketing efforts.

Even so, it helps to understand some SEM basics:

- **Keyword bidding and pricing.** Not surprisingly, many advertisers want to be associated with the same words—after all, there are a lot of companies selling cell phones or car insurance or financial planning. For this reason, the price of a paid search engine advertisement is based on an auction system. Advertisers indicate how much they're willing to spend per click through, and those that make the highest bids for keywords show up at the top of the ad section on the results page. Different search engines have various ways of suggesting amounts to bid or to let you know what your competitors are bidding for those keywords.

- **Click through rate (CTR).** The ratio of the number of times a searcher has clicked on your ad to the total number of times your ad was displayed. In other words, if your ad was displayed alongside one thousand search results but only 30 people clicked it to go to your website, your CTR would be 3%. The CTR is a measure of response to the ad and gives you an easy way to compare the effectiveness of different keywords and ad language.

- **Cost per click (CPC).** Bidding for keywords is done on a "cost per click" basis. Advertisers pay each time a user *clicks through* to the link they put in a search engine ad. Cost per click varies widely, depending on desirability of the keyword. Obviously, the most expensive keywords are those that are in the most demand. Typically, keywords for business-related terms are more expensive than those for popular consumer items. Looking at the CPC helps you determine the efficiency of your search engine marketing efforts and the return on your investment (ROI).

- **Monthly budget.** With most search engines, the advertiser specifies a monthly budget—or maximum number of clicks—they're willing to pay for. This way, a sudden barrage of ad-generated site traffic won't result in higher-than-anticipated costs.

- **Quality.** When determining an ad's ranking in their results, some search engines rely not only on keyword bid price but also on how well matched that ad is to a searcher's intent. Google calls this a Quality Score (QS)—and it's something the company assigns to keep spammers from being able to buy their way into top spots in search engine results. Generally, quality is determined by factors such as click through rates, the average length of time searchers remain on sites, and algorithms measuring the nature of the link's landing page. (For example, does it appear to have real content? Does it use the keywords repeatedly and in relation to real content?)

Improving Your SEM Results

When thinking about how to improve your SEM results, you need to ask the following questions:

■ How can you make your website appear higher in search results?

■ How can you improve click through rates?

■ How can you increase your *conversion rate*—meaning the number of searchers who actually take an action that you want (such as making a purchase, registering for a newsletter, or requesting info)?

An entire industry is devoted to improving these types of SEM results, but here are a few key concepts to keep in mind:

■ **Choose narrowly defined keywords.** By purchasing very narrowly defined keywords, you improve your chances of showing up higher in results (and thus finding the right prospects) while decreasing your costs (since fewer competitors are likely to be bidding on the same terms). If, for example, you make handmade Windsor-style chairs and you bid on the terms *furniture* and *chairs,* you're likely to be bidding against a huge variety of companies. Even keywords such as *handcrafted wood furniture* will return many results and should only be chosen if you have a substantial budget. If you have a limited SEM marketing budget, instead choose a very descriptive, narrow term such as *handmade Windsor chairs.* Sure, fewer people will type in such a narrow string of keywords, but those who do will be very qualified customers, and thus more likely to click through to your website.

■ **Go local**. You're more likely to get a higher ranking if you add a specific geographic area to your keywords. For example, an office furniture business in Des Moines, Iowa, might want to find customers looking to buy Aeron brand desk chairs. If they bid on the keywords *Aeron desk chair,* they'll find themselves competing with national, international, and online companies. And the overwhelming majority of people who see that listing will be nowhere near Des Moines. If, however, this Iowa company specifies *Aeron desk chair Des Moines* as its keywords, the company will likely find itself competing—and bidding—against fewer businesses for those terms. Thus, the company will show up higher and pay less per click—and the searchers are likely to be in close proximity to the company.

■ **Experiment.** Try different headlines and ad copy in your search engine ads. You only have a few words, so you need to make each of them work for you. Because it's so easy (and usually quick) to evaluate the performance of individual ads (thanks to search engine analytics; see page 289), you can try out a number of different wordings to see which headlines and ad copy bring you the best results. Also, experiment with different offers or products/services to see which ones are best suited for your SEM efforts.

■ **Improve your quality ratings.** Since major search engines consider quality—and not just bid prices—when determining a page's ranking in paid search listings, it's wise to figure out ways to make your ad's quality score as high as possible. That means, first, continually working to improve your click through rate. It also means that you need to be sure you have appropriate, high-quality content on the page your ad links to.

■ **Eliminate or disable negative keywords.** Since you pay for every click through, you want to not only maximize the number of qualified prospects who come to your site but also minimize the number of people who will never take the action you desire. To do this, you must evaluate conversion rates, or the ratio of the number of people who click through to your site to the number who actually take an action you desire (such as making a purchase). Search engine analytic software makes it fairly easy to perform this type of analysis. For instance, while the term *free* works well for attracting visitors, you need to ask yourself whether the people who clicked through on the word *free* will be willing to pay for what you're selling. With search engine programs, you can choose to identify *negative keywords* such as *free*, and your ad will not be shown to searchers typing in those terms.

■ **Create different landing pages.** Once searchers click through, are you driving them to the right page? By creating different "landing pages," you can respond to varying interests of the searchers who click on your ad. If, for example, you run a general travel agency, but you're using SEM to advertise your eco-adventure tours to Belize, searchers should click through to a Web page solely about Belize (perhaps one created just for that ad campaign), not to the home page for the rest of the tours you offer.

SEO and SEM Costs

The price of SEO and SEM varies widely, depending more on how committed you are to these online marketing techniques than the techniques themselves. For instance, doing a bit of SEO as you are developing your site may cost you virtually nothing. On the other hand, if ranking high in search results is critical to the success of your business, you may need to hire full-time SEO staffers and an SEO marketing firm to work with you, which could be quite expensive. Likewise, you could spend as little as $50 to $100 per month on SEM, bidding on just a few critical keywords. Or you could spend more than a million dollars a year on SEM.

The amount of money you spend on SEO and SEM should be based on how important Web traffic is to the income of your business. If you run an e-commerce site and almost all of your sales will come from online visitors, you should invest fairly heavily in both SEO and SEM.

The following SEO/SEM Affordability Scale is based on a company that's fairly committed to these online marketing techniques and is designed to reflect the relationship of costs for a company with a significant SEO and SEM budget.

SEO and SEM Return on Investment

As with every other aspect of your marketing plan, you should carefully evaluate the return on investment (ROI) of your SEO and SEM marketing efforts. Fortunately, this is one area of marketing where ROI is extremely easy to measure.

The reason for this is Web *analytics*—software that provides you with detailed data analyzing your ad and website traffic. Analytics quantifies website traffic and every action taken in your SEM activities and by your website visitors. It can tell you how many times your ad was shown to searchers (called *impressions)*, how many times it was clicked through, what Web pages users visited once they clicked through, how long searchers stayed on your site, whether they took certain actions (such as making a purchase) after they had clicked through to your site, and more.

As part of your SEM program, the companies selling you keywords (for example Google and Yahoo) typically provide a great deal of analytics FREE. By taking advantage of it, you can tell how well your ad campaign is going—or not going—so that you can tweak it accordingly, making your ads more and more successful. In most cases, you'll find this information relatively easy to access, use, and understand—meaning you don't have to be a techie to use analytics to improve your Web advertising results.

You can also purchase Web analytics programs or services from third parties if you want more detailed analysis or need help analyzing your SEO activities.

Web analytics software is powerful stuff. It gives you significant insight into what's happening as a result of your SEO and SEM efforts. And it will help you evaluate whether the traffic generated by search engine pay-per-click ads translates to revenue that covers the cost of these clicks.

Learning to use and understand search and website analytics is a critical part of your SEO and SEM marketing efforts. And it's the only way to truly measure your ROI.

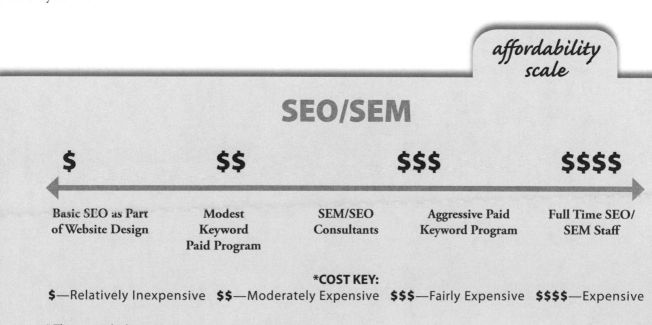

affordability scale

SEO/SEM

$	$$	$$$	$$$$
Basic SEO as Part of Website Design	Modest Keyword Paid Program	SEM/SEO Consultants	Aggressive Paid Keyword Program	Full Time SEO/ SEM Staff

*COST KEY:

$**—Relatively Inexpensive   **$$**—Moderately Expensive   **$$$**—Fairly Expensive   **$$$$—Expensive

* These symbols represent general rate estimates.

Calculating Your SEM ROI

The following worksheet can help you get started on your own ROI analysis. For the purposes of this analysis, start small—that is, with the results you can expect to achieve from purchasing just one keyword (or phrase). Then, simply describe your site, your goals (financial and non-financial), and your market, and fill in the rest of the requested data to get an idea of the ROI you can expect to achieve from your search engine marketing campaign.

Note also that although search engine *optimization* is theoretically free—that is, you're not paying anybody to place ads for your site—there are still costs associated with it if you plan to pursue it on a grand scale, especially if e-commerce represents a significant component of your website. If this is the case, calculate the costs of hiring consultants or dedicating staff to the function, purchasing Web analytics software, and so on to perform a similar ROI analysis for search engine optimization.

Here are some tips for using the worksheets (and calculating your ROI):

- **Use narrowly defined keywords to achieve optimal results.** Thus, if you're an antiquarian bookseller in Santa Barbara, California, who recently acquired a trove of military history titles, you could use "Antiquarian Books Santa Barbara" as your keywords if your primary goal was to get local bibliophiles into your store by offering information on your location, hours, and product offerings. Conversely, you could use "Antiquarian Books Military History" if your goal was to get warfare history buffs from all over the globe to come to your site and check out (and ultimately purchase online) your military history first editions.

- **Create separate landing pages/Experiment.** Once someone clicks through from your ad, you want to make sure they immediately find what they're looking for. Drive them to the appropriate page of your website or create separate pages just for your ad campaign. If you're finding that people are clicking through to your website but then not buying, you need to keep making changes to your landing page and marketing language and continue to evaluate the nature of your offer—until you find a combination that results in higher levels of conversions to sales.

- **Remember non-financial goals.** While you may not be able to put a cash value on things like brand awareness and customer perception, these are important components of any marketing campaign, and as such must be considered when calculating return on investment—especially on websites where e-commerce is not the primary function.

RETURN ON INVESTMENT

YOUR SEARCH ENGINE MARKETING ROI

Your business: _____

Your target market: _____

Your keyword(s): _____

Description of website: _____

GOALS

Financial: _____

Non-financial: _____

PROJECTED COSTS

Ad cost per click: _____

Total ad purchase budget per month: _____

SEM keyword/strategy consultants: _____

SEM tech consultants: _____

SEM writers/consultants: _____

Internal staff dedicated to SEM: _____

Additional web analytics software/services: _____

Total cost: _____

PROJECTED RETURNS, FINANCIAL

Number of click throughs: _____

Number of click through conversions (i.e., number of users of who take desired action after clicking through to site: _____

Amount of revenue generated per conversion: _____

Monthly revenue generated from SEM conversions: _____

Total annual revenue generated from Web search customers:_____

Total cost: _____

Total projected net financial gain (annual revenue minus total cost): _____

PROJECTED RETURNS, NON-FINANCIAL

Total number of impressions: _____

Number of non-converting click throughs:_____

Other brand building, awareness benefits: _____

TOTAL ROI (Total Net Financial Returns Plus Total Non-financial Returns):_____

SEO/SEM BUDGET (12 MONTHS)

	JAN	FEB	MARCH	APRIL	MAY
Professional Assistance					
SEO technology consultants					
SEO keyword/website writer consultants					
SEM technology consultants					
SEM keyword/strategy consultants					
SEM writers					
Web analytic services					
Other consultants					
Ad Buys					
SEM pay-per-click keywords					
Other ad buys					
Supplies/Cost of Goods/Manufacturing					
Analytic software					
Other supplies/goods/manufacturing costs					
Other					
SEO					
SEM					
TOTAL					

! **NOTE:** An electronic version of this worksheet is available as part of the Planning Shop's Marketing Budget Templates package.

JUNE	JULY	AUGUST	SEPT	OCT	NOV	DEC	TOTAL

Lingo

AUTO RESPONDER: A part of a computer program that automatically communicates with someone via email, typically in response to an action or on a certain date or dates.

EMAIL MAILING LIST: A collection of email addresses to send communications to; typically made up of customers, prospects, and other business associates.

EMAIL NEWSLETTER: Similar to print newsletters, a communication sent via email to customers and prospects providing information and advice—usually on a recurring basis.

FILTERS: Software programs that prescreen email messages to block email considered to be spam, or junk email.

OPT-IN: A procedure whereby an individual must choose to receive email communications before something will be sent to them.

OPT-OUT: A procedure whereby an individual must choose not to receive email communications in order to prevent email communications from being sent to them.

PERMISSION-BASED MARKETING: Sending marketing communications only to those prospects and customers who have given their approval to receive such communications.

SPAM: Unwanted, unrequested email—typically bulk email sent from strangers.

TRIGGER EVENT: An action, date, or other item that causes an email to be sent via an auto responder.

Email Marketing

A financial planning consultant sends an email newsletter containing ten investment tips to her customers. A retail store sends an announcement of an upcoming sale via email. A dentist's patient gets a notice in his email inbox alerting him that it's time for a checkup. All of these represent ways businesses can stay in touch with customers and prospects via email.

Like their print counterparts, email marketing communications are extremely effective when it comes to building your business and retaining customers. They also have the advantage of being fast, easy, and inexpensive to produce.

Of course, people are deluged with email, and as with any kind of marketing piece, there's the possibility that your communication may well just get tossed—after all, it's easy to hit that Delete button. But if an email communication comes from a recognized and trusted source and offers something of interest to the recipient, there's a good chance it will be opened—and perhaps even viewed as something valuable.

Email marketing is:

- **Effective.** Customers and prospects look at their email continually.
- **Affordable.** Email is significantly less expensive than print communication.
- **Quick.** Messages can be prepared and sent virtually immediately.
- **Easy.** A variety of email communication services make it a snap to stay in touch via email.

But a word of caution about all email marketing: be careful not to abuse it. Send email only to those who've signed up to receive email from you or have had some dealings with you. Limit the frequency of your messages. And make sure your mailings are meaningful, valuable, and don't contain offensive content or language. If not, recipients will soon block your email, and if too many people report you as sending undesirable bulk email (or *spam*), Internet email filters will block your messages to many larger servers. You may also be violating the law in some countries.

Email Marketing Basics

While most people send emails every day, if you're going to begin email marketing in earnest—as part of your overall marketing plan—it's useful to understand a few basics that apply to virtually all types of email marketing.

Words to Get You Bounced

Email filters look for certain words often associated with spam email. Using these words or punctuation marks in your subject line (or repeatedly in your text) increases the chance that your email will get sent to the "junk" folder in an email box or blocked altogether.

- *Free*
- *Instant*
- *Order now*
- *Money-back guarantee*
- Advertisement or ADV
- *Your bills/debt/credit*
- *Lose pounds/lbs/weight*
- *XXX*
- *Sex*
- *Over 21*
- *Adults*
- Dollar signs ($)
- Multiple exclamation points (!!)
- Exclamation points and question marks together (?! or !?)
- Lots of spaces
- All capital letters
- G.a.p.p.y-T.e.x.t

"Opt-in" vs. "Opt-out"

How do people get on your mailing list and end up receiving your email communications? Do they have to give their permission for you to send them an email—or do they have to actively take a step to get their name removed from your mailing list? That, in essence, is the primary difference between an opt-in versus an opt-out mailing list. For instance, if you become a member of an online group or social networking site, will they *ask* you if you want to receive email announcements from their advertisers or sponsors, or do they automatically send you those announcements, merely allowing you to "unsubscribe" or get off their lists if you later choose to do so?

Opt-in email marketing—also referred to as *permission-based marketing*—is the only type that is allowed in some countries, and many email newsletter services (described later in this chapter) will only allow you to send to opt-in mailing lists.

Sender Identification

One of the most important pieces of information you can put in an email communication is the name of the sender. Most recipients decide whether to open an email based on who it's from. Personal names are usually the best bet. If you have an existing relationship with a recipient—or that person is likely to know who you are—the best sender identification is your own name. And if a celebrity is associated with your business, using that person's name is almost certain to get your email looked at. If, however, your name is unlikely to be known to your email recipients, it's generally best to add some kind of identification along with the company's name (for example, "Chris Jones, TrailBikes, CEO").

Subject Line

A recipient of an email message is going to decide in a split second whether an email is worth opening. To make that decision, they're going to look at two things: who sent the email and what it's about. This means you have to make your subject line work for you.

To do this, make sure your subject line promises some value to the reader. That value can take the form of a financial incentive ("$25 cash back") or, more likely, information a reader might find useful ("7 weight-loss tips"). You can also make your subject line more inviting by showing an immediate benefit to the reader ("7 tips for losing 3 pounds by Saturday!") or, better yet, by putting the reader in the headline and teasing them a bit ("You can lose 3 pounds by Saturday! Don't believe it? Here's how"). But remember, though: subject lines still need to be believable and credible to be opened.

Generally, shorter subject lines are more effective (studies have shown that subject lines with fewer than 50 characters are best); however, longer subject lines can also be effective—as long as they have very specific details and are enticing to the recipient.

Spam, Email Filters, Junk Email

If you've been getting email for any length of time, you're familiar with spam—unwanted bulk email. It's so easy and cheap to send email that the Internet is overwhelmed by spam email. As a result, software programs—called *filters*—have been developed to detect and block spam. For this reason, it's important that you learn what email filters are looking for in their effort to detect spam emails—and then make sure you avoid using similar terms in your marketing emails. Sure, you might attract a reader's attention with a subject line that reads, "FREE! FREE! FREE! SAVE YOUR $$$!!!" However, there's also a pretty good chance your email won't ever make it to users' inboxes. Thus, it's important that you familiarize yourself with some of the basic terms and practices that set off alarms with email filters so that you can avoid them.

Company Identification and Taglines

If you're sending bulk email, you should make it standard practice to identify your company and include a link to your website in every email you send. Many online email services require this—and it's the law in Europe—but it's a good idea in every case, adding credibility, driving traffic to your website, and helping your email make it through email filter programs. In addition, many recipients simply delete any email communication that doesn't include a clear company identification.

Remember: Every email you send can serve as an ad for your business—all you have to do is tack on a tagline at the bottom (beneath your signature) and provide a link to your website. Don't let this valuable piece of real estate be wasted. In most email programs, you can automatically add a "signature" line to every outgoing email—on bulk emails you need to remember to include your contact information and a link to your website.

Graphics, Length, and Appearance

One of the most important rules of email marketing is to make your emails attractive and easy to read. People tend to be in a hurry—which means that many email recipients will decide whether to read something solely by how it looks. The lesson: make your email inviting.

Another important rule for your marketing email: keep it short. Use brief, concise sentences and short paragraphs. This means you'll need to edit your communications to include only the most important information. Remember: you can always include a link to your website or to a *landing page*—that is, a Web page that's been put up just to respond to that email (though to be fair, the percentage of readers who will click on links is likely to be very small).

Better yet, make your emails graphical. Include images and use an attractive font (though not too many fonts). This means you'll have to lay out your email in HTML (the format that enables graphics) rather than use just plain text. Keep in mind, though, that using HTML will make your email message a bit longer and not everyone will be able to see the graphics. However, for most recipients this shouldn't be a problem.

When to Send Your Email

You want your emails to arrive in readers' inboxes when they're likely to be at their computers (or other email devices) and in a position to respond. The more time that elapses between when an email is received and when a recipient is likely to read it, the lower your response rate.

For instance, if you're sending marketing emails to business customers late Friday night, there's a good chance your customers won't see that email until Monday morning—at which point your email will be buried in an overflowing inbox. And on Monday morning as your customers wade their way through dozens of emails, your email is likely to receive little attention. In contrast, if your email arrives at 10 a.m. on Tuesday, your recipients are much more likely to read and respond to it.

There have been many studies of the best times to send email, but generally for business customers, the best days are Tuesdays, Wednesdays, and Thursdays—preferably mid-morning and mid-afternoon. However, you typically cannot control exactly when bulk email will be delivered. If you're targeting consumers, evenings and weekends are often preferable, since they may not be checking personal email during the day—or may be less likely to take action then even if they are checking.

When sending email, also keep time zones in mind—especially if you're sending to recipients across countries and time zones. Try to time your mailing to be received when the overwhelming majority of your readers are most likely to open and respond to their email.

Mailing Lists

As with all mail marketing communications—whether in printed or electronic form—the quality of your mailing list is key in getting your message to the right customers or prospects and determining whether your mailing will be a success.

Just as with print mail, you can either rent or build your mailing. Generally, when you "rent" an email list of prospects, you do so in a partnership or advertising relationship. This means that a company that has an email list that might be of interest to you will send out an email to its list on your behalf. For instance, an outdoor/adventure magazine might send out an email about your white water rafting trips. It's also possible to rent from email list brokers lists containing names of recipients that have been screened and agreed to receive advertising email.

Renting email mailing lists, however, is a bit more problematic than renting mailing lists comprised of physical addresses. The reason for this is that many online mailing services will only allow you to use opt-in addresses you've compiled yourself or addresses of those you've had at least some business connection with (this includes those who've given you their business cards as well as customers).

Thus, you're likely to be building your own mailing list. People to add to your mailing list include:

- Current customers
- Past customers
- Prospects, visitors to your store/office
- Business colleagues/connections such as vendors and referral sources
- People you've met at networking events
- Visitors to your trade show booth
- Website visitors who've given you their email addresses
- Customers and prospects who've signed up to receive your email newsletter
- Anyone who's given you their business card

One of the best ways to collect highly targeted addresses is to entice those who visit your website to give you their email addresses—either to receive email newsletters (see page 300) or to obtain other information. A catering company, for instance, might offer to email several quick-and-easy gourmet recipes, or an online advertising agency might offer a white paper on the most effective search engine marketing techniques for download. It's entirely appropriate to solicit email addresses in exchange for valuable information of this sort.

You can also put a sign-up sheet at your trade show booth, store, or any other venue where you come in contact with potential customers. Alternatively, you could conduct a drawing or sweepstakes for a valuable prize. People often need an incentive to provide their email addresses—another reason that email newsletters serve as an effective tool for building your email mailing list.

In all cases, avoid spamming, or sending email to people who have had no interest in or contact with you or your products. People who don't want your mail will not be your customers, so do your best to avoid sending messages to them. As with direct mail, carefully qualify the customers on your list. And *always* offer an opt-out option for those who don't want your emails.

Banned Spam?

The laws covering bulk email vary from country to country. In the U.S., the CAN-SPAM Act (Controlling the Assault of Non-Solicited Pornography and Marketing Act)—which covers commercial messages only—requires a clear opt-out option (that is, the sender must remove the recipient's email address within ten days, if requested) and accurate identification of the sender, as well as limits certain content, including misleading or inaccurate subject lines. In Canada, the Personal Information Protection and Electronic Documents Act (PIPEDA) protects the privacy of email addresses and limits the use of email addresses for unrequested email. In Europe, all bulk email messages (including charitable and political ones) require recipients to opt in (that is, give their permission to receive a message) or have an existing business relationship with the sender. European bulk email messages are also required to have an opt-out option and must provide specific details (such as full name and address) about the business sending email.

❝ Think of your readers as an audience and think of yourself as a publisher. Create short, informative, and/or entertaining, compelling content. Once you've done that it's perfectly acceptable to weave promotions into the text, sidebars, landing pages, even occasionally a little more center stage.❞

Matt Blumberg
CEO
Return Path
(Email Services Company)

Email Newsletters

Sent by email to prospective customers and others, email newsletters provide a digital counterpart to print newsletters. The best ones contain useful information (beyond sales pitches) that positions their senders as experts in a particular field.

Like their print counterparts, email newsletters contain information and tips your customers can use, short articles, business updates, special announcements, and (sometimes) coupons and other special offers. What they *should not* contain is lots and lots of sales information about your products and services. In other words, you need to provide recipients with benefits for opening your newsletter—not just a heavy-handed sales pitch. That way, recipients are more likely to open your next email newsletter.

Because of their informational format, newsletters are particularly useful for building your credibility as an expert in your field. They also place your contact information in front of customers and prospects on a regular basis, making it easy for them to find and do business with you when they're ready.

Newsletter Frequency

To be effective, a newsletter must be sent regularly—but not so frequently that recipients view it as a nuisance and hit the "Unsubscribe" or "Block Sender" button.

The frequency of your email newsletter will depend on two factors:

- How eager recipients are for your information
- Your ability to prepare and send a newsletter on a regular basis

Generally, a monthly email newsletter is just right: recipients are happy to get the information, and most businesses can manage to prepare one newsletter per month. If, however, you can't pull one together that frequently, try sending a quarterly email newsletter instead—any less frequently, and your results are likely to be less than stellar. Remember, the point of a newsletter is to get your name in front of customers and prospects with enough regularity that they don't forget you.

Depending on your business, customers may want to get information from you even more frequently—say, on a weekly basis. If, for instance, customers truly want to see your weekly sales figures in a newsletter format, great: just make sure you can actually manage sending a newsletter that often. And make your newsletters brief and easy to read—just like their print counterparts.

Preparing Your Newsletter

Be aware that preparing and sending out a newsletter can be a time-consuming undertaking—especially if you plan to handle all aspects of it in house.

Before launching a newsletter, determine:

- Who will gather information
- Who will write it
- Who will design it
- Who will manage laying out the content
- Who will manage the mailing list (removing un-subscribes and bounce-backs)
- Who will manage the software and hardware necessary to physically send it out
- Who will evaluate responses and determine what's working

But this sounds more arduous than it has to be. That's because you'll find many reasonably priced online email newsletter services available to help you create your newsletter, providing a host of turnkey templates and tools, as well as additional support for designing and sending your newsletter.

These automated online email newsletter services handle many of the functions listed above, making it easy to send regular email newsletters, manage your mailing list, and analyze what's working and what's not. And because these email services perform all of the technical tasks associated with sending your newsletter, all you need is an Internet connection. Moreover, such services also continually clean up your mailing list, deleting those people who've chosen to unsubscribe and evaluating "bounce backs." They'll put up links on your website (and/or others' websites) so people can sign up to receive your newsletter, making it easy to maintain your mailing list.

In addition to technical services, these online services also provide newsletter templates, which you can use to speed and simplify the design of your own newsletter. They also suggest ways you can improve responses to your email mailings, and they can generally provide a wealth of information about your newsletter's performance (for example, who's opening it, how many people are clicking on which links, and so on)—information you can use to experiment to continually improve the effectiveness of your newsletter.

Moreover, most of these online email newsletter services are quite affordable; prices depend on the size of your mailing list and how frequently you are sending newsletters. Even large corporations use these types of services because they have become experts in managing newsletters.

Even if you use an online email newsletter service, if you plan to produce a regular newsletter, you'll need someone on your staff to manage the process. You'll also need staff members (or contractors) to write each newsletter. Keep in mind that to be most effective, you need to send your newsletter regularly—no less than once a month. So you need to dedicate the staff time to be able to get a newsletter prepared and sent on an ongoing basis.

E-Newsletters Made Easy

Many companies provide easy-to-use, turnkey online email newsletter services to help you create and send email newsletters in a snap. Here's a short list of some:

- AWeber (www.aweber.com)
- Campaign Monitor (www.campaignmonitor.com)
- Constant Contact (www.constantcontact.com)
- Emma (www.myemma.com)
- JangoMail (www.jangomail.com)
- MailChimp (www.mailchimp.com)
- WebMail.us (www.webmail.us)

BRAINSTORMING

YOUR EMAIL NEWSLETTER

Use this worksheet to outline the specifics of an email newsletter your business could produce and distribute to current and potential customers.

What kinds of useful information and tips will it contain? _____

How will you promote your products or services without driving readers away? _____

Who will be responsible for developing and writing the content? _____

How will you develop your mailing list? _____

How frequently will you produce and send a newsletter? _____

Will you use an online email newsletter service to send your newsletter and maintain your mailing list?
If so, which one? _____

If not, who will be responsible for the technical aspects of sending your newsletter and maintaining your mailing list? _____

If not, who will be responsible for maintaining and updating your mailing list, getting rid of un-subscribes and bounce backs? _____

How will you evaluate whether your email newsletter is serving as an effective marketing piece? What are the criteria for success? _____

What other aspects of your email newsletter must you consider? _____

Other Email Communications

While email newsletters are among the most effective regular email marketing techniques, there are a variety of other ways you can communicate with a large number of customers and prospects via email.

Product Launches, Announcements, and Press Releases

Have you just launched a new product line? Was your company just featured in a magazine as a leader in your industry? Will celebrities at the Oscars be wearing your products? If you have news that's likely to be of interest to your customers and prospects or that will enhance your company's credibility, send out an email to your entire email mailing list to announce it. And if you're sending a press release to let the media know about something, make sure your own mailing list gets a copy of that press release too!

Remember, each of these occurrences gives you a legitimate reason to keep your name in front of people.

Such announcements are commonly used to:

■ Introduce new products or services

■ Announce partnerships with other companies

- Introduce new company leadership or staff
- Announce new locations, store openings, and moves
- Announce a newsworthy event or statistic that relates to your company or product
- Highlight the popularity of your products

When sending an email announcement, be sure to state the news you're sending in the subject line. And if possible, use that line to indicate how the news benefits your customer. For example, in emails to your own mailing lists, the subject line might read, "Just Launched - New Hats with Patented Sun-blocking Fabric in Time for Your Summer Vacation." In contrast, the subject line of the press release for the media headline might say "Top Designer Elizabeth Smith Launches New Line of Hats with Patented Sun-blocking Fabric."

Sales and Discounts

Everyone loves a bargain. That means that many of your customers and prospects will appreciate hearing from you when you have sales or special offers, or are offering discounts. If, for instance, you have a loyal group of customers who like your camping equipment, they're going to love hearing about your end-of-season special sale and will appreciate hearing about it before the general public.

If you're launching a new product, you can give it a good push by offering your mailing list a special "introductory offer" that entices them to at least give it a try.

Some stores and companies have regular monthly specials that their customers look forward to seeing. For instance, an advertising specialty salesperson who sells promotional items (such as mugs, calendars, pens, and T-shirts) might want to see what specials manufacturers are offering each month to increase their own sales and profit margins.

Be careful, however: sending sale announcements too frequently—that is, more than once a month—will result in people only shopping your sales or deleting your emails as a nuisance. In other words, they won't feel a need to act quickly on your special offers—and you'll be diluting your own message.

If you're sending a message with a special sales incentive to entice a customer to visit your site, be sure to clearly state that in the subject line and lead off the message with that information. However, take care to avoid subject lines with words like *free, on sale now, special offer,* and *discount,* because use of these terms often results in email being flagged as spam (unwanted email). You can include in your message special online coupon codes that customers can type in to receive a discount or print coupons they can bring to a physical store. Your message might announce the availability of products that have sold out quickly in the past, like "Velvet Scarves Have Arrived!" The key is to offer a substantial benefit—one that will keep your message from being marked as "junk" and blocked in the future.

Surveys, Contests, and Sweepstakes

Another way to stay in touch with your mailing list is to conduct a survey or hold a contest or sweepstakes.

Surveys are popular with customers because they provide a fun way of finding out what other people—like them—are thinking, and they show that the vendor is looking to serve them better.

Your survey can be:

- **Fun.** Just something amusing—perhaps dealing with some aspect of popular culture.
- **Product- or service-oriented.** An attempt to improve your products or services and determine your customers' wants and needs.
- **Current event–oriented.** An effort to take the pulse of your customers on newsworthy topics to attract media attention.

A number of online survey software companies make the process of conducting and compiling surveys fairly easy.

Contests and sweepstakes are often very popular with the public. If you conduct a drawing for something valuable, you're likely to attract a lot of attention. However, many people who respond to sweepstakes simply like getting something for nothing—which doesn't exactly make them great prospects. Thus, make sure you're reaching qualified prospects with your contests or sweepstakes.

BRAINSTORMING

YOUR OTHER EMAIL COMMUNICATIONS

Other than email newsletters, what types of bulk emails might you send to your mailing list—and how often?

TYPE OF COMMUNICATION	NATURE OF CONTENT	FREQUENCY
ANNOUNCEMENTS		
SALES/DISCOUNTS		
SURVEYS/ SWEEPSTAKES		
OTHER		

"Trigger" Marketing

In addition to sending newsletters, announcements, or other communications to your entire mailing list, email services and software can automatically generate email when an individual takes an action that "triggers" a response—such as filling in an online form.

Let's say a customer signs up to get announcements of future sales: you can set a trigger—or auto responder—to thank that person for signing up. That's a basic auto-response; however, you can get far more creative (from a marketing standpoint) with your triggers. You can, for instance, set triggers to send a thank-you email one week after someone has placed an order, to shoot off a congratulations email on someone's birthday, or to send a "Time for your next check-up" email a year after a patient's last appointment. By setting up your triggers carefully, you can stay in touch with customers and prospects on a personal level without a great deal of time or effort.

The great thing about trigger marketing is that it feels very personal. Without much work on your part, you can create and maintain a one-on-one relationship with a customer, prospect, or business contact. You can follow up on a prospect who's made an inquiry without having to remember to make a call or send an email.

Most online email marketing services—as well as many customer contact software programs—can handle trigger marketing activities for you.

BRAINSTORMING

YOUR TRIGGER EVENTS

List actions/events (in each category, if applicable) that you could use to trigger a communication via an auto responder. What would you say in your email?

TRIGGER EVENT/DATE	WHAT YOU'D SAY IN YOUR EMAIL
EARLY/FIRST CONTACTS	
PRE-PURCHASE INQUIRY	
AFTER PURCHASE	
BIRTHDAYS/ANNIVERSARIES	
MEETING/APPOINTMENT FOLLOW-UPS	
OTHER	

Email Communications ROI

As with other online marketing activities, email newsletter and communication services and software include analytics that enable you to see how your efforts are paying off. With online email newsletter marketing services, you can easily see how many people opened your newsletter, which links they clicked, whether they forwarded the newsletter to others, or chose to unsubscribe—all data that's extremely helpful in figuring out the return on investment (ROI) you're getting out of your email marketing efforts. Moreover, these analytics help you figure out what's working and what's not, so that you can continually improve your email marketing efforts and increase your response rates.

Remember, however, that there are more things to consider than just click throughs when it comes to evaluating your newsletter (or other email) response rates. You're also using these email communications to keep your name in front of customers and prospects and to enhance your credibility.

Email marketing communications generally represent an inexpensive, effective way to market your business. For this reason, all businesses should consider including at least some form of bulk email marketing in their overall marketing plan.

Calculating Your Email Communications ROI

The following worksheet can help you get started on your own ROI analysis. Simply describe your email marketing efforts, your goals (financial and non-financial), and your market, and then fill in the rest of the requested data to get an idea of the ROI you can expect to achieve from your email marketing campaign.

Here are some tips for using the worksheets (and calculating your ROI):

■ **Make Web analytics work for you.** Online email newsletter services offer a wealth of analytics that you can employ to find out not only how many people are opening your newsletter but which links they're clicking, whether they're forwarding your newsletter to friends, and more—all information you can use to target your market more successfully (offering just the right enticements to get recipients to take the action you desire). And it's all information you can use in calculating your ROI.

■ **Remember non-financial goals.** While you may not be able to put a cash value on things like brand awareness and customer perception, these are important components of any marketing campaign, and as such must be considered when calculating return on investment—especially when it comes to something like email marketing, where the primary goals are keeping your name in front of customers and heightening your credibility.

RETURN ON INVESTMENT

YOUR EMAIL MARKETING ROI

Your business:_____

Your target market:_____

Description of your email communications (newsletter, announcement, contest/sweepstakes, etc.):

_____

GOALS

Financial: _____

Non-financial: _____

PROJECTED COSTS

Newsletter writers: _____

Newsletter designers: _____

Newsletter manager:_____

Email mailing list rental (if applicable): _____

Email mailing list manager:_____

Customer support team: _____

Email newsletter marketing service: _____

Total cost: _____

PROJECTED RETURNS, FINANCIAL

Number of click throughs:_____

Number of click through conversions (i.e., number of users of who take desired action after clicking through to site): _____

Amount of revenue generated per conversion: _____

Monthly revenue generated from conversions: _____

Total annual revenue generated from email communications:_____

Total cost: _____

Total projected net financial gain (annual revenue minus total cost): _____

PROJECTED RETURNS, NON-FINANCIAL

Total number of impressions: _____

Number of non-converting click throughs: _____

Other brand building, awareness benefits: _____

TOTAL ROI (Total Net Financial Returns Plus Total Non-financial Returns):_____

EMAIL MARKETING BUDGET (12 MONTHS)

	JAN	FEB	MARCH	APRIL	MAY
Professional Assistance					
Writers					
Graphic designers Photographers/Illustrators					
Email list manager					
Email newsletter manager					
Email newsletter marketing service					
Customer support team					
Other consultants					
Supplies/Cost of Goods/Manufacturing					
Email mailing list rental					
Contact management software/database					
Other supplies/goods/manufacturing costs					
Other					
TOTAL					

! NOTE: An electronic version of this worksheet is available as part of the Planning Shop's Marketing Budget Templates package.

JUNE	JULY	AUGUST	SEPT	OCT	NOV	DEC	TOTAL

Lingo

AD NETWORKS: Companies that aggregate websites and accept paid advertisements. Ad networks host and serve up ads for advertisers on participating websites.

AFFILIATE PROGRAM: An ad program that pays other organizations to place your ads on their sites, giving them a commission on sales that originate from their websites.

BANNER ADS: These are the equivalents of display ads in the world of traditional media—that is, an ad of a specific size, typically including graphics or photos as well as text, placed adjacent to the content of the page itself.

CONTEXTUAL ADS: Text ads (just like SEM ads) that are automatically placed adjacent to relevant content on websites, mobile devices, social networking sites, and other digital locations.

FLOATING ADS: Ads that float atop Web page content, often interfering with users' ability to read that content until they've clicked on the ad.

INTERSTITIAL ADS: Ads that appear between (or before) other content and websites (such as when you click on a website address only to be taken to an ad before the site itself opens).

ONLINE AUCTION SITES: Web-based marketplaces where online shoppers can bid on and buy products sold by companies and individuals. The best-known online auction site is eBay.

ONLINE CLASSIFIEDS: Digital versions of print classifieds where goods and services can be promoted to a local audience using the Web. One of the best-known examples is Craigslist.org.

POP-UP/POP-UNDER ADS: Ads that open up and appear in a new browser window over or under existing Web page content.

PORTAL SITE: A website that serves as a hub, providing content and advertisements based around a particular industry, location, interest, or other unifying concept.

SKYSCRAPER AD: A long, narrow vertical banner ad that runs the length of a Web page and often remains in the user's sight for the duration of time they linger on a page.

WEB DIRECTORY: A listing of companies—which usually share some common factor (such as industry or location)—including brief business descriptions, contact info, and links back to the company sites (sometimes including reviews and ratings).

CHAPTER 25

Other Online Advertising

Online ads: you'll find them on just about any commercial website you visit. They're either lurking at the side of the page or incorporated right into the design. Some are static; others blink or flash messages at you; and some even float across the page. Then there are those that pop up in front you, often obscuring the website you're trying to view until you can figure out how to get rid of them. Online ads are everywhere, and many of them are annoying. Still, the name of the company in the ad is likely to stick—and if the ad is appealing enough, you might actually click on it.

Even if you find some online ads bothersome, it's a good bet that there are others you're happy to see. For instance, if you're looking for environmentally sensitive products—solar-powered heating, energy-efficient lights, recycled building materials, and so on—and come across a website listing and describing suppliers of such products, you'll be thrilled. You won't care that these companies paid to be listed; you're just glad to find all of these resources in one location.

Online ads work. What's important is that you design them to attract (not annoy) your target customers and then place them where potential customers are most likely to see them.

Some major types of online website advertising opportunities include:

- Website ads

- Sponsorships

- Portal sites/directories

- Online classifieds

- Auction sites

- Contextual ads

- Affiliate programs

Website Ad Sizes and Shapes

The world of Web advertising is constantly evolving, but for the moment these are the primary types of ads now playing at your favorite website:

■ **Banner ads.** Fixed rectangular ads, usually horizontal, which appear at the top, bottom, side, or middle of a Web page.

■ **Floating ads.** Ads that float atop Web page content, often interfering with users' ability to read that until they've clicked on the ad.

■ **Interstitial ads.** Ads that appear between content or websites.

■ **Pop-up/Pop-under ads.** Ads that open another window or Web page and that appear on top or beneath the intended website.

■ **Skyscraper ads.** Vertical fixed ads that appear on the side of a Web page, often enabling a viewer to see the ad the entire time they're on a page.

There are also ads you can create that won't seem like ads at all—things like videos, blogs, and social networking site applications; however, those marketing opportunities are discussed in the next chapter.

Website Ads

In the early days of the Internet, the typical Web page ad looked much like what you'd see in a newspaper or magazine—what's called a *display* ad in the world of traditional media: an ad of a specific size, typically including graphics or photos as well as text, placed adjacent to the content of the page itself. On the Internet, this type of ad came to be called a ***banner ad***, and it had the added advantage (over print ads) that a reader could actually click through to an advertiser's website.

Over time, a variety of ad types have developed on websites. One of the earliest—and most annoying—was the ***pop-up ad,*** which appeared when you clicked on a Web page and opened an additional Web page or window. These got in your face, obscuring the website you wanted to see—and thus another variation emerged: the pop-*under* ad. These ads, too, opened an additional window, but you didn't see it until you closed the original website. Recognizing that users were finding pop-up *and* pop-under ads annoying, browser makers began incorporating software that blocked such ads entirely. Although advertisers still use these types of ads, they do so with the under-standing that many potential prospects will never see them (because they have pop-up blockers enabled)—something you should keep in mind as well if you're considering using pop-up (or pop-under) ads.

Another form of Internet advertising that's caught on over the years is ***interstitial ads***—that is, ads that appear between (or before) other content and websites. A classic example of interstitial advertising is the television commercial—appearing, as it does, in the middle of a TV show, this type of ad has a captive audience. You've also experienced an interstitial ad if you've ever typed in a website address only to be taken to an ad before the site itself opens—just like the TV viewer, you're represent a captive audience as you wait for the site to appear.

When creating your website ad, consider ways of making it *do* some-thing—though be careful not to annoy in the process. You can attract atten-tion by adding animation, video, music, or sounds. You can also make your ad interactive—enticing viewers to play a game, answer a question, or take a survey. The goal is to get people to notice your ad *and* to want to take action.

While these kinds of website ads can be intrusive and annoying, they're also very effective at capturing viewers' attention—often enticing them to click on the ad, which then takes them back to the advertisers' website. In other words, *mission accomplished.* But even if users don't click on the ad (and only a small percentage will), the ad has still generated numerous *impressions*—meaning it's been viewed by a large number of people.

That's why these kinds of ads—annoying as they may be—are particu-larly good for brand-building and awareness-building campaigns. They get the word out about a product or service and help raise company visibility.

Where they're *not* as effective is in getting viewers to take a specific action—such as clicking on the ad or making a purchase.

This is the reason such ads are often priced on a cost-per-impression or CPM (cost per thousand viewers) basis rather than on a cost-per-click (CPC) rate (as is typical with search engine marketing)—a practice that can make your online advertising campaign fairly expensive, and without any guaranteed results. To get the most for your money with these kinds of online advertisements, try to negotiate prices based on click through rates (CTRs) rather than CPM.

You can purchase a website ad from the website itself or through an ad network—a company that aggregates websites which accept advertising. These companies often feed a number of ads to particular sites, making the advertising more interesting to readers and allowing ads to be shown on many more sites. These networks are often aggregated around a common theme—for example, sites catering to women, sports fans, pet owners, and more.

BRAINSTORMING

YOUR WEBSITE ADS

Use this worksheet to plan your website advertising campaign, brainstorming where your ads should appear, what form they should take, what you hope to gain from them, and more.

What websites will you advertise on? _____

What form will your web advertising take (banner, floating, interstitial, pop-up/pop-under, skyscraper)? _____

What will your website do (i.e., will it be interactive—containing a game, survey, or the like—or contain animation, video, music, or sounds)? _____

What is your ad's primary function—building brand and heightening customer awareness, or prompting users to take specific action? _____

Briefly describe your ad's content and appearance and explain how it will help you achieve your advertising goals without annoying website visitors: _____

Who will design your website ads? _____

How will you measure their efficacy? _____

Will you purchase advertising space through an ad network, or will you purchase directly from the websites you want to advertise on? _____

Sponsorships

Sponsorships are very similar to advertisements—the term *sponsor,* in fact, is often used synonymously with *advertiser* (for example, "And now a word from our sponsors" or "Sponsored Links"). On the Internet, however, sponsorships are viewed slightly differently than other forms of advertising.

With a sponsorship, an advertiser pays to support a website, portion of a website, content within a website, or the organization behind the website. In return, the website gives the advertiser visibility and recognition on the site. Often, this visibility takes the form of a static banner ad; however, it can also mean displaying the sponsor's name, logo, or tagline in immediate proximity to content—placement that can sometimes make sponsorships even more visible than banner ads.

Sponsorships are most often employed to support the websites of non-profit organizations, community groups, sports teams, and special content websites—and they often entail other financial commitments to the organization as well. The advantage of sponsorships is that they provide high visibility with a desired target market, and they're less likely to be viewed as ads.

Say, for example, you make a line of hair care products, and you help sponsor an industry trade association for hair stylists. Your name and company logo might appear on the association's website, as well as at its annual trade show or in the organization's quarterly journal—all providing positive associations with your products without you having to advertise them directly. Likewise, a restaurant may want to help sponsor the website of the local chamber of commerce, or an eco-tourist travel agency might help sponsor the website of the Wildlife Conservation Network.

Keep in mind, however, that you're not likely to get information about click through rates or other analytics from website sponsorships—meaning it will be much harder to measure your return on investment in this area. That said, there are many less immediately measurable benefits associated with this type of online marketing—such as increased credibility and visibility within your market and association with a cause or organization you believe in—so it's still a marketing route worth pursuing.

Portals and Directories

Portals and directories serve as online hubs—usually grouped around a common theme, topic, product, or location—where users come to look for information, products, and services. As such, portals can provide effective (and affordable) places to advertise your product or service—especially if you have a clearly defined target market and are using a portal or directory site that generates a lot of traffic.

For example, DeliciousItaly.com is a portal for visitors interested in travel, food, and culture centered on Italy. As such, the portal features ads and descriptions of hotels, restaurants, tours, and others things related to that target market. This means that if you operate cooking (or eating!) tours to Italy, this is probably an excellent place to advertise—likely to bring you a far better return on your marketing dollars (ROI) than advertising on a more general site or even perhaps buying keywords on search engines.

Likewise, if you own a condo in Puerto Vallarta, Mexico, which you rent to tourists, you'll probably want to pay for a listing on VRBO.com (Vacation Rental By Owner)—a directory listing vacation properties rented out by owners. Or find a portal site aimed at tourists to Puerto Vallarta.

One advantage of advertising on portal and directory sites is that visitors to such sites are more likely to consider your ads useful resources than simple annoyances (as they might on other sites). After all, if a Web user is looking for a cooking tour to Italy, they're likely to be happy to find an in-depth description of your tour on DeliciousItaly.com—and they won't care that you've paid to have it placed there.

In fact, many portal "ads" don't really look like ads at all but rather just more site content. This means that what appears to be a simple text description of an offering could actually be a paid ad—and your cooking school listing might be indistinguishable from editorial content put together by the website's staff. Other ads, however, are more obviously advertisements, looking much like any other banner ads.

There are loads of general portal sites—such as news sites and search engine sites—which serve as entry points for many Web users; however, from a marketing point of view, portals and directories focused on a specific theme are typically the most cost-effective locations for ads.

Some Web portals and directories also include reviews and ratings. Working to get good reviews on those is discussed in the next chapter.

Online Classifieds

Surprisingly, some of the most effective ads don't contain any graphics, music, or moving images. Instead, they're pure text (or, perhaps, text augmented with a few pictures)—these are the equivalent of online "classified" ads.

A number of online consumer sites operate much like the print classified ads traditionally found in newspapers (and, in fact, many of these classified sites are run by local newspapers). Users take advantage of these sites to sell things, offer services, advertise job openings, and more—just as they do with traditional classified listings in newspapers.

One of the most popular—and successful—of these online classified sites is Craigslist (www.craigslist.org). Divided into sections targeted to cities and geographic areas, Craigslist listings are grouped into easy-to-use categories, and the listings themselves tend to be straightforward: descriptive text accompanied by a few photos or a link to a website. Some online classifieds are more sophisticated, including video as well as text and photos.

While classified sites are aimed at e-commerce—that is, making sales—they also serve as an effective advertising medium, especially since you can link back to your own website. Say, for example, you sell guitars: you can list a particular guitar on Craigslist; however, within that product description you can also describe and provide photos of other guitars that you sell, as well as provide a link to your online store or website. Keep in mind, too, that you can use online classifieds to sell both new and used products. Although people often associate Craigslist (in particular) with used goods being sold by individuals, businesses regularly use the service to advertise new products.

Advertising on Craigslist and other online classified sites offers many advantages:

- **It's FREE.** Yep, in most cases ads on Craigslist are free. And most other online classified sites are quite inexpensive as well.

- **It's easy.** Because most listings are composed of straight text, it takes very little time or money to create an ad. While you can enhance your listings with photos, videos, and other media, it's not necessary.

- **It's a great way to reach a large number of people.** A huge number of consumers—and businesses looking for employees, office space, products, and a variety of other goods and services—check out Craigslist or their local newspapers' websites.

- **It's location-specific.** You can often narrow your listing to particular neighborhoods (if appropriate). Thus, if you only want to offer math tutoring services in the York region of Toronto, you can do so. On the other hand, you can reach out across the world by posting listings on sites of areas you'd like to target.

- **It's personal.** Employing a grassroots, community-oriented approach, classified sites bring you close to prospects and customers. You'll probably engage in at least an email conversation with anyone who answers your ad.

- **It's a good way to learn about your market.** Online classified sites often contain discussion forums that you can participate in to locate or learn more about your target market.

Online classified sites can also serve as testing grounds for marketing products and services on a larger scale. Although you're generally asked to identify a community and place ads locally, you can also place ads in multiple areas. Therefore, using Craigslist and similar sites can provide a good means of determining whether a market exists for your products or services in a particular area.

One downside of Craigslist listings is that they're posted chronologically—which means that your ad can get buried fairly quickly. To make sure that your listing is seen, you'll need to update and repost it as frequently as Craigslist allows. This means that managing your Craigslist postings may take ongoing, frequent attention—unlike other types of advertising. However, this may not be the case on all classified sites.

Online Auction Sites

Online auction sites, such as eBay, are more than just places for individuals to auction off used goods to the highest bidders. Representing huge online marketplaces, such sites have created myriad marketing opportunities for entrepreneurs.

Sure, such auction sites are designed for e-commerce—that is, the direct selling of products—but that doesn't mean you can't also use them as marketing tools. Since you can set up "stores" on these sites or list products as "Buy It Now" without conducting an auction, you can use auction sites as an advertising medium—just as you would online classified sites.

All you need to do is register, pay the fees, and upload some photos to get your products—and your business—in front of a marketplace that consists of millions of eyeballs.

Here are some of the benefits of marketing your product or service on auction sites:

- **Prospects are generally highly targeted,** since they have to search for you by category or keyword.

- **They represent a relatively inexpensive form of advertising.** Although you must pay fees to be listed and sell products, these fees are typically far less than those associated with advertising in other media.

- **You can include links back to your website,** enabling prospects to see other products you're offering.

- **They provide easy and secure systems for accepting customer payments** (such as through the Web payment service PayPal).

Marketing on eBay, however, also comes with its own considerations and limitations—chief among them is the fact that you need to be set up to actually ship out products quickly and safely. Some other things to consider before establishing a marketing presence on eBay (or any other auction site):

- **You will have lots of competition**—which means your listings can get overlooked. And you don't want to drive your own customers to auction sites because they'll learn about your competitors there.

- **Setting up and managing online stores or auctions as well as shipping goods can be time consuming.**

- **Auction sites aren't particularly effective marketing tools for service-based businesses.**

The bottom line: if your company targets customers who are likely to be shopping on auction sites, such sites represent a fairly low-risk/low-effort way to market your wares and are probably worth trying.

BRAINSTORMING

YOUR OTHER ONLINE ADVERTISING TACTICS

Use this worksheet to plan your other online advertising tactics, brainstorming your ads, affiliate programs, sponsorships, and more.

SPONSORSHIPS

List some organizations whose websites you might consider sponsoring, along with your reasons for doing so (i.e., their fit with your target market):

1._____
2._____
3._____
4._____
5._____

What form will your sponsorship take? Banner ad? Your name, logo, or tagline placed in close proximity to relevant content? Other?_____
_____

What do you hope to achieve from your sponsorship? Heightened customer awareness? Association with an organization or cause you believe in? Other?_____
_____

WEB PORTALS AND WEB DIRECTORIES

List some Web portals and directories that you could place ads on, along with your reasons for doing so (i.e., their fit with your target market):

1._____
2._____
3._____
4._____
5._____

What form will your Web portal or directory ads take? Will they look like ads (for example, simple banner ads), or will they be nearly indistinguishable from text (for example, simple narrative descriptions of offerings likely to be of interest to site visitors)?_____
_____
_____
_____
_____

Who will create your Web portal and directory ads?_____
_____

How will you measure their efficacy?_____
_____

ONLINE CLASSIFIED SITES

Do you plan to use online classified sites to advertise your company or offerings? _____ _____

If so, how will you use such sites to drive customers to your website and beyond single-product purchases?_____
_____

Will your online classified ad be pure text, or will it contain images or video? _____
_____

Who will manage your online classified listing, making sure it remains at the top of the list and viewable by the greatest number of people? _____
_____

ONLINE AUCTIONS

List any auction sites you might like to list and sell your offerings on, along with your reasons for doing so (i.e., their fit with your target market):_____
_____

Who will manage your online auction presence (i.e., creating listings, arranging shipping, keeping content current, etc.)?_____

How will you drive auction customers to your website? _____
_____

CONTEXTUAL ADS

Do you plan to use contextual ads as part of your online advertising campaign? If so, list the types of content you'd like your ads to appear by: _____ _____

Now list some keywords appropriate to your products, services, or target market:_____

What contextual ad network will you use to place your ads? _____

Contextual Ads

One of the most important tenets of marketing is that you've got to advertise to your target market. If, for instance, you're selling dental supplies, you'll want to make sure your ad gets in front of dentists rather than optometrists.

An effective (and easy) way to make sure your ads are hitting their target is by using contextual ads—text ads, just like your SEM ads (described in Chapter 23), automatically placed adjacent to relevant content on websites, mobile devices, social networking sites, and other digital locations. Here's how it works: you simply design the same type of ad that you would for your search engine marketing program. Then, you sign up to be part of a contextual ad network (two of the best known being Google's AdSense and Yahoo's Publisher Network) and select keywords appropriate to your products, services, or target market. These networks then find websites that fit your specified keywords and target market and that have agreed to accept ads. (These programs are aligned with Google's and Yahoo's search engine marketing programs. You can sign up for SEM and contextual ads together or separately.)

A particularly appealing feature of these contextual ad programs is that, generally, you pay for your ad on a *pay-per-click* or *click through* basis. In other words, you only pay when someone clicks on your ad and is taken to your website or landing page. This means that you can easily evaluate the effectiveness of your contextual advertising campaign (using the programs' analytic tools) as well as determine the ROI for your investments.

Since contextual ads are so similar to SEM ads, refer to Chapter 24 for more information.

Affiliate Programs

Want to advertise your products or services on other people's websites without paying——or at least waiting to pay until you've made a sale? One way to do so is by setting up an affiliate program (which can also be thought of as pay-per-sale advertisements, since the hosting website only gets paid if the ad results in a sale).

Affiliate advertising offers incentives for others to place your ads on their sites in exchange for a piece of the action—usually in the form of a sales commission on customers who come through their site. For instance, let's say you were selling your brand of tennis accessories. Other websites—such as those for tennis magazines, tennis clubs, or sporting goods retailers— could agree to place your ad (including a link back to your website) on their Web pages. Then, if one of their site visitors clicks the ad, goes to your site, and makes a purchase, the originating site gets a commission on the final sale. (In most cases, they get a commission on any other sale that customer makes for a set period of time, perhaps 7 to 30 days.)

Many major sites, such as Amazon.com, have well-developed affiliate programs, allowing participants to easily "grab" the ads and programming code, and plop them right onto their sites. In addition, many shopping cart programs make it easy to develop and offer affiliate programs.

Typically, you'll pay a commission of from between 5% and 15% of the sale, which is generally considered a very affordable sales commission. And since you're not paying for the ad but are getting the exposure to Web readers in any case, affiliate programs generally have very high return on investments (ROI) regardless of the number of sales they generate.

The key to a successful affiliate program is to offer a number of products that affiliate sites can choose from to advertise—depending on the nature of their users. You'll need to market your affiliate program to get other website owners to include your ads on their sites—and you'll only succeed if you're consistent in your sales efforts and target sites that cater to an appropriate market for your products.

If done well, affiliate programs can be a win-win both for you and for the site that accepts your ad.

BRAINSTORMING

YOUR AFFILIATE PROGRAM

Use this worksheet to plan your affiliate program.

What websites will you target for your affiliate program?

_____

_____

_____

What percentage commission will you pay/what other incentives will you offer to get websites to participate in your affiliate program?

_____

_____

_____

Describe the range of ads that affiliates will be able to choose among:

_____

_____

_____

How will you enable affiliate program participants to easily incorporate your ads into their websites (i.e., via a shopping cart program, by plopping ads and programming code right into sites, etc)? And who will handle the technical details on your end?

_____

_____

_____

_____

Online Advertising ROI

As with every other aspect of your marketing plan, you should carefully evaluate the return on investment you can expect to achieve from your online advertising efforts. For some campaigns—such as website and portal advertising as well as affiliate programs and contextual ads—this will be easy thanks to Web analytics software. Other activities—such as sponsorships—will present more of a problem, since it's difficult to place a monetary value on simply associating your name with a site. In such cases, you will have to pay special attention to the increased credibility and visibility within your market that such associations can provide.

Calculating Your Online Advertising ROI

The following worksheet can help you get started on your own ROI analysis. Simply describe your online advertising plans (where you plan to advertise, what form your ads will take, and so on), your goals (financial and non-financial), and your market, and then fill in the rest of the requested data to get an idea of the ROI you can expect to achieve from your online advertising campaign.

One thing to note: Because so many divergent online advertising tactics are described in this chapter, you should complete the following worksheet for each type (website, portal, contextual, sponsorship, affiliate, and so on) you plan to employ.

Here are some tips for completing the worksheet (and calculating your ROI):

- **Make Web analytics work for you.** Using the wealth of information provided by Web analytics software, you can determine how many times your ad was shown (*impressions*), how many times it was clicked through, what Web pages users visited once they clicked through, how long users stayed on your site, whether they took certain actions (such as making a purchase), and more.

- **Remember non-financial goals.** While you may not be able to put a cash value on things like brand awareness and customer perception, these are important components of any marketing campaign, and as such must be considered when calculating return on investment.

RETURN ON INVESTMENT

YOUR ONLINE ADVERTISING ROI

Your business: _____

Your target market: _____

Type of online advertising (website, portal, contextual, classified, auction site, etc.): _____

GOALS

Financial: _____

Non-financial: _____

PROJECTED COSTS

Ad design and production: _____

Cost per ad: _____

Total number of ads: _____

Commission (for affiliate programs): _____

Total number of ads: _____

Technical support: _____

Total cost: _____

PROJECTED RETURNS, FINANCIAL

Number of click throughs: _____

Number of click through conversions (i.e., number of users of who take desired action after clicking

through to site): _____

Amount of revenue generated per conversion: _____

Monthly revenue generated from conversions: _____

Total annual revenue generated from online advertising: _____

Total cost: _____

Total projected net financial gain (annual revenue minus total cost): _____

PROJECTED RETURNS, NON-FINANCIAL

Total number of impressions: _____

Number of non-converting click throughs: _____

Other brand building, awareness benefits: _____

TOTAL ROI (Total Net Financial Returns Plus Total Non-financial Returns): _____

OTHER ONLINE ADVERTISING BUDGET (12 MONTHS)

	JAN	FEB	MARCH	APRIL	MAY
Professional Assistance					
Writers					
Graphic designers/Illustrators					
Photographers/Videographers					
Ad agencies					
Marketing/Ad consultants					
Other consultants					
Ad Buys					
Website pop-up or interstitial ads					
Website sponsorships					
Portal ads					
Web directory listings					
Online classified ads					
Contextual ads on websites					
Online auction program costs					
Affiliate ad program costs					
Other online ad buys/costs					
Other					
TOTAL					

NOTE: An electronic version of this worksheet is available as part of the Planning Shop's Marketing Budget Templates package.

JUNE	JULY	AUGUST	SEPT	OCT	NOV	DEC	TOTAL

Lingo

FEED: Distribution of content over a network, wire service, or syndication service. The term has come to be used to refer to frequently updated content sent to subscribers, particularly blogs.

FRIEND: A person you invite to connect with you in a social networking community. It can also be used as a verb: "I'll friend you," for example, means you'll invite someone to be part of your network.

PODCAST: Combining the words *iPod and broadcast*, podcast refers to content designed to be played on an iPod or other digital device and distributed through an online syndication service or via downloads. Podcasts typically contain audio content, but they can also contain video and text.

RSS FEED: RSS—or Really Simple Syndication—feeds comprise a system for easily distributing and subscribing to frequently updated content (such as blogs, podcasts, and website updates), which is aggregated from many sources into one location.

SMARTPHONE: A mobile phone equipped with features such as Internet access, email, full computer operating systems, audio/video capabilities, and more.

TEXTING: Short text messages sent to mobile phones. The technology used for this—SMS, or Short Message Service—is available on almost every phone.

WEB 2.0: A term used to describe the supposed second generation of the Internet, based heavily on user-generated content, social networking and online communities, and online collaboration.

CHAPTER 26

Social Networking, Blogs, and Other Online Tactics

Facebook. MySpace. LinkedIn. YouTube. Blogs. Podcasts. TripAdvisor. Smartphones. Once the Internet took root in people's lives, communications and interactivity exploded as new digital technologies emerged, making it possible for people to not only get information on the Web but to communicate instantaneously, create communities, be entertained and informed, and find new friends.

Sometimes referred to as Web 2.0—to represent the second generation of the Internet—this new digital universe is based on the concept of user-generated content combined with continuous interactivity and connectedness. The result has been that a huge number of people are constantly attached to the Web, their phones, and each other. And as any good marketer will tell you, any time millions of people are communicating, a marketing opportunity exists.

In this chapter, you'll learn about some of the intensely personal and persistent ways people are using the Web to create communities, inform, entertain, and communicate—and how you can leverage those activities as part of your marketing plan.

Some of the ways these digital platforms are bringing people together include the following:

- Social and professional networking sites
- Blogs
- Podcasts
- User review sites
- Video sharing sites
- Mobile devices
- Virtual reality sites

> *We started going out to bloggers and participating in social communities several years ago and learned a really important lesson from these experiences: Be a part of the conversation. People want to hear from you more. To win in today's marketplace, to really be heard, you have to participate.*
>
> **Kira Wampler**
> **Marketing Manager**
> **Intuit (Maker of QuickBooks)**

> *" The more instances people mention your website online, the higher your relevancy rating will be in Google's search engine results. Buzz about your business is always good, especially if there are links back to your website. Blogs and online social networks are the chamber of commerce meetings of the world—attend. "*
>
> **Alan Luckow**
> **President**
> **Luckow Communications**

Social and Professional Networking Sites

When you think of social networking sites, the first ones to come to mind are probably those aimed at a broad consumer audience—sites like MySpace and Facebook, which were first embraced by teens and young adults and eventually became enormously popular with the rest of the population. Yet networking sites don't begin and end with MySpace and Facebook. Today, there exist a huge number of social networking sites—active Web communities offering participants a forum for sharing personal or professional information and interacting with each other, often on a virtually continual basis. Some of these sites are aimed at a business audience, some at specific industries or professions, some at particular interest groups. *All* offer marketing opportunities.

Members of these online communities exchange information about themselves, their activities, and their interests. Most importantly, they constantly pass along to other members of their communities—referred to as *friends*—things that have piqued their interest, such as quizzes, videos, and contests. Community members can also post items that intrigue them on their own pages, and they can buy and give virtual "gifts," which will be displayed on their friends' pages.

All of which is to say that community members communicate *a lot*. This means that if you can connect your product or service with something of interest (such as a cute quiz, an interesting event, or a new product announcement) to someone in the community, there's a good chance that person will forward it to others—in essence, doing your marketing for you.

Social networking sites can be divided into three general categories:

- **Mass market.** This group includes sites like Facebook, MySpace, Friendster, Orkut, and Hi5—all good for reaching a large consumer audience, particularly one made up of younger adults and teens.

- **Special interest.** Got an interest? Bet you can find a social networking site formed around the topic. There's Chowhound for people who are interested in food, LinkedMusicians.com for lovers of live music, and on and on. Primarily consumer-focused, such sites provide an excellent means of reaching a highly engaged target audience. You can become a frequent contributor to and participant in these sites, many of which accept advertising.

- **Business or professional.** This category includes both general sites such as LinkedIn and industry- and profession-specific sites such as NurseLinkUp.com (a social networking site for nurses) and JumpUp. com (for small businesses). Such sites can serve as excellent vehicles for reaching a target market as well as for developing professional references and referrals.

The marketing campaign you develop for social networking sites will depend on your target market and product or service; however, picking the right site (or sites) is the first step. Be certain that the audience of any site you're considering is truly interested in your offerings. Are you trying to reach consumers or businesses? Do you need a mass market for your offering? Or would a more focused site better suit your needs?

Once you've identified the right social or professional networking site, the key to your marketing campaign's success will be providing content that appeals to your target audience. If you provide relevant, interesting, and entertaining content, you can raise your (and your company's) visibility by being an active participant in the community. You can even from time to time include a call to action in your content (which could be something as simple as a "Click here to learn more" button that links to your site).

Ideally, you will create something compelling enough that someone will send it on to a friend or colleague—so that your campaign can become *viral*, spreading from one person to another like a physical virus.

You can use online networking sites to:

■ **Spread the word.** Use social networking sites to create buzz and get the word out about your products or services—particularly if those products or services are aimed at fervent users of these sites. Keep in mind, though, that you need to be clever: participants in networking sites (like their blog counterparts) tend to be less receptive to heavy-handed sales approaches. One way to get people's attention is by creating a quiz (for example, asking, "What kind of race car would you be?" for a product aimed at young men). Other options include contests, product samples, and giveaways.

■ **Advertise.** Just as you can choose contextual ads for websites (see the previous chapter in this section), you can run ads on individual pages of social networking sites targeting exactly the kind of people you want to reach. You can target your marketing campaigns by age, gender, location, and interests. For instance, if you run a matchmaking service in Vancouver, you could run ads for singles over 40 that would be displayed on pages of individuals who've indicated they're single, over 40, and live in British Columbia.

■ **Create your own group/community.** It's easy to set up a group in most of these social networking sites, and if you have a product or company that is likely to generate a great deal of interest from consumers, you might even want to set up a site to help foster a sense of community. You can also set up a group if you're holding an event to help participants connect with each other, or if you're launching (or have just launched) a new product and want to get feedback from customers. Creating your own group is free and takes almost no time. It does, however, invite others to make comments—which means you better be prepared to deal with some negative ones.

■ **Build referral sources and networking connections.** Social networking sites provide a great venue for reconnecting with people you've lost touch with or with whom you share something in common (for example, fellow alumni of your school or college), and could become future clients

> *One suggestion for small businesses is to put pages or profiles on Facebook, LinkedIn, or JumpUp. These social networking sites attract large, targeted audiences, and being visible on them can improve your results on search engines.*
>
> **Kira Wampler**
> **Marketing Manager**
> **Intuit**

or referral sources. You can also identify individuals to contact by doing keyword searches on these sites. Professional networking sites, such as LinkedIn, employ mechanisms that let you use the network of people you know to connect with others you'd like to meet. For example, if you'd like to meet someone who's an editor at the *New York Times,* you could do an "Advanced Search" on those keywords. The result would show you how you're connected to people who know editors at the *New York Times.*

■ **Enhance your credibility.** By contributing meaningful content to social networking sites and interest groups, you can gain visibility and credibility with a target audience. With some sites, such as LinkedIn, you can also ask individuals to give you a recommendation—which is especially useful for consultants who ask former clients to recommend them so others have greater confidence in their skills.

BRAINSTORMING

YOUR SOCIAL NETWORKING STRATEGIES

Use this worksheet to identify social networking sites you might be able to use to market your products and/or services and to describe the ways you might leverage those sites.

List the networking sites your tarket audience uses regularly:

Social networking sites: _____
_____
_____

Interest-oriented sites: _____
_____
_____

Business and/or professional sites: _____
_____
_____

List the ways you could use networking sites to market your products and/or services:

Would you contribute content? _____

Advertise? _____

Create quizzes, contest, and other viral content? _____

Create groups? _____

Identify potential clients/referral sources? _____

Other: _____

Blogs

Typically created by individuals, blogs—short for *Web logs*—are online journals whose contents are updated frequently (sometimes as often as multiple times per day). Blogs can contain text, audio, video, graphics, and photos, and while many people create blogs to share news about themselves, their friends, and their family, many others create blogs about specific topics (such as politics, business, technology, hobbies, music or the arts, industries, lifestyles, and more).

Some of the best blogs attract a sizable readership among those who are interested in the blog's topic. Thus, if you have a product or service that's likely to appeal to people interested in a particular blog topic, blogs can serve as an effective marketing vehicle.

Once you identify a blog that serves your target market, you can use it to:

- Build name and brand recognition
- Establish yourself as an expert
- Attract customers and clients
- Create links to your website
- Generate buzz around a new product
- Tap into a committed market

Let's say, for instance, that you run a company specializing in employee benefits, and your target prospects are human resource (HR) directors within large corporations. You discover an HR blog that's frequently read by just such people. By becoming an active participant in the blog discussion—responding to blog entries, adding content and links, and including contact info (and a link back to your website) in your entries—you can both establish your company as a benefits expert and entice prospects to contact you. In other words, blogs can provide a great deal of visibility into a highly specialized market.

Blogs can also be used for more traditional marketing tactics. For example, if the owner of a barbecue restaurant located near Fenway Park in Boston wanted to make sure fans visiting the ballpark knew about her eatery, she could identify blogs that reach large numbers of Red Sox fans and then send free samples of her barbecue ribs to some of the most popular Red Sox bloggers—thereby encouraging them to mention her restaurant in their blogs. She could even make blogs part of her advertising program by taking out banner ads on a few of the Red Sox Nation blogs that accept advertising.

As part of your overall marketing plan, you can do the following to leverage the power of blogs:

- Create your own blog
- Submit press releases and sample products to popular blogs
- Contribute content (including commentary) to existing blogs
- Suggest links (including your own) and content to existing blogs
- Advertise on existing blogs

Myth ⊘ Buster

To Blog or Not to Blog?

MYTH: Blogs serve as excellent, free business marketing tools!

BUSTED: Blogs aren't necessarily effective for every type of business, and they're not truly free for any business. If your target audience consists primarily of very busy people who are not likely to be avid blog readers, why bother? You may be tapping just a small community of blog enthusiasts instead of reaching a more profitable target market.

Blogs are also time-consuming to maintain and update—meaning you'll have to devote resources to the tasks if you're to create a compelling blog. And remember, it's difficult to track your return on investment in a blog.

THE BOTTOM LINE: While blogs can serve as good marketing tools, they're not the right tools for every business.

Finding Blogs to Reach Your Niche

How do you find blogs that reach your target market? You check out blog directories or blog search engines, which highlight the most popular blogs and help you find your niche. Here are a few to investigate:

- www.Blogorama.com
- www.Blogsearchengine.com
- www.Readablog.com
- www.Technorati.com

Or try this site, which features a more comprehensive list:

- www.aripaparo.com/archive/000632.html

From a marketing perspective, blogs work well for businesses in which expertise is valued—such as for consultants, technology service providers, professional service businesses, and so on. Whether you create your own blog or regularly contribute to a popular blog in your field, your blogging efforts can greatly enhance your visibility and credibility. If you offer readers something of value (beyond a sales message), it's likely you'll attract people looking for your services (or products).

Keep in mind, though, that most blog communities have little tolerance for sales pitches masquerading as content. This means that the majority of your content must be of great value to readers, and that you should mention your company, products, or services subtly and within the context of the content, such as in sharing an experience that answers a question or sheds light on a problem.

On the other hand, if you don't have much information to offer beyond a sales message, blogging is probably not worth the time and effort.

If you decide to create a blog, make sure that it:

- Showcases your (or your company's) talents and strengths in a subtle yet frequent way

- Employs a conversational tone (not stiff, academic, or "business-y" language)

- Is well-designed (in terms of layout, photos, and video)

- Is regularly updated (certainly no less than once a week and as frequently as a few times a day)

- Contains numerous links to other sites and sources (blogs derive much of their traffic and usefulness from links in and out)

- Is responsive to postings (in the spirit of creating an online community)

Other Online Marketing Tactics

A huge range of marketing opportunities exists online, and new ones are being developed virtually every day as new technologies emerge and entrepreneurs create innovative ways to communicate. Add to this the fact that people are now connected to the online universe virtually all the time via their smartphones and mobile devices—and you begin to see what a gigantic and growing marketing opportunity the online world represents.

The following subsections outline some of the other online marketing opportunities that exist on the Web today.

Podcasts

The term *podcast* is a combination of *iPod* (Apple's popular MP3 player) and *broadcast*. Not surprisingly, then, a podcast is a program (radio or TV show) created expressly for download to individuals' MP3 players, computers, or mobile devices. You don't need an iPod per se to receive a podcast, since the term really just describes a digital program (not one specific to the iPod) typically delivered regularly via the Internet. The most effective podcasts are broadcast regularly (just like ongoing radio or TV programs), allowing

BRAINSTORMING

YOUR BLOG MARKETING STRATEGIES

Use this worksheet to develop a blog marketing strategy for your business. Do a search for blogs that might serve your target market; identify those you might advertise on or participate with; and clarify whether blogging would be good for your business.

List the blog topics your prospects might look for/read (interest areas, industries, demographics, location, and so on):

_____

_____

List the existing blogs on these topics that seem to reach a large/committed number of readers. List whether they accept advertising:

Blog: _____ Accept ads?_____

Blog: _____ Accept ads?_____

Blog: _____ Accept ads? _____

Blog: _____ Accept ads?_____

In what ways other than advertising might you participate in some of the blogs you've identified? What kinds of content/links/comments might you contribute?

_____

_____

Would creating/writing a blog appear to be a good marketing strategy for your business? If so, list the reasons why:

_____

_____

If you created a blog, what would the nature of the content be?

_____

_____

If you created a blog, who would maintain it?

_____

_____

If you created a blog, how often would you add new content, update it?

_____

_____

Feed Your Content to the Masses

You've created a blog or podcast, and you're continually creating fresh, updated content to keep users paying attention. But how can you guarantee that your content will get in front of users? Let's face it: most people are too busy to return to your site again and again to see whether you've added anything. And if you have added content but no one's seeing it, you've expended a lot of effort for nothing. RSS feeds helps solve this problem by automatically distributing your content (or notices of new content) to people who've signed up to be notified.

individuals to subscribe to them so that they get downloaded on an ongoing basis. And there are podcast directories (one of the most popular being on Apple's iTunes), which you can scan to find podcasts of interest.

So how do you go about using podcasts for your marketing efforts? Creating your own podcast is one possibility—and a good option for individuals (such as consultants) or businesses that have compelling content (or entertainment) *and* whose target prospects are likely to subscribe to podcasts. Topics that seem to attract the most committed podcast subscribers are technology, politics, and business.

If you provide valuable information in your podcast, you'll likely be able to regularly and repeatedly engage with a highly qualified target audience. Say you run an SEO (search engine optimization) consulting company: if you create a really good weekly podcast covering the latest in SEO techniques, you could develop quite a following, some of whom are likely to be prospects (such as online marketing officers of large companies).

Creating a podcast—particularly an audio podcast—is not particularly difficult or expensive: it's basically a matter of recording a broadcast and uploading the audio file. However, it does entail a lot of work to develop and maintain a podcast, since you have to be committed to doing it on a regular basis, and your podcast has to be of value to the listener if you're to keep and grow an audience. And finally, your target market has to be the kind that listens to podcasts—which is why for most smaller companies podcasts simply don't justify the time commitment.

Another option, though, is to identify podcasts that reach your target market and advertise in or sponsor them. This puts you in front of prospects on a regular basis, and the cost of advertising on podcasts is likely to be lower than advertising in most other traditional media.

Videos

YouTube transformed the world of videos, making it easy for individuals—and companies—to share them. While YouTube is the best known of the video sharing sites, there are many others out there as well, and some of them are focused on "how to" videos, providing a perfect opportunity to showcase your expertise. If, for example, you're a dog trainer, you could create and upload a video on how to get a dog to stop barking. Your instructional video could easily find its way to people who need to quiet their dogs, and they in turn might forward it to others in need of your services.

You can also use these video-sharing sites to upload interviews with company executives and staff as well as recordings of speaking engagements or events. Even if the general public isn't likely to find these videos, you can still direct prospects to your YouTube (or other video) link to get a more personal sense of you and your company.

User Review Sites

People turn to the Internet regularly before buying products or using services. A traveler heading to a new town, for example, will likely check out hotels online, looking at websites like TripAdvisor to find out what others have to say about local hotels. Likewise, someone who's looking for a plumber may check out Yelp.com or Angie's List to find recommendations, and a mom-to-be in the market for a baby stroller might look for reviews on Epinions.com or check out the discussion boards on BabyCenter before heading out to the store.

Review and community sites give users the opportunity to rate and post comments about the products, services, and companies they use. These comments and reviews can then become powerful marketing tools for your business—or they can result in disaster.

Best-case scenario, people who've used your products or services will rave about your company on such sites, providing powerful testimonials and viral marketing of your products and services as word spreads. People who are enthusiastic about how clean, convenient, and comfortable your affordably priced motel is, for example, will likely encourage other budget travelers to make reservations there.

On the other hand, people who've had less-than-positive experiences with you or your company can just as easily post negative comments on such sites. And even if these customers never told *you* they were unhappy, they can easily let the rest of the world know how dissatisfied they were just by turning on their computer and tapping in their comments on a review site—comments that unfortunately are likely to sway more potential customers than are the positive ones. Indeed, research has shown that customers are far more likely to be influenced by negative comments than positive comments. Thus, while it only takes one negative comment to keep someone from buying from you, it may take five or ten positive comments to convince someone to give you their money.

That said, here are some ways you can use these review sites as effective marketing tools:

- **Stay on top of what's being posted.** Check these review sites regularly to see what's being said about you—especially if you're in an industry or profession (such as travel, restaurants, contractors) where prospects check such sites regularly.

- **Encourage satisfied prospects to post.** Many happy customers never think to go to a site and make positive comments. (In fact, unhappy customers are far more likely to make an entry than those with no complaints.) Thus, it's not inappropriate to remind satisfied customers to add their comments to such sites—being careful *not* to provide them with any kind of payment or incentive to do so, since this is against the rules of most such sites (and will likely get you kicked off).

- **Clarify inaccurate comments.** If you read a comment you know to be untrue—let's say someone says your hotel doesn't offer king-size beds when half of your rooms have them—add your clarification to the postings. *Do not,* however, get into an online spat with someone who has posted negative comments—this will only make you look bad.

- **Advertise.** These sites accept advertisements, and the people using them are typically highly qualified prospects. Such sites can serve as excellent places for you to place ads—especially if you have good ratings.

Flak Your Stuff Online

Even if you're not actively engaged in online communities, writing a blog, or developing a podcast, you can leverage the influence of those who are. In fact, you need to include online media in your overall public relations and marketing campaigns just as you do "traditional" media such as newspaper, radio, and TV. And this, of course, means identifying and sending press releases and samples to online key influencers such as bloggers and organizers of key online groups.

There are public relations agencies that specialize in reaching online communities and blogs—and you may want to consider hiring one if you're planning a major media announcement. Whatever way you approach the task, keep in mind that members of the online media can be even more influential than members of the traditional media—depending on your target market.

Keep in mind, however, that you can also learn from negative feedback. If the comments seem legitimate—as unpleasant as they may be to read—they can help you identify and solve problems, allowing you to improve your products and services over time.

Virtual Reality Sites

Entire parallel worlds exist online in virtual reality sites such as Second Life. In these universes, participants buy and sell virtual merchandise in exchange for real money, leading many people to set up businesses in these sites.

Companies are also finding these virtual worlds to be interesting venues for advertising their real-world products and services, especially if their target audience spends a lot of time participating in them. If your prospects are likely to be heavy users of virtual reality sites, you should consider investigating the marketing possibilities they afford.

Web Marketing Strategies

With so many interactive online marketing tools to consider, how do you choose the right one for you?

■ **Make sure that your target market is actually participating in these online activities.** Do your customers read blogs? Listen to podcasts? Join social networking groups? If so, you need to carefully identify *which* blogs, podcasts, and social networks. Sure, you may find a social networking site for garden enthusiasts—and you hope to target its members for your high-end gardening tools—but are site participants really the kind of people who'll pay a premium for such tools?

Read the blos, listen to the podcasts, participate in the community before you decide to spend a great deal of time and money on any particular site. You'll want to get a sense of the quality of the participants and content to make sure you're comfortable being associated with it.

■ **Determine whether you have the time to develop and maintain an active online presence.** Your business must be willing to put in the time not only to launch an interactive Web presence (whether in a social network, podcast, or blog) but also to maintain it and drive traffic to it—all of which can be a distraction, especially if your audience isn't on the Web much.

■ **Understand that some of these online activities come with pitfalls—most notably unfavorable comments.** By establishing an interactive Web presence, you're inviting comments. Whether you're on a social networking site, writing a blog, or getting mentioned on a user review site, people can post comments about you and your business—and chances are not all of them will be fair or even honest. Make sure that you're ready for this kind of exposure.

■ **Keep experimenting.** With the Web itself continually evolving, so too are the marketing opportunities it presents. Because the Internet is a fast-moving medium, you can quickly adapt marketing strategies to find the approaches that work best for you.

Mobile Devices

Once upon a time cell phones were simple devices used to make and receive phone calls. Over the years, however, mobile phones have morphed into *smartphones*—wireless, ubiquitous digital devices that allow users to connect to the Internet, send email, play video and music, take and store photos, provide global positioning and mapping, and much, much more.

With all of these new capabilities—not to mention a huge global market of consumers and businesspeople tethered to their mobile devices—comes a world of marketing opportunities. Just as the Internet grew into a powerful marketing medium, so too are smartphones.

One of the ways marketers are using smartphones is through *texting*—that is, by sending short text messages to mobile phones. The technology used for this—SMS, or *short message service*—is available on almost every phone. Although most people use text messages primarily for personal and business contacts, some companies are beginning to use them for promotional purposes as well. Examples include offering phone content like wallpaper, ring tones, video downloads, horoscopes, jokes, and news; sending coupon codes for free and discounted products or services; sponsoring contests, games, and other chances to win prizes; giving users a chance to vote in surveys, political polls, and more; and announcing events and concerts.

Popeyes Chicken & Biscuits, for example, used text messaging to get its Houston-area customers to try its new chicken sandwich. A sign outside the restaurant offered potential customers a free drink and fries if they would text the code "popeyes" to a particular number. In return, respondents received a reply text "coupon," which they flashed at the counter to get their freebies.

Other examples of creative text message marketing include a ski resort notifying regular guests that fresh powder has fallen overnight; a real estate agent alerting clients that a desirable type of home has come on the market; and a political group motivating party members to vote for their candidate and identify polling places.

Key for any company considering using SMS for marketing is that their target market is familiar and comfortable with the technology. Here are some additional tips:

- **Only send text messages to those who "opt in."** Texters opt in by responding to a company's earlier SMS promotion (as with the Popeye's sign), through a website, or through their phones. The opt-in part is important to the success of the promotion, because mobile phone users who don't like getting these messages are likely to be unreceptive, and even hostile, to companies sending them.

- **Make messages timely.** If you're announcing a grand opening, send your message out the day before, or that day. If you send it a week in advance, your customers will probably delete the message and forget the event.

- **Offer a value proposition.** Your customers won't want to read a text message that contains nothing but advertising. Instead, offer worthwhile benefits, like prizes, discounts, freebies, or at the very least, a bit of fun (like an interesting mobile phone game).

You'll find plenty of SMS companies ready to help you set up your text messaging campaign: just go to any search engine and enter "Text message marketing" or "SMS marketing" for a list of providers.

Other mobile marketing opportunities arise from the ability to link your ad to search results on mobile phones. This can be especially powerful for phones equipped with Global Positioning System (GPS) software. For example, a person doing a search on their mobile phone (either through a Web connection or by calling an "information" line) for a yogurt shop in Palo Alto, California, might see an ad for your Palo Alto yogurt shop alongside their results.

YOUR OTHER ONLINE MARKETING TACTICS

Use this worksheet to develop a strategy for the other types of online marketing tactics you could employ for your business.

What other online activities can you employ to market your company, products, or services? Podcasts? User review sites? Video sharing sites? Virtual reality sites? Mobile devices?

_____

_____

_____

List the podcast topics your prospects might look for or read (interest areas, industries, demographics, location, and so on):

_____

_____

_____

Do any of the podcasts on these topics accept ads? If so, list some that might be appropriate for you to advertise on:

_____

_____

_____

What kinds of content/links/comments might you contribute?

_____

_____

_____

Would broadcasting a regular podcast be a good marketing strategy for your business? If so, list the reasons why and the types of content/links you would include:

_____

_____

_____

List the types of user review sites your prospects would be likely to visit:

_____

_____

_____

_____

Describe how you could generate positive buzz about your products/services on such sites, as well as how you might be able to dispel negative views.

_____

_____

_____

Describe the types of videos your prospects would be interested in viewing (how-to's, product demos, and so on):

_____

_____

_____

Are there any virtual reality sites that would serve as appropriate venues to advertise your products/ services?

_____

_____

_____

Are your prospects tech-savvy enough to benefit from marketing to mobile devices?

_____

_____

_____

If so, what kind of benefits and incentives could you offer to make text message marketing successful for those devices?

_____

_____

_____

If you created a podcast or video, what would the nature of the content be?

_____

_____

_____

If you created a podcast, how often would you broadcast new ones?

_____

_____

_____

Other Online Marketing ROI

As with every other aspect of your marketing plan, you should carefully evaluate the return on investment you can expect from blogs, social networks, and other online marketing tactics. Although many of these activities don't *appear* to cost much money, all of them take *time*. And time, as everyone knows, equals money, so be sure to factor in the time—yours, your staff's, and any consultants'—that goes into writing a regular blog, preparing a podcast, and so on.

If, on the other hand, your primary marketing activity involving blogs, social networks, and the like revolves around placing ads there, they can represent a very affordable way to market your products and services—especially in comparison to traditional advertising venues such as radio, TV, and newspapers.

Calculating Your Other Online Marketing ROI

The following worksheet can help you get started on your own ROI analysis. Simply describe your online marketing venue (blog, podcast, social networking site, mobile device, and so on), your goals (financial and non-financial), and your market, and then fill in the rest of the requested data to get an idea of the ROI you can expect to achieve from your online marketing campaign.

One thing to note: Because so many divergent online marketing tactics are described in this chapter, you should complete the following worksheet for each type (mobile devices, podcasts, blogs, social network, review sites, and so on) you plan to employ.

Here are some tips for completing the worksheet (and calculating your ROI):

■ **Make Web analytics work for you.** Although it may be difficult to calculate your return on investment for writing a blog, sharing a video on YouTube, or broadcasting a regular podcast, it's *not* difficult to calculate your ROI for advertising on such sites—thanks to Web analytics software. Using the wealth of information provided by such software, you can determine how many times your ad was shown (*impressions*), how many times it was clicked through, what Web pages users visited once they clicked through, how long users stayed on your site, whether they took certain actions (such as making a purchase), and more.

■ **Remember non-financial goals.** While you may not be able to put a cash value on things like brand awareness and customer perception, these are important components of any marketing campaign, and as such must be considered when calculating return on investment—especially when it comes to activities like maintaining a blog, sending out regular podcasts, and participating in social networking sites, where the primary goals are keeping your name in front of customers and heightening your credibility. Thus, to return to an example from earlier in the chapter, if a dog trainer creates a how-to video on how to silence barking canines, she may not see any *immediate* financial gain. However, if the video is a good one—and yelping rascals suddenly turn into serenely quiet pups when owners employ the methods demonstrated therein—that dog trainer could soon be known as the next *dog whisperer,* as the video is shared and word spreads.

RETURN ON INVESTMENT

OTHER ONLINE MARKETING TACTICS ROI

Your business: _____

Your target market: _____

Description of your online marketing tactic (blog, social networking site, podcast, etc.): _____

GOALS

Financial: _____

Non-financial: _____

PROJECTED COSTS

Writers: _____

Designers: _____

Videographers: _____

Technical support: _____

Other consultants (SMS specialists, community managers, online PR agency, etc.): _____

Total cost: _____

PROJECTED RETURNS, FINANCIAL

Number of click throughs: _____

Number of click through conversions (i.e., number of users of who take desired action after clicking through to site): _____

Amount of revenue generated per conversion: _____

Monthly revenue generated from conversions: _____

Monthly revenue generated from online marketing activity: _____

Total annual revenue generated from online marketing activity: _____

Total cost: _____

Total projected net financial gain (annual revenue minus total cost): _____

PROJECTED RETURNS, NON-FINANCIAL

Total number of impressions: _____

Number of non-converting click-throughs: _____

Other brand building, awareness benefits. _____

TOTAL ROI (Total Net Financial Returns Plus Total Non-financial Returns): _____

BLOGS, SOCIAL NETWORKS, AND OTHER ONLINE TACTICS

	JAN	FEB	MARCH	APRIL	MAY
Professional Assistance					
Online marketing ad agency					
Online PR agency					
Blog writers/researchers					
Social networking consultants					
Community managers					
Mobile ad consultants					
Photographers/Illustrators/Videographers					
Podcast/Audio assistance					
Programmers/Tech assistance					
Other consultants					
Ad Buys					
Blogs					
Social network sites					
User review sites					
Video sites					
Mobile devices					
Other online ad buys					
Supplies/Cost of Goods/Manufacturing					
Blogging services/software					
RSS feed services/software					
Quiz/contest services/software					
Audio/Video equipment					
Other supplies/goods/manufacturing costs					
Other					
TOTAL					

! **NOTE:** An electronic version of this worksheet is available as part of the Planning Shop's Marketing Budget Templates package.

BUDGET (12 MONTHS)

JUNE	JULY	AUGUST	SEPT	OCT	NOV	DEC	TOTAL

BUILDING YOUR MARKETING PLAN

ONLINE MARKETING

Drawing from the Brainstorming worksheets in this section, plan the strategies you will use in your online marketing campaign.

1. What type of website—brochure, e-commerce, content, lead generation, portal, social networking, customer service—will best serve your marketing needs, and why? _____

2. Provide a brief description of your planned website.

Goals: _____

Audience: _____

Content: _____

Functions (e-commerce, customer service forms, newsletter sign-up, search box, etc.): _____

Overall design: _____

_____

_____

3. What SEO/SEM keywords will you use? _____

4. Will you use SEO/SEM consultants? _____

5. Do you plan to use email to market your products and services? If so, what form will it take (email newsletters, sales announcements, product launches, press releases, etc.), and how will you come up with your mailing list (i.e., develop vs. rent)? _____

6. What types of Web advertising or sponsorships do you plan to take advantage of? (Briefly describe your plans for each type.)

Website ads: _____

Sponsorships: _____

Portals/Directories: _____

Online classifieds: _____

Auction sites: _____

Contextual ads: _____

Affiliate programs: _____

7. Who will create your ads? _____

8. Will you use online social and professional networking sites to market your products and services, and if so, how (contributing content, advertising, creating groups, etc.)?

_____

_____

_____

_____

9. Will you use blogs to market your products, and if so, how (creating your own blog, submitting press releases, contributing content, suggesting links and content, advertising, etc.)?

_____

_____

_____

_____

10. Can you incorporate mobile devices into your marketing plans (i.e., is your audience comfortable enough with the technology to make it worthwhile)? If so, what kind of immediate benefits can you offer to inspire "texters" to take action?

_____

_____

_____

_____

11. Describe any other online marketing tactics you intend to employ (podcasts, video-sharing sites, user review sites, etc.):

_____

_____

_____

_____

12. How will the online marketing tactics you choose bring you closer to your marketing goals?

_____

_____

_____

_____

_____

SECTION VI

Other Types of Marketing

Lingo

AUDIO SPOTLIGHT: A recorded advertising message beamed to either an individual or a small group in a public place.

CAUSE-RELATED MARKETING: Involving your company in a cause you believe in and that your customers relate to as a way of raising your visibility with your target market.

GUERILLA MARKETING: No-cost or low-cost marketing strategies, typically involving grassroots and local activities.

IN-STORE MARKETING: Displays, signage, and ads that aim to attract customers and influence their purchasing decisions while they're in a store.

OUT-OF-THE BOX MARKETING: Marketing focused on non-traditional venues in an attempt to capture customer attention in places they're likely to live, work, shop, or travel.

PROMOTIONAL ADVERTISING: Items—often small and relatively inexpensive (though they can also be substantial)—given to customers and prospects with your company name and info printed on them (for example, calendars, mugs, pens, T-shirts, and so on).

TRANSIT ADVERTISING: Advertising placed on or near vehicles that transport people from one place to another, such as buses, trains, taxes, and subways.

CHAPTER 27

More Ways to Reach Your Customers

You're browsing the shelves of a bookstore, minding your own business, when you hear a voice whispering in your ear, "Hey you, can you hear me? Do you ever think about murder?" You look around to see who's talking to you or wonder if you're dreaming. No one else seems to have heard the voice. It turns out that it's an ad for a Court TV murder mystery television show. Using a new technology called "audio spotlight," it's a method of directing sounds directly to one person's ear rather than broadcasting to an entire area, and it's just one of many new forms of marketing.

During the dot-com era, when young companies with huge marketing budgets were desperately trying to get a foothold, it was not unheard of to see an ad for a dot-com company on an orange in your supermarket or on a seat back at a Major League ballpark. Such companies might even have offered to pay you to name your new baby after them.

In a world where people are bombarded with ad messages virtually every waking moment of every day, it's a huge marketing challenge to cut through all of this clutter. How do you get the attention—not to mention affection—of customers when so many other companies are vying for their hearts and minds as well?

This section examines a number of marketing techniques—none of which fall neatly into the other categories discussed in this book—which you can employ to get your name, message, and brand in front of customers. The tactics discussed here tend to be deployed *closer* to the customer than more traditional methods—perhaps taking the form of stacks of canned pumpkin placed at the end of the supermarket aisle before Thanksgiving, free samples of soap coming to you in the mail, or a company's name on the back of your kids' Little League uniform. These are marketing vehicles that show up where you are—managing to get in your face without being offensive. They subtly or overtly grab your attention and compel you to buy.

Such marketing vehicles include both time-tested methods such as signs and samplings and new techniques like the above described audio spotlight. Regardless of the form they take, all of these marketing activities share the same goals: to get the attention of prospective customers, reinforce your brand, and get your message out.

The marketing tactics discussed in this section include:

- **In-store marketing.** Marketing aimed at attracting customers and influencing their purchasing decisions precisely when they're making a choice about what to buy.

- **Sampling.** Giving a small amount of your product or service to a prospect to entice them to buy

- **Promotional items/Giveaways.** Small gifts—such as calendars, mugs, and pens—that carry an advertising message but are perceived as presents.

- **Signs.** Fixed signs, movable signs, banners, posters, and other physical announcements.

- **Product placement.** Having your products placed or featured where prospective customers are likely to see them (such as public places and on TV shows) or giving them to celebrities or popular community members.

- **Event marketing.** Hosting or sponsoring events to attract your target audience or to make your name and brand visible to that audience.

- **Transit advertising.** Advertising on buses, taxis, planes, trains, and their associated facilities (such as bus stops and train stations).

- **Yellow Pages and directories.** Paid listings and advertisements in phone or business directories.

- **Community marketing.** Getting involved in community activities to help raise the visibility of your company.

- **Cause-related marketing.** Associating your business with a cause you believe in (and to which your customers relate) to raise your visibility with a target audience.

- **Guerilla marketing.** Low-cost, innovative strategies for marketing to customers, usually at the grassroots level.

- **Other non-traditional advertising.** Things such as advertising in movie theaters.

Other Marketing Costs

The Affordability Scale below compares the costs of the various forms of marketing discussed in this section. Keep in mind, however, that because these marketing activities vary widely (even within categories), this cost comparison is based on very rough estimates.

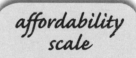

affordability scale

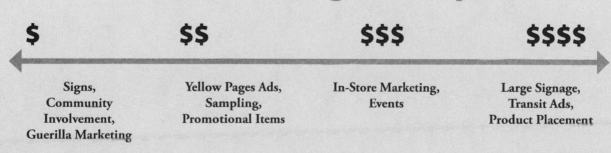

Other Marketing Techniques

$	$$	$$$	$$$$
Signs, Community Involvement, Guerilla Marketing	Yellow Pages Ads, Sampling, Promotional Items	In-Store Marketing, Events	Large Signage, Transit Ads, Product Placement

*COST KEY:

$—Relatively Inexpensive $$—Moderately Expensive $$$—Fairly Expensive $$$$—Expensive

* These symbols represent general rate estimates.

Lingo

DEMO: A demonstration (or trial version) of a product, software, technology, or service.

ENDCAPS: Special displays of merchandise—usually at the end of an aisle—designed to bring attention to a specific product.

PLANOGRAM: A floor plan detailing the products each store location will carry as well as their placement and display.

SHELF TALKERS/BARKERS/DANGLERS: Printed signs affixed to a shelf to bring attention to a product located there—often printed with phrases like *New Product!* or *Buy One, Get One Free!*

SKU: Short for stock keeping unit, SKU refers to the product number that a retailer assigns to an item (individual or bundled) to keep track of it in inventory.

SLOTTING FEE: A fee companies pay to retailers to carry and sell their products.

TEAR-OFFS: Coupons for a product attached to the shelf where it is displayed. Customers can tear one off and use it at checkout.

In-Store Marketing and Sampling

A s you're walking through a supermarket, someone offers you a sample of a new Thai peanut sauce for pasta. You may never have thought about putting peanut sauce on pasta, but heck, it actually tastes pretty good. So when you come across a whole stack of that peanut sauce at the end of the aisle, you throw a bottle in your shopping basket. Or perhaps you're looking for a way to keep your contacts organized in a database: when an online service offers a month's free trial, you decide to give it a try. Then, when that month is up, you decide to keep the service because you've grown to like it.

For entrepreneurial companies, some of the most effective marketing activities are the ones that get them close to customers. Marketing often works best, in fact, when it brings you in direct contact with your customers—especially if it allows you to reach them when and where they're making purchasing decisions. This is why in-store marketing and sampling are two particularly important marketing tactics for entrepreneurial and new businesses.

Not only are these marketing tactics effective, they're also often relatively inexpensive. Sampling—whether of a tangible product, a Web application, or a service—can be a great way to build a market at minimal cost. And in-store marketing—especially if you start with local stores (or even farmers' or crafts markets in your area)—helps you increase your revenues as well as learn about what your prospective customers want and how they respond to your marketing message.

In-Store Marketing

Step into any supermarket, department store, superstore, or even corner convenience store, and you'll find shelves crammed with products vying for your attention. Some products, however, stand out. Perhaps there's a big stack of them at the end of an aisle or in a rack or table at the front of the store. Maybe there's a window display of a newly released product, or perhaps there's a poster announcing a two-for-one sale on a certain brand.

It's hard enough to get retailers to carry your products; you also have to convince them to *continue* selling them. To do this, you must attract attention to your product or service and persuade customers to buy it—thereby convincing retailers to continue selling it. Luckily for you, there are numerous in-store marketing techniques you can use to achieve this goal.

In-store marketing refers to any type of display, fixture, or signage that makes a product stand out in a store. Using bright colors; graphics; concise, compelling language; and (occasionally) audio and video, this kind of marketing aims to catch a shopper's eye (or ear), draw them to a product, and convince them to put that product in their cart.

The nature and availability of in-store marketing options will vary greatly depending on the stores carrying your merchandise and how well your products are likely to sell. Retailers are selling *products,* not just space, so you'll need to convince them—usually by a past sales track record—that your products will sell well if they allow you more in-store promotional opportunities.

Common In-Store Marketing Vehicles

There exists an enormous—and ever-growing—range of in-store display opportunities, with marketers continually searching for new ways to make their signage and devices stand out. The following represent some of the most popular types:

- **Audio spotlight.** In this up-and-coming technique, in-store audio technology beams a compelling message directly into the ear of a nearby customer.

- **Electronic coupon devices.** Shelf-mounted coupon machines that automatically release a coupon when a customer nears and triggers a light sensor.

- **Endcap displays.** Signage at the end of a store aisle promoting and displaying products on shelves, hooks, or in other formats.

- **In-store radio.** In-store announcements (via loudspeaker or audio system) directing shoppers to special displays or product offerings.

- **In-store sampling.** Small amounts of products offered for people to sample while shopping (for example, tastes of food items).

- **Point-of-purchase displays.** Signage and/or shelving promoting a product at or near the point of purchase (for example, by the cash register) or elsewhere in the store where a customer is likely to make an impulse purchasing decision (say, at the produce counter or magazine rack).

- **Shelf talkers.** Bright, simple signs attached to a shelf saying something like "New Product!" "Try Me!" or "Buy One; Get One Free!" Some rest against the shelf, while others stick out perpendicular to it so that customers don't need to turn their heads toward the product to see them.

- **Shopping cart ads.** Ads on the inside of shopping carts at grocery stores, typically for local businesses.

- **Tear-offs.** Coupon stacks attached to a shelf with savings offers customers can tear off to get a discount on a nearby product.

- **Video displays.** Monitors that display video messages, generally on a continuous loop.

- **Window displays** Prominently featuring a product in a store's front window or other windows.

If you have the opportunity to promote your products in stores, and you can come up with an appealing in-store marketing strategy that separates you from the crowd, you're likely to significantly increase your product's visibility and sales.

Getting Shelf Space

With tens of thousands of new products per year vying for limited shelf space (already occupied by hundreds of thousands of existing products), one of the biggest challenges for manufacturers is simply getting their products on retailers' shelves.

Given this scarcity of retail shelf or display space, then, how do you get your products into stores?

- **Go straight to the top.** First, recognize that you're not likely to walk into a local branch of a huge national chain—such as a Target, Wal-Mart, Sports Authority, or Petco—and get that retailer to agree to carry your product. Product decisions for mass-market stores are almost always made at the national level. Thus, if you want to be carried by one of those mega-stores, you need to present your products at national headquarters—and it's not easy to get a meeting with a buyer.

- **Pay your fees.** In addition, some large stores— particularly supermarkets— may charge slotting fees, requiring payment just to be carried on their shelves. Large retailers say this fee is required to help offset the costs of adding new products to their inventory management systems and to reduce the risk of new products failing.

- **Do your research.** By researching how specific stores choose what products to carry, you can increase the chance that the store will carry your products. Many store buyers attend trade shows (such as fancy food shows, sporting goods show, and so on) looking for new products to feature. Thus, if you're interested in getting your product on the shelf at a particular large retailer, try to identify which trade shows their buyers attend.

Even if you're lucky enough for a large store to express interest in carrying your products, if there are hefty slotting and promotional fees involved, you'll want to make sure getting into a big store is worth your while, especially if yours is a new or smaller company. Find out the fees, estimate your potential profits, and do an ROI to make sure it makes sense to play with the big boys.

In-Store Displays

If you're fortunate enough to get your products onto a retailer's shelves, you must do everything you can to help sell those products. In most cases, this means carrying out all of the other marketing activities you would normally do to drive customers into stores, such as advertising and PR. This also means helping your products stand out from the competition. If you're lucky—and you ask—you may be able to have an in-store display.

Of course, you will have to pay for these in-store displays—and not just for the cost of the physical display itself (such as a free-standing special rack).

Strategies for Getting Your Products into Stores

Here are some ways to make sure your products make it onto retailers' shelves:

- **Start local.** Local stores, especially smaller ones, are far more likely than national retailers to give a new vendor a chance. In rare instances, even local stores within a national chain will be permitted to carry some products from local vendors. Being carried by local stores helps you build a sales record that you can later use to convince larger stores of your marketability as well as to build income.

- **Sell your products directly.** By peddling your wares through local farmers, crafts markets, and fairs, you help build credibility for your products that you can later use to convince retailers to carry them. This works especially well for foods, jewelry, crafts, and the like.

- **Get press coverage for your product.** Retailers respect vendors who are able to generate publicity about and market interest in their products. In addition, press coverage increases their confidence in your ability to provide the marketing support necessary to drive sales. The better known you are, the more confidence you inspire in store representatives.

- **Get a distributor.** If you're a small manufacturer looking to get your products into large stores, one way of doing so is by working with a distributor who provides products to the retailers you're interested in.

- **Partner with a larger manufacturer.** For example, if you make sippy cups for children, consider a dual packaging arrangement with an apple juice manufacturer.

- **Offer retail exclusives.** Make your product available at only one store.

Get with the Plan

A *planogram* is the floor plan that all stores in a chain follow in laying out their stores, planning their displays, and placing merchandise on their shelves. It shows exactly what each store will carry and where it will be placed. Decided upon by headquarters, planograms are generally drawn up every six or twelve months for major stores and every season or quarter for specialty stores. If you're not in a company's planogram, you're not likely to be in that store. If, however, you pitch your product or special display to a company's main buyers when they're determining their planogram, you greatly increase your chances of success. Thus, it's important to find out when a store changes its planograms so that you can pitch your product to the corporate office about six months in advance of that.

Promos Mean Orders

One compelling reason to participate in any kind of retail promotion—commonly referred to as a *promo*—is to get more of your product ordered and out there for customers to see and purchase. Let's say, for example, that a discount department store chain normally carries a few dozen of your toy electric guitars per store. If you negotiated an endcap display for a month, that retailer would have to significantly increase its inventory of your toy guitars to keep that endcap supplied for the entire month.

You have to pay for the privilege of having that display space—and these costs can be substantial. If you're working with a regional or national chain, you'll pay on a per-store basis, and they'll usually want the promo/display in all of their stores. That means that if you're offered a display in a store with 220 locations, and they charge you $1,000 per location, you will pay $220,000 just for the display space. Thus, you must think carefully about whether such a display will pay off in terms of additional sales.

Keep in mind, too, that not all in-store displays are equally effective. Window displays, for example, may be good for generating interest and even drawing traffic into a store (such as in a mall), but they're not as immediate as some other types of in-store displays.

One of the most effective types of in-store displays are those located right near the checkout or cash register—referred to as POP, or point-of-purchase, displays (or sometimes as POS, or point-of-sale, displays). These work especially well for small, impulse items that a shopper may choose to add while they're waiting in line.

Endcap, or end-of-aisle, displays are also extremely desirable. For starters, they make your product very visible within a store, since customers coming from all directions—not just up and down one aisle—will see your products. In addition, retailers usually have to order a lot of your product to stock the endcap.

Big retailers have a large range of display options available to vendors, and they're sometimes open to being pitched more creative ideas as well.

In-Store Ads

Retailers have come to realize that once people are in a store, they become a captive audience for advertising. Not surprisingly, then, stores have come up with ways to sell some of their space for ads.

Retailers, however, *do not* want their stores to become as cluttered with ads as sports stadiums. Instead, they're likely to offer more discreet advertising options that can still be very effective.

In-store ads include:

- **Shopping cart ads.** Typically, these ads are used for extremely local businesses, such as realtors advertising in grocery shopping carts.
- **In-store "radio" ads.** These take the form of announcements over a store's public address system, drawing attention to a product or special sale.
- **Banners/Posters/Signs.** These can be free standing, affixed to a wall, or hung from the ceiling to draw attention to a product.
- **Video displays.** In these types of ads, monitors with promotional messages or instructional information generally run a continuous loop.

RAINSTORMING

YOUR IN-STORE MARKETING

Use this worksheet to plan your in-store marketing efforts.

List the retailers where you would *like* to get shelf space for your products: _____
_____

List some places—including local stores and other options such as crafts and farmers' markets—where you could *most easily* get your products carried:_____
_____

Indicate which of the following in-store marketing vehicles might work for your product(s) and describe how you could use them most effectively:

POP displays: _____

Endcaps: _____

Freestanding displays: _____

Window displays: _____

Other displays: _____

In-store ads (specify): _____

Why Are the Corn Flakes Talking to Me?

Marketers have a new way of bending customers' ears: *Audio spotlight* technology beams audio marketing messages directly into customers' ears as they shop, sit in waiting rooms, or pass by a booth at a trade show. The audio beams reach people as they enter specific zones; however, they *cannot* be heard by others standing just a couple of feet away.

Marketers are finding all sorts of ways to leverage this technology to improve the shopping or browsing experience. Auto dealers, for example, have used the technology to promote the features of their cars to prospective buyers. Museums have used it to promote various parts of their exhibits. And supermarkets are experimenting with the technology to alert customers to new products and inform them of the nutritional value in products like cereals and vegetables.

Developed by Holosonic Research Labs in Watertown, Massachusetts, the technology offers a way of advertising to customers directly—without disturbing anyone else in the vicinity (and thus avoiding the audio assault of blaring in-store loudspeaker systems). Prices for the service vary widely, based on the type of audio package purchased, but the media has reported on some packages priced at around $1,000 to $2,000.

As for customers' reactions, some admit finding the technology a bit creepy. After all, hearing voices hawking products can be frightening. However, once customers figure out what's going on, they tend to be amused, which makes them more receptive to those marketing messages.

> *Sampling can be very labor-intensive, but the best recipe for selling something in the food business is putting a consumable in a consumer's mouth. If the product is good, it's going to sell.*
>
> **James Parker**
> **Associate Global Coordinator**
> **for Produce**
> **Whole Foods Markets**

Sampling

Try it; you'll like it!

This classic marketing message nicely sums up the theory behind sampling—namely that if customers are given a chance to try a product, they're more likely to buy it. For new products and technologies, in fact, there may be no more effective marketing technique than sampling. Since you don't have to overcome a customers' natural reluctance to spend their own money on an unknown product, you have a chance to overcome their sales resistance. In fact, many products consumers now take for granted first gained popular acceptance due to free sampling. Take PostIt Notes: consumers had never seen an adhesive that could stick and then come unstuck cleanly before the introduction of PostIts, so it took a lot of free samples to get them used to the idea.

One form of sampling most people are familiar with comprises the taste of food vendors use to entice customers to buy their edible offerings. However, the table in the supermarket or warehouse store represents just one form of sampling. A company can also sample its software, Web services, just-introduced products, and even business and personal services.

Some of the many types of samples include:

- **Trial-size products.** For example, a small box of a new kind of detergent.
- **Trial versions of software.** For example, a download of a new game that expires after a month.
- **Free, limited time memberships.** For example, a free week's membership in a gym.
- **Free, limited time use of online services.** For example, two weeks of free access to an online music service.
- **Free testing.** For example, a free makeup application at a cosmetics department counter or a test-drive of a car.
- **First time free.** For example, free cans of a new energy drink distributed outside of a sports. stadium.
- **Free trial of a service.** For example, a first visit to a chiropractor.

While sampling is often associated with product marketing, it can also work for service-related businesses. Potential clients considering hiring a consultant, using a personal service provider, or paying for some other intangible service have little information on which to base their decision unless they've received recommendations from other clients. (In contrast, those purchasing products can usually see, feel, and sometimes hear the merchandise before buying.)

Offering a sample of your service serves as a great way to build a buyer's confidence in your expertise or abilities, to influence a client to buy a full service, and to generate powerful word of mouth (when clients sampling the service tell their friends and colleagues). Consider these strategies for offering service samples to potential customers:

- Offer a free first-time consultation or a free first-time service, such as a first manicure at a new nail salon.

Offer an abbreviated version of a service, such as a half-hour meeting for an attorney or a five-minute neck massage for a spa.

If you have an opportunity to speak before a group, include the type of advice you would give your actual clients in your speech.

Give employees at a corporation a free consultation or treatment in exchange for being allowed to distribute your business cards.

If you have an opportunity to deliver your service—even for free—to a person who's known and respected by your target market, and that person lets you use their name in your marketing materials, those free hours of service can translate into a tremendous amount of marketing mileage. This person doesn't have to be a celebrity (though that would be great)—even a local business leader or local radio or TV personality can add clout to your marketing efforts.

Although sampling can be one of the most affordable marketing techniques, it still has its costs. First, there are the costs of the samples themselves (though allowing prospects to sample your software or Web services may cost you virtually nothing). Then, there's the cost of any handouts or packaging you distribute along with those samples. On top of that, there are distribution costs such as paying retailers for in-store sampling, paying mailing houses for direct mail sampling, and even paying people to hand out samples (if you choose that form of distribution). Keep these costs in mind as you prepare your sampling budget and calculate your return on investment.

> ## Giving It Away
>
> The following are some of the methods you can employ to get your samples to customers:
>
> - **In-store samples.** This usually involves paying a fee to the retailer.
> - **Mailed samples.** You may have to use a mailing service or fulfillment house for these.
> - **Bundled samples.** These could include samples bundled with a morning newspaper or packaged with another product.
> - **Online samples.** With this type of sampling, customers are often required to sign up and provide credit card info to receive the free trial.
> - **Handouts.** Free samples distributed in public places such as ballparks, concert venues, busy streets, and transit terminals.

BRAINSTORMING

YOUR SAMPLING ACTIVITIES

Use this worksheet to determine what kinds of samples and free trials might serve as effective marketing vehicles for your products or services.

List three places you could you offer samples of your product or service: _____

_____

_____

Explain how you would distribute your samples: _____

_____

_____

What supporting materials/handouts—if any—would you include with your samples? _____

_____

_____

What other support/staff/assistance will you need for your sampling activities? _____

_____

_____

Calculating Your In-Store Marketing and Sampling ROI

The following worksheet can help you get started on your own ROI analysis. Simply describe what your in-store marketing tactics and sampling efforts will entail, and fill in the requested data to get an idea of the ROI you can expect from your in-store marketing and sampling.

Here are some tips for using the worksheets (and calculating your ROI):

■ **Be sure to break out all of your costs.** While sampling and in-store marketing tactics represent some of the most cost-effective ways to entice customers to purchase your products or services, they still have associated costs. Thus, don't forget to include, for example, the costs of distributing your samples (for example, the fee you pay retailers to let you set up a sample table), the costs of the samples themselves, and the amount you pay retailers to set up an endcap or window display of your offerings.

■ **Remember non-financial goals.** While you may not be able to put a cash value on things like brand awareness and customer perception, these are important components of any marketing campaign, and as such must be considered when calculating return on investment.

In-Store Marketing and Sampling Return on Investment

For many in-store promotions, it's relatively easy to work out the return on investment (ROI) because the retailer will order and purchase an increased amount of your product to support the promotion—meaning all you have to do is determine how much it's going to cost you in relation to the number of increased items the retailer plans to purchase. In most cases, these orders are non-returnable, so these promos can pay for themselves—even if they appear to be relatively expensive.

For example, if you were offered the chance to provide a back-to-school endcap display of the backpacks you manufacture at a regional discount department store chain, that chain might charge you something like $3,000 per store. With 30 stores in the chain, this would mean your promo would cost $90,000. However, the chain will now order 300 backpacks per store, instead of the 50 they'd order if you didn't have the endcap—which means you'll be selling 250 more backpacks for each of the 30 stores, or an increased order of 7,500. If you charge the stores $20 for the backpacks, this increase would amount to $150,000, and you'd have a profit of $60,000—in addition to the increased exposure for your brand and your other products on their shelves.

Although it's more difficult to calculate the ROI for some of the other in-store marketing techniques described here, in-store advertising can significantly enhance your sales. Recent studies have indicated that about 66% of all purchasing decisions are made *while* shopping (rather than in advance), and 53% of those in-store purchases are made on impulse.

Is in-store advertising worthwhile for *your* business? A good way to find out is to gauge your sales at a particular store before and after you've implemented an in-store advertising tactic. Then use the worksheet on the following page to do an ROI on the costs of the promotion itself to see if it was worthwhile.

Sampling typically has a fairly high ROI—and once again is fairly easy to measure in terms of short-term returns. After all, you can track how many people who downloaded your trial software actually bought it, how many jars of peanut sauce you sold in the store where you were sampling it, or how many clients returned for future chiropractic visits. What's harder to measure is how many of these customers continued to buy from you and what their lifetime value is—which may mean you have a significantly higher ROI than your short term results would indicate.

RETURN ON INVESTMENT

YOUR IN-STORE MARKETING AND SAMPLING ROI

Your business: _____

Your target market: _____

Description of your in-store marketing tactics and sampling activities: _____

GOALS

Financial: _____

Non-financial: _____

PROJECTED COSTS

Store slotting fees: _____

Endcap/window displays: _____

Point-of-purchase displays: _____

Freestanding displays: _____

Cost of samples: _____

Sampling/demo tables: _____

In-store ad buys (including radio ads): _____

Printing and reproduction (for shelf talkers, coupons/handouts, posters/banners, and more): _____

Shipping and postage (including mailing and fulfillment services): _____

In-store marketing consultant: _____

Product demonstrators/distributors: _____

Writers: _____

Graphic designers/photographers: _____

Other consultants: _____

Total cost: _____

PROJECTED RETURNS, FINANCIAL

Annual revenue generated from in-store promotions and advertising: _____

Annual revenue generated from sampling and trial versions of products/services: _____

Total cost: _____

Total projected net financial gain (annual revenue and sales minus total cost): _____

PROJECTED RETURNS, NON-FINANCIAL

_____

_____

TOTAL ROI (Total Net Financial Returns Plus Total Non-financial Returns): _____

IN-STORE PROMOTION & SAMPLING BUDGET (12 MONTHS)

	JAN	FEB	MARCH	APRIL	MAY
Professional Assistance					
In-store marketing consultant					
Product demonstrators/distributors					
Writers					
Graphic designers/Photographers/Illustrators					
Other consultants					
Ad Buys					
Store slotting fees					
Endcap/Window displays					
Point-of-purchase displays					
Free-standing displays					
Other in-store ad buys					
Printing/Reproduction					
Shelf talkers					
Coupons/Handouts					
Posters/Banners					
Other printing/reproduction costs					
Shipping and Postage					
Mailing/Fulfillment services					
Other shipping and postage costs					
Supplies/Cost of Goods/Manufacturing					
Cost of displays/cost of samples					
Sampling/demo tables					
Other supplies/goods/manufacturing costs					
Other					
TOTAL					

! NOTE: An electronic version of this worksheet is available as part of the Planning Shop's Marketing Budget Templates package.

JUNE	JULY	AUGUST	SEPT	OCT	NOV	DEC	TOTAL

Lingo

ADVERTISING SPECIALTY ITEMS: Another term for promotional giveaways imprinted with your company name and info (such as calendars, mugs, pens, and shirts).

PRO BONO: Short for *pro bono publico*, or "for the public good," *pro bono* refers to free services—usually performed by professionals such as attorneys, though the term can be applied to any free services—which are donated to help the community, needy individuals, or causes.

PRODUCT PLACEMENT: The act of placing products in highly visible or respected venues—such as in a movie, luxury hotel, or industry conference—where your target market is likely to see them and be enticed to use them.

SEEDING: Giving your product or service to individuals who are likely to influence others to buy.

SPONSORSHIP: When a for-profit business provides funds, services, mentorships, or other types of support to a nonprofit in an effort to be socially responsible and to generate positive publicity.

TSCHOTKES: Promotional advertising giveaways. Pronounced "tshots-keys," the term is Yiddish for unnecessary playthings or gizmos.

YELLOW PAGES: The term used for the business section of the phone book or a business phone directory; also occasionally used to refer to online business directories. In some countries, the term *Yellow Pages* is trademarked.

CHAPTER 29

Signs, Other Ads, and Out-of-the-Box Marketing

By now, you've likely come to realize that a huge number of marketing options exist for entrepreneurial companies. This chapter explores some additional marketing techniques that can be highly effective for new, small, and growing companies. It covers some of the oldest—as well as the newest—forms of marketing.

As you develop your own marketing plan, don't forget to start with some of the tried-and-true marketing methods discussed in this chapter. After all, there's a reason these marketing tactics are still in use—they work! Putting a sign over your store or on the side of your truck isn't rocket science, but it certainly helps make prospects aware of your existence. Likewise, giving a customer a pen imprinted with your company's name isn't the kind of thing that takes an MBA in marketing; however, that pen plays an important role in keeping your name fresh in that customer's mind.

Those are the tried-and-true techniques. It's also a good idea to be clever and creative—to try some marketing techniques that are a bit outside the normal box of print, TV, and Web advertising. Sponsoring an event or getting involved with a social cause not only helps you reach your target market, it also lets you connect with that market in a more meaningful way.

In this section, you'll learn about:

- Signs
- Other ads, including transit and Yellow Pages ads
- Guerrilla/Low-cost marketing (including advertising specialty items and product placement)
- Events
- Cause and community marketing

Making Your Signs Work

When considering putting up signs for your business, be sure to think carefully about their appearance and placement. Here are a few things to keep in mind:

- **Make your sign consistent with your corporate identity and branding** in terms of its colors, type style, logo, and tagline

- **Make your message brief—** perhaps as few as seven to ten words. People can only process a small amount of information as they pass by.

- **Use large type.** Your sign should be legible from the street (or farther).

- **Make sure your sign is visible from any direction** (if possible).

- **Use high-contrast colors.** Black text on a yellow background is considered the most readable combination, followed by black text on white, and white on black.

- **Make sure your sign can be distinguished from its surroundings.** If trees will surround your sign, avoid using too much green. Also try to make your sign different in shape, size, and style from any signs around it.

- **Provide good lighting** if you want your sign to be seen at night.

Signs

With the exception of standing in a town market hawking your wares, signage likely represents the oldest form of marketing. From a sign placed over the front door of your store to neon billboards in New York's Times Square to a business name painted on the side of your van, signs serve as an effective way to let others know your business exists and to get your message out.

One advantage of signs is that they're *persistent.* Unlike TV or website ads, which are gone in 30 seconds, or a trade show booth, which disappears after a few days, signs usually remain in place for a long time. You invest in them once, and they stick around (with the exception of billboards and other advertising signs in which you rent space for a limited time).

Another advantage of signs is that they're relatively inexpensive. Sure, a huge neon sign next to a major highway can cost big bucks, but a magnetic sign on the side of your construction truck serves as a fairly cheap way of letting the world know about your business.

The following subsections list the range of choices available for using signs in your marketing plan:

Place-of-Business Signs

- Awnings, with your business name and addresss painted on them
- Painted signs, identifying your business
- Neon and electronic signs, visible from a distance, attracting attention
- Banners, announcing a special sale or grand opening
- Window placards, drawing attention to a new product or sale
- Inside-store signs/posters, highlighting certain products, discounts, new offerings
- Entryway signs, enticing people to enter your store, particularly useful in malls and highly trafficked locations
- Large signs on the top or side of your building, visible from a distance or nearby road or highway

Vehicle Signs

- Name and contact information painted on the side of the vehicle
- Magnetic signs attached temporarily (though they may be left on for extended periods)
- Top-of-vehicle signs (such as for pizza delivery vehicles)

Signs in Public Locations

- **Posters.** Paper signs put up in highly trafficked areas such as sides of buildings, campuses, and construction barriers.
- **Sandwich boards/Sign wavers.** Temporary signs usually held up by individuals in well-trafficked locations.
- **Electronic signs.** Placed in public places.

BRAINSTORMING

YOUR SIGNS

Describe the type of signs you can use to announce and advertise your business.

Place-of-business signs: _____

_____

_____

_____

Vehicle signs: _____

_____

_____

_____

Signs in public locations: _____

_____

_____

_____

Other Types of Ads

Ads are everywhere; you can't avoid them. With virtually all public places (and many private ones) plastered with ads, you'll find yourself bombarded by them wherever you go—whether you drive down the highway, go to a sporting event, or wait at a bus stop. We're so used to ads being part of everyday life that we hardly seem to notice them. But, in fact, we do—and we remember the companies that advertise. That's why ads continue to proliferate: *they work.*

Ads are particularly pervasive where there's a *captive audience*—that is, anyplace where a group of people is likely to remain for a period of time. You may hate the ads that come on before a movie starts, but you don't get up and leave. Instead, you sit there eating your popcorn—and watching the commercial—while you wait for the feature film to begin.

Of course, there's one place where people are actually seeking out ads— the Yellow Pages, or phone directories of businesses. If you want to order a pizza or need a plumber on Sunday, you might look first to Yellow Pages ads for help with your choice. Sure, you could turn to the Internet or your mobile phone, but many people still try the Yellow Pages first.

Post No Bills

Just because a location seems like a great place for a sign doesn't mean you can put your sign there. Even at your own place of business, it's likely that your city or town has regulations limiting the size and nature of the sign you can put up—its dimensions, whether it can be lit, at what hours, and so forth. It's also illegal to post signs and posters in most public locations or on private property. And you can't just put up a poster at a bus stop; instead, you must pay the transit authority for that privilege. Thus, if you're going to be hanging up a sign or poster, be sure to check out the rules before you spend a lot of money.

Short and Sweet

When you use advertising in a transit setting, be sure to keep it simple. Since your audience is on the go, you need to keep both your message and your graphics clean and minimal, so that your audience can absorb them as they hurry to reach their destination. You should also try to tailor your ad to the transit type or location it appears in. Thus, for example, if you were running an ad on a subway train, you might reference the appropriate stop for your business rather than just the street address.

Transit Ads

Want to reach people who can't get away from your ad? Look for places where people are in transit—sitting in a taxi, waiting for a bus, standing in line at an airport terminal, or stuck in rush hour traffic.

Transit advertising has the advantage of reaching a large captive audience. The size of that audience—especially in a busy place like an airport terminal—means that the reach of these ads can rival that of even television ads. In most cases, the prospect can't escape. If, for example, an ad appears on the back of a passenger's airline seat tray table, that traveler is going to be looking at it for hours. And even though drivers pass highway billboard ads quickly, they're still going to see them day after day on their commutes to work—meaning the information they contain is bound to stick.

What's more, transit ads can be highly localized. You can place them just on the bus stops in the neighborhood where your restaurant or insurance brokerage firm is located (rather than paying to place them all over town). Your transit ads can even be interactive—for example, a computerized ad display in the backseat of a taxi can let prospects choose the category of information (and thus ads) they want to see.

For all of these reasons, transit ads can be highly effective marketing vehicles—particularly for the following types of entrepreneurial companies:

- **Companies whose target customers are likely to use the type of transit where the ads will appear.** For instance, if your target audience is made up of corporate executives, airport and airline ads represent good advertising choices because your customers are likely to be frequent flyers.

- **Companies whose primary business is local.** If you cater to a very specific area, you can choose a transit ad program that serves just your neighborhood.

- **Businesses people are likely to patronize soon after being in transit.** These include restaurants or food establishments, hotels (for airline travelers), and more.

- **Companies that target tourists.** If tourists are your target customers, airlines, taxis, and trains are great places to advertise.

Most transit ads are charged based on the number of people who are likely to come into contact with your ad on a CPM, or cost per thousand, basis. You'll pay to have your ad displayed for a period of time—typically a month at minimum; however, many transit agencies require longer contracts. And don't forget the expense of designing and producing the ad.

Some of your options for transit advertising include.

- **Buses.** Bus stops, sides of buses, bus interiors.
- **Subways.** Subway terminals, inside subway trains.
- **Airlines.** Airport terminals, airline magazines, airline in-flight "radio."
- **Billboards.** On highways and roads.
- **Taxis.** Taxi tops, taxi seat backs (including video displays).
- **Trains.** Train stations, inside some trains.

AMPLE: **SUBWAY AD**

TIME FOR A SWEET STOP?

Aldo's

Your Dessert Destination

At 4ᵗʰ & Pine
Subway Stop: Central Square

555-EAT-CAKE
(555-328-2253)

RAINSTORMING

YOUR TRANSIT ADVERTISING

List the type of transit your target audience uses regularly: _____

_____

_____

List the transit advertising options that could work well for your business: _____

_____

_____

Draft the wording or sketch a design of an ad that could work in a transit setting for your business:

_____

_____

Designing an Effective Yellow Pages Ad

Here are some tips for designing an effective Yellow Pages ad:

- Attract customers' attention by using a large headline focused on their needs and your competitive advantage. Some examples include "24-Hour/7-Day Service," "We Can Be There in an Hour," "The Largest Selection on the North Side," and "Open on Sunday."

- Bring to the fore your unique selling proposition; show prospective customers what sets you apart from competitors. Remember, your competitors are listed here as well.

- Briefly list your most important services or products.

- Use large type for your business name, phone number, website, and physical address (if relevant).

- List hours of operation—especially if they differ from the standard workday.

- Use photos or graphics (if appropriate) to grab people's attention.

- Negotiate with your ad rep for good placement, preferably near the top of the page and on the right side. You may need to pay for this placement, but sometimes you can negotiate preferred placement into your ad deal.

Yellow Pages and Other Print Business Directories

One type of advertising you should carefully consider when developing your marketing plan is that which appears in Yellow Pages directories. Since so many people turn to Yellow Pages directories for a wide variety of services and products, if you choose *not* to advertise in a Yellow Pages directory, you should at least be able to explain the reasoning behind your choice.

The Yellow Pages—the phone directory listing business numbers printed on yellow paper—used to be the No. 1 source for business information. As a result, the directories expanded from just a list of phone numbers to include display ads, providing readers with additional information—such as business hours, location, special services, and the like—and providing the phone company with extra revenue.

Eventually, the Internet began to offer much of this information; however, many people still turn to the Yellow Pages. The reason for this is threefold:

1. They're widely distributed (and typically free to every household or phone subscriber).

2. They're convenient and easy to use (organized by category and focused on just one city or even one neighborhood in a big city or metropolitan area).

3. They stick around. Your ad stays in a directory for a year, and most businesses and households hold on to them for at least that long.

Many of the major companies that print Yellow Pages directories also offer online and mobile phone counterparts as well as discounted (or perhaps even free) ad space in these venues for companies that advertise in the print edition.

While Yellow Pages were originally printed only by the phone companies today, many competing companies develop and offer business phone directories. (In the U.S., the term *Yellow Pages* can be widely used; however, in Canada and many other countries it's trademarked.) Business directories also exist for ethnic groups (for example, the Korean-American Yellow Pages) and specific industries (for example, a Yellow Pages directory for dentists). And there are also business directories purporting to include only prescreened or approved businesses.

When choosing whether to advertise in a Yellow Pages or business directory, keep in mind the following:

- This type of directory is best used to advertise services or products that people always need (rather than discretionary purchases). They're a particularly good choice if one of the key purchasing drivers is location. They're also a good choice if the customer is likely to need the service immediately (think plumbers, taxis, airport shuttles, locksmiths, appliance repair, pizza delivery, and so on). Some people will also turn to the Yellow Pages for professional services like dentists, accountants, and lawyers.

Yellow Pages display ads are typically not necessary for professional services or products—such as business consulting, engineers, and scientific instruments—which aren't in demand by the general public.

Unlike Internet ads, Yellow Page ads don't work particularly well for most personal consumable products and products that people enjoy shopping for (such as clothing, accessories, consumer electronics). The same holds true for the stores that sell such items.

Yellow Pages ads are good for companies targeting older customers—that is, those who grew up using the Yellow Pages and are thus less likely to turn to the Internet for the same information.

Your listing will appear on the same page and in the same section as your competitors' listings, making it easy for customers to call all of the numbers and comparison shop. That, in turn, means that unless your products and services are competitively priced, the Yellow Pages may not be the appropriate venue for them.

Although not necessarily cheap, Yellow Pages ads are affordable for most businesses, ranging in price from free (for a simple listing, sometimes offered if you have a business account with the phone company that publishes the Web pages) to thousands of dollars per month for a full-page print ad. Billing structures also vary: some may ask you to pay in full up front; however, most charge on a monthly basis. Be sure to check before you commit.

If you decide that a Yellow Pages listing is likely to benefit your business, choose your directory company carefully. In cities and larger communities, there tend to be many to choose from. You'll get more bang for your buck if you choose one that includes:

■ **An online component.** Web listings increase the chances that potential customers will find you through search engines.

■ **A print edition that's the most widely viewed Yellow Pages directory in your community.** Be aware, however, that this option may be more expensive. As with media ads, be sure to ask for CPM (cost per thousand exposures).

■ **Your competitors' listings.** If you're in one directory and all of your competitors are in another, you may not be viewed as a player in the field. (On the other hand, the lack of competition in the first directory may result in more business. You might want to experiment with both to see which brings you the most calls.)

What's in a Number?

If you're starting a business and need to get a phone number, ask your telephone company for one that your customers are likely to remember. This is especially useful if you plan to put the number on signs, ads that customers are only likely to view for a short time (for example, transit ads), and in the Yellow Pages.

If possible, get a number that corresponds to a word, since people remember words much more easily then they do numbers. Then work out what the digits of the number will spell. For example, if you're advertising a service for children, try to get the last four numbers to spell out *KIDS, TOTS,* or *4FUN.* If you're in the loan business, you might want the digits to spell out *CASH.* It's ideal if you can get the whole number to spell out your business name. A consultant with the name Joe Bell would do well with the number 563-2355 (or J-O-E - B-E-L-L).

If you're able to get a number that relates to your name, be sure to include the actual numbers in parentheses wherever space allows in your marketing pieces. Although a great phone number can enhance your credibility and help customers remember your business, you want to make it as easy as possible for them to call. Thus, you should avoid making them figure out what letters correspond to which numbers on your phone pad.

If you can't get a phone number that correlates to your name, always include a memorable Web address along with the phone number. That way, even if customers can't write down or remember the number, they're likely to remember the word-based Web address (like JoeBell.com).

YOUR YELLOW PAGES AD

Will your business advertise in a Yellow Pages or other business directory? _____

If so, why? If not, why not? _____

List the directories that serve your area and business type:_____

List the products or services you plan to feature in your Yellow Page ad: _____

What need would customers be looking to fill when they turned to the Yellow Pages looking for a company like yours?_____

What competitive advantages would you highlight?_____

Draft the wording for a Yellow Pages display ad for your business. Make sure it includes:

■ **The need you fill for customers**

■ **Your name, phone number, address, and website**

■ **Your key products and services**

■ **Your competitive advantages and unique selling proposition**

_____

_____

_____

Coupons That Pack a Punch

One form of advertising that businesses have used for decades are coupons. Of course, coupons for discounts on products or services can be included in your print or even online ads, or they can be part of your direct mail program—all of which are covered elsewhere in this book. However, there are also many companies that create and distribute coupon packages directly to consumers—generally to every household in a neighborhood. One of the best known of these coupon packaging/direct mail companies is Val-Pak, which sends billions of coupons a year in more than a half-billion mailings. According to Val-Pak's owner, Cox Target Media, 85% of all adult consumers use coupons.

One advantage of being included in these coupon packages is that you get to participate in a direct mail program directed at a targeted community—without all the expense and trouble of creating your own program (including mailing list rental, printing, and so on).

These coupon packages are best for businesses catering to very local consumers, particularly in a specific neighborhood—companies like restaurants, dry cleaners, and house cleaners as well as personal service providers such as nail salons and optometrists.

Other Ad Venues

As companies have come to realize that by accepting ads they can get additional revenue with little work, virtually every business, building, and venue has come to accept them.

Some of the additional places you can advertise include:

- **Movie theaters.** Theater chains accept expensive, high production–value commercials from national advertisers that they run before feature films; however, many *local* movie theaters also run inexpensive, simple ads from local businesses.

- **Gas station pumps.** Realizing that people aren't going anywhere while they're filling up their tanks, many stations have now begun to include video monitors displaying ads on gas pumps.

- **Bathrooms.** Yes, bathrooms! There really is no escaping ads. Many bathrooms in public places like restaurants, sports stadiums, and public buildings have ads, typically for local businesses.

If you're going to advertise in any non-traditional location, remember to make your ad simple and straightforward. Many people in such locations will be aggravated to encounter ads, so it's best to make your ad as inoffensive and matter-of-fact as possible.

Guerrilla Marketing, Out-of-the Box, and Other Alternative Marketing Tactics

Over the years, a lot of terms have been used to describe inexpensive or unconventional approaches to marketing. *Guerrilla marketing* generally refers to inexpensive marketing tactics that are typically fairly grassroots. *Viral marketing* refers to marketing approaches that inspire one person to share information with others—spreading your message like a physical virus. *Out-of-the-box marketing* refers to any kind of creative and unique—even in-your-face—marketing tactic.

All of these terms arose in an attempt to describe marketing tactics that don't rely on the conventional advertising or public relations techniques typically employed by major corporations. While these tactics were once used primarily by startups and small businesses lacking huge ad budgets, some of them have proven so effective that large businesses have come to adopt them as well. In fact, mainstream advertising agencies have even set up divisions to run alternative marketing strategies for large corporations.

Some of the many guerrilla and out-of-the-box marketing strategies are described in the following pages. Keep in mind, however, that alternative marketing strategies are limited only by your imagination, your budget, and the tolerance of your target market. If you can come up with a unique and clever way to capture your prospects' attention and get your message out, go for it!

Marketing: It's All in Your Head (Hands, Belly, Legs, and Teeth …)

When it comes to finding ad space, nothing is sacred anymore, including the human body. That was the thinking of the folks at Kapust-Allen Enterprises In the early 2000s when the company hired college students to advertise for companies by printing temporary tattoos on their heads. Was it successful for the advertisers? It's hard to tell beyond the initial media frenzy it provoked, and Kapust-Allen is now defunct. The move did, however, generate significant buzz, and some marketers have already begun to experiment with full-body advertising, while others are using eBay auctions to seek bidders for ad space on hands, pregnant bellies, feet, ears, hair, teeth, and more!

> ❝ *Everyone loves getting tschotkes. People see them as little gifts. They bring them to their homes or put them on their desks in their offices where they look at them— and your message—all the time.* ❞
>
> **Janice Hill**
> **President**
> **Concepts in Advertising**

Advertising Specialty Items

Advertising specialty items—also known as giveaways, promotional items, swag, or *tschotkes*—are things you give away to customers and prospects. They're often very inexpensive (consisting of toys, knickknacks, and office supplies); however, they can also be fairly nice and relatively expensive (for example, a leather portfolio, an electronic device, or a carry-on suitcase). The key is that they are imprinted with a company's name, logo, and perhaps its tagline or a message related to the item itself. For example, a flashlight distributed by a management consulting firm might have the following emblazoned on it: "We light the path to your success."

Advertising specialty items offer many advantages. First and foremost, they're perceived as gifts rather than ads—which means your customer or prospect won't mind getting them. In fact, they may even stand in line at a trade show to get the blinking ball you're handing out so that they can bring it home to their kids. It's not unusual for employees returning from trade shows to boast about the *swag* they've taken away. Take advantage of this: it's a rare thing when people are happy to receive an ad.

Another advantage of this type of advertising is that it's *persistent*. People are much less likely to throw away a gift—even an inexpensive, relatively meaningless one—than an ad. They may already have a drawer filled with pens or a closet full of tote bags, but they're not going to throw yours away.

As with all marketing tactics, you'll want to be sure to consider the needs and behavior of your customer, as well as your marketing message, when choosing and distributing advertising specialty items. In other words, what will your customers want to pick up? Is it useful, attractive, and/or fun?

It also helps to think about the kinds of things your customers are likely to need in their daily lives (or at least are inclined to keep around)—whether you're targeting other businesses or consumers. The reason that so many giveaways take the form of office supplies is that people are likely to keep them on their desks. However, you can also relate your giveaway to your customers' professions or hobbies, or to your business. A mortgage company, for example, could give nice calculators to realtors. Likewise, a cooking supply store could give away measuring cups or jar openers.

Telemarketing

Unsolicited telephone calls to prospects—or *telemarketing*—is one of the least popular forms of marketing from the prospects' perspective. No one wants to get a interrupted by a phone call sales pitch. But does telemarketing work, and should you consider it for your business?

First, recognize that regardless of how the word sounds, telemarketing is more of a sales technique than a marketing technique. So think of it as *telesales* instead. After all, the goal of the cold call sales call is to get someone to sign up for a magazine subscription, donate to a charity, book a vacation package—it's rarely just to build a company's brand name and get a message out.

Part of the reason for this is that telemarketing is relatively expensive. Even though there are automated programs that dial numbers until they reach a live person, you have to pay for a person to be on the phone making

BRAINSTORMING

YOUR GIVEAWAYS

List three promotional items that would reflect your business:

_____
_____
_____

List three promotional items that would work with your audience:

_____
_____
_____

Why would they work? What would be their appeal?

_____
_____
_____

How would they deliver your brand message?

_____
_____
_____
_____

the pitch. Although response rates for telemarketing calls may be higher than direct mail response rates (a Direct Marketing Association showed a response rate of more than 5% for telemarketing compared to less than 2% for direct mail), the costs are far higher as well.

Cold call telesales work best for products and services that can be sold by someone using a script. After all, the people hired to make sales for these companies are unlikely to know much more about the product or service than what's available to them in a pre-prepared script. Thus, telesales works best for large companies that can afford professional telemarketing services or that can hire a telemarketing staff.

It's also become more difficult to perform cold call telemarketing since the creation of the National Do Not Call lists in the U.S. and Canada, because consumers can now register to keep telemarketers from calling.

The one situation in which telemarketing can work well for entrepreneurial companies is when they have their own lists of prospects to call. These prospects can include former customers, prospects you've met at trade shows, and individuals who've signed up to receive more information. In these situations, having in-house staff who can follow up with phone calls can be a very effective way of both raising your company's visibility and making sales.

Sources of Ad Specialty Items

Looking for cheap ad space in your customer's home or business? Try these sites for a good selection of promotional items:

- **Concepts in Advertising:** http://imprintedeverythings.com/
- **4imprint USA:** www.4imprint.com
- **Epromos:** www.epromos.com

What's the Best Marketing Tool? *A Waiting List*

It's simply human nature: if a lot of people want something, you're likely to want it too. If you see a line of people around the block waiting for the new Apple iPhone or spending the night outside the store before the release of a book or game, your desire for that iPhone, book, or game is likely to increase. That's why some companies enhance demand through *intentional shortages*. No company, of course, will admit to this practice—after all, it's terrible PR to say you're willing to disappoint your customers. However, some companies do manage their inventories of in-demand products (for as long as customers are willing to wait) to limit the number available at any one time. In this way, they create a "must have" aura for these products. Of course, if your customers aren't willing to wait, you're going to lose all of those sales.

Party On!

Sick of being the one throwing parties? Then invite your customers to throw one for you! When a spa opened recently, it decided to forego advertising or a big grand opening and instead invited key influencers—primarily prominent women in the area—to host "parties" at the spa on various evenings. At these parties, the spa provided mini-services—short pedicures, facials, and massages—along with wine and cheese. This enabled the spa to be introduced to a much wider group than it would have reached with just one grand opening—and the parties cost less than newspaper or radio ads.

Product Placement

Everyone's seen celebrities using brand name products such as computers, soft drinks, cars, and sunglasses in the movies, on TV, or when they're snapped in photos for magazines. What you may not have realized is that companies either paid to have those products shown or gave them to the celebrities in return for the exposure. This is called *product placement* .

Although high-profile product placements involving movies or celebrities can cost a lot and take a great deal of time and effort to achieve, you can do a low-cost version of the same thing by getting your products placed in well-respected venues where your customers and prospects are likely to see them.

For example, a florist could give a weekly bouquet to a high-end salon with a "Flowers provided by …" placard or business cards nearby, since the salon is likely to attract the type of customers who are likely to buy lavish floral arrangements. Likewise, the maker of a new fitness drink might donate bottles of its product to speakers at an industry conference so that the audience would see industry leaders consuming the drink.

Ideally, you want to place your products at prominent venues or with *influencers*—individuals who are highly regarded in their sphere and help drive others' choices. One way to do this is through *seeding,* or giving your product to well-respected leaders of a particular demographic, group, or network (whether social or business) to influence others to try the product. If the members of a high-tech industry association, for example, see their chairperson using your new hand-held device, they're more likely to start up a discussion about it and perhaps purchase it themselves.

Events/Happenings

Everybody loves a party. Events can be an excellent way to attract customers and increase your company's name recognition. Entrepreneurial companies—especially those just being launched—can use events to let the world at large know they exist.

If you're opening a new restaurant, a great way to let the community try out your offerings and introduce them to your menu is to host a grand opening. Naturally, you'd invite friends, family, and colleagues so that they could serve as better referral sources for you in the future; however, you'd also want to invite staff from businesses in nearby buildings, concierges and other staff from area hotels, and even taxi drivers. Think about your grand opening as a way to cultivate your referral network as well as to attract future customers. By inviting industry leaders, members of the media, and potential clients, you can generate buzz and excitement about your product or service offering.

Other events you may want to consider hosting include:

- Holiday parties
- Parties/Hospitality suites at trade shows
- Concerts/Fashion shows/Sporting events
- Footraces and golf tournaments

While hosting your own events can be costly and time consuming, you also have the option of sponsoring other groups' events or piggybacking with another company to put on an event together.

BRAINSTORMING

YOUR EVENTS

List five events you could hold or host that would help attract prospects and increase your company exposure to your target audience:

1. _____

2. _____

3. _____

4. _____

5. _____

Community- and Cause-Related Marketing

People want to feel good about the products they buy and the companies they patronize. Sure, they want the best product at the best price, but when presented with similar products at similar prices, they're likely to choose the one they can feel good about purchasing. For some segments of a market, choosing a product or company that reflects their values trumps even price considerations.

That's where cause and community marketing come in.

In *cause-related marketing*, a for-profit business lets it be known that it's giving part of its proceeds or some other benefit (for example, a donation of goods or materials) to one or more nonprofit organizations or that it's committed to a social cause. The cause will focus on a mission likely to interest the for-profit's target customer. For instance, a natural food energy bar enjoyed by hikers might give part of its proceeds to an organization that protects the environment. The for-profit company will also make it known that it donates a portion of its profits to a particular charity or to an organization that reflects certain values. For example, a company that cares about animals might indicate the following on its website: "A portion of our pre-tax profits are donated to Wildlife Conservation Network (www.wildnet.org)." Or it might include the statement "No animal testing."

It's also important to note that contributions aren't limited to money. Businesses can also donate employee time, expertise, office space, and other assets as a means of assisting their nonprofit partners, or they can source raw materials or products in a way that reflects their values, such as "We use only Fair Trade coffee beans."

> *"A product with a purpose is infinitely more marketable, but it has to be good. You can't market something that feels good but tastes terrible. It can't just be a good story; it has to be a great product."*
>
> **James Parker**
> **Associate Global Coordinator for Produce**
> **Whole Foods Markets**

Closely related to cause marketing is *community marketing*—associating your for-profit business with community nonprofit organizations. Giving a Little League team the money for uniforms and then getting the name of your plumbing company sewn on back of the uniforms may not seem like it has much in common with helping to save the habitat of the snow leopard by putting a picture of the snow leopard on your website; however, both tactics positively associate your company and products with something that consumers value.

The following are some examples of cause- and community-related marketing:

- A maker of children's craft toys donating some of its products to underprivileged children

- A gourmet coffee company sponsoring a sustainable farming program in the communities where it sources its beans

- A tool company donating hammers and other tools to Habitat to Humanity

- A grocery store participating in a scrip program in which it donates a portion of your expenditures to the school of your choice

- An attorney doing pro bono work for a community homeless organization

- A pet food manufacturer supporting animal adoption programs

- A dry cleaner laundering business clothes donated for low-income first-time workers

Usually, cause and community marketing creates a win-win situation for all concerned: the for-profit business, the nonprofit, the constituents or cause the nonprofit is serving, and the consumer. In general, the for-profit business, in addition to feeling good about the impact of its sales, may see a marketing boost from attracting customers who feel good about what the company is doing. The nonprofit, its constituents, and the cause it is championing get more donation dollars, volunteer time, and exposure. Consumers like the fact that they're getting a good product while improving a community or the environment at the same time.

Of course, to get a marketing boost from cause and community activities, you have to actually let customers and prospects know about your actions. You could quietly give money or time to a cause you and your company believe in, but that wouldn't be marketing, it would be a charitable activity or a socially responsible activity that helped your employees feel good about working for you.

If you want to leverage your cause and community activities to have a *marketing* impact, you have to let people know about them—on your products, websites, and ads; with posters or banners at events; and the like.

Keep in mind that customers can often sense when a company's heart is not in its cause-related marketing effort—that is, when its motives are focused on the revenues generated from its supposedly good deed rather than on actually making a difference. A company that is sincere in its efforts will reflect that in its *overall* approach to the problem or cause. For instance, if a clothing company is giving proceeds to a children's safety organization but having its merchandise made in factories that use child labor, the media and the public will eventually catch on—which could be disastrous for the company.

At the same time, a good cause is no substitute for a bad product. If your cereal box is plastered with messages about your support of organic farming, but the cereal itself tastes like cardboard, people aren't going to buy it. For cause-related marketing to work, the following four factors must be in place:

- A good cause
- A partnership with a reputable organization
- A good product
- A sincere goodwill effort to support the cause and make a positive impact.

BRAINSTORMING

YOUR CAUSE- AND COMMUNITY-RELATED MARKETING

List five charitable or community organizations or causes whose mission and goals would be a good fit for your product, service, or company and describe the ways you could work with those organizations.

1. _____

2. _____

3. _____

4. _____

5. _____

List three ways your company could let prospects know about your commitment to a cause without turning them off:

1. _____

2. _____

3. _____

Return on Investment for Signs, Other Ads, and Out-of-the-Box Marketing

As with every aspect of your marketing plan, you'll want to carefully monitor the return on investment you receive from your signs, other types of advertising, and out-of-the-box marketing efforts. While some of the marketing methods that fall into this category—such as Web directory listings (for which you can employ Web analytics)—lend well to ROI analysis, many of them do not. For example, how can you measure your ROI for the fancy sign that hangs above your door announcing your business without taking it down completely—and thus risk losing a huge number of prospective customers (including all of those people who can't find your business once your sign is gone). And how do you know how many more people are patronizing your pizza parlor because they're happy to see your name emblazoned across the backs of the local Little League team's uniforms?

Still, it's worth attempting to figure out your ROI for these activities because it will help you break out their costs, analyze their results (both financial and non-financial), and then plan your marketing activities accordingly.

Calculating Your Signs, Other Ads, and Out-of-the-Box Marketing ROI

The following worksheet can help you get started on your own ROI analysis. Simply describe what your signs, ads, and out-of-the-box marketing efforts will entail, and fill in the requested data to get an idea of the ROI you can expect from these marketing tactics.

Here are some tips for using the worksheets (and calculating your ROI):

- **Be sure to break out all of your costs.** While many of the techniques described in this chapter represent some of the most cost-effective ways to entice customers to purchase your products or services, they still have associated costs. Thus, don't forget to include things like the cost of printing and mailing coupon books, the value of your time if you're donating your services to a local charity, or the expense of feeding an army of Little Leaguers if your restaurant is sponsoring the local championship.

- **Remember non-financial goals.** While you may not be able to put a cash value on things like brand awareness and customer perception, these are important components of any marketing campaign, and as such must be considered when calculating return on investment.

RETURN ON INVESTMENT

SIGNS, OTHER ADS, AND OUT-OF-THE-BOX MARKETING ROI

Your business:_____

Your target market:_____

Description of your signs, ads, and out-of-the-box marketing tactics:_____

GOALS

Financial: _____

Non-financial: _____

PROJECTED COSTS

Cost of signs: _____

Cost of ads:_____

Cost of giveaways: _____

Parties/Events: _____

Printing and reproduction (for coupons):_____

Shipping and postage (for coupons):_____

Sponorships/Donations: _____

Writers:_____

Graphic designers/photographers:_____

Other consultants: _____

Total cost: _____

PROJECTED RETURNS, FINANCIAL

Annual revenue generated from signs, other ads, and out-of-the-box marketing tactics: _____

Total cost: _____

Total projected net financial gain (annual revenue and sales minus total cost): _____

PROJECTED RETURNS, NON-FINANCIAL

_____

_____

TOTAL ROI (Total Net Financial Returns Plus Total Non-financial Returns):_____

SIGNS, OTHER ADS, AND OUT-OF-THE-BOX MARKETING BUDGET (12 MONTHS

	JAN	FEB	MARCH	APRIL	MAY
Professional Assistance					
Writers					
Graphic designers/Photographers/Illustrators					
Sign painters					
Ad agencies					
Event planners/staff					
Other consultants					
Ad Buys					
Transit ads					
Yellow Pages/Directories					
Billboards					
Other non-traditional ad buys					
Printing/Reproduction					
Magnetic signs					
Banners/Posters					
Coupons					
Event flyers/Handouts					
Other printing and reproduction costs					
Supplies/Cost of Goods/Manufacturing					
Place-of-business signs					
Ad specialties/giveaways					
Other supplies/goods/manufacturing costs					
Other					
Event sponsorships					
Cause sponsorships					
Donations					
TOTAL					

NOTE: An electronic version of this worksheet is available as part of the Planning Shop's Marketing Budget Templates package.

JUNE	JULY	AUGUST	SEPT	OCT	NOV	DEC	TOTAL

BUILDING YOUR MARKETING PLAN

OTHER TYPES OF MARKETING

Drawing from the Brainstorming worksheets in this section, plan the other types of marketing tactics (including in-store marketing, sampling, signs, additional ad types, and out-of-the-box marketing techniques) you'll use in your campaign.

1. List the retailers (including chains as well as local stores, craft fairs, farmers market, and so on) where you plan to procure shelf space for your products, and explain why they're a good match for your products/services:

_____

2. List the in-store marketing techniques you plan to use, and explain why they're a good choice for your products/services:

_____

3. Is your product or service suitable for sampling? If so, list three places you plan to sample it and explain why each venue serves as a good marketing vehicle for your product or service:

_____

4. What will your samples entail, and will they require any supporting materials or handouts?

_____

_____

5. Who will distribute your samples and how?

_____

6. List the types of signs (place of business, vehicle, public location) you plan to use to promote your business and briefly describe their contents and specific locations:

_____

7. What type of transit ads will you use to promote your products or services (buses, subways, airlines, billboards, taxis, trains)? Briefly describe why each type you chose is a good fit for your business

_____

8. Do you plan to advertise in a Yellow Pages or other business directory, and if so, why?

_____

9. List the directories you plan to advertise in and your reasons for choosing each:

_____

10. What products/services and competitive advantages will you feature in your Yellow Pages ads?

_____

11. List some non-traditional locations you could place ads for your business (for example, movie theaters, gas pumps, bathrooms):

_____

12. Will you use coupon packages to promote your products or services?

_____

13. Do you plan to give away promotional items to market your business? If so, list and describe them:

_____

14. Do you plan to use telemarketing—or more accurately, telesales—as one of your marketing tactics? If so, who will be on your call list?

_____

15. Will you use product placement to promote your business? If so, what will you place, and where?

_____

16. Will you hold any parties or events to promote your business? If so, describe the events and their functions:

_____

17. Will you associate your business with or contribute to a cause, charity, or community organization? If so, list the organizations and describe how you'll work with them as well as how you'll make customers and prospects aware of your involvement:

_____

18. How will the additional marketing tactics described in this section bring you closer to your marketing goals?

_____

_____

_____

_____

_____

_____

_____

SECTION VII

Pulling It All Together

CHAPTER 30

Creating Your Marketing Plan

You've now worked your way through all of the sections in this book. You've set your goals. You've learned which marketing tactics are available to you. You've filled in worksheets and brainstormed about the possibilities. And you've probably narrowed down your list of tactics to those you think will be most effective for your business. Ideally, you've also started to develop a budget, evaluating which marketing tactics offer you the best return on investment (ROI).

Now, it's time to pull it all together in an overall marketing plan. That means revisiting your goals, reviewing your tactics, and revising your budget. Most importantly, it means making some tough decisions—because unfortunately you can't pursue every marketing tactic, and you're likely to have chosen more than you have the money, time, or personnel to actually execute.

So how *do* you decide what stays and what goes when it comes to your final marketing plan and budget? You won't go wrong if you base your decisions on these critical components:

■ **Your goals.** Your choice of tactics and activities must fit the goals you set in Section I, Marketing Essentials. Are your goals to get customers to take a specific action? To drive sales? How much of your marketing efforts are aimed at brand building or generating investor interest? Keep in mind both your quantitative (numerical) and qualitative (more subjective) goals as you make your marketing plan decisions.

■ **Your milestones and metrics.** Once you've executed on your marketing plan, how will you know if you've achieved success? You need milestones to measure your progress along the way and metrics to evaluate how well you've done. Back in Section I, you completed a Brainstorming Your Marketing Milestones worksheet (page 83), where you laid out specific achievements and the date by which you hoped to accomplish them. Go back to those milestones now—review them—and create a final milestone list to be included in your marketing plan.

■ **Your brand.** You must project a consistent image in all of your marketing efforts if your brand is to remain strong. That means you must be clear

Let's Go Over This One More Time ...

The key to any successful marketing campaign is repetition, repetition, repetition. Remember: it takes multiple exposures for your message to be absorbed by its intended recipients—and even longer to build a brand. This means that you must choose a few tactics that you can employ repeatedly on the same market rather than adopt a scattershot approach in which you try one tactic after another on different audiences.

about all of your brand elements, and you must spell them out in your marketing plan. Go back to Section I, Chapter 6 ("Your Brand and Core Image"), and review the core aspects of a brand. Then, in your plan, remember to delineate the following brand elements:

— **Name(s).** Although it seems obvious, the nomenclature you use for your company, products or services, special features or advertising campaigns, and more must be consistent. (For instance, do you label your largest size offering Large, Extra Large, or Giant?) Make sure that everyone in your company uses those names consistently.

— **Colors.** Identify which colors will be used in all of your marketing and branding activities. Be very specific—choosing the exact PMS (Pantone Matching System) colors and using them consistently on every marketing piece you produce, including your website, packaging, ads, brochures, business cards, and so on.

— **Typefaces.** Choose consistent typefaces for your marketing materials. While you may add to or change some of these for certain marketing materials, the typeface for your brand name—on your packaging, website, and so on—should remain consistent. It's part of your brand.

— **Graphics/Images.** Likewise, key graphics, such as logos, should be used consistently in your marketing efforts. Include a copy of key corporate graphic images and logos in your marketing plan.

— **Look and feel.** If you've been consistent in the above-described elements, you will have achieved a general "look and feel" that's evident in all of your marketing components. However, there may be additional components that add to your look and feel, such as the use of unbleached recycled cardboard for all of your packaging or playful language that appears across your marketing components.

■ **Your brand promise and message.** One of the most important things for you to spell out in your marketing plan—and reinforce in all of your marketing activities—is your brand promise. You must be very clear on what your company stands for and what differentiates it from competitors. Moreover, you must have a clear and compelling core message—what it is you want customers and prospects to remember about you. You may also develop this core message into a tagline, which you can then use to reinforce your message time and again.

■ **Your budget.** Face it, the best marketing plan in the world won't work if you don't have the funds to carry it out. In new and growing companies, money is always an issue. For this reason, you should focus on affordable tactics that will enable you to maintain an ongoing marketing presence. When it comes to budgeting, be conservative. It's tempting to plan a marketing campaign based on the increased money you think your marketing efforts will bring in; however, that's not necessarily realistic. Instead, be cautious: consider how much money you *know* you can afford to spend on marketing, and then ask yourself, "Which other business activities will I have to curtail to spend money on marketing?" Conversely, you should also ask yourself, "What will happen to my income if I *don't* spend sufficient funds on marketing?" There's always a trade-off; that's why it's important to have a marketing planning process in place.

■ **Your other resources.** If your marketing efforts are to be successful, you must have enough time, personnel, attention, and support to manage them effectively. However, entrepreneurial companies can rarely afford the luxury of a full in-house marketing staff. For that's reason, it's important to recognize the other demands on your time and that of your staff when making final decisions about your marketing plan.

Developing Your In-House Marketing Staff Budget

There's one final budget worksheet you'll need to complete before finalizing your overall marketing budget—your in-house marketing staff budget. For each of the marketing tactics described in this guide, you've already developed a budget and accounted for any consultants or outside experts you'll need to hire. However, you also need to financially account for the time that your own staff will be spending on marketing activities.

Let's face it: in most entrepreneurial companies (especially small ones and newer ones), staff members often do more than one job. Thus, you may have one or several full-time marketing employees—such as a marketing director—but you'll likely need to call upon others in your company to help out with certain marketing activities. For example, you're unlikely to have employees whose sole job it is to staff your trade show booth. Thus, some of the people helping out in your trade show booth today may be assisting you ship products tomorrow.

This means that many of the people you list in your in-house staff marketing budget may only spend 10%, 5%, or even less of their time on marketing. That's OK—just indicate what *portion* of their time they'll be spending on marketing activities.

The Planning Process

Now it's time to actually put together your marketing plan.

First, set aside time to focus on your marketing plan. Ideally, you should allow at least a day—every year—to develop an annual marketing plan. If this is the first time you've created a marketing plan for a particular company (or product/service), the process will take a bit longer. After all, you have to decide on key issues, such as your brand identity, target market, message, and so on—however, you won't have to revisit these issues every year. Even if yours is only a one-person company, having an annual marketing plan in place will save money and insure that you use your limited marketing dollars more effectively.

Second, review the Brainstorming worksheets from each section of this book. You should have been working through these as you progressed through the book, but if you haven't, now is the time to fill in the critical worksheets for the marketing tactics you're most likely to use.

Third, pull together the final Building Your Marketing Plan worksheets from each section of this book. These worksheets are designed to serve as the basis of your marketing plan, making it quick and easy to

---

The Best Marketing Staff for Entrepreneurial Companies

So you know you can't hire a full-on marketing department for your entrepreneurial company. What, then, should you look for in your few key marketing employees?

■ **They must be flexible.** Since your marketing staff will inevitably be performing a range of marketing tasks—not to mention helping out wherever else your company needs assistance—they must wear many hats ably and willingly.

■ **They must be sales oriented.** Entrepreneurial companies are typically more focused on sales than on brand building—a key difference from large corporate marketing departments, where staff can often perform their jobs with little eye on the company's bottom line. In addition, entrepreneurial companies may have other objectives, such as increasing awareness and impressing potential investors or strategic partners.

■ **They must be energetic.** Your marketing staff must have the same drive as your company overall—especially important given the fact that they often serve as the public face of your company.

finalize your plan. You may have to make some changes—now that you've completed all of the sections—but these will serve as the foundation for your marketing plan.

Next, fill in the budget worksheets. If you have the Electronic Marketing Budget worksheets (which come with the Deluxe Binder Edition of this book or can be downloaded from www.PlanningShop.com), the process will go much faster. If you haven't already, you may need to gather critical information—such as the specific costs of the marketing techniques you're considering (for example, advertising, direct mail, SEM, and so on).

Then, bring together all of the people who will help carry out the marketing plan. Involve all key players, including:

- Those who set the strategic direction of your company, such as the president or CEO
- Those charged with responsibility for your marketing success, such as your marketing staff
- Those charged with executing your marketing plan, such as your outsourced consultants and administrative staff

It's important that everyone involved in your marketing activities agrees with and understands your overall marketing plan.

Finally, and most importantly, set dates and deadlines for your marketing activities. Give staff members assignments and responsibilities so that you can turn your marketing plan into a plan of action.

Conclusion

Now comes the most important part: *executing on your plan.*

Just going through the process of preparing a marketing plan is incredibly useful. It gives you an opportunity to think through critical aspects of your branding, positioning, strategy, target market, and more. Plus, it provides an opportunity to look at *all* of the marketing tactics available to you, consider which are right for your business, and then focus and direct your marketing campaigns.

To make a real impact on your income, bottom line, and overall success, though, you must now take action. Make your marketing plan a living document. Keep it visible where you can refer to it often. Bring it to staff meetings and review your action plan and milestones. Throughout the year, review what's working and why—as well as what's not and why.

You now have your Successful Marketing Plan: use it and see the positive effects it will have on your bottom line. You're on your way to success!

In-House Marketing Staff Budget

Use this worksheet to create an annual budget for your expenditures on in-house marketing staff. Figure out how many staff people will carry out marketing tasks and determine the percentage of their time they'll be spending on marketing tasks.

IN-HOUSE MARKETING STAFF BUDGET (12 MONTHS)

	MONTHLY SALARY	% OF TIME DEVOTED TO MARKETING	JAN, FEB, MARCH, ETC	TOTAL
Marketing Staff				
Marketing director				
Marketing assistants				
Public relations staff				
Trade show/Events manager				
Writers				
Graphic/Web designers				
Website manager				
SEO/SEM managers				
Social networking manager(s)				
IT/Tech management/support				
Administrative support				
Non-marketing Staff				
Non-marketing staff/Others				
Title of non-marketing position				
Title of non-marketing position				
Other In-house Staff				
TOTAL				

Note: Because of space constraints, this 12-Month Budget does not include a column for each month. Instead, you will have to use another piece of paper to include those figure, then add them up and insert the result in the Total column here. However, in the Electronic Marketing Budget Templates, all 12 months are included.

! **NOTE:** An electronic version of this worksheet is available as part of the Planning Shop's Marketing Budget Templates package.

TOTAL MARKETING BUDGET (12 MONTHS)

	JAN	FEB	MARCH	APRIL	MAY
Print Advertising					
Radio Advertising					
TV Advertising					
Networking					
Word-of-Mouth Marketing					
Trade Shows					
Public Relations					
Print Collateral					
Direct Mail					
Website					
Search Engine Marketing & Optimization					
Email Marketing					
Other Online Advertising					
Blogs, Social Networks, and Other Online Tactics					
In-Store Promotion & Sampling					
Signs, Other Ads, and Out-of-the-box Marketing					
In-house Marketing Staff					
TOTAL					

NOTE: An electronic version of this worksheet is available as part of the Planning Shop's Marketing Budget Templates package.

JUNE	JULY	AUGUST	SEPT	OCT	NOV	DEC	TOTAL

TOTAL MARKETING BUDGET BY EXPENDITURE TYPE (12 MONTHS)

	JAN	FEB	MARCH	APRIL	MAY
Professional Assistance					
Ad Buys					
Printing/Reproduction					
Shipping and Postage					
Media Services					
Membership/Subscription Fees					
Trade Show Fees					
Travel					
Entertainment					
Referral & Loyalty Programs					
Website Hosting					
Supplies/Cost of Goods/Manufacturing					
Other Expenses					
In-house Marketing Staff					
TOTAL					

! **NOTE:** An electronic version of this worksheet is available as part of the Planning Shop's Marketing Budget Templates package.

JUNE	JULY	AUGUST	SEPT	OCT	NOV	DEC	TOTAL

Index

About the Contributors

Rick Allen

Vice President, Cabovillas.com

Rick Allen is a search engine marketing and Web design specialist, as well as vice president of Cabovillas.com, which specializes in luxury villa rental and travel in Cabo San Lucas, Mexico.

Loni Amato

President, Ingenious Solutions

Loni Amato heads Ingenious solutions, a full-service advertising firm in Los Gatos, California. Her company plans and creates ad campaigns for a variety of media, specializing in commercial TV ad placement and production.

Adryenn Ashley

Media Strategist

Adryenn Ashley is a media strategist, entrepreneur, actress, and award-winning filmmaker who uses well-honed media and publicity techniques to market entrepreneurs through radio, TV, print media, and the Internet.

Veena Bhasin-Naszady

Account Executive, The Kingston Whig-Standard

Veena Bhasin-Naszady is a seasoned print advertising professional and account executive with *The Kingston Whig-Standard* in Ontario, Canada. Tracing its roots back to 1834, the newspaper is considered Canada's oldest continuously published daily.

Matt Blumberg

Chairman & CEO, Return Path, Inc.

Matt Blumberg heads New York email marketing firm Return Path, Inc., which has helped some of the world's most successful companies use email more effectively. He is also the author of *Sign Me Up!: A Marketer's Guide to E-mail Newsletters that Build Relationships and Boost Sales.* Previously, he served as the vice president of marketing and Internet services for MovieFone.

Janice Hill

President, Concepts in Advertising

For 27 years, Janice Hill has helped companies develop innovative advertising and branding strategies using imprinted promotional items. Based in Jacksonville, Oregon, Concepts in Advertising offers a wide range of branded novelties, from breath mints to yo-yos.

John Jantsch

Author, Duct Tape Marketing and Owner, Jantsch Communications

John Jantsch is a marketing and digital technology coach, award-winning social media publisher, and author of *Duct Tape Marketing: The World's Most Practical Small Business Marketing Guide*. His Duct Tape Marketing Blog was chosen as a *Forbes* favorite for small business and is a Harvard Business School featured marketing site. His "Hype" column can be found monthly in *Entrepreneur* magazine along with his podcast on Entrepreneur.com.

Alan Luckow

President, Luckow Design

Al Luckow has been creating marketing materials ranging from business cards to websites for more than two decades, and designs from his studios in Ben Lomond, California, just south of Silicon Valley. His extensive client list includes Apple Computer, Canon Systems, The Fillmore in San Francisco, Joe Satriani, Logitech, Mitsumi Electronics, the National Association of Broadcasters, and more.

Julie McHenry

President, Communications Insight

Julie McHenry has provided strategic business communication services to a broad array of corporations for more than 20 years. She specializes in helping companies move through various points of corporate change, devising strategic, thoughtful plans of action. Julie has provided public relations and marketing communications services for such companies as Microsoft, Symantec, Intuit, Excite, Toys "r" Us, and Regent Pacific Management Corp.

James Parker

Associate Global Coordinator for Produce, Whole Foods Markets.

James Parker of Whole Foods Markets has been working in various merchandising, marketing, and strategy roles with the company for 22 years. In that time, he developed extensive expertise in in-store marketing, socially responsible marketing, and building customer loyalty, and has been instrumental in helping the company grow from one small store in Austin, Texas, to more than 270 stores in North America and the United Kingdom.

Mark Ramsey

President, Hear 2.0

Mark Ramsey is author of *Fresh Air: Marketing Gurus in Radio* and president of Hear 2.0, an audio entertainment strategy company. For nearly a quarter of a century, Mark has been a key strategic advisor to top broadcasters nationwide, including CBS Radio, Clear Channel Communications, Entercom Communications, Entravision Communications, Saga Communications, Susquehanna Radio, Corus Entertainment, and many others.

Susan Schwartz

Owner, You Who Branding

As a facilitator, speaker, writer, and coach, Susan Schwartz has more than 20 years of experience helping clients define who they are in everything they do. As head of You Who Branding, Susan has created award-winning ad campaigns for a wide range of businesses, with an extensive client list that includes 3-Com, AT&T Wireless, Oracle, SBC, Sun Microsystems, and United Health Care.

Kira Wampler

Marketing Manager, Intuit

As a marketing manager at Intuit, Kira Wampler has helped the QuickBooks team build its word-of-mouth programs. A survivor of several startups, she recently launched the QuickBooks Women's Small Business Center to provide women with the tools, networking, and resources they need to achieve success.

Sandra Yancey

Founder and CEO, eWomenNetwork

Sandra Yancy is one of the leading authorities on networking and relationship building. Since starting eWomenNetwork with just 20 women in her personal database in 2000, she has grown the organization into a powerful entrepreneurial force with 113 chapters throughout the U.S. and Canada, and a database of more than 500,000 women business owners and professionals. Sandra is also the author of *Relationship Networking: The Art of Turning Contacts into Connections* and has been featured in *Chicken Soup for the Entrepreneur's Soul*. In addition, Sandra hosts the eWomenNetwork Radio Show, out of Dallas, TX.

Acknowledgments

Rhonda Abrams would like to thank:

Julie Vallone, whose research and writing skills helped make this book possible. This was a huge project, and Julie helped me tackle it with energy, good humor, and a flair for clear and engaging writing. Julie has worked on a number of book projects for The Planning Shop, including *Business Plan In A Day.*

Jill Simonsen, Editorial Project Manager, who took over this project mid-stream and saw it to its successful conclusion. Without Jill, and her organizational skills, editorial excellence, and years of professional publishing experience, this book might still be sitting on my computer. Aloha, Jill!

Sue Raisty-Egami, Electronic Marketing Budget Worksheet Project Manager. Sue took charge of quickly and accurately creating the Electronic Marketing Budget Worksheets that accompany this text. Sue's extensive years of project management of electronic products make her an invaluable addition to The Planning Shop team—as well as the fact that she's a joy to work with.

Rosa Whitten, Office Manager and all-around go-to woman of The Planning Shop's team. Rosa makes sure that everything in The Planning Shop actually works and that the bills get paid. She is an organizational champion and is invaluable—in terms of both her skills and her positive outlook. We are fortunate, indeed, to have her.

Diana Van Winkle, who now oversees the design of all books in The Planning Shop line and brought her graphic expertise to the design of this book. She is talented, responsive, and a delight to work with. Diana's skills ensure that The Planning Shop's books continue to be easy and pleasurable for readers to use.

Maggie Canon, Managing Editor. Maggie shepherded this book from conception. Maggie's professionalism was an invaluable addition to The Planning Shop. She was founding editor of *InfoWorld* and numerous other technology magazines and was also managing editor of the bestselling *America 24/7* series.

Mireille Majoor, Editorial Project Manager, who oversaw the bulk of the editorial process of this book. Mireille is a consummate professional and both The Planning Shop's books and readers have benefited from Mireille's commitment to excellence.

Kathryn Dean, who brought her eagle eye to the proofing process, ensuring that our books are pristine and error free, as well as developing a thorough Index, making it easy for readers to find exactly what they need quickly.

Arthur Wait, who originally designed the overall look and feel of The Planning Shop's line of books and products and developed our first website and electronic products. We are always amazed (though no longer surprised) by the range of Arthur's talents.

Julie Vallone would like to thank the following people for their expertise on a range of topics relating to marketing:

Marsha Fischer

Randy Peyser, AuthorOneStop

Electronic Marketing Budget Templates

Save Time. Save Hassles.

Electronic Marketing Budget Templates

Create a professional overall Annual Marketing Budget on your computer—quickly and easily. Just use the Electronic Marketing Budget Templates designed especially to accompany this book. These Excel-based templates comprise all of the marketing budget worksheets from this book in electronic format—as pre-formatted Excel spreadsheets.

Included:

- Each and every budget worksheet from this book
- Internal Marketing Staff Budget
- Final budget automatically totaled by marketing tactic
- Final budget automatically totaled by type of expenditure (for example, professional services, ad buys, and such)
- Charts and graphs automatically created so you quickly see how you're spending your money
- "Flow through financials"—enter your figures just once and they automatically flow through to the annual budgets

These worksheets automatically total the individual budget worksheets to create an overall Annual Marketing Budget. If you've purchased the Deluxe Binder Edition of *Successful Marketing: Secrets & Strategies*, the Electronic Marketing Budget Templates are included. Purchasers of the paperback version of this book can download the Electronic Marketing Budget Templates (for a modest fee) at www.PlanningShop.com.

Download today!
Available only from
www.PlanningShop.com

the**Planning**shop

Grow Your Business with The Planning Shop!

We offer a full complement of books and tools to help you build your business *successfully*.

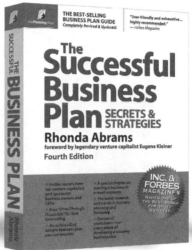

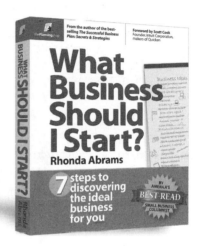

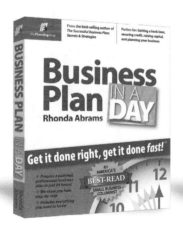

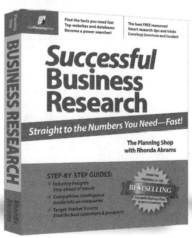

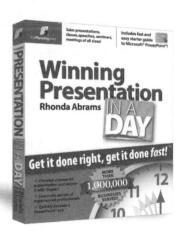

Ask your bookseller about these titles
or visit www.PlanningShop.com

the**Planning**shop

Every successful business starts with a plan.

If you're starting a business, you need to make sure you've accurately assessed your market potential, costs, revenue, competition, legal issues, employee needs, and exit strategy *before* you start investing your (or someone else's) money.

Fortunately, *The Successful Business Plan: Secrets & Strategies* by Rhonda Abrams will show you how to develop a well-crafted, clear, meaningful business plan—step-by-step—that will help ensure you don't end up facing any costly surprises down the road!

Named by *Inc.* and *Forbes* magazines as one of the top ten essential books for small business, *The Successful Business Plan* is the best-selling business plan guide on the market, used in the nation's top business schools and by hundreds of thousands of successful entrepreneurs.

Whether you're seeking funds from outside investors or bankrolling your start-up on your own, *The Successful Business Plan* will be your guide to planning your business in a sound, profitable manner.

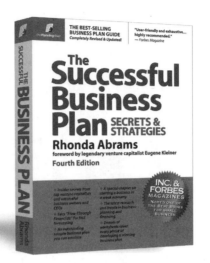

Book features:

• 99 worksheets to help you get started quickly, taking you through every critical section of a successful business plan

• Sample business plan offering guidance on length, style, formatting, and language

• The Abrams Method of Flow-Through Financials, which makes easy work of number crunching—even if you're a numbers novice

• Special chapters addressing issues of concern for service, manufacturing, retail, and Internet companies, plus advice on starting a business in a challenging economy

• Nearly 200 real-life insider secrets from top venture capitalists and successful CEOs

"User-friendly and exhaustive...highly recommended."
Forbes Magazine

"There are plenty of decent business plan guides out there, but Abrams' is a cut above the others..."
Inc. Magazine

Available from your bookseller or at www.PlanningShop.com

the**Planning**shop